THE GLORY OF HERA

Greek Mythology and the Greek Family

by Philip E. Slater

BEACON PRESS : BOSTON

Grateful acknowledgment is made to the following for the explicit use of their publications: ATHENEUM PUBLISHERS, New York, New York, for Peter Weiss, *The Persecution and Assassination of Jean-Paul Marat as Performed by the Inmates of the Asylum of Charenton under the Direction of the Marquis de Sade.* G. BELL & SONS, LTD., London, England, for Florence Stawell, translator, Euripides' *Iphigenia in Aulis*; and for Oates and O'Neill, editors, *The Complete Greek Drama*, Volume II. COLLINS-KNOWLTON-WING, INC., New York, New York, for Evelyn Lancaster and James Poling, *The Final Face of Eve*, published May 26, 1958 by McGraw-Hill Book Company. E. P. DUTTON & Co., INC., New York, New York, for Richard Crawley, translator, Thucydides' *The History of the Peloponnesian War*, Everyman's Library Edition. NORMA MILLAY ELLIS, for "Benediction" in *Flowers of Evil*, published by Harper & Row, Publishers, New York, New York, copyright 1936, © 1963 by Edna St. Vincent Millay and Norma Millay Ellis. HARPER & ROW, PUBLISHERS, New York, New York, for Howe, Harrer and Epps, *Greek Literature in Translation.* HARVARD UNIVERSITY PRESS, Cambridge, Massachusetts, for Evelyn-White, translator, Hesiod, *The Homeric Hymns and Homerica: The Homeric Hymn to Apollo*; for Frazer, translator, *Apollodorus*; for Smyth, translator, *Aeschylus*, Volume II; and for Way, translator, *Euripides*, Volume I, all from the Loeb Classical Library. HILL & WANG, INC., New York, New York, for Arthur L. Kopit, *Oh Dad, Poor Dad, Mamma's Hung You in the Closet and I'm Feelin' So Sad.* MRS. BENJAMIN KARPMAN, for Dr. Benjamin Karpman, *Case Studies in the Psychopathology of Crime*, Volume II. THE MACMILLAN COMPANY, New York, New York, for Bruno Bettelheim, *Truants from Life*, copyright © 1955 by The Free Press. RANDOM HOUSE, INC., New York, New York, for Butcher and Lang, translators, *The Odyssey of Homer*; for Lang, Leaf, and Meyers, translators, *The Iliad of Homer*, copyright 1950; for Oates and O'Neill, editors, *The Complete Greek Drama*, Volume I, copyright 1938; and for John Crowe Ransom, *Chills and Fever*, copyright 1924 by Alfred A. Knopf, Inc., and renewed 1952 by John Crowe Ransom. SCHOCKEN BOOKS, INC., New York, New York, for Franz Kafka, "The Green Dragon," *Parables and Paradoxes*, copyright © 1946, 1958. THE UNIVERSITY OF CHICAGO PRESS, Chicago, Illinois, for Richmond Lattimore, translator, *The Iliad of Homer*, copyright 1951; for Richmond Lattimore, translator, *Greek Lyrics*, copyright 1949, © 1955, and © 1960; and for the following plays from David Grene and Richmond Lattimore, editors, *The Complete Greek Tragedies*: Aeschylus' *The Libation Bearers* (copyright 1953, Lattimore, translator), *Prometheus Bound* (copyright 1942, Grene, translator), Sophocles' *Oedipus the King* (copyright 1942, Grene, translator), *Women of Trachis* (copyright © 1957, Michael Jameson, translator), *Electra* (copyright © 1957, Grene, translator), Euripides' *Heracles* (copyright © 1956, William Arrowsmith, translator), *Iphigenia in Aulis* (copyright © 1958, Charles R. Walker, translator), *Electra* (copyright © 1958, Emily Townsend Vermeule, translator), *The Bacchae* (copyright © 1958, William Arrowsmith, translator). THE VIKING PRESS, INC., New York, New York, for Horace Gregory, translator, *Ovid:* The Metamorphoses, copyright © 1958 by The Viking Press, Inc.

International Standard Book Number: 0-8070-5795-9
First published as a Beacon Paperback in 1971.

THE GLORY OF HERA

TO *John Elliot Slater*
AND *Pauline Holman Slater,*
WHO PROVIDED ANOTHER MODEL

CONTENTS

vii

PREFACE

A DESCRIPTION of the origins and purpose of a book, if it is logical enough to be of any use to the reader, cannot help but distort history. This book was not intended at all, and my only purpose in writing it was to get to the end of it. Indeed, I have never intentionally written a book, for although papers are pleasant enough to write, I find writing books unpleasant. Yet one thing leads to another. This book began as a little paper, a short version of Chapter I. A peripheral interest in folklore and myth had led me to consider the fact that my knowledge of the richest mythology of all was unusually inadequate, and I began to read various compendia. I was struck by certain of the trends which are discussed in this volume and I wrote a little paper on it. Feeling that my knowledge of the field (which my education had slighted) could not support even so modest an endeavor, I began to explore it more deeply, abandoning it only when I had achieved sufficient familiarity to perceive its limitlessness. From the very start I felt I was beyond my depth and swam continually toward what I mistook for the nearest land, ending, nine years later, on the other side.

But this description, although accurate, does not help the reader who wishes to know something about the interests and assumptions that directed the enterprise, or who wants some kind of guide to assist him through the book. I shall deal very briefly with the first and third of these, saving the more complex issue of assumptions and techniques for the last.

My primary interest has always been in the motivational

structure of the human organism and its evolution. I have approached the problem in terms of collectivities because the individual organism is not a very meaningful entity (evolution affects species, not individuals). I am particularly interested in the relationship between individual and group demands on the finite motivational resources available to them, and in changes in this relationship.

In pursuing these interests I have always regarded the interpersonal structure of the family and the early socialization of the child as strategic. It is here that patterns are formed and here that they are changed, for the motivational plasticity of the organism decreases rapidly with age.[1] While I would see few changes as immanent in the family pattern, I suspect that an outside force rarely produces enduring change unless it affects that pattern in some way.

In the first chapter I attempt to reconstruct, from the scanty evidence available, a central interpersonal pattern in the modal Greek family of the classical period, and to show how this pattern relates to several familiar characteristics of Greek culture. The second chapter explores an elemental psychological conflict, universal to mankind, but peculiarly aggravated by the Greek family pattern. These two chapters comprise Part I, and are necessary for understanding the more detailed analyses which follow.

Part II shows how these processes are reflected in Greek mythology. A number of gods and heroes are discussed, each exhibiting one or more psychological techniques for mastering the conflicts described in Part I. Comparative data are introduced from time to time, and some additional concepts, but by and large Part II is an elaboration and exemplification of Part I.

Part III attempts to inject some statistical rigor into the proceedings (Chapter XIII), then to assess the cross-cultural gen-

[1] The phenomenon of conversion is often mentioned as evidence in contradiction to this view, but I have discussed elsewhere the reasons why I regard conversion as a very small change indeed [Slater, 1967, pp. 570–76].

eralizability of the hypothesized relationships (Chapter XIV), and finally, to explore the implications of the study for cultural evolution in general and modern society in particular.

From this description it should be clear that my purpose in writing the book was not to make a contribution to classical scholarship, although I would naturally be pleased were this to occur. My attitude toward the field is not without ambivalence, for reasons which will become clear at the close of this preface. I should like first, however, to spell out some of the strategies, assumptions, and reservations that have influenced the construction of this book.

A good part of the volume is devoted to myth-interpretation—an occupation which perhaps requires some defense. Greek mythology as a field has been ravaged by more barbarian invaders than ancient Mesopotamia, and classical scholars are wisely skeptical of any and all claims. Most of these outsiders presume far too much, particularly the various psychoanalytic ones (who, armed with Freud's concept of overdetermination, should know better). Yet all have added something, and it is as foolish to throw up one's hands and dismiss the whole effort as it is to embrace any one interpretation exclusively. Worst of all is the conventional academic trick of ridiculing all interpretation by presenting a series of waspish caricatures of each school (e.g., ". . . and a recent interpretation even goes so far as to attribute the triumphs of the Periclean Age to a fear of pubic hair"). The folklorist of this persuasion ends by caricaturing himself as a knownothing, stubbornly maintaining the folly of inquiry ("if God had meant us to interpret myth he would have given us a codebook").

My own view is resolutely polytheistic. An old myth is of necessity an elaborately condensed product—no matter how many layers one peels off there will still remain much to be explained. To ask which interpretation is "correct" is manifestly absurd. To try to ascertain how much of the variance can be accounted for by each is premature. At present all we can do is uncover as many contributory strands as possible. History, religious ritual, psychology, social structure, and artistic embellishment all contribute to the formation of a myth (and even of a folktale[2]) and none should be arbitrarily excluded.

My emphasis here is on the part played by the Greek family system and the preoccupations which it seems to have engendered. My analysis of a given myth makes no attempt to be "complete," even within a narrow psychological framework. It often presupposes interpretations made by other scholars, and in no case should be viewed as attempting to supersede them.

To demand an exclusive interpretation is equivalent to insisting that a Spanish peasant, a tropical flower, the Hudson River, an oyster, and the fountains of the Villa d'Este are identical because they contain H_2O. It is a point in common, yet it hardly exhausts their significance. If a dream, a symptom, or a slip of the tongue by an individual is overdetermined, how very much more so is a myth, which must condense the wishes, thoughts, feelings, and experiences not of a single person but of several nations. If, for example, we see in a myth distorted history—the conquering of one people by another, or the spread of a religious cult—we have still left unexplained the basis for the selection of symbols to represent these events. Similarly, if a myth represents the forces of nature, changing seasons and celestial movements, it is not immediately obvious why these processes should appear in the costume of fornicating and incestuous anthropomorphic beings rather than something else. And a bright mythmaker engaged in explaining a ritual or misinterpreting an icon could concoct at least a dozen myths to do the job; therefore this selection must also be explained. Just as the raw material for a dream may come from bodily stimuli or the recent experi-

2 For the purposes of this analysis I have ignored these distinctions.

ence of the dreamer, but is activated by his most fundamental needs and wishes, and molded and shaped by an enduring structure of conflicting intrapsychic forces, so, too, a myth draws material from events in the history of a group, but orders it according to the desires and stresses common to those participating in the culture of that group. Some myths retain their appeal in cultures foreign to the one in which they were born; others become mere antique curiosities, a fact which can only be explained by multiple determination.

In this context, arguments over which is the "best" interpretation become ridiculous. Fromm's attempt to repudiate Freud's interpretation of the Oedipus myth and to substitute a nonsexual one—an attempt which forced him to exclude the incest theme as unimportant [Fromm, 1957, pp. 196–231]—seems a gratuitous waste of ingenuity. It stands in sharp contrast with a similarly nonsexual reinterpretation by Ferenczi, which makes no claim for exclusive possession of the truth, and no attempt to displace earlier interpretations [Ferenczi, 1912, pp. 253–69].

The purpose of this book is, in any case, not to "interpret" the Greek myths, but rather to make certain inferences about Greek family life with reference to these myths. It is of no concern to me what "caused" these myths to come into being, or what their "essence" is. Artists often paint ancient heroes in costumes contemporary with the artist, and whatever the "core meaning" of the Greek myths, they were dressed up in accordance with the family relationships current at the time of their telling. I am therefore as interested in the accidental, "retouched," secondary elaborations as in the original myths. What may be regarded as most trivial by the scholar concerned with the historical antecedents of Greek religion may tell the most about psychological preoccupations. How and why does a military tale of dynastic struggle become translated into a family romance, acquiring a psychological significance which the original myth did not have?

This approach, however, is not without its problems. I make the basic assumption that a myth tells us something about the people who listen to it. The authors are lost in obscurity, and what each teller contributed can never be known. This yields some simplification, since the Greeks of the fifth and fourth century constitute the audience I wish to understand. In some cases we are on firm ground. We know, for example, that the Greeks of this age revered Homer and frequented the theater. Indeed, modifications of Homeric myths by the dramatists provide the strongest data of all, since the changes are most likely to reflect the psychological preoccupations of the theater-goer. On the other hand, many myths or parts of myths appear only in the works of late compilers, writing well past the time of Alexander, some of them not even Greek. Should these be ignored? Some scholars, such as Fontenrose [1959, pp. 4–5], have argued that these late myths, drawn from oral tradition and perhaps from the lower classes, are of greater antiquity than the Homeric ones, and it is impossible to reject this view out of hand. But this raises other difficulties. Were the myths and folktales of the various social strata the same or different? And what of the family system? Did this retain its essential character all the way from the Dorian conquest to the Christian era? And did it not vary from region to region and class to class? The Spartans and the Athenians certainly thought their family arrangements differed markedly, although the differences may not have affected the variables under consideration here.

To be rigorous with regard to these questions is to abandon the enterprise. It is difficult enough, for example, to construct a coherent picture of Athenian upper-class family life of the classical period from the fragments of evidence available without trying to pinpoint its temporal, social, or geographical limits. Gomme shows, with devastating humor, the hazards of such analyses [1937, p. 113]. What I have tried, *faute de mieux*, is to describe the family constellation which seems to have obtained at some period and at some places, related it to myths which were enjoyed at some times and at some places, and hoped that I have not exaggerated the area of overlap. Since my major arguments rest most heavily on the dramatists, the problem is not as serious as the previous statement implies. Yet it must be admitted that I have on many occasions made minor interpretations of myths whose relation to fifth-century Athens is entirely unknown. I have preferred to draw the portrait as vividly and with as much elaboration as possible, at the risk of increasing the number of individual errors.

My reason for making this choice is based on a second difficulty—one which has to do with the special character of psychological interpretations. It can reasonably be argued that without strong psychological relevance a myth will, in time, simply die, unless some compulsive priest or pedant is on hand to preserve it. But the importance of the psychological factor is a two-edged sword. A completely psychological approach, such as that embraced by the Freudians and Jungians, fails to account for differences between myths, or systems of myth. Some Greek myths, for example, are enjoyed by inhabitants of our own society, while others are primarily of antiquarian interest. The same may be said of the Grimms' collection, of which some half-dozen or so are a fundamental part of our own culture. A great many myths of our primitive contemporaries, on the other hand, generate in the average European layman an almost excruciating boredom. Psychological explanations as such account only for what is universally appealing but tell us nothing about the more specific fascination they hold for individual societies.

The family constellation which I describe for classical Greece is by no means peculiar to it. It can be found in individual families in almost any society, and aspects of it are prominent as modal cultural patterns in many historical and contemporary social systems. Thus, what I have to say is in part peculiar to Greece and in part universal, and while I may be in error as to the relevance of a particular myth item for classical Greece, it may yet throw some light on the more general issue. In Leach's terms [1965, p. 575] I am both symbolist and functionalist. At present we can only begin to distinguish between the unique and the universal (one can certainly see quantitative differences, for example). We can also note that the kinds of issues dealt with in *Oedipus Rex* and *Antigone* seem almost as interesting to modern Europeans as to the Greeks, while those involving Orestes seem a good deal less so, and myths like that of Procne scarcely at all. I shall make comparative statements whenever I feel able to, but in general I must leave the boundaries somewhat blurred for the present.

My strategy, then, has been to make sweeping approximations, naturally with as much care and rigor as possible, but with the clear recognition that many specific examples and connections may prove, on more informed examination, to be useless or misleading. I myself am altogether convinced, of course, that when this debris has been cleared away, the main outlines of my thesis will still stand as strongly as before. But I am well aware of the absurd errors into which psychiatrists and other nonexperts often fall in their attempts to draw parallels between classical history and literature on the one hand and their own subject matter on the other, and the lay reader should be warned not to mistake abundance for expertise, but to treat details with caution.

It is perhaps not necessary to add that my interpretations are just that, and that if I have occasionally fallen into the terminology of demonstration and proof, it is purely for stylistic reasons—to avoid the cumbersomeness of constant qualification.

One of my underlying assumptions is that the modal familial experiences of members of a given society play an important part in shaping the fantasy products of the culture. Lloyd Warner goes even further than this: "Religious symbols . . .

are formed by, express, and reinforce the family structure." He argues, with respect to contemporary Christianity, that, "the Church, its rites, beliefs, and practices, would not exist if the family failed to survive. The Church, forever dependent on the family for its existence, expresses more concern about, and exercises greater moral influence on, the family than on any other human institution" [1959, p. 353]. This statement would have to be sharply qualified for Greek religion, but it is not without significance. Warner points out that the family organizes the emotional life of the individual, and is hence the referent for much of his symbolic life [*Ibid.*, p. 345]. A similar assumption is made by Whiting in a somewhat different context [1961]. Warner, however, is thinking of the universal rather than the differential effects of familial life. He argues that the spread of world religions necessitates symbols which evoke universal sentiments, and sees the family as "the only social institution which provides men of all cultures with such powerful and compelling experiences" [1959, p. 345]. But the family is not the *same* social institution in all societies, and I will therefore assume that the experiences and symbols differ correspondingly. While the influence of many other variables may blur this differential effect (which is presumably less compelling than the universal similarities), it should be visible in its broad outlines.

A second assumption I have made is that the conglomerate whole formed by the surviving fragments of a myth has some meaning as such—that some psychological cohesive has formed and preserved this juxtaposition. Greek mythology was frozen into a literary mold at a rather peculiar juncture, as many authors have pointed out. It is a curious mélange of local histories, legends, folktales, epics, literary and dramatic inventions, religious and philosophical revision, and so on. Generalizations about origins are therefore very difficult to make. But by the same token, the psychological relevance of this inelegant mixture must have been intense, indeed, to resist rationalization, purification, and integration as well as it did. The authority of Homer may have been great, but this in itself requires some explanation, and cannot in any case account for the preservation of that which was not Homeric.

I have, then, following Lévi-Strauss [1965, pp. 567–68], treated all surviving versions and fragments surrounding a given god or hero as more or less a totality, and interpreted them as such. In so doing I of course run the risk that any specific totality might include truly anachronistic elements and invalidate the interpretation. To avoid this difficulty as much as possible I have placed far more weight on some sources than others, so that the thinnest ice supports the least important detail. The greatest weight I have placed on the dramatists, and, indeed, my main arguments could rest on their evidence alone, although naturally I feel equally secure with other sixth-, fifth-, and fourth-century sources; and Homer and Hesiod clearly still had relevance for the classical period. Of the later sources I have depended most heavily on Apollodorus, who inspired confidence even before I became aware of his almost total reliance on fifth- and fourth-century authors [cf. Frazer's introduction to the Loeb Apollodorus, pp. xviii–xx]. I have generally assumed all of Apollodorus to be relevant to the classical era.

One cannot make this assumption with Pausanias, yet I have usually felt his allusions to refer to myths of genuine antiquity, partly, perhaps, because they have such clear local roots. Least reliance of all has been placed on Diodorus Siculus and Ovid, who seem to betray the most interest in rationalizing or romanticizing their material to suit their audiences. Still, I have used them all to some extent, and on a few occasions have even relied on secondary sources when the primary sources were not available to me. For all of his liberties and lack of authenticity (from a fifth-century viewpoint), Ovid often captures the emotional quality of a myth so vividly and with such rich imagery that I have been unable to resist quoting him.

Since I do not read Greek, I have also had to worry about relying on translations, which I compensated for whenever possible by reading the work in at least two, and often as many as four, different versions. In addition, I have struggled through many passages in the original, dictionary in hand, trying to assure myself that a crucial concept was not generated by the translators as a concession to modern patterns of thought.

A word should also be said about the technique of myth-interpretation, which often relies on psychoanalytic theories and may seem entirely arbitrary to those not familiar with these ideas. In Chapter XIII, where I have used quantitative methods for testing hypotheses derived from the main body of the book, the rules of procedure are made quite explicit, but interpretations of specific myths make additional assumptions.

First, the formal structure and temporal order of the myth are largely ignored, since I am interested in emotional factors and not the cognitive elements. Instead, the more primitive principle of mere contiguity in time or space is utilized. Second, since I am interested in correlates with the family, all characters in a story are equated with either father, mother, sister, or brother—different characters representing different aspects of the same figure. This is not to say that Hera or Medusa or Demeter *is* the Greek mother, and that when I have made this equation I have exhausted the significance of a goddess or monster—the device is specific to this mode of analysis. The validity of the equations cannot be proved, but they can perhaps be justified by the usefulness of the results.

In general, symbolic equations are easy to make and even easier to ridicule. Yet one must keep trying, since there is no simple formula for translating an associative, metaphorical, nonlogical language into a formal one. Indeed, the greatest absurdities in psychoanalytic interpretations of myths and folktales have sprung from the tendency to be too literal and mechanical in the treatment of symbols—assigning one and only one meaning to a given symbol. Often it is only when we put two contradictory interpretations together that we begin to make sense out of the material. In light of the condensed nature of fantasy, we must be additive in our approach to it. A symbol perhaps cannot mean everything, but it can mean a great many things, and some consideration of the elements associated with it is necessary. Lévi-Strauss argues: "If there is a meaning to be found in mythology, this cannot reside in the isolated elements which enter into the composition of a myth, but only in the way those elements are combined" [1965, p. 564]. I would agree with this statement as it applies to symbols. I would disagree only in that (a) a pattern which is repeated in a number of myths for a given culture may also reflect itself in the frequencies with which specific elements are associated, and (b) the statement subsumes Lévi-Strauss' determination to find an *explicit* logic in nonlogical material, a determination which is admirable but often strained.

My third assumption is that interpersonal patterns appearing in poetic and dramatic treatments of myth will mirror directly the modal patterns of the culture. Unfortunately, we expect a fantasy to include not only an interpersonal reality and the feelings it evokes but also techniques for managing these feelings, and these techniques may involve a negation of either the reality or the feelings. Does this mean one must adopt the heads-I-win-tails-you-lose posture so often attributed to the psychoanalyst? How can one refute an interpretation which includes opposites?

The answer is not difficult: one evaluates the interpretation in terms of whether or not the dimension of polarization seems significant. We may say that size is an important issue in a fantasy if it includes dwarfs *or* giants, so long as there is a size discrepancy. By the same token, my interpretation of the birth of Apollo, as both denying and expressing dependence upon the mother, could be rejected, not on the grounds that it must be one or the other, but on the grounds that I have magnified into polarized opposites what is actually a minor variation around a mean. An awareness of the vagaries of psychoanalytic myth-interpretation scarcely justifies reviving the simpleminded eighteenth-century notion that a feeling cannot coexist with its opposite. The censor is fascinated with pornography, the McCarthyite with Communism, the rebel with tyranny, and so on. To say that a thing must be one or the other is to miss the significance of the whole. I will attempt to show this total constellation in each interpretation, arguing that the *issue* is important—and will thereby open myself to the counterclaim that it is in fact trivial. It would be absurd, for example, to reject my argument that the Greeks were narcissistic on the grounds that the whole notion of *hubris* betrays a profound fear of narcissism. The two are indissolubly linked. The proper debate is whether or not the Greeks were unusually preoccupied, as I have maintained, with issues of pride.

We would be amused if some learned man were to announce that a moth, contrary to previous opinion, does not fly at all, but is merely a worm; if a controversy over this were to rage for years in the journals; and if university professors, with self-congratulatory impartiality, were gravely to inform their students (after reviewing the arguments of both sides) that the truth lay somewhere in between—that a moth neither flew nor was a worm. Yet most scholarly dispute fits this model with sad precision. While science seems by and large to proceed on an additive basis, humanists still maintain an assumption of intellectual scarcity: an assertion by one is viewed as taking away from the assertions of others.

Lastly, I would like to mention the peculiar discomfort I have experienced in my very heavy dependence on classical scholars. Anyone who seeks to study a field not his own has a delicate balance to maintain. Not to recognize his lack of sophistication would be arrogant and foolish, but a posture of humility would be belied by the endeavor itself, and the occasional advantage that derives from an alien vision would be forfeited. Like a short-term ethnographer, I cannot hope to understand Greek culture in its entirety, and in setting more segmented goals, I run the risk of making errors by an inattention to context. Thus, I cannot trust too fully my own observations, but must rely heavily on native informants—in this instance, classical scholars. Yet, at the same time I must be aware that the consuming patriotic ardor of these informants and the enveloping familiarity of their surroundings will at times engender a bias which may lead me astray, and vitiate the benefits of detachment. When a lecturer in some branch of history or one of the behavioral sciences insists upon placing an event, a custom, a trait, or an image "in context," the wise student suspects that the lawfulness of the universe is about to be renounced in order that the speaker may caress his subject matter, to which, after all, he has devoted a large part of his life.

Many scholars will no doubt be outraged, for example, by my emphasis on the social pathology of Greek civilization, and will feel that it is a negation of the Hellenic achievement. I can barely comprehend this attitude, but, as I have seen it expressed many times, I feel obliged to assure the reader that the one-sided emphasis found in this volume does not imply that ancient Hellas can somehow be "reduced" to these concerns. But neither can it be reduced to the ethereal land of sunshine to which all too many classicists have consigned it —a stereotype which seems to me a far more profound derogation. When Murray tells us that "Greek thought, always sincere and daring, was seldom brutal, seldom ruthless or cruel" [p. 67]; or Nilsson feels obliged to apologize for rejecting the preposterous notion that the Greeks were not superstitious [1961, p. 111]; or Rose tells us piously that "the Greeks were in general a people of clean life" [1959, p. 126], they are asking us to share a vision which is not only false but emasculated and bloodless. To recreate Greece in the image of Plato is to reduce a rich and vibrant society to its most arteriosclerotic by-product.

The Greeks were both sublime *and* ridiculous. The story of the Sicilian Expedition cannot exclude Nicias' superstition and still arouse in us the anguished sense of contrast between human aspiration and human limitation. Nor would I care to see Professor Rose bowdlerize Aristophanes in accordance with his views on Greek character. Greece is exciting precisely because it included such disparate elements: reason, superstition, humanity, brutality, imagination, pedantry, originality, conservatism, and so on. One of the many springs of my admiration for the work of Jane Harrison is that she valued Hellenic civilization for what it was rather than for what she wanted it to be [yet, see Harrison, 1924, p. 25], and those who have no affection for the effete and cerebral travelogue offered by traditionalistic scholars will not share the latter's contempt for her "enthusiasm."

I confess that I do not fully understand those who feel that a man is somehow reduced if one calls attention to his feelings. An awareness of Lewis Carroll's pedophilia does not lessen my admiration for him—on the contrary, it adds depth and poignancy to his work.[3] There have been millions of pedophiles but only one *Alice in Wonderland*, and pedophilia was certainly not a sufficient condition for its creation. Yet it was nonetheless a necessary one—had he not been an expert at attracting and sustaining the interest of little girls the story would never have been created.

The idealizing attitude gives rise to many absurdities in description and interpretation. Kitto [1960] repeatedly asks

---

[3] I have not been able to ascertain whether or not Dodgson's early family history contained any of the elements discussed in Chapter I. For later biographical data on Carroll see Collingwood [1899], Gardner [1960], Green [1953], and Lennon [1945]. Note especially the photographs.

how it happens that the Greeks, who were never childish or stupid or vulgar or irrational or superstitious, could ever have done all the childish, stupid, vulgar, irrational, and superstitious things they did, and contrives many ingenious explanations without ever questioning his postulate. His explicit assumption, which he shares with many others, is that beautiful architecture, sculpture, literature, and so forth, is somehow incompatible with ordinary human folly (he is apparently unacquainted with any creative people).

Another expression of this attitude is a kind of Un-Hellenic Activities Committee, which attributes to alien influence everything that does not fit the classicist stereotype.[4] Thus, of the birth of Dionysus, Rose remarks, "Clearly we have here a barbarian myth; Greek legend does not lend itself to such grotesques" [1959, p. 150]. And again, "it is not surprising, considering how little the Greeks liked monstrosities," that their huge gallery of bogies, *"products of an imagination not their own* are represented as living in the lower world" [*Ibid.,* p. 31. Italics mine]. One might wonder why these "alien" products were adopted with such avidity, why there were so many of them, and why they appeared so often in art and drama. It is also curious that precisely these bogies, which "are rather horrors lurking in the background than clear-cut figures of the generally sunny Hellenic mythology" [*Ibid.,* p. 32] have survived to modern times [Lawson, 1964, pp. 130ff.], while the "clear-cut figures" have been submerged in an alien religion.

Rose's position is best expressed in the following quotation:

The Greeks at their best were sane, high-spirited, clear-headed, beauty-loving optimists, and not in the least otherworldly. Hence their legends are almost without exception free from the cloudiness, the wild grotesques, and the horrible features which beset the popular traditions of less gifted

[4] For an interesting interpretation of the idealizing tendency, compare Gouldner [1965, p. 39].

and happy peoples. Even their monsters are not very ugly or uncouth, nor their ghosts and demons paralysingly dreadful. Their heroes, as a rule, may sorrow, but are not broken-hearted; on occasion they are struck down by an adverse fate, but not weakly overwhelmed; they meet with extraordinary adventures, but there is a certain tone of reasonableness running through their most improbable exploits. As for the gods and their supernatural characters, they are . . . on the whole neither irrational nor grossly unfair in their dealings [1959, p. 14].

One is surprised to find this statement followed by a relatively uncensored presentation of the Greek myths, in dazzling contradiction to each of his remarks. Indeed, few mythologies show us more madness, more weak, depressed, uncouth, and suffering heroes, more grotesque and terrifying monsters, more vicious and vindictive deities. Since I shall concentrate my attention on these latter aspects, however, Rose's statement may be read as a kind of antidote to the rather one-sided impression one might obtain from this volume.

I should also add that my impatience with the classicists' idealizing proclivities gains its intensity by contrast with the admiration and indebtedness which predominate in my feelings toward them, and which increase my intolerance of their occasional lapses. My efforts are indeed an epiphenomenon of the classicists' achievement.

I would like to acknowledge an intellectual debt, long outstanding, to Robert W. Hyde, perhaps the most exciting teacher I ever encountered. While never an admirer of the kind of approach I have used here, his influence on my work was fundamental and pervasive.

Chapter XIV was based on a study made possible by a grant from the National Institute of Mental Health (MH–08128–01). The planning and execution of the study were done in collaboration with Dori Appel Slater. Advice and assistance were also provided by William Stephens, Robert Textor, and John Whiting.

I would like also to express my appreciation to Jean Durling Berraras, who made it possible for this work to begin, and to Brandeis University for financial assistance in preparing the manuscript.

Finally, I am most particularly indebted to Dori Appel Slater, who read and criticized the manuscript at several stages, and who sustained the agonies of its completion.

P.E.S.

Nice, France
May, 1968

Part One

ORIGINS AND
CONSEQUENCES

⟦ CHAPTER I ⟧

The Greek Mother-Son
Relationship: Origins
and Consequences

> . . . they are adventurous beyond their power, and daring beyond their judgment. . . . Thus they toil on in trouble and danger all the days of their life, with little opportunity for enjoying, being ever engaged in getting. . . . To describe their character in a word, one might truly say that they were born into the world to take no rest themselves and to give none to others [Thucydides: i. 70].

WE HAVE FEW OBJECTIVE PORTRAITS of the Athenian character, so thorough was their monopoly of the literature which has come down to us. Even the descriptions put into the mouths of aliens and enemies by Thucydides and the dramatists quiver with self-satisfaction and pleased wonderment. The literature they have left us, however, is far too rich for this lack to be very acutely felt. We have too much rather than too little data about this curious society and its inhabitants—enough to characterize them in virtually any way one wishes. At this distance most people find the Athenians (and indeed the Greeks generally, for with a few exceptions the local variations are merely quantitative) rather appealing;

but if I try to envision them at close range, I find myself back-
ing off a bit. If I imagine an individual I know with these
characteristics, the word that comes to mind is "difficult." At
times I might even share the ambivalent opinion of Thucydides' Corinthian envoy, and change the word to "impossible."
They were quarrelsome as friends, treacherous as neighbors,
brutal as masters, faithless as servants, shallow as lovers—all
of which was in part redeemed by their intelligence and
creativity. But the core of both what is most admirable and
what is most "impossible" about them is a kind of grandiosity—an ability not merely to conceive, but also to *entertain*,
in every sense of that term, an outrageous idea, an outlandish
scheme.

The Greek phenomenon was an accidental product of the
confluence of many forces, most of which I am not competent to discuss. There are a few strands, however, on which
a social scientist can throw considerable light. We know something about the extent to which personality characteristics,
values, behavior patterns, ideas, and fantasies are shaped and
molded by early familial experiences, and an inquiry into the
nature of the Greek family might well add to our understanding of the brilliant episode to which we owe so much.

The Role of Women in Athens

When I first turned my attention to this problem I was struck,
as so many have been before, by a paradox. On the one hand,
one is usually told that the status of women in fifth- and
fourth-century Athens achieved some kind of nadir. They
were legal nonentities, excluded from political and intellectual
life, uneducated, virtually imprisoned in the home, and appeared to be regarded with disdain by the principal male
spokesmen whose comments have survived [Kitto, 1960, pp.
219–22; Blümner, n.d., *passim*]. On the other hand, as Gomme
points out: "There is, in fact, no literature, no art of any

country, in which women are more prominent, more important, more carefully studied and with more interest, than in
the tragedy, sculpture, and painting of fifth-century Athens"
[Gomme, 1937, p. 92]. Gomme rejects the traditional view
on these grounds and shows how one might arrive at a similar
assessment of our own era by the appropriate selection of
sources.

Gomme's essay is a healthy antidote to the intoxications
that historical inference can induce in the unwary, but the
dilemma cannot be laughed away. One may grant the absurdity of using polemical statements (e.g., "a woman's place
is in the home") as indices of reality [1937, pp. 97–102]. One
may grant that the legal position of women need not reflect
their social position [*Ibid.*, p. 90]. One might accept the
inference that at least some women—perhaps only hetairai
[Licht, 1963, p. 153]—attended the theater [Ehrenberg, 1951,
p. 27; Gomme, 1937, p. 233; but cf. Aristophanes: *Thesmophoriazusae* 395–97], and were generally *au courant* [Gomme,
1937, p. 102; Kitto, 1960, pp. 226–27]. It is also likely, as
Ehrenberg argues, that the lower classes never participated
very fully in this social pattern: that it was aristocratic males
who first wore long hair and became enthusiastic pederasts
and misogynists, forcing their wives into adultery [1951, pp.
97, 100–2, 112, 180, 193; cf. also Thomson, 1950, p. 366].
The cultivation of bizarre and inconvenient social patterns
is at all times and in all places a luxury which the lower
classes often cannot afford, and the poor Athenian woman
could not remain secluded in the home if peddling vegetables
in the marketplace was her only source of livelihood [Ehren-
berg, 1951, pp. 114–15].

But when all of these qualifications have been made, a core
of derogation and sex antagonism still remains. Women were
legally powerless—a man could sell his daughter or even his
sister into concubinage [*Ibid.*, p. 198]. Women of the upper
classes could not maintain this status and go out unattended,

and their social life outside the home was largely restricted to religious festivals and funerals [Lysias: On the Murder of Eratosthenes; Licht, 1963, pp. 31–32; Thomson, 1950, p. 366; Kitto, 1960, pp. 219–20; Blümner, p. 133; Flacelière, 1960, p. 114; Ehrenberg, 1951, pp. 200–2]. Among the well-to-do, men and women usually ate, and in some cases, slept apart [Lysias: *loc. cit.*; Flacelière, 1960, pp. 114–15; Ehrenberg, *loc. cit.*; Licht, *op. cit.*, p. 57], and a wife who dined with her husband's guests was assumed to be a prostitute [Kitto, 1960, p. 219]. This separation obtained even in Macedonia [Herodotus: v. 17ff.].

Since this is the generally accepted view of the status of women, it is perhaps unnecessary to accumulate further examples. Instead, let us examine more carefully the dissenting voices of Gomme and Kitto, to see if we can find in their arguments a way of resolving the dispute. Kitto, after reviewing the evidence in favor of the majority opinion and admitting its force, rejects it on the grounds of "the picture it gives of the Athenian man. The Athenian had his faults, but pre-eminent among his better qualities were lively intelligence, sociability, humanity, and curiosity. To say that he habitually treated one-half of his own race with indifference, even contempt, does not, to my mind, make sense" [*Ibid.*, p. 222]. This statement typifies the sentimentality which classical scholars on occasion permit themselves, and we need spend little time over it. Leaving aside the peculiar limbo into which it casts many brilliant and creative homosexuals and misogynists of all eras, and the absurd insistence that intelligence precludes eccentricity, Kitto's way of stating the argument—"one-half of his own race"—is peculiarly ironic. On the contrary, the Greek was quite capable of treating *any* segment of his race, male or female, with consummate brutality and callousness—abandoning or killing his allies, betraying his city to the enemy and joining gleefully in the ensuing slaughter of his neighbors, and so on. The only thing unique about his rejection of "one-half of his own race" was its consistency.[1]

When we examine the remainder of Kitto's argument, however, we notice a more interesting regularity. In addition to echoing Gomme's stress on the powerful role played by women in tragedy, he cites a number of facts which argue the importance of the woman's role in the home [*Ibid.*, pp. 227ff.].

At once it becomes clear that the entire controversy rests on a false assumption shared by all the combatants.[2] This assumption might be called the "patriarchal delusion": the notion that power follows deference patterns—or that a sizable power differential between the sexes is possible. Once one has shed this illusion, the combination of derogation of and preoccupation with women ceases to be a paradox and becomes an inevitability.

The issue is too complex to discuss in detail here, and it will perhaps suffice to point out the most important flaw in the fantasy of male dominance. Rejection and derogation of women mean rejection and derogation of domesticity—of home and family life, and hence of the process of rearing young children. The Athenian adult male fled the home, but this meant that the Athenian male child grew up in a female-dominated environment. As an adult he may have learned

[1] An amusing parlor game of the "famous-last-words" variety would extend this thinking to other societies, e.g., "The Germans were too civilized to ————," "The Americans were too egalitarian to ————."

[2] The social scientist has no cause to be smug about this, however. The tendency to confuse marital and parental roles has by no means disappeared from sociology, and researchers still seem surprised to find that children from fatherless families and those from "patriarchal" (even polygynous) ones resemble each other. But from the child's viewpoint, the father is unimportant insofar as he is not present, no matter how exalted and dictatorial a stance he maintains, and no matter how much prestige males have in the society at large. Luigi Barzini seems to be responding to the same stimulus when he refers to the Italian family as a "crypto-matriarchy" [Barzini, 1967, pp. 208–13].

that women were of no account, but in the most important years of his psychological development he knew that the reverse was true. Men were at that time trivial to him—all of the most important things in his life were decided, as far as he could see, by women.

Nor was his view simply a function of his ignorance of the outside world. We know from studies of the modern American family that participation and power go hand in hand. A working mother, for example, has more power in economic decision-making than a non-working mother, but *less* power in decisions regarding household activities—the husband not only participates more in domestic activities but exerts more control over them [Hoffman, 1963; Heer, 1963; Blood, 1963. Cf. also Mace and Mace, 1964, pp. 92–116; Briffault, 1931, pp. 188–89, 248–49; Nemecek, 1958, pp. 5–6]. Conversely, the more the male imprisons the female in the home and takes himself elsewhere, the more overwhelmingly powerful is the female within the home.

The social position of women and the psychological influence of women are thus quite separate matters. The Greek male's contempt for women was not only compatible with, but also indissolubly bound to, an intense fear of them, and to an underlying suspicion of male inferiority. Why else would such extreme measures be necessary? Customs such as the rule that a woman should not be older than her husband, or of higher social status, or more educated, or paid the same as a male for the same work, or be in a position of authority— betray an assumption that males are incapable of competing with females on an equal basis; the cards must first be stacked, the male given a handicap. Otherwise, it is felt, the male would simply be swallowed up, evaporate, lose his identity altogether [cf. Plutarch: "Dialogue on Love" 752e–f, 753c–d].

I shall try to show how the low status of women and the male terror of women were mutually reinforcing in Hellenic society, but before describing this cycle we must establish that women were in fact powerful in the house. The strongest datum comes from Aristophanes. In *Lysistrata*, the fact that wives control the management of household finances is advanced as an argument for their assuming political control [493–94]. Xenophon confirms this, saying that while the husband earns the money, the wife dispenses it [*Oeconomicus* iii. 15]. Kitto points out that the home was also a factory, and that the woman's position was thus one of great responsibility [1960, p. 230]. The house being divided into men's and women's quarters, her control over her own domain, which included the children, most of the slaves, and the economic heart of the household, was largely unchallenged, and made the male vulnerable indeed [cf. Xenophon: *op. cit.*, ix. 5; Lysias: *op. cit.*]. As Flacelière observes: "*Son mari est d'ailleurs trop occupé au-dehors pour désirer lui contester la direction de son intérieur, dont elle est comme le ministre . . .*" [1960, p. 104]. And Ischomachus, in attributing the outdoor life of the male and the indoor life of the female to a god-given division of labor, likens the wife's role to that of the queen bee, who supervises not only interior but also outside workers [Xenophon: *Oeconomicus* vii. 22–42]. This is not to say that this division of labor completely eliminated marital power struggles—Ehrenberg points out the frequency of allusions to sexual competition in comedy [1951, p. 207]. But one cannot be a family patriarch at a distance. The role is an active one, involving the acceptance of interpersonal responsibility. The alcoholic who returns home only at midnight to beat his wife and children is not the important figure in the daily life of the home.

Arnold Green [1946] was one of the first of a series of social scientists to discuss the overwhelming involvement of mother and child in our own middle class. The involvement is due in part to the absence of the commuting father; and Greek fathers appear to have been even less in evidence [cf. Blümner, *loc. cit.*, p. 147]. While the presence of slaves may have mitigated this maternal involvement somewhat, the child's world before the age of six or seven was an almost entirely feminine one.

This seems to me to explain adequately the presence of active, aggressive women in Greek tragedy. Gomme points to the great freedom of action that women have in drama, and argues that women like Jocasta and Antigone must have been modeled on contemporary women [1937, pp. 93, 96, 107]. Kitto makes the same point, observing that the women are usually more enterprising than the men—that the tragic heroines are striking in their vigor, intelligence, vindictiveness, and uncontrollability [1960, pp. 228–29]. But while one may agree that these women had contemporary models, one need not assume that such modeling extended beyond the narrow range of the household. All that a playwright requires for drama is a vivid memory for his own childhood and family— especially Greek drama, which is most intensely concerned with intrafamilial conflict. If this were not true, one would be hard put to explain how so many of the great heterosexual dramas of Greek, Elizabethan, and modern theater could have been written by homosexual playwrights.

Attempts to homogenize Greek attitudes toward women are thus thoroughly misguided. The combination of fear, awe, and contempt is too pervasive. One of the best expressions of this totality is in Herodotus' description of the Battle of Salamis. We find the Athenians so resenting the fact that a woman, Artemisia, commanded a ship against them, that they offered a large reward for her capture alive [viii. 93]. Yet of the same battle there was a popular legend that the phantom of a woman appeared in the midst of the fighting and asked contemptuously, "in a voice which could be heard by every man in the fleet . . . if they proposed to go astern all day . . ." [*Ibid.*, viii. 84]. The belief that an Athenian woman's place is in the home does not in the least prevent them from imagining her in virago form.

This same contradiction appears on Olympus. Despite the patriarchal superstructure we find there, the goddesses are more intimately involved in the lives of men than are the gods. In particular, the enduring wrath of Hera is far more often the mainspring of mythological action than are the brief tantrums of Zeus, and has more far-reaching consequences. Like the Greek husband, Zeus wanders and philanders, but, as the Greek wife was almost forced to be, Hera is faithful. This is in marked contrast to Teutonic mythology, in which gods and goddesses are equally promiscuous. Hera works out her jealous feelings primarily through the vindictive pursuit of her stepchildren, and there are several instances (e.g., Medea, Procne) in Greek mythology in which a mother kills her own children to spite her husband for his infidelity. Is it not possible that this phenomenon, too, reflects (in style if not in intensity) a situation obtaining in the Greek home? Is it not usual to expect the frustrated mother to work out some of her feelings upon her children? It seems likely that some such tendency is responsible for the menacing aspect of women in so much of Greek myth.

Much has been written about homosexuality among the Greeks. We may perhaps pass over the anticipated efforts to idealize this feature of Greek life as "platonic," since as usual the argument appears to be based not on evidence but on some imagined incongruence between homosexuality and various Greek virtues. Actually, there is no source, from comedy to philosophy to litigation to history, which does not indicate with compelling clarity that physical homosexuality was widespread and generally accepted; and that among the upper classes it competed successfully with heterosexuality [cf. Licht, 1963, pp. 133ff., 411–98]. Furthermore, far from being incongruent, we shall see that the tendency toward homosexuality is an essential part of a total pattern of response—that, indeed, one would even predict its existence knowing the rest of the pattern.

Modern studies of the family patterns of male homosexuals indicate that most often the household is "mother-dominant and father-avoidant," with the mother-son relationship "of the close-binding, intimate type, where often it seemed that the mother might select the son as a kind of surrogate husband." The homosexuality is then seen as "a defense against hidden but incapacitating fears of the opposite sex" (Gundlach and Riess, 1966). We shall see that this description fits the Greek case rather well, although obviously one cannot equate a cultural pattern with a clinical one without some qualification.

Greek fear of women, however, was more particularized than this. It was mature, maternal women who were most feared, and regarded as most dangerous. In the tragedies it is young women and virginal goddesses who are helpful and benign, while the mature ones tend to be jealous, vindictive, and destructive. In Greek religion we find two goddesses, Athene and Artemis, being transformed, over the centuries, from mother-goddesses to youthful virgins. And in the daily life of Athens, we find a tendency for males to marry barely pubescent girls, and to encourage their women to practice depilation of all body hair [Aristophanes: *Lysistrata* 85ff. 148ff. and 828; *Ecclesiazusae* 60–67; *Thesmophoriazusae* 215–67 and 532–39; cf. also Ehrenberg, 1951, pp. 34, 179; Licht, 1963, pp. 12, 506]. As Licht observes, it was on *women* that pubic hair was considered ugly.

Now it may be objected that both of these practices are widespread in the Eastern Mediterranean [cf. Linton, 1959, p. 229], and that therefore no special conclusions can be drawn for Hellenic culture. To this I would make two answers. First, the Greeks were not totally Mediterranean; they had received many waves of Northern invaders, who presumably did not share these patterns. The mixture of these cultures provided several opportunities for choice, and thus for psychological motivation to enter the picture more directly.[3] Second, and more important, it is not necessary for us to distinguish Greece from surrounding cultures on every cultural item. In fact, a large portion of the constellation I shall describe was and is characteristic of other Mediterranean cultures. It is only the totality which is unique.

At the clinical level, one would tend to regard the desire for pubic depilation as phobic. Bettelheim mentions, for example, the frequency with which disturbed boys are concerned about the "hairy vagina," and suggests that it is "related to fear of the vagina dentata" [1955a, pp. 232–33]. We may also recall that during the persecutions which periodically convulsed Europe between the thirteenth and seventeenth centuries, witches were often shaved in order to uncover the mark of the Devil.

The reader may feel, at this point, that we are pursuing a course which is at best trivial, and that the equation of clinical psychopathology and cultural patterns is a misleading and dangerous enterprise. The classicist has perhaps already abandoned us. Since, however, this analysis was in fact inaugurated by my recollection—touched off by reading Aristophanes—of a long-forgotten case study in sexual pathology, I must ask the reader's indulgence while we retrace a series of what may seem like dubious and improbable con-

---

[3] This is a point usually ignored both by diffusionists, who never explain why some items are accepted and others rejected when tribes interact, and by those scholars prone to assigning Greek traits to barbarian influence. Since Greece was something of an ethnic goulash, this is rather easy to do, but it is a little difficult to determine what is to be considered truly Hellenic, since each of the contributing cultures was responsible for only a part of the totality, with probably the richest single strand coming from the indigenous (and hence barbaric, by some strange reasoning) Mediterranean culture. The effort is quite familiar to an American, accustomed to having the United States defined as a white Anglo-Saxon Protestant culture (despite the relatively small cultural contribution of this ethnic fragment during the twentieth century), and to having undesirable traits assigned to immigrant influence. Thus, despite the venerable tradition of WASP violence and brutality in the South and the old West, this trait is often projected onto "foreigners."

nections, suspending judgment until we have crossed over to firmer ground. The similarities to be discussed should not be interpreted as intending in any way to slight the profound differences—they are to be regarded solely as a means to an end.

The Case of Kenneth Elton

The preference for immature women did not end with the Greeks, but has always existed in its most extreme form as a type of deviant sexual behavior called pedophilia.[4] In the criminological literature there is at least one highly detailed case study of a pedophile, containing considerable fantasy material as well as reports of behavioral patterns. The patient, "Kenneth Elton," was treated in a brief but apparently successful psychoanalysis by Karpman during the nineteen-twenties [Karpman, 1944, 516–636]. Elton was convicted three times on various charges involving assaults on little girls, and was analyzed while in prison following the third of these convictions.

During the early weeks of the analysis, Elton attempts to minimize the psychological significance of his acts, and to demonstrate that his sexual life, marked by two marriages and many casual affairs, has been for the most part a normal one. As the analysis progresses, however, he gradually reveals, first, that he has seduced many more children than those for whose seductions he was convicted, and second, that his "normal" heterosexual relationships were made possible largely through the fulfillment of certain conditions. Toward the end, this statement appears: "if my second wife had allowed

[4] This term is used in its modern psychiatric sense of "an erotic craving for a child of the same or different sex on the part of an adult," or "an abnormally accentuated fondness for children," or "gratification from sexual intimacies with children" [Karpman, 1954, pp. 14–15], not in its original Greek sense of "love of boys." The Greek preference was for adolescent boys; seduction of pre-pubescent boys occurred but was considered a crime [Licht, 1963, pp. 414–18].

me to shave her, I don't think I would have ever bothered any little girl" [*Ibid.*, p. 605]. He says, however, with masterful understatement, that "generally, I don't care to look at woman's genitalia" [*Ibid.*, p. 595], and he employs a variety of devices—darkness, clothing, shaving the pubic area, and the pedophilia itself—to transcend this discomfort:

"My first wife was a brunette—she had a pretty good sized backside . . . seeing that would give me a peculiar feeling. She had a large amount of hair on her genitals—it worried me . . ." [*Ibid.*, p. 599].

"I always felt exceedingly peculiar whenever I'd see this portion of my wife's anatomy, but I had no idea what caused this queer sensation to come over me whenever I so beheld her. I was bothered so much by the sight of this hair that I never had intercourse with my wife during the daytime, as I simply couldn't bear to see her naked; and even when I had intercourse at night the contact of my body with her hair gave me the 'creeps'; so one day I got to kidding with Vera, and while she was in a good humor I proposed that she let me shave the hair from around her vagina, and to my surprise she consented" [*Ibid.*, p. 630–31].

"I enjoyed the intercourse more—you might think it was because she would resemble a little girl—I don't know. . . . I told you once I prefer adult girls at night—that I wouldn't see their box—perhaps that's the reason why I like underwear rather than nude, so as not to see the hair. . . . I wonder whether the fact that the little girls didn't have any hair was the reason for my liking them. I had with them a peaceful feeling—girls up to fourteen, fifteen—different from that with adult—at ease, while with mature girls—the hair—different feeling—rather peculiar . . ." [*Ibid.*, p. 599].

Let us now consider some of the possible origins of this sexual attitude, beginning with one of Elton's dreams:

". . . I was sailing this boat up a small stream which was awfully crooked and full of sea grass. The latter caused me considerable trouble by becoming entangled in my propeller and causing me to stop every few minutes to 'clean' the propeller. After I had put up with this annoyance for what seemed to me an hour, or thereabouts, during which time I had made about a dozen stops for the purpose of removing this miserable sea grass, I sighted an island about half a mile away from where I was, and as I headed for this island the boat suddenly ceased its forward progress and I knew that, though the motor was functioning properly, my propeller wasn't 'pulling'; so I 'cut off' the motor and bent over to examine the propeller again; and this time, instead of it being full of sea grass it was full of long, black hair which seemed to have been plaited around the blades of the propeller, as well as its shaft. And as I gazed down towards the bottom I could see that *it* was covered with this long, black hair, the sight of which, as the movement of the water made it wave (as it were) to and fro, absolutely made me feel 'creepy'; in fact, it looked to me like so many thousand snakes straining to get at me. I evidently was rather frightened by seeing this very extraordinary sight, as immediately thereafter I awakened and found that my heart was beating rapidly and that I had had a night sweat" [*Ibid.*, p. 598].

The boat made powerless by the hair strangling its propeller dramatizes Elton's sexual difficulties. The uncanny feeling that he reports, together with the comparison of the hair to snakes and the inability to move, brings to mind the Medusa myth, about which psychoanalytic theorists have had a good deal to say. Ferenczi, for example, reports, "in the analysis of dreams and fancies, I have come repeatedly upon the circumstance that the head of Medusa is the terrible symbol of the female genital region, the details of which are displaced 'from below upwards.' The many serpents which surround the head ought—in representation by the opposite— to signify the absence of a penis, and the phantom itself is the frightful impression made on the child by the penis-less (castrated) genital" [Ferenczi, 1923, p. 360].

Freud elaborates on this somewhat, suggesting that "to decapitate = to castrate. The terror of Medusa is thus a terror of castration that is linked to the sight of something . . . the female genitals, probably those of an adult, surrounded by hair, and essentially those of his mother" [Freud, 1922, p. 105]. But why, one might ask, should an adult female seem more "castrated" than an immature one? There seems to be something incomplete about this formulation. Freud and Ferenczi both stress the defensive nature of the fantasy, "castration" being denied by the "multiplication of penis symbols" (snakes) and by the idea of erection, suggested to Freud by the theme of being turned to stone [Freud, 1922, p. 105] and to Ferenczi by the "alarming starting eyes of the Medusa" [Ferenczi, 1923, p. 360]. Freud argues that, "however frightening (the snakes) may be in themselves, they nevertheless serve actually as a mitigation of the horror" [Freud, *loc. cit.*].

But if this interpretation is correct, and snakes may be equated with hair, one would expect that a prepubescent girl would be more terrifying than a mature one to a male with castration anxiety. One wonders if there may not be a less oblique interpretation of this fantasy. Elsewhere, Freud associates the ideas of staring and immobility with the primal scene [Freud, 1918a, pp. 498ff.], and one might ask whether it is the idea of castration which is primary, or whether it is the child's being confronted with the sexuality of the mother.

In this connection one of Elton's associations is of interest. He twice denies, rather gratuitously, that he ever witnessed parental intercourse, although he admits having slept in the same room with his parents. He then states, "can't possibly recall anything like that; besides I don't think it would have made any impression on me. I can recall far back, when I was a kid, father crossed a bicycle, a snake—it wiggled and wiggled. But I can't recall anything of sexual nature until I was about eleven years old" [Karpman, 1944, pp. 526, 534]. Here a snake is associated directly to the primal scene, but whether the usual equation between snake and phallus should be made is not at all clear.

Freud continues his discussion of the Medusa's head by pointing to its reappearance on the aegis of Athene: "thus she becomes a woman who is unapproachable and repels all sexual desires—since she displays the terrifying genitals of the Mother. Since the Greeks were in the main strongly homosexual, it was inevitable that we should find among them a representation of woman as a being who frightens and repels because she is castrated" [Freud, 1922, p. 106]. But it is somewhat misleading to talk of Athene as someone who "frightens and repels," inasmuch as she emerges as the most personal, most helpful, and least punitive of all the major Olympian females. Why, furthermore, should a virgin goddess display the "genitals of the Mother"? Historically, of course, the answer would be that Athene is fundamentally a patriarchalized Earth-Mother goddess, and the aegis might represent a remnant of this tradition. But one may also resolve the psychological problem by pointing out that the only "repellent" aspect of Athene *is* the aegis, suggesting that from the Greek viewpoint kindness could be anticipated from a woman only so long as she remained a virgin. Perhaps the inhibitory value of the aegis lies in the fact that it is a reminder that the alternative to a helpful Athene is a vindictive Hera.

Freud's idea that the primary psychological significance of the female genital derives from that of the male is peculiarly myopic—a kind of psychoanalytic version of Adam's rib. There is something rather strained and cumbersome about his interpretation, even allowing for the usual distortions created by repression.

A more compelling interpretation is suggested by Karen Horney's paper, "The Dread of Woman," in which the fear of female genitalia is derived from a fear of maternal envelopment. She describes typical dreams of male homosexuals: falling into a pit, sailing a boat in a narrow channel and being sucked into a whirlpool, being in a cellar full of "uncanny, blood-stained plants and animals"; and she comments upon the widespread myth of the pool maiden (there are several in Greek mythology) who lures the male to his death. She also gives an account of an experiment in which a slit was cut in a rubber ball and children of both sexes asked to put a finger in it. While all were somewhat uneasy, the boys showed far more fear, and many refused altogether. Menstrual and defloration taboos are also related to this fear, and the "state of lethargy—even the death—after mating which occurs frequently in male animals." She rejects Freud's notion that all of this fear is based merely on the absence of the penis, but argues that, on the contrary, the attempt to find a penis in the woman is an attempt to deny the existence of the intrinsically "sinister female genital." She suggests two techniques for denying this dread: disparagement and idealization. With the first, which we recognize as the Greek solution (although it is in fact widely diffused), the male reassures himself that nothing is to be feared from so poor a creature. With the second, which seems to have evolved somewhat more uniquely in modern Europe [cf. Watt, 1964], he concludes that there is no need to fear so saintly a being [Horney, 1932, pp. 349–53].

Missing from Horney's analysis is any clear indication of the conditions under which this fear is likely to become prominent, for although she implies that it is universal, it is obviously trivial for many individuals and cultures, and utterly incapacitating for others. One would assume, however, that it would be related in some way to the mother-son relationship. We might find a clue in the mythology of the Trobriand Islanders, who also practice pubic depilation [Malinowski, 1929, pp. 299–300]. The Trobrianders believe in a mythical island on which there are a number of villages in-

habited only by beautiful women. (So strong is their belief
that they land their canoes on desert reefs rather than risk an
encounter.) On this island, appropriately given a name which
means "the fill of copulation," the women do not dep-
ilate, and their pubic hair grows long enough to form a kind
of grass apron. They are very fierce, and sexually insatiable.
"When they cannot have intercourse, they use the man's
nose, his ears, his fingers, his toes—the man dies." Boys born
on the island are treated in the same way, become tired and
sick, and die before growing up [*Ibid.*, pp. 422–23]. For the
Trobrianders, then, pubic hair is associated with being over-
powered by a mature and lustful female, a theme we will encounter again in the case of Kenneth Elton.

First, however, let me summarize. I have suggested that both
the practice of pubic depilation and the preference for immature females might derive from a phobic attitude toward the
maternal genitalia. I have accepted the view of Freud and
Ferenczi that the head of the Medusa is a representation of this
fear, but rejected the notion that the fear itself is based on the
absence of the penis, or that the many snakes necessarily represent phallic symbols. Despite Freud's ingenuity in dealing
with the problem, it seems more likely that the snakes of the
Medusa head are not compensatory, but are a *source* of fear,
and represent an aspect of the vagina itself.[5]

I would suggest that the horror associated with these symbols of the maternal genitalia, if they be such, is attributable
not to the notion that the mother is "castrated" but rather to
her being experienced as "castrating," by virtue either of her
hostility or her seductiveness toward the male child. This

[5] Women in some Australian tribes make magic by cutting off their
pubic hair and making of it a long string. By anointing it with vaginal
blood, it is "transformed" into a snake which is then sent to destroy their
victims. Roheim views this snake as a substitute penis [Campbell, 1959, p.
303]; for now, I will merely note the association between hair and snake.
The complex symbol of the serpent will be discussed in detail in the next
chapter.

interpretation has the advantage of accounting for *variability* in "Medusa-dread," in terms of maternal behavior and its correlates.

To explore this possibility, let us return once more to the case of Kenneth Elton. Elton tells us that both parents were both loving and strict, but it was his mother with whom he had the most involved relationship [Karpman, 1944, p. 618]. Unfortunately there is too little information to infer that she was "castrating" in either of the ways suggested; but one does find almost a caricature of the castrating female in the neighbor who seduces Elton when he is six years old. I feel that this "trauma" is only a small part of Elton's difficulty, and is etiologically important only because it has some resonance with the maternal relationship, but again the evidence is scanty. I can only point out the surprising readiness of young Elton to place himself in the power of a woman of whom he was supposedly deathly afraid.[6]

Elton describes the woman as young (about twenty-two) but powerful, aggressive, determined, and quick-tempered. He recalls her chopping wood, and recounts incidents in which she caught him and teased him. Despite his fear, however, she later tempts him into her house, and he gives a graphic account of his frightened reaction to her powerful

[6] As Freud discovered quite early, one must always consider the possibility that these childhood seduction recollections are fantasy rather than reality. If it is fantasy, there is little doubt that it is displaced from the mother. If reality, one must take note of his (perhaps unconscious) complicity. This is, of course, not unusual—the majority of sexual encounters between adult and child are mutual and often repeated, with the initiative coming from the child in some cases. The popular stereotype of the innocent child assaulted by a total stranger accounts for only a fraction of the cases. In most cases (72 per cent) the adult is a neighbor, friend of the family, or relative [Karpman, 1954, pp. 66ff., 104ff.]. Barring physical injury, the effect of these experiences need not be traumatic. Abraham feels that guilt is the primary danger—that a resisted and reported physical attack produces less emotional disturbance than an encounter in which the child at first shows interest but later breaks off without reporting it [Abraham, 1907, pp. 50–53].

limbs and hairy body [*Ibid.*, pp. 615–16, 624–26]: "And as she advanced toward me a feeling of horror pervaded me, and if the floor could have opened up and swallowed me I would have been glad. . . . some two or three months previously I was wading in the water of a small pond when I stepped into a small bed of quicksand or extremely sticky mud which held me for several minutes before I could extricate myself. During the time that I was held in this mud . . . I thought I was a 'goner.' Of course I was greatly frightened *then*, but my fright on this occasion was as nothing compared to the feeling that swept over me while lying on top of the Howard woman. It just seemed to me that I was going to be swallowed up within this mass of hideous hair, and I was so frightened I was unable to talk or move" [*Ibid.*, p. 626].

Note that despite his fear of being swallowed up by the woman and the quicksand, he wishes "the floor could have opened up and swallowed" him, an expression, perhaps, of the same ambivalence that drew him into the situation. His association to the quicksand reflects the common equation of earth and mother—a symbolism particularly frequent in Greek myths. As we shall see, even Heracles becomes helpless under such conditions. Elton's inability to talk or move mirrors the notion that all who gazed on the Medusa head were turned to stone.

The quicksand episode is in turn associated with still another childhood sexual experience, occurring when Elton was "less than three years old—a woman . . . Negress—nineteen years—used to bathe me—I didn't then have any realization of nudity and certainly not of color—used to put my arms around her . . . she used to take me to water—I don't recall whether she let me swim . . . she used to play with me, put my legs on her shoulders, throw me up in air. Once I nearly sank in mud, scared me" [*Ibid.*, p. 607]. In this instance, however, the associations are largely pleasant and gratifying ones, the Negro woman representing perhaps (as is so common in the South), the more positive aspect of the maternal image [Smith, 1961, pp. 109ff.].

It seems likely that the mother's body becomes menacing to the child only as a function of what she does. A recent cross-cultural study by Stephens [1962, pp. 80ff., 124ff.), for example, found a positive correlation between variables suggesting sexual arousal of the child by the mother and a number of sexual anxieties and taboos (e.g., menstrual taboos, sexual prohibitions, desexualization of breasts, kin-avoidance); and a study by Baruch [1952] provides an excellent illustration of this relation in a child unable to cope with the mother's sexual needs. Thus we may say that wherever one finds a mother unfulfilled in her sexual life, one may expect also to find a mother whose aspect is menacing to her child. But Stephens also finds a relationship between indices of "castration anxiety" and the severity of menstrual taboos, and one may infer not only that menstrual taboos presuppose high castration anxiety among males, but also that in a society with severe menstrual taboos, penis envy and resentment of males by females is likely to be strong. Hence, one might also hypothesize that wherever one finds a mother who, by virtue of being a woman, is deprived in some way of self-expression or forced to endure narcissistic wounds of various kinds, one may expect also to find a mother whose aspect is menacing to her male children.

Marital Strains and Maternal Scapegoating

If sexual deprivation and humiliation by males both lead to anxiety-provoking maternal behavior toward sons, we would expect Greek males to be doubly fearful, since these phenomena seem to have been combined in the Greek household.

However much she may have looked forward to it in fantasy, as young girls do everywhere, marriage for a Greek maiden was somewhat traumatic. She moved abruptly from the life of childhood and the security of her family into the seclusion of a stranger's house. Her husband was chosen by her father [Ehrenberg, 1951, p. 193] and was probably never seen by her before the marriage, since deception in marriage contracts seems to have been common [Licht, 1963, p. 39]. Marriage also involved a religious change—the relinquishing of the household gods of her youth: "She must abandon her religion, practice other rites, and pronounce other prayers. She must give up the god of her infancy, and put herself under the protection of a god whom she knows not" [Fustel de Coulanges, 1956, p. 43]. These sudden changes took place, furthermore, when she was still very young [Ehrenberg, 1951, p. 193]. The bride of Ischomachus in Xenophon's *Oeconomicus* is only fourteen, and he points out that she could not be other than ignorant, since she was well brought up, under strict surveillance, and taught neither to see nor hear nor to ask questions [vii. 5–6; cf. also iii. 13]. (The effects of this neglect were, of course, later used—as in the case of racial and religious discrimination—to justify such treatment.) Hesiod recommends that the girl *wait* four years after menarche, which in Mediterranean countries would make the age of marriage seldom later than sixteen [*Works and Days* 697–99]. Blümner notes that "it was not uncommon, since Greek girls married very early, for them to play with their dolls up to the time of their marriage, and just before their wedding to take these discarded favourites, with their whole wardrobe, to some temple of the maiden Artemis, and there dedicate them as a pious offering" [Blümner, p. 92]. A nuptial song of Theocritus [xviii. 9ff.] chides the drowsy bridegroom and suggests that if sleep was all he wanted he should have gone to his bachelor's bed and left his bride nestled in her mother's arms or playing with her playmates. When we realize that this girlish bride is Helen, the most beautiful woman in the world, we can gauge the depth of Greek misogyny. If the poem were history one would have to conclude that no one more deserved the cuckolding he was later to receive than this sluggish bridegroom.

The bride, then, is an ignorant and immature teen-ager, totally dependent upon a somewhat indifferent stranger for all her needs—a stranger who regards marriage at best as a necessary evil, but certainly a tiresome, if only partial, interruption of a pleasant and well-established pattern of daily living, in which his social and sexual needs are already being satisfied, the latter through hetairai and young boys. Semonides of Amorgos thus concludes a long tirade, in which women are compared to sows, vixen, bitches, donkeys, weasels, and monkeys, by saying: "No one day goes by from end to end enjoyable, when you have spent it with your wife" [Lattimore trans., 1961, p. 11]. The husband has normally had little say in choosing his bride, marriage being defined as having a purely procreative function. This is expressed in a famous quote from Demosthenes, which the reader will for once be spared [cf., instead, Xenophon: *Memorabilia* ii. 2, 4–5].

Licht makes much of the oft-verbalized reluctance of Greek males to marry [1963, pp. 33–39, 71–73], but such material is open to the objection that these dour jokes about exchanging freedom for slavery or equating marriage with death may be found in our own society, as well as in many others. They receive greater force, however, when we see the structural realities associated with them. Many Greek cities, for example, punished celibacy as a crime, and at one time Sparta denied the rights of citizenship to the man who did not marry. While Athens had no such law—perhaps Solon's own homosexuality played a part in this—custom forbade bachelorhood, and it was everywhere viewed as impious. Athens did have a law, however, which made it a duty of the city's magistrate to prevent any family from becoming extinct. Only a man who had an elder brother with children could avoid the general rule without incurring disapprobation [Plutarch: *Lycurgus* xv. 1–3; Solon: i. 1–3 and xx. 2–3; Fustel de

Coulanges, *op. cit.*, pp. 49–50; Flacelière, 1960, p. 106; Licht, 1963, pp. 34–35, 69].

These laws and customs, which were based on the traditional attitude that the family rather than the individual was the basic unit of society, and that happiness and preservation beyond the grave for the male (there was no arrangement for females) depended upon the funeral libations of his male descendants [Fustel de Coulanges, *op. cit.*, pp. 34–39], betray the strength of the reluctance so vigorously assailed. Licht argues, however, that despite this pressure, the proportion of old bachelors and old maids in Greece was high [Licht, 1963, pp. 34–37; but cf. Ehrenberg, 1951, p. 193]. At any rate, the age at which the male married was probably around thirty—more than a dozen years later than that of his bride [Hesiod: *Works and Days* 695–99; Blümner, p. 136]. In the case of some, it was apparently a great deal more; when Socrates, for example, was over seventy, Xanthippe was still at or near childbearing age [Plato: *Crito* 45, 52 and *Phaedo* 60, 116]. This age difference was viewed as desirable since the beauty of the female was of briefer life than the strength of the male [Licht, 1963, p. 40]. Since for some Greek males, as for Humbert Humbert, beauty and maturity could not coexist, this period of desirability was brief indeed.

On her side, the bride was equally unprepared for a mature heterosexual relationship. Her relationship with her father had probably been rather tenuous, partly because of his emotional distance from familial life, but also because of his overriding concern with his daughter as either a highly marketable commodity or a serious economic liability—a concern which necessitated preserving her chastity by means of strict control and seclusion. The pervasive segregation of, and antagonism between, the sexes prevented her ever transferring her major cathexis from mother to father, and she understood of men only that they had the best of things. In the Greek wedding ceremony it was the mother and not the father who performed the ritual analogue of giving the bride away [Blümner, p. 139].

Even if the paternal relationship was rather limited, however, and even if an unmarried girl led a "retired and . . . joyless existence," and even though marriage often may have brought "somewhat greater freedom" [Licht, 1963, pp. 28–29], it was nevertheless a disappointment: "When we are young, in our father's house, I think we live the sweetest life of all; for ignorance ever brings us up delightfully. But when we have reached a mature age and know more, we are driven out of doors and sold, away from the gods of our fathers and our parents, some to foreigners, some to barbarians, some to strange houses, others to such as deserve reproach. And in such a lot, after a single night has united us, we have to acquiesce and think that it is well" [Sophocles: *Tereus* fragment 524 from Nauck; quoted by Licht, 1963, pp. 39–40]. However restricted her childhood years, maternal protection and affection were hers, as well as the companionship of siblings and playmates. The marital relationship provided little compensation for the loss of these advantages. Socrates can ask Critobulus, "are there any men to whom you entrust more matters of importance, or with whom you have less conversation, than with your wife?" [Xenophon: *Oeconomicus*, iii. 12] and feel secure in the answer.

This shallowness of the marital bond is not new with the classical period—Finley points out that in Homer there is no marital relationship which contains the emotional intensity found in the attachment between father and son or between male friends [Finley, 1959, pp. 137–38]. But in most societies or subcultures in which the marital bond is weak, the partners are deeply invested in other relationships which are strong and enduring and supported by a stable and permanent environment [Bott, 1957, pp. 52–113]. When this external stability breaks down the marital bond becomes more important, and if marital roles are still structured along the older principle, substantial misery can result. This seems to have happened in fifth-century Athens, particularly for the wife; the husband still had many, if shallow, external ties [cf. Gouldner, 1965, pp. 26, 60–64, 68–70]. Whereas in Victorian England one could talk of a *wife's* "marital duties," in Athens it was more likely to be the male who would view marital sexuality in this light—not, of course, for prudish reasons. While Plutarch may be unduly generalizing from a law which seems fundamentally to be the same one violated by Onan [*Solon:* xx. 3; *Genesis* 38:8], he nevertheless captures something of the spirit of the Greek male's attitude toward marriage in his discussion of a law of Solon: "that a man should consort with his wife not less than three times a month—not for pleasure surely, but as cities renew their agreements from time to time . . ." [Plutarch: "Dialogue on Love" 769]. When marital love occurred, even between newlyweds, it excited special comment [Xenophon: *Symposium* viii. 3].

The marital relationship thus came to resemble that of an older brother and younger sister, when the brother has been unwillingly entrusted with his sister's care at a time when he would rather be out adventuring with his friends, and she is longing for her mother and resents his coldness, irritability, and contempt. But in the case of brother and sister, the mother will eventually return, and the sister can even complain of her brother's ill-treatment. The wife is alone among strangers and will remain so. As a child she could perhaps vent her feelings in doll-play. As a wife she vents them on her children.

This is particularly likely to affect the male child. If the wife resents her husband's superiority, she can punish arrogance (or even masculinity) in her son [cf. Vogel and Bell, 1960, p. 387]. Such vengeance is especially appropriate, inasmuch as the son is the sole means of perpetuating the father's lineage and property. Furthermore, lack of a son meant not only lack of an heir but also the disappearance of the family religion and rites, and condemnation of the father to eternal unhappiness beyond the grave [Fustel de Coulanges, pp. 48ff.]. Since the direct expression of hostility toward the husband would be inhibited by the wife's dependence upon him, her youth, and her social inferiority, destructive unconscious impulses toward male children must have been strong. Both the impulses and the need to deny them would be increased, furthermore, by the greater value assigned to male children. A woman who failed to produce an heir for her husband was viewed as not having performed her most elemental function, and women could be divorced for barrenness.

The male child was thus of vital importance to the wife —her principal source of prestige and validation. Yet how much she must secretly have resented the callous and disparaging male attitude toward female children, who were an economic liability, a social burden (i.e., guarding their chastity), and of no redeeming religious significance to the household, of which they were, in any case, only a temporary member. The mother-daughter bond seems nonetheless to have been the closest, most affectionate, and least conflicted of all familial dyadic relationships, as is true in most sex-segregated societies. One sees it in the Demeter-Kore myth, which is unique in having parental affection as its primary motivational theme. Yet it was considered perfectly acceptable, even at Athens, for a healthy female infant to be exposed, even if the family were rich, if the father willed it [Ehrenberg, 1951, p. 199; Flacelière, 1960, pp. 111–12; Licht, 1963, p. 37].[7] When the dramatists based Clytemnestra's

---

[7] The infant was exposed by placing it in a clay vessel and leaving it in a temple or in the wilderness. Many so abandoned were taken by childless women and passed off as their own to prove their fertility. Children were also sold for the same reason. From Aristophanes we know that women often succeeded in making their husbands believe that they had themselves given birth to infants thus acquired [*Thesmophoriazusae* 407–9]. It would be difficult to find a more dramatic demonstration of the social and emotional distance between husband and wife.

hatred of Agamemnon on his having casually murdered Iphigenia to further his military adventures, they were tapping
a contemporary emotion. To be a woman was to be "nothing"
[cf. Licht, 1963, p. 39], and if women consciously and automatically shared this social assumption, this did not prevent
them from resenting it. The male child aroused both feelings,
and the casualness with which female children were denied
found its negative counterpart in the mother's ambivalent
overinvolvement with the son. His life, in other words, was
given preference at a measurable cost. One does not know
how common child-exposure was in Athens—classicists often
gloss over it as they do with so many other unpleasant facts
—but however infrequent it was, the sexual preference was an
emotional reality.

Lucile Dooley suggests, following Freud [1933, pp. 171–
72], that penis envy prevents marriage from ever being
entirely satisfying to the female—that complete emotional gratification can only be derived from the mother-son relationship
[Dooley, 1938, p. 182]. In orthodox psychoanalytic thinking,
of course, this is a universal statement, but it can be usefully
modified to mean that in societies where sex antagonism is
strong, the status of women low, and penis envy therefore
intense, the woman's emotional satisfactions will be sought
primarily in the mother-son relationship; while in those societies in which these social characteristics are minimally
present, the marital bond will be the principal avenue for
need-gratification. Classical Greece certainly fell into the
former category. For sex antagonism is a two-edged sword,
and if men could only feel secure in a heterosexual relationship in which they were unambiguously superior, the same
was true of the woman. The male child was hers—under her
control and subject to her whims, and it was here that her
feelings could be given full expression, within the limits of
incest and murder laws.[8] The male child was at one and the

---

[8] Exposure required paternal consent, and could not, in any case, be
done once the child was named.

same time a scapegoat for and an antidote to the penis envy of the mother.

In myth the use of the son as a scapegoat for the father is both well-known and baldly expressed. Medea kills her sons in jealous rage against Jason [Euripides: *Medea* 803ff. 1021–1080 and 1236–1414], while Procne, for identical motives, kills her son and serves him up to his father in a stew [Apollodorus: iii. 14. 8]. Ovid captures the feelings when he has Procne express the desire to burn, blind, and castrate her husband, and then remark pitilessly, upon seeing her son walk by, "how like your father you are!" [*Metamorphoses* vi. 613–22].

But the positive side of the ambivalence was no less difficult for a child to handle. Imprisoned and isolated by her indifferent and largely absented husband, some of the mother's sexual longing was turned upon her son.[9] Along with, and in direct contradiction to, her need to belittle and discourage his masculine striving, she attempted to build him up into an idealized replacement of her husband, fantasying that "her little man" would grow up to be the perfect hero and take care of his mother all of her days [cf. Baruch, 1952, 202ff.]. Such fantasies would also gratify her own masculine strivings —though *she* might be confined and restricted, her son, an extension of herself, was free and mobile, and she could live her life through him. This may be an additional reason why Greek men married at such an advanced age, and also why the mother of the groom played such an important part in the marriage ceremony.

This maternal ambition for the son is reflected in myths such as those of Danaë and Perseus, and Thetis and Achilles.

[9] Adulterous relationships did, of course, occur, often with slaves, but were difficult to negotiate, risky, and, in all probability, emotionally perfunctory [cf. Blümner, p. 148; Lysias, "On the Murder of Eratosthenes"; Xenophon: *Memorabilia* ii. 1. 5]. In general it seems fair to say that the separation between sex and marriage applied only to males. Women were expected to make do with the little that the marital relationship provided them.

In both cases the mother has been slighted or injured in some way by a male (Danaë by Acrisius and Polydectes, Thetis by Peleus) and the exploits of the son serve directly or indirectly to compensate for this. An analogous relationship is that between Hera and Jason, the goddess using the hero to revenge herself on Pelias.

The myth of Perseus[10] is particularly instructive, inasmuch as it involves the repeated theme of the mother's imprisonment by adult males, whom her son ultimately kills. As his unmarried mother's champion, it is no coincidence that he must face the Gorgon Medusa—symbol of the mother's sexual demands upon the child. The myth thus represents a solution not only to the mother's problems but also to the resulting difficulties of the son.[11]

Another theme related to that of the son-savior or son-extension, but less elaborated, is that of the proud mother who boasts that her children are more beautiful than some group of immortals (Niobe is of course the most famous of these). We can summarize the contradictory attitudes of these various myths by saying that stories which reflected an entirely narcissistic attitude of the mother toward the child appealed to the Greek mind. There are, in fact, very few instances of maternal affection toward sons in the Greek myths. Leaving aside the several cases of incest, parental affection for the same-sex child is generally greater than for the cross-sex child, reflecting the generally disturbed relationship between the sexes in classical Greece (see Chapter XIII), but the mother-son relationship seems to be particularly disturbed.

The ambivalence of the Greek mother toward her son was, in other words, not a normal reactive ambivalence, involving an object-oriented affection and an object-oriented irritation,

---

[10] These myths will be discussed in detail in subsequent chapters.

[11] Thetis, the mother of Achilles, also has Medusa-like qualities, for not only does she transform herself into a serpent and a squid when Peleus, the father of Achilles, attempts to ravish her, but she also turns a wolf to stone by making a Medusa-like face at him [cf. Pausanias: v. 18. 5; Apollodorus: iii. 13. 5 and note; Graves, 1955, I, pp. 271–72].

but a deeply narcissistic ambivalence in which the mother does not respond to the child as a separate person, but as both an expression of and a cure for her narcissistic wounds. Her need for self-expansion and vindication requires her both to exalt and to belittle her son, to feed on and to destroy him.

Since this constellation is unique to classical Greece only in its completeness and intensity, I might mention in passing Freud's remark that the mother-son relationship was least "liable to disaster," and provides "the purest examples of unchanging tenderness, undisturbed by any egoistic considera-tion" [1920, p. 183]. This is surely the most inaccurate state-ment he ever made—a breathtaking piece of sentimental denial by a man rarely given to it. A good argument could be made that all of the major defects of his theory—the patriarchal bias, the overemphasis on oedipal as opposed to "oral" inter-pretations, the limited understanding of female sexuality—can be traced to this blind spot.

Greek Narcissism

Present knowledge of psychopathology permits us to antici-pate two consequences of this ambivalent attitude of the Greek mother. The first is a generally narcissistic personality structure in the child. This springs in part from the mother's own narcissism—the child has no model for the development of simple object-love.[12] But it also follows from the pressure of the mother's ambivalence. Since she alternately accepts him as an idealized hero and rejects his masculine pretensions, one would expect him to develop an abnormal concern about how others view him, and to have an extremely unstable self-concept. He will feel that if he is not a great hero he is noth-ing, and pride and prestige become more important than love. This is perhaps the basis of the Greek idealization of and preoccupation with the body; and we may also assume

---

[12] As Grace Stuart says: "We love out of our leisure from self-concern, and we are always self-concerned unless we know that someone other than ourself is prepared to maintain the significance of our being" [1955, p. 45].

that the homosexuality of the Greeks rests on a firm narcissistic foundation: an unknown poet says, "Seeing a kindred
shape I swooned away" [Plutarch: "Dialogue on Love"
769b]. It is, after all, his physical maleness on which his
mother's ambivalence is focused, and it is his childish pride in
it which she is unable to tolerate with the relaxed indulgence
of an unenvious mother, and yet which she continually stim-
ulates and encourages. Consequently, his physical maleness becomes of enormous importance to him. The male body
dominates his art and his sexual life.

Bieber suggests that the more precocious and more frequent sexual activity of homosexuals may be oriented toward
release rather than pleasure—an attempt "to discharge in
homosexual behavior the anxiety-laden sexual excitation
evoked by the mother. The continued obsessive preoccupation with sexuality is evident in the concentration on sexual
anatomy seen in the exhibitionistic and narcissistic presentation of genitals and buttocks by some homosexuals and the
voyeuristic interest shown by others" [1965, pp. 254-55].
This emphasis on male exhibitionism was striking in Greek
culture, and expressed itself through athletics as well as art.
Homosexual love in Greece centered very much on the
gymnasium, and many pederastic love affairs began with the
admiration of bodily grace. The Greek word *gymnos*, in fact,
means "naked," for naked athletes were a Greek innovation,
dating apparently from "not long" before the Peloponnesian
War, and looked upon askance by non-Greeks [Licht, 1963,
pp. 86-91, 411-98; Plato: *Republic* v. 452; Thucydides: i. 6;
Herodotus: i. 10]. But women, except in Sparta, were excluded from this world of male bodily display. They were
forbidden to watch athletic performances, and were themselves rather fully covered [Licht, 1963, 83-93].[13] The nude

13 Plato, in his prissy way, remarks how ridiculous it will seem, in his
Spartanesque Utopia, to see naked women, especially old ones, exercising in
the gymnasium with the men [*Republic* v. 452].

forms that one sees in Greek art are, until rather late, almost entirely male forms.

But Greek vanity was not only physical. It expressed itself in the preoccupation with honor and glory, in boastfulness, and even perhaps in the willingness of Athenians to spend the better part of their daily lives in myriad and tedious official positions. It appears early: in Achilles' willingness to trade a long uneventful life for a brief one filled with honor and glory, and in Agamemnon's willingness to trade several months of his life for an honorable death on the battlefields of Troy [Homer: *Odyssey* xxiv. 18ff.], a sentiment strongly endorsed by his surviving son:

> Ah, would that 'neath Ilium's walls, my father, thou hadst been slain, gashed by some Lycian spear! Then hadst thou left fair renown for thy children in their halls, and in their going forth hadst made their life admired of men . . . [Aeschylus: *The Choephori* 345–50. Smyth trans.].

One sees it also in the comical discomfiture of Eurymachus at his inability to string Odysseus' bow:

> . . . we dread the speech of men and women, lest some day one of the baser sort among the Achaeans say: "Truly men far too mean are wooing the wife of one that is noble, nor can they string the polished bow. But a stranger and a beggar came in his wanderings, and lightly strung the bow . . ." [Homer: *Odyssey* xxi. 316ff. Butcher and Lang trans.].

Here the scale of values is made quite clear, for despite the years he has devoted to the enterprise Eurymachus says:

> Not for the marriage do I mourn so greatly, afflicted though I be; there are many Achaean women besides, some in sea-girt Ithaca itself and some in other cities. Nay, but I grieve, if indeed we are so far worse than godlike Odysseus in might, seeing that we cannot bend the bow. It will be a shame even for men unborn to hear thereof [Homer: *Odyssey* xxi. 252ff. Butcher and Lang trans.].

Perhaps the most dramatic demonstration of Homeric narcissism is Achilles' willingness to sacrifice his comrades to his own glory. When Patroclus goes out to do battle, he instructs him carefully to "win, for me, great honour and glory in the sight of all the Danaans, so they will bring back to me the lovely girl, and give me shining gifts in addition." But he cautions him not to diminish Achilles' honor by winning the entire war without him. And he concludes his instructions by praying to the gods that not one of the Trojans *or the Greeks* would survive the war save Patroclus and himself [Homer: *Iliad* xvi. 80–100. Lattimore trans.].

What was merely an exaggeration of a trait one would expect to find in any aristocratic warrior culture did not, however, diminish as the Greeks became more civilized; instead it was generalized to embrace all of life. "Nothing defines the quality of Greek culture more neatly than the way in which the idea of competition was extended from physical prowess to the realm of the intellect, to feats of poetry and dramatic composition" [Finley, 1959, pp. 128–29]. Indeed, as Huizinga remarks, "The Greeks used to stage contests in anything that offered the bare possibility of a fight"—beauty (male, of course), singing, riddle-solving, drinking, staying awake [Huizinga, 1955, p. 73]. Nothing seemed to have meaning to the Greek unless it included the defeat of another.

This Runyonesque hypertrophy of Greek narcissism, however comic it appears from a distance, had disastrous consequences for Greek civilization. The insatiable striving for honor and prestige, and the devouring envy of the successes of others continually sapped and disrupted their collective existence and prevented the formation of an enduring social order.

This phenomenon has been brilliantly described in a recent study by Gouldner [1965, pp. 41–74]. Gouldner pulls together a number of Greek traits, such as the obsession with fame and honor, the emphasis on competition and achievement, envy, pessimism, their fear of being guilty of *hubris* (a term that originally meant simply impropriety or not knowing one's place, but as the society became more urban and less traditional, ultimately came to attain the more diffuse significance of arrogance and pride), their rationalism, their loose attachments to both people and possessions, their treachery and duplicity, and their homosexuality; and relates them to what he calls the Greek contest system, a zero-sum game, in which someone wins only if someone else loses. In such a game there is simply a "redistribution of assets without any increase in their total." Gouldner shows how the internal logic of the contest system necessarily generates such peculiarities as Achilles' lukewarm commitment to his own side's victory, and the inability to tolerate the success of one's own leaders, so that almost all of the great men of Greece are eventually punished, exiled, or executed [*Ibid.*, pp. 52–57].

Gouldner does not maintain that the contest system "causes" all of the Greek traits which he describes, but only that it is "one of the major factors . . . underlying the total configuration: pull this strand out, it seems, and much of importance comes in its train" [*Ibid.*, p. 48].[14] The metaphor is extremely apt, and could also be applied to my thesis in this book concerning the correlates of the family constellation. Both systems are self-perpetuating, as we shall see, so that the question of direction of causation becomes even more difficult than usual. If one attempts to relate the two systems, the circle is simply enlarged, without providing an obvious point of entry. For as the reader proceeds, it will become apparent that the Greek family constellation is both maintained by, and generates the motivation for, the contest system.

Whatever the origins of Greek narcissism, its intensity can

[14] The chauvinistic response of classicists to Gouldner's contribution was somewhat saddening [cf. Finley, 1966]. Gouldner unfortunately neglected to take into account the fact that his analysis of the Greek contest system also reproduces, with utter fidelity, the world of academic humanism.

scarcely be ignored. Life in fifth-century Athens seems to have been an unremitting struggle for personal aggrandizement—for fame and honor, or for such goals as could lead to these (wealth, power, and so forth). Since, as Gouldner points out, this was a zero-sum endeavor in which the rewards had to come from one's competitors, the struggle was a somewhat futile one [Gouldner, 1965, pp. 53–55]. Nevertheless it went on, in the accelerative fashion of unquenchable motives. Personal ambition was often impossible to control, as Kitto observes, and three of Greece's most famous leaders —Themistocles, Pausanias, and Alcibiades—were eventually driven by it to betray their homelands and to intrigue with the archenemy, Persia [Kitto, 1960, pp. 248–49]. Indeed, it is even more characteristic of Greek history than of Greek tragedy that men and cities constantly overreached themselves in moments of success, and were destroyed. The most striking example is, of course, the Sicilian Expedition during the Peloponnesian War, in which the Athenians, already hard-pressed by Sparta, essentially risked everything by taking on a second and equally powerful enemy. The willingness, even the compulsion, to risk everything, including one's life, for fame and glory, is stressed by many scholars [cf., e.g., Kitto, *op. cit.*, p. 246; Gouldner, 1965, pp. 43, 48–49]; and Thucydides makes it quite clear that it was in part the very foolhardiness of the adventure which made it so appealing to the Athenians. The more its hazards were stressed, the more they favored it. They competed with one another to provide and equip the various forces involved in the Sicilian Expedition, with the result that it was the largest and most expensive military expedition ever fielded by a Greek city—one directed against the most remote and irrelevant enemy Athens had ever attacked, at a time when they were under siege in their own city. An unusual time to want to "thoroughly upset the Hellenic estimate of their strength and audacity" [Thucydides: vi. 22–25, 31–32, and vii. 28]. The result of this orgy of grandiosity was a disaster from which Athens never fully recovered.

Thucydides' description of the results of the war and the exacerbation of class hatreds can be viewed as merely an intensification of familiar Greek characteristics:

> Words had to change their ordinary meaning and to take that which was now given them. Reckless audacity came to be considered the courage of a loyal ally; prudent hesitation, specious cowardice; moderation was held to be a cloak for unmanliness; ability to see all sides of a question, inaptness to act on any. Frantic violence became the attribute of manliness . . . Revenge also was held of more account than self-preservation. Oaths of reconciliation . . . only held good so long as no other weapon was at hand; but when opportunity offered, he who first ventured to seize it and to take his enemy off his guard, thought this perfidious vengeance sweeter than an open one, since, considerations of safety apart, success by treachery won him the palm of superior intelligence. Indeed it is generally the case that men are readier to call rogues clever than simpletons honest[15] . . . The cause of all these evils was the lust for power arising from greed and ambition . . . [Thucydides: iii. 82].

Even before the Peloponnesian Wars political intrigue and wars between cities were constant [Thucydides: i], and this chronic international condition is mirrored by continual machination and litigation within Athens [cf. Kitto, 1960, pp. 216–18]. So absorbed were the Greeks in the quest for the unwilling admiration of their peers, so universal were vanity, boastfulness, ambition, competitiveness, and invidiousness, that there was neither a need nor an attempt to hide the

---

[15] Thucydides' complaint apparently applies also to modern Greeks, who would still prefer being accused of mendacity and deceit to being honest and deceived [Friedl, 1964, p. 80]. "Honesty and truthfulness are not the national virtues. To lie, or even to steal, is accounted morally venial and intellectually admirable. . . . Anyone may be honest; but to be . . . shrewd. . . . This is Greek and admirable" [Lawson, 1964, p. 31].

feelings of envy and vindictiveness which the success of another aroused. To achieve revenge and arouse envy were the twin delicacies of everyday life [Thucydides: ii. 43; Kitto, 1960, pp. 244ff.; Gouldner, 1965, pp. 43, 53–58]. In Thucydides' sober account of the war with Sparta, one is impressed with the Greeks' willingness to betray tomorrow what they were willing to die for today; with their equal capacity for humane treatment of prisoners and the most savage butchery; with their extraordinary geographical mobility—perhaps unequaled until modern times;[16] with the willingness of citizen-soldiers to spend many years of their lives in military camps, much of the time without engaging in battle. While placing little value on a life after death, they seemed to place little value on life itself when questions of personal vanity were at stake. To honor, everything was sacrificed, and honor is an insatiable god.

As Gouldner points out, the Greek concern with limits derives from a sense of the insatiability of these needs [1965, p. 59]. "They had a maxim, 'nothing too much,' but they were in fact excessive in everything" [Russell, 1945, p. 21]. Their obsessive narcissistic preoccupations kept them from understanding either themselves or their environment to the degree that their intellectual adroitness would lead one to hope [Linton, 1959, pp. 343–46].[17] Their need to surpass prevented them from rational appraisal of their own actions, and led them to attribute behavior they could not accept to external influence (e.g., divine agency)—a trait which they certainly share with most of mankind, but which even today is so extreme as to arouse ethnographic comment [Nilsson,

16 I am not thinking here of nomadic behavior, in which a whole tribe continually moves together in a more or less fixed circuit, occasionally disturbed by ecological conditions, but of individuals or subgroups voluntarily pulling up stakes with the intention of permanently changing residence.

17 Sachs shows how even the pure *body* narcissism of the Greeks may have prevented them from achieving technological innovations [1933, pp. 404ff.].

1949, pp. 159, 163–64; Friedl, 1964, p. 86]. Worst of all, as every schoolboy knows, Greek narcissism continually sabotaged the formation of any enduring system of voluntary cooperation, particularly on the "international" level. So desperately were the Athenians frustrated in this regard that many of them formed what seems to me an outlandish respect for Spartan institutions—a respect which can only in part be attributed to oligarchic partisanship. Sparta, a grotesque and deformed society which was culturally barren, and ineffectual at everything but warfare (and usually even in warfare when it mattered), while hardly free of narcissistic preoccupations, was able to achieve somewhat more stable patterns of cooperation in everyday life. This puny accomplishment corresponded to an aching need among the other Greeks—a need for stability, for a respite from the contest system, for security and trust [Kitto, 1960, pp. 92–95].

I have, of course, been making rather gross generalizations which, while customary in discussions of The Greeks, should at least be recognized as such. Any society, however perverse, produces the usual wide range of individual variation, and I am talking about dominant or socially accentuated rather than universal traits. The same applies at the familial level. Not every marital bond was weak, nor every mother so intensely ambivalent toward her male child, nor every Greek narcissistic in the manner I have described.[18] Nor

---

[18] Indeed, one can best sense the pervasiveness of a trait when one observes it in individuals in whom it seems incongruous—not fully integrated with the rest of their personality. Thus it would be difficult to imagine two men who seem more modest, sensible, unpretentious, and free from self-aggrandizement than Thucydides and Xenophon. The former seems almost un-Greek in his self-effacement from the record of his times, and in his disinterest in justifying his own military performance. But it is as a historian that Thucydides seeks the applause of posterity, and he does not let one forget the fact that he is writing what he considers (correctly, it should be added) to be the greatest historical work ever attempted up to that time. [Thucydides: i. 1. 20–24; cf. also his "signatures" at the close of each year of the war]. Xenophon's *Anabasis* is a more explicitly self-justificatory

would we expect the effect of maternal ambivalence to be uniform. In some instances, with little real affection present to dilute the syndrome, it may have been altogether crippling, but such cases do not make history. Slaves, too, must have moderated the effect in a variety of ways that one can only guess at. In other cases, the narcissism of the son may have been rooted in a firmer maternal foundation, producing sufficient confidence to survive the first shocks of the contest system and find some success in it. Men like Themistocles, Alcibiades, and Alexander, with all the narcissistic failings of their contemporaries, obviously had something more as well. The mother of Themistocles, for example, was alleged to have been a Thracian courtesan, and one assumes that the overweening ambition of Themistocles was not unrelated to her inferior social position [Plutarch: *Themistocles* 1–3, 5]. But all of this is mere speculation.

When we come to Alexander we are on somewhat firmer ground, for we have a little more information about the family. Like many of the other famous Greeks in Plutarch's *Lives*, Alexander is obsessed with ambition and glory, reacts violently to the most paltry slights, and demands adulation, to the point of insisting, in the final years, that even his own soldiers take seriously the ritual farce of his godhood. Of the family conditions which might be conducive to this pattern there are only a few rather dramatic incidents; these, however,

effort, the hero of which is the author—continually under attack, always unjustly so, but always extricating himself with honor from every situation. If one believes even half of this account, Xenophon emerges as a likable person, deserving of our respect and admiration; but there is a certain discrepancy between the selflessness of the hero and the smug, self-congratulatory tone of the author, who is writing, we cannot forget, for the main purpose of commending himself to history.

An even more amusing example, presumably fictitious, is found in the First *Alcibiades* attributed to Plato, in which Socrates, after calling attention to the hopelessly insatiable nature of Alcibiades' narcissistic ambition, reveals his own fantasy of being the power behind the throne—of controlling the would-be-world-conqueror [*op. cit.*, 103–5].

accord well with expectations. Olympias, his mother, was a Dionysian devotee—a jealous and vindictive woman who seems deliberately to have poisoned an initially amicable father-son relationship, and generated exalted ambitions in her son to satisfy her own needs. Her famous claim that Alexander was fathered not by Philip but by Zeus-Ammon, in the form of either a thunderbolt or a serpent, expresses this. Philip, on the other hand, was frightened by his wife's maenadic proclivities, and upon finding her sleeping beside a serpent one day, avoided her company ever afterward, and sought new wives and concubines [Plutarch: *Alexander* 2–3, 9, 23, 27–28, 39, 42, 60, 62, and 74].

An early psychoanalytic interpretation of Alexander's narcissism, by Clark, while based on a different etiological theory of narcissism, is quite consistent with the thesis offered here. Clark stresses Olympias' jealousy and Alexander's seclusion in the women's quarters prior to his tutelage under Leonidas, and suggests that Alexander "received not only maternal love from his mother but conjugal love as well." This love, however, was not for Alexander alone, but sprang from a desire to thwart Philip's ambitions [Clark, 1923, pp. 62–65]. The continued machinations of Olympias throughout Alexander's career do nothing to detract from this family portrait.

It is easy to see how this combination of overdetermined love, exploitation, and aggrandizement, laced with a bit of antagonism toward men and maleness (the near-parthenogenetic birth fantasy expresses this), would produce a man who is generally confident, even reckless, but with his self-regard always problematic, his sensitivity to criticism acute, and his need for respect, honor, and glory exaggerated to insatiability. Alexander's strenuous efforts to achieve the acceptance of the Athenians express this nagging doubt.

For, as Aristotle observes, men pursue honor in order to assure themselves of their own worth ["Ethica Nicomachea"

i. 1095b. 26]. This need, which is surely one of the motivational pillars of the contest system, must derive in large part from a mother-son relationship in which the most grandiose self-definitions are at once fomented and punctured. Gouldner shows how the incessant Greek striving after honor and glory is closely linked to a deep pessimism, and notes that the self is conceived "as a precarious entity which is difficult but vital to maintain . . . an entity that might perish with only one discrepant, unfitting act," such as one of the many seizures of madness with which Greek mythology is dotted [Gouldner, 1965, pp. 43–44, 58, 98]. Feelings of weakness, dependence, passive surrender, desires to be protected, must all be hidden from consciousness, forming, as Gouldner notes, the hidden "underside" of the Greek self-image, achieving expression in the weak, dependent, anxious, fearful, and submissive tone so often taken by Greek choruses [*Ibid.*, pp. 108–11]. These feelings are also expressed, as we shall see, in the anomalous fact that the misogynistic heroes of Greek myth can rarely achieve any of their goals without extensive feminine assistance. The rejection of and dependence upon women mirror the mother's own ambivalence.

This phenomenon is familiar to the psychoanalyst: "unsublimated, erotized, manic self-inflation easily shifts to a feeling of utter dejection, of worthlessness, and to hypochondriacal anxieties. *'Narcissists' of this type thus suffer regularly from repetitive, violent oscillations of self-esteem"* [Reich, 1960, p. 224]. Such a patient tends to be preoccupied with, and overvaluate, the phallus, while regarding the female organs as dirty, injured, and repellent. His attitude toward the female analyst varies inversely with his self-esteem, ranging from contempt to abject dependence, the latter being set off by any minor setback: "The tiniest disappointment, the slightest physical indisposition, the most trifling experience of failure can throw the patient into extreme despair. . . . The grandiose body-phallus fantasy . . .

turns *suddenly* into one of total castration . . ." [*Ibid.*, pp. 222, 224, 226–27].

This syndrome, at a cultural level, both generates and is generated by penis envy in the mother. A society which derogates women produces envious mothers who produce narcissistic males who are prone to derogate women. The anxiety that success aroused in Greek males had its origins in the nursery. For was not *hubris* fundamentally masculine pride and phallic self-satisfaction, even exhibitionism? And was not the divine *phthonos* at bottom the resentful envy of the mother? Baruch describes graphically such intolerance of maleness and male exhibitionism [1952, pp. 64–69; see also pp. 57, 75, 108, 124–25], and Hellenic society seems to have been ideally constructed to induce both responses. It is significant that the name of one of the avenging Erinyes, who were primarily, if not exclusively, agents of *maternal* revenge (perhaps personifications of maternal curses), connotes not merely anger but also envy.

Use of the term "penis envy" in discussing this attitude is justified by several considerations. If women are derogated in a society it seems reasonable to assume that their resentment would focus on differentiating sexual characteristics. This would be particularly accentuated in a society in which male exhibitionism was encouraged and female exhibitionism prohibited. The female child learns early that her brother is a far more important and valued being than herself, and why. In such a society one is not surprised to find that a common mode of feminine revenge consists of magic spells designed to render the male victim impotent. Concomitantly, a variety of devices are used by males to protect or guarantee potency [Licht, 1963, pp. 370–71, 513ff.]. Such spells were still being employed by jealous women, and being anxiously counteracted by fearful males, when Lawson studied Greek folklore at the turn of the century [Lawson, 1964, pp. 18–21].

Horney argues that the fear of derision is universal in males, and that this is rooted in the fact that the small boy's narcissism is so centered in the penis, which he knows is inadequate in relation to the mother. She cites chronic male preoccupations with penis size and potency, which she ties also to the fact that a woman can bear a child by simply *being*, while the man must *perform* [Horney, 1932, pp. 356–59]. That the adjective "castrating" has come to be applied popularly to women who ridicule or disparage male pretensions supports this view. But it also seems likely that the incidence of "castrating" behavior by mothers toward sons would depend heavily on social conditions aggravating tension between the sexes.

The dynamics of the process were ably described by Abraham [1920, pp. 368–69]: "A mother with this kind of aversion to the male sex injures the narcissism of the boy. A boy in his early years is proud of his genital organs; he likes to exhibit them to his mother, and expects her to admire them. He soon sees that his mother ostentatiously looks the other way, even if she does not give expression to her disinclination in words. These women . . . are most careful to avoid touching and even mentioning the penis, [but] they tend to caress the child's buttocks. . . . They also take an excessive interest in the child's defecatory acts. The boy is thus forced into a new orientation of his libido. Either it is transferred from the genital to the anal zone, or the boy is impelled towards a member of his own sex—his father in the first instance—to whom he feels himself bound by a bond which is quite comprehensible to us. At the same time he becomes a woman-hater, and later will be constantly ready to criticize very severely the weaknesses of the female sex. This chronic influence of the mother's castration complex seems to me to be of greater importance as a cause of castration-fear in boys than occasionally uttered threats of castration."

All three of these outcomes are found together in Greek

culture. Abraham's analysis, for example, helps account for the modal preoccupations of Aristophanes, in whose comedies defecation, buggery, and the vulgarity of women are pervasive. Since one may reasonably assume that a comic writer competing for a prize does not devote his energies to material that is not entertaining to his audience, it seems fair to say that the Greeks were exceptionally fond of scatological humor. The boy analyzed by Baruch showed a similar fondness, feeling that all body protuberances aroused his mother's displeasure, but that "brown penises" pleased her greatly. The mother in turn reported great ease with bowel training but a fierce struggle over bladder control. "A mother often unwittingly betrays through hands or shoulders or face how she feels about him and his body" [Baruch, 1952, pp. 64–69], and such preferences and priorities are easily and effectively transmitted. Anxiety about injury to the penis is expressed in the Greek practice of infibulation, and one might conceivably make a case that the Greeks centered their erotic interest in the buttocks to an unusual extent [Licht, 1963, pp. 27, 507, 512]. Evidence for the latter is scant and unconvincing, however, except with regard to homosexual attachments, which I shall discuss shortly.[19]

What is perhaps more characteristically Greek is an outcome not mentioned by Abraham, but discussed by other psychoanalytic writers: a "genitalization" of the entire body. Thus Katan suggests that when a small boy's phallic exhibitionism is rejected by the mother, "instead of cathecting an organ that seems worthless, the boy cathects his whole body as if it were a penis." This will be the case particularly if the mother treats him as a narcissistic extension of herself. Katan describes such a case, in which the mother, a domineering woman, made her son perform for guests on every possible occasion, and treated his body as her own property, for ex-

---

[19] What is required is evidence that this was the *only* part of the anatomy considered attractive, and this is surely lacking.

ample, giving him frequent enemas. The patient, who was terrified of women, and in particular of the vagina, which he imagined as huge and bloody, was absorbed in homosexual fantasies involving young blond boys without pubic hair. He thought of himself as an extension of his mother, as her penis [Katan, 1960, pp. 211–14]. In still another case, "The aggressive, mocking and sneering way in which his mother had rejected the little boy's exhibitionistic genital wooing" led to a passive homosexual orientation toward the father, since "every approach to a woman meant a melting together with her" [Lampl-de Groot, 1957, pp. 121–22]. Since the mother's hostility is focused on the phallus, her displeasure is avoided by generalizing phallic narcissism to the whole body. Furthermore, the boy's separation from her is problematic—both desperately desired and as desperately feared—and the "whole-body" orientation expresses both of these feelings: his body is integral, intact, yet simply a part of hers. I shall discuss these feelings in more detail in the next chapter.

Harnik applies this degenitalization of the boy's narcissism specifically to Greece. He argues that the displacement of exhibitionistic tendencies from the genitals to the whole body is expressed in Greek sculpture, particularly in representations of Heracles, with a small de-emphasized penis and intense concentration on secondary sexual characteristics [Harnik, 1924, pp. 74–75].[20] Whether or not this is so, degenitalization clearly provides a solution to the Greek mother's ambiva-

[20] Opposition between manly strength and organ size is a common theme in bawdy jokes, and I can recall from my own childhood in a suburban community a curious folk belief which was shared by boys just entering puberty. This was during the golden age of Charles Atlas and his body-building plans, and advertisements involving "97-pound weaklings" having sand kicked in their faces by sturdy bullies at beaches appeared in every comic book and newspaper. Despite references in these ads to books and courses of training, the miraculous transformations supposedly achieved were alleged to lie in the mysterious principle called "dynamic tension," and many boys believed that this term was nothing else than a euphemism for castration. According to this extraordinary idea, the energy bound up

lence, since the boy can at once strive to approximate his mother's exalted ambitions for him and yet de-emphasize that aspect of himself of which she is intolerant.

The connections between these various components of Abraham's syndrome—genitalization of the body, misogyny, anality, homosexuality, and attraction to the father—will become clear when we discuss the Greek homosexual pattern. We must first pause, however, to complete a line of thought left dangling at the beginning of this section, where I suggested that narcissism was one of two outcomes which might be predicted from the kind of maternal ambivalence previously described.

Greek Madness

The second consequence one would anticipate from the ambivalence of the Greek mother is an increase in the incidence of schizophrenia. Such an expectation derives from the theory of Bateson and his associates [1956] that schizophrenia originates in what they call the "double bind." A "double bind" is said to obtain when a mother deals with ambivalent feelings by explicitly or covertly directing the child to respond to two contradictory ideas, and punishing him for failure to do either. The situational factors operating in the Greek family accord well with the contributory conditions discussed by Bateson, and the maternal injunctions he outlines might be expressed somewhat as follows:

(1) You must be a strong and adult male, treat me as a

---

in the testicles would, after castration, be released to the rest of the body to assist in muscular growth. It is not accidental that this primitive libido theory was popular among boys entering puberty, who were experiencing the opposite, as it were, of their hypothesized "dynamic tension" process: i.e., a concentration of libido in the genitals, and the decay of the latency-period pattern (boastful hypermasculinity and muscular activity) as they entered the "spring fever" era of their lives. The underlying notion, in any case, is that sexuality is enervating.

woman, and by your conspicuous male achievements express my own aspirations.

(2) You must not aspire to maleness nor flaunt your masculinity before me nor remind me that I am a woman.

(3) You must not desert me nor find any contradiction in my demands.

But is there any evidence for the rather heretical notion that schizophrenic tendencies occurred with particular frequency among the Greeks? They probably experienced as much psychosis as other societies during this period [Dodds, 1957, pp. 64–82; Kisker, 1941, 535ff.], but there is no way of comparing illness rates, and no clues to indicate a special predisposition. It may be that all the conditions of the "double bind" did not hold: I have already suggested a partial "way out" of the dilemma through the elaboration of secondary narcissism, and the boy's exodus from the nursery at seven or so may have provided another mitigating factor.

Whatever the reality may have been, the prediction achieves a shadowy confirmation from Greek fantasy. No other mythology with which I am familiar contains so many explicitly designated instances of madness.[21] All of these, of course, involve a superhuman agent, but the agents are thereby few in number, and certain characteristics easily identified.[22]

The most striking fact is that of all the clear instances of madness deliberately produced in one being by another, none can be said to be caused by a truly masculine or paternal agent. Most are inflicted by goddesses, and the remainder by the effeminate Dionysus, himself a previous victim at the hands of Hera [Euripides: *The Cyclops* 1–4; Apollodorus: iii. 5. 1]. Nor is the relationship between the sex of the agent and the

[21] While it must be admitted that Christian myth, legend, and official history provide the highest yield of madmen to be found anywhere, they are not identified as such in the materials themselves.

[22] The method of choosing cases is presented in Chapter XIII, along with a rudimentary quantitative analysis.

sex of the victim a random one: in the overwhelming majority of cases madness is induced in persons of the opposite sex.
The pervasiveness of narcissism in Greek life (where else but
in Greece could the myth of Narcissus have been born?) is
reflected in the motives for these inflictions. Direct insult to
the god or goddess is the overwhelming favorite, with jealousy second.

The symptoms of madness are reasonably consistent, but
vary somewhat by the sex of the victim and the identity of
the agent. The most general symptoms are wandering, raving,
visual hallucinations or distortions, and acts of aggression.
Men hallucinate far more often than women, while women
(as Maenads) have a monopoly on eating children raw. Men
are more often self-destructive, but men and women are
equally prone to kill their children. The peculiarly frequent
symptoms of killing and dismembering one's own children
are entirely restricted to the two most inveterate psychotogenic agents, Hera and Dionysus.

Several themes emerge from these cases. The first is the
antagonism between the sexes, already discussed. The second
is the notion, shared by much of modern psychiatry, that
madness comes primarily from the mother (assuming the god-
mortal relationship to be a symbolic equivalent of the parent-
child relationship). The third is that madness consists
primarily of aggression, i.e., killing or injuring someone—an
idea which has always been popular and which finds expression in the double meaning of the English word [cf. Plato
(?): *Alcibiades* ii. 139].

That children are so often the victims of parental attacks
of madness is an indication both of the narcissistic nature of
the disease and of the tendency for narcissistic disorders to
be emotionally contagious, particularly between parents and
children. Hera's injured narcissism leads her to persecute her
stepson, Dionysus, whose injured narcissism in turn leads him
to persecute Lycurgus, Agave, and the women of Argos, who

express their madness in the destruction of their children [Apollodorus: iii. 5. 1–2]. This cycle has its milder counterpart in the dynamics of the Greek family. The jealous, neglected mother injures the narcissism of the young boy. He, upon reaching adulthood, selects, because of doubts about his adequacy with mature women, an immature, inadequate wife, whom he treats with contempt and neglect, thus ensuring a malignant disturbance in the mothering of his own sons, and so on. His precarious self-respect compels him to disparage women and to choose "a feminine type which is infantile, non-maternal and hysterical, and by so doing . . . expose each new generation to the influence of such women" [Horney, 1932, p. 360].

Now it may be objected that all this talk of mythical madness is inappropriate, since many of the myths involved are merely a misunderstanding by sophisticated urban Greeks of shamanistic survivals and ecstatic cults. There are two answers to this objection. First, it is impossible that any educated Greek was unfamiliar with religious ecstasy, which was an important part of the Eleusinian initiations, Bacchic rites, and the utterances of the Delphic Pythoness—institutions in relation to whose durability the classical age was but a lightning flash in a long night. Many leading Athenians were initiated into the Mysteries, and even Socrates was not above consulting the Delphic Oracle.[23] They were perfectly capable of distinguishing between such temporary and structured possession and "spontaneous" psychosis; Plato does so at some length [*Phaedrus* 244]. Second, regardless of the origins of the myths, their survival in the form given must be accounted for in terms of contemporary meanings, which is what I am attempting here. As Gouldner points out, the Greeks were

[23] By our standards, the Greeks were hopelessly superstitious. Even so sensible a man as Xenophon never made a move without consulting his diviners. At one point during the Persian Expedition the army was in danger of starving to death because Xenophon would not act with unfavorable omens [*Anabasis* vi. 4. 12–22].

"deeply concerned about their capacity to go murderously berserk" [1965, p. 109]. Their rational self-possession was precarious and brittle, and they worried constantly about impulse control. Part of their difficulty arose from the fact that while this control was exerted in the service of narcissistic ambition, their need for self-aggrandizement was itself out of control. Thus the instances of madness cited by Xenophon both involve grandiose notions of self-capacities [*Memorabilia* iii. 9. 7 and iv. 7. 6].

Homosexuality and the Role of the Father

Bateson [1956] maintains, as have many others, that in the family of the schizophrenic child the role of the father is primarily a negative one; that he is important, to the male child at least, primarily through his weakness and inconsequence, his physical or emotional distance; and that he is unable to provide an alternative and less overcharged source of support for the child, to moderate the pathogenic impact of the mother, or to form an adequate role model [Lidz, et al., 1966, pp. 50, 103–5, 262–63, 266–67].

In the case of the Greeks the father's role was minor by virtue not so much of weakness as of physical withdrawal and detachment. Although for most purposes this distinction is an unimportant one, physical absence does tend to produce one additional effect, i.e., idealization. This relationship is stressed by Bach [1946], who found that father-separated boys tended to have an idealized father image, somewhat similar to the normal feminine view of the father as a nurturant, rewarding protector. This image was a more ambivalent one, however, insofar as the mother of the father-separated boy presented a negative picture of the father to him.

Such an ambivalence characterizes the Greek image of Zeus: on the one hand he appears often as wise and just, a benevolent protector. On the other hand he is often portrayed as capricious and irresponsible. The first group of traits might be seen to represent the kind of father the Greek boy wanted, as an antidote to the conflicting demands made upon him by his mother. The second group perhaps shows the father more as the mother tended to see him and portray him to the child.[24] Yet both may, in part, describe the father as he actually was, if my thesis is correct. The female-dreading narcissism of the Greek male indeed made him a somewhat capricious being, yet also helped to free him from traditional customs and loyalties, thus providing the groundwork for a more universalistic orientation to the world [cf. Gouldner, 1965, pp. 64–74].

The readiness of the Athenians to exalt and depose leaders is another expression of the search for the idealized father, which Abraham mentions in the work quoted above. This homosexual quest (cf. also Xenophon: *Symposium* iv. 15–17) helps to explain the willingness of the Athenians to follow and forgive Alcibiades despite his uncertain loyalty, his lack of any significant skills that we know of, and his tendency to flout their most cherished and pristine superstitions. Narcissist that he was [cf. Thucydides: v. 43 and vi. 15–19], Alcibiades was faithful only to himself, but he knew how to make his own narcissism work for that of all men, as in this speech "quoted" by Thucydides:

> Athenians, I have a better right to command than others
> . . . The things for which I am abused, bring fame to my
> ancestors and to myself . . . The Helenes . . . concluded [our
> city] to be even greater than it really is, by reason of the mag-
> nificence with which I represented it at the Olympic games,

[24] Many scholars would no doubt argue that these contradictions merely represent a developmental trend in the religious life of the Greeks from a more primitive, magical, shame-culture orientation to a more ethically oriented one. One must then ask, however, why the more primitive conception survived? Certainly the two views of Zeus appear side by side in the *Iliad* as well as in very late works. Here, as elsewhere, there is room for many interpretations of the material.

when I sent into the lists seven chariots, a number never before entered by any private person, and won the first prize, and was second and fourth, and took care to have everything else in a style worthy of my victory . . . Again, any splendour that I have exhibited at home . . . is naturally envied by my fellow-citizens, but in the eyes of foreigners has an air of strength . . . persons of this kind and all others that have attained to any distinction, although they may in their lifetime be unpopular with their fellow-men . . . leave to posterity the desire of claiming connexion with them even without any ground, and are vaunted by the country to which they belonged, not as strangers or ill-doers but as fellow-countrymen and heroes. [Thucydides: vi. 16].

This speech plays upon the injured narcissism of the Greek male by offering him a hero model with whom he can identify and of whose glory he can partake. The homosexual search posited by Abraham is in part a search for a more neutral, non-devouring protector, but it is also a search for a more heroic self-image. This is sought through a male identification and an attempted purging of maternally induced conflicts, such as is described by Campbell in his discussion of the "atonement with the father" [cf. Campbell, 1956, pp. 138ff.].

What is perhaps somewhat unique to Greek culture is that this search was to a degree successful. At the age of six or seven both Spartan and Athenian boys entered the male world of school and gymnasium, albeit in quite different styles [Blümner, pp. 99ff.]. Thus they were removed from those factors operative in the nursery and provided to some extent with male role models. As they grew older, furthermore, strong, institutionalized emotional attachments to adult males became more and more significant.

It is important to recognize what this did and did not do for the Greek male's psychological development. There has been much recent discussion of the existence of certain common

characteristics among cultures and subcultures in which a
male child grows up in a "matrifocal" household, and then
makes an abrupt transition into a male world [Burton and
Whiting, 1961; B. Whiting, 1965], and the Greeks shared in
these traits, as we shall see. It seems likely, however, that the
Greek patterns of transition were somewhat more successful
in achieving a comfortable masculine identification than patterns such as the harsh puberty rites of many primitive tribes,
or the rigid male peer-group attachments of the modern slum
—providing an earlier and more gradual attachment than the
former and more access to adults than the latter.

At the same time, it should be recognized that the transition
still occurred too late to *undo* the effects of the ambivalent
and close-binding mother-son relationship—it could only construct a reasonable neurotic compensation. It did not, for example, change the relationship between mother and son, but
only reduced its importance long after the "damage" had
been done. Neubauer, in his study of the one-parent child,
concludes that the effect of parental seductiveness toward the
child will be insignificant if the loss of the other parent occurs "after he has reached the oedipal position"—presumably
four to five years old [1960, pp. 287ff., 303]. Conversely, one
might assume that the effects of such seduction cannot easily
be erased by events occurring after that period. In any case,
nothing has been resolved or worked through in either the
marital or the mother-son relationship: all of the old fearful
and sex-antagonistic assumptions are still operative, with the
boy simply stepping from one camp to the other.

Yet it may have been precisely this marital separateness and
the son's ability, as he grew older, to relate to each parent
separately, which protected the son from more serious pathology. We know today that the most typical family constella-
tions of schizophrenic males and homosexual males resemble
one another to a considerable extent, both featuring an intense, close-binding, mother-son bond and a remote father.

It has even been argued that the two are functionally related—homosexuality being a defense against latent schizophrenia. Bieber argues that they are independent, however, and points out that the schizophrenics in his study differed from the nonschizophrenic homosexuals in having a disturbed father-son relationship [1965, p. 264]. Now, most of the more recent studies of the etiology of schizophrenia have stressed the role of the total family constellation—in particular the willingness to falsify reality and sacrifice the psyche of the child in order to preserve a spurious family integration [Wynne, *et al.*, 1958; Lidz, *et al.*, 1966; see also Vogel and Bell, 1960]. This would suggest that the child may be protected somewhat by social arrangements which permit the parents to be as separate as they really feel. The Greeks did not expect the family to be a close, intimate unit, and this perhaps gave the child more psychic maneuverability than in a society like ours, in which a family identical to the Greek ideal-type I have posited would be forced to operate at very close range.

Another consequence of the Greek system was that the father did not compete with his son within the family. What is "disturbed" about the father-son relationship in the families of schizophrenics is that the father is often seen entirely through the contemptuous eyes of the mother, or is a highly narcissistic individual intensely jealous of the care received by the child, or both. Lidz and his associates found that in their male patients "the most striking findings concern the very poor masculine model provided the son by his father, and the mother's dependency upon this son for her own emotional satisfaction and completion, often with failure to set ego boundaries between herself and the boy."[25] Many of the fathers "behaved more like sons to their wives than husbands," while others "filled rivalrous rather than paternal roles toward their sons." The mothers, meanwhile "made it clear to their sons that they were dissatisfied with their hus-

25 A question I will discuss in detail in the next chapter.

bands," and in their behavior toward the sons "tended to be engulfing and, at times, highly seductive." As a result, "the original mother-son symbiosis with its erotic components and the initial identification of the boy with his mother were never properly surmounted . . . The son found himself more important than the father to his mother . . ." [Lidz, et al., 1966, pp. 104–13, 266–67].

Now, the Greek son may have had the same dissatisfied, engulfing, seductive mother, and the same difficulty in breaking the symbiotic tie with her. But it seems clear that he *did* have an adequate if somewhat remote masculine model, and a father or father substitutes who filled paternal rather than rivalrous roles. Unlike the father of the schizophrenic, the Greek father did not look to the mother for the satisfaction of his needs, but sought them outside the family. Hence competition between father and son in this deepest sphere was avoided. In addition, father and son had a separate relationship of some sort *outside* the family, as common participants in the male world. This meant that the impact of whatever angry, disparaging feelings the mother may have had toward her husband was reduced by the fact that the son had an independent experience with and perception of him.

In the modern schizophrenogenic family a derogated father tends to have little relationship of any kind with the son. Thus despite (and in some ways because of) their profuse narcissism, Greek males could genuinely love their sons, and, indeed, young boys in general, without these relationships being incapacitated by rivalry. Gouldner discusses the ways in which homosexual relationships mitigated, although they were ultimately infected by, the contest system [1965, pp. 60–63]; and this seems to be rooted in the need to preserve the solidarity of the father-son relationship. Greek homosexuality always had, as Gouldner observes, a decidedly nonreciprocal quality, consisting of an older lover who pursued, protected, and gave, and a younger love-object who received, begged, and simply existed as a beautiful object [cf. Xenophon: *Symposium* i. 8–10 and viii. 21–22; Strato: "Musa Puerilis" 228; Plato: *Charmides* 154–55]. Plato makes this quite explicit by insisting that Achilles must have been the beloved and not the lover of Patroclus (as Aeschylus had erroneously maintained), since he was younger and prettier [Plato: *Symposium* 179–80]. Indeed, there is some evidence that only pretty boys with homosexual lovers to look after them received an adequate education in Athens [Plato (?): *Alcibiades* i. 122; cf. also *Symposium* 178], and this was more fully institutionalized at Sparta [Licht, 1963, p. 441].

One does not know, of course, how close the typical father-son relationship actually was. The passage from the *Alcibiades* just cited implies that it was not close, but other evidence suggests the contrary [cf. Xenophon: *Symposium* iii. 12–13]. It seems most likely that the relationship was typically affectionate but somewhat attenuated, and that the emotional intensity of the later homosexual attachments both expressed and redressed its limitations. Insofar as he felt neglected by his father's absorption in political or social affairs or warfare, the boy was receptive to the more or less nurturant lover, and when he grew still older, loved his own childhood image in a new youth, as compensation for his own deprivations [cf. Stuart, 1955, pp. 129–30]. These themes of self-love and yearning for a paternal protector are occasionally fused, as in Critobulus' love for Cleinias [Xenophon: *Symposium* iv. 10–18], but are more typically kept separate.

Thus pederasty was far from being a trivial by-product of Greek society; it became an almost vital institution, diluting the mother-son pathology, counteracting rivalry between father and son, and providing a substitute father-son bond. As is not unusual with social institutions, the same pattern—sex segregation—both caused and mitigated social pathology. It is basically a system of compartmentalization, with all the clumsy inconveniences of such systems. Its Rube Goldberg rigidities impeded internalization and self-awareness, encouraged denial and projection of personal feelings, and facilitated the drawing of artificial distinctions. Yet these defects cannot be separated from the essential compensatory functions that they also served.

Some writers, misled by Socrates' alleged asceticism, have assumed the pederastic relationship to have been an entirely sublimated one, which is a little like trying to argue that Americans are only interested in spiritual prosperity. Pederasty is indeed strongly romanticized by the Greeks, and they were no different from modern homosexuals in their fondness for viewing homosexual relationships as more spiritual than heterosexual ones (cf. Henry, 1948). But women and boys are continually discussed as interchangeable alternatives, and in contexts where there can be no doubt that copulation is at issue, and not some vague spiritual connection [cf. Xenophon: *Anabasis* iv. 1. 14–15; Plutarch: "Dialogue on Love" 751c; Plato: *Symposium* 191–92]. Even more frequent are references to physical contact which will lead, or not lead, or is in danger of leading, to some physical consummation, the most famous of which is Alcibiades' engagingly candid account of his vigorous but unsuccessful effort to seduce the pious Socrates [Plato: *Symposium* 217–19; cf. also *Charmides* 155 and *Phaedrus* 255–56; Xenophon: *Symposium* iv. 25–28]. Finally, if there had been no physical sexuality involved, it is a little difficult to understand why parents found it necessary to keep young boys chaperoned in the presence of older males who were potential lovers [Plato: *Charmides* 155 and *Symposium* 183]. While male prostitutes were looked down upon, and even prohibited by law (unsuccessfully), it was clearly only the mercenary aspect of it that was scorned [Licht, 1963, pp. 436–38]. A similar attitude is held with regard to sexual relationships with slaves—it is equated with heterosexual intercourse and scorned as devoid of higher feelings [cf. Plutarch: "Dialogue on Love" 751b].²⁶

The preferred style of homosexual contact was apparently anal intercourse, with the younger boy assuming the passive role—some shame being attached to accepting this role at too late an age [Plutarch: "Dialogue on Love" 751d–e and 768f; Xenophon: *Symposium* viii. 21–22; Strato: "Musa Puerilis" 7, 206, 210, 213, 228, 238, and 251].²⁷ This is what one would expect, for the Greeks, like ourselves, were rather anxious about assuming the feminine role. Effeminate men and transvestites were viewed much in the same manner as in our own society (although, to be sure, much less punitively), being a frequent butt of Aristophanes' humor [cf. Licht, 1963, pp. 493–94]. On the whole, at least until very late, the Greeks were homosexuals of the black leather variety—compulsively masculine, scornful of womankind, phobic about all things feminine, and very concerned with maintaining a dominant and aggressive self-image. By substituting a young boy for a woman the Greek male could realize all of these needs simultaneously—still playing a phallic male role but avoiding the dangerous female.²⁸

For the younger partner the response was more complex. His youth reduced the shame attached to his role, as did the fact that he was the pursued, the flattered, the sought after. Furthermore, it was common for youths his age to be thus initiated into manhood. Indeed, the incorporation of feminine characteristics is a frequent paradox of such transitions [cf. Bettelheim, 1955a]. But the assumption of a passive, feminine

²⁶ Not only the most prominent Athenians but even the gods themselves were much addicted to pederasty [cf. Licht, 1963, pp. 434, 493].

²⁷ Some of these materials are very late, but they resemble in all respects the quality of homosexual interaction in fifth-century sources.

²⁸ The old phobia regarding pubic hair plays a not inconsiderable role in the preference for youthful objects, even when male [cf. Strato: "Musa Puerilis" 30, 220, and 229. Note especially the pun in the latter].

role at this moment of approaching maturity also fulfilled two other symbolic needs: the need to counteract competitive feelings toward the father and other males, and the need to identify with and feel a part of them.

It is common among mammals for males to assume a feminine copulatory posture toward other males when wishing to express submission or surrender. Ovesey has suggested that many homosexual feelings and fantasies among humans are to be similarly understood, and tend to be aroused in competitive situations when assertion is required and failure threatened [1965, pp. 212ff.]. Gouldner points out a perfect example of this phenomenon in the *Iliad*, when Hector considers trying to appease Achilles [see Gouldner, 1965, p. 60]. Taking an adult role in as highly competitive, contentious, and invidious a society as urban Greece of the classical period must have been a somewhat fearful prospect for a young boy, although also an exciting and venturesome one, and the temptation to assume a placating attitude must have at times been strong. The institutionalization of a feminine sexual role—being courted, pursued, and surrendering passively—served to ease the transition.

Even more important, and closely related to this anxiety over assertion, was the need for some paternal support, some borrowing of paternal potency and strength. Often such a need takes the rather literal form of fantasies of being the father's penis or being anally violated by the father—acquiring in this symbolic way the father's power so as to be able to function as a man [cf. Katan, 1960, pp. 210ff.; Reich, 1960, p. 227; Ovesey, 1965, pp. 213–15].

Part of this need arose from the Greek boy's felt inadequacy in relation to his mother's unstated sexual demands. In wishing to borrow his father's potency he was merely requesting the redress of a prior imbalance; for had the father been adequate in fulfilling the mother's sexuality in the first place, the son's feeling of impotence would not have arisen.

This constellation is common in the family histories of homosexuals today. The mother is often extremely seductive toward the son, sleeping in the same bed with him at a late age, exhibiting herself to him, making him a confidant and an ally against the father, punishing his heterosexuality, and so on [Bieber, 1965, pp. 250–53; Gundlach and Riess, 1966, Tables I and III]. The son wishes the father to be stronger, to protect him against these overpowering feminine needs [Ovesey, 1965, p. 226; cf. also Baruch, 1952, pp. 205–9]. The mother's seductiveness is frightening—she "expects too much" [*Ibid.*, pp. 135–36], and her behavior is retrospectively viewed with disgust. She is fantasied as a prostitute and the vagina is viewed as dirty, polluted—a toilet [cf. Thompson, 1950]. It is the homosexual's aversion toward the vagina which enables one to categorize homosexuality as a phobia [Bieber, 1965, p. 253; Gundlach and Riess, 1966, Table III; Ovesey, 1965, pp. 222, 228–29, 230]. The Greeks clearly shared this phobic attitude, as we have seen, so that to attempt to pass them off as exhibiting nothing more than a healthy sexual diffuseness, as Finley does [Finley, 1966], is merely the usual whitewash.

Maternal Bogies

While paternal figures tend to be idealized in Greek fantasy, the exact reverse is true of the mother. Blümner points out that "naughty children were brought to obedience or quiet by threats of bogies, but, curiously enough, these Greek bogies were all female creatures" [Blümner, p. 88]. Similarly, there were witches but no sorcerers in Greek folklore, and the statue of Fear was a woman [Nilsson, 1961, p. 97; Rose, 1925, p. 95]. Thalia Feldman also comments upon this feminine near-monopoly of the realm of fear, and contrasts it with the situation in the West today, which is almost exactly the opposite, with male bogies prevailing [Feldman, 1965, pp. 490–

94]. In rural Greece, however, the ancient pattern remains, with malevolent female deities omnipresent [Lawson, 1964, pp. 130–90].

These female bogies—Lamia, Gorgo, Empusa, Mormo, and so forth—are fundamentally nothing more than that; they are often named plurally, and have little attached myth. When they are assigned characteristics, however, their connection with fear of the mother's sexuality becomes apparent. That they should prey on children is intrinsic, but what is important is the sense of deprivation that often attaches itself to them. They have lost their own children, they are devouring and cannibalistic, and, above all, they are sexually ravenous and insatiable [Kerényi, 1960, pp. 39–40; Lawson, 1964, pp. 172–76].[29] Whatever the origin of these bogies, it seems apparent that at some point they were infused with meanings derived from the child's fear of the emotional needs of the mother, needs often directed toward himself, and in relation to which he felt helpless, inadequate, and frightened. This is one reason why intense feelings which are difficult to control tend to be viewed as having a feminine origin. Thus Socrates refers to passions and vices as "despoinae" and sees them as more malevolent and less straightforward than a severe master, insatiable and deceitful and capable of destroying a man ut-

---

[29] Many interesting parallels may be found in the witches of other cultures. Among the Gusii, for example (who are also strongly sex-antagonistic as well as patriarchal and polygynous, with children brought up in separate mother-child households), fear of female sexuality is expressed in the practice of clitoridectomy. The wedding night in this society is defined as a contest, in which the wife wins if she makes the husband impotent or prevents penetration, while he wins if he successfully performs intercourse many times and inflicts pain and exhaustion on his bride. Any active role on the part of the wife during foreplay or coitus is punishable by ancestor spirits. Witches among the Gusii are always female, and are believed to run about naked at night, and to be cannibalistic. One becomes a witch by having lost, like Lamia, many children, or by deliberately killing one's own child [B. Whiting, 1963, pp. 65–72, 114ff., 183ff.].

terly [Xenophon: *Oeconomicus* i. 20 and ii. 1]. Indeed, even when he is trying, in his sophistical way, to talk a young man out of his hatred for his mother, Socrates automatically compares the latter to a wild beast [Xenophon: *Memorabilia* ii. 2, 7–10].

In support of Socrates' equation of impulse with female dominance, the extreme forms of maternal seductiveness are often accompanied by schizophrenia, as is, almost invariably, consummated mother-son incest. Wahl points out that feelings of being devoured or drained by intercourse are not uncommon, and suggests that these are enormously magnified in the case of incest with "the all-encompassing mother who gives not only the breast but takes, as the female spider takes —leaving the hollow husk of her mate as a memento of their ecstasy." He suggests that it is not surprising that the cases of mother-son incest he describes (both of which involve absent fathers and promiscuous mothers who are alternately seductive and rejecting toward the male child) "are associated with the most seriously disorganizing and ego-shattering illness which we know" [Wahl, 1963, pp. 182–89]. The Greek male generally escaped this outcome, as I have suggested, but never entirely lost sight of the danger nor the sense of fear, and his defiant narcissism expressed his fervent need for autonomy, ego integrity, and control.

Thus we find that what Licht calls the first Greek love-tragedy—Sophocles' lost *Phaedra*—consists of a chaste and prudish boy being pursued by his passionate stepmother, who responds to his refusals with vindictive and lethal rage [Licht, 1963, pp. 150–51]. Aristophanes treats the same interpersonal constellation farcically in the *Ecclesiazusae* [1015ff.], in which a law is passed requiring any man who wishes to copulate with a young girl first to satisfy some old hag, and as a result, a young man is almost torn to pieces by two old harlots.

Mature and conspicuous female sexuality was in itself sufficient to call bogies to mind. Courtesans were frequently
called names like Lamia and Charybdis [Licht, 1963, pp. 345,
348], Sphinx [Fontenrose, 1959, p. 309], or Phryne ("toad")
—names which expressed depth of avarice as well as sexuality
[Aristophanes: *Ecclesiazusae* 1101]. Indeed, even married
women were frequently called *lamiae* or *empusae* if they
showed any spirit [Licht, 1963, p. 59]. It was only young
girls who escaped these epithets.[30] The feminine ideal in art
was correspondingly youthful—even boyish [*Ibid.*, p. 427],
and benevolence among goddesses was highly correlated with
virginity. As Kitto points out [1960, p. 18], the two oldest
cities in Greece worshiped mother-goddesses (betraying the
matriarchal substructure of Greek civilization): One of these
goddesses, Athene, was "dematrified," and became not only
virginal and boyish, but also the most helpful female deity in
the Greek pantheon; the other, Hera, retained her maternal
form, and became the most vindictive and persecutory. Finley describes her, with magnificent understatement, as "the
complete female . . . whom the Greeks feared a little and
did not like at all" [1959, p. 140]. It is in fact fair to say that
Greek males, as a group, were terrified of any female who
was a whole woman.

Before abandoning the topic of Greek bogies, a word or
two might be said about the maternal bias of the Erinyes, who
not only appear in feminine form, but seem to be concerned
only with avenging wrongs inflicted upon the mother. The
most familiar examples are those of Alcmaeon and Orestes,
but the most instructive is that of Oedipus, whose forthright
slaying of his father fails to rouse the Angry Ones from their
infrequent slumber, but who is later attacked by them for
having indirectly brought about his mother's suicide [Homer:
Odyssey xi. 270ff.]. This bias is not very surprising, since the

[30] Today even this sanctuary has disappeared, and women of all ages are
casually called "Gorgons" [cf. Clift, 1956, pp. 93ff.].

Erinyes are a product of the older, chthonic religion [Harrison, 1957, pp. 213ff.].[31] The myth of the origin of the Erinyes from the blood of the castrated Uranus is presumably a later patriarchal amalgamation.

The association with blood and castration bears upon our theme, however. In Aeschylus' *The Eumenides* [778ff.], when Orestes is rescued from them by Athene and Apollo, the Erinyes threaten to cause pestilence, blight, and sterility in the land by letting their "heart's-blood" fall on the earth. Robert Graves, who is not usually given to this sort of thing, suggests that this threat is a mildly disguised form of the familiar taboo of menstrual blood, which is so widely believed to have a similar blighting effect [Graves, 1955, II, p. 72; Stephens, 1962, pp. 85ff.]. Elsewhere in *The Eumenides* [182–84], however, the "heart's-blood" is seen as having been sucked from the wounds of men, thus forming another link with the castration theme. Perhaps it would not be too speculative to imagine that the Erinyes, originally undifferentiated spirits of the dead, like the Keres [cf. Harrison, 1957, pp. 212ff.], were later the recipients of projective masculine fantasies about women. From colorless spirits they eventually came to represent the vindictive, castrating female who avenges with fury her own symbolic "castration." Thus Ovid sees Envy as having a similar blighting effect [cf. *Metamorphoses* ii. 791ff.]. This accords with Stephens' cross-cultural finding, mentioned above, of a relationship between menstrual taboos and castration anxiety.

It is obvious that menstruation, like the pubes, connotes maturity, as Bettelheim has so strongly emphasized [1955a, pp. 27ff.], and menstrual taboos will arise wherever there is fear

[31] It bothered Greeks of the classical period, however, since it was so opposite to their own conscious prejudices. All three of the dramatists seem to be complaining of the Erinyes' failure to serve Agamemnon's ghost as they later serve Clytemnestra's; the passages in question, however, are subject to more than one interpretation [Aeschylus: *The Choephori* 400–9 and 924–25; Sophocles: *Electra* 276; Euripides: *Orestes* 58off.].

of the mature woman. Thus in some tribes it is believed that the glance of a menstruating woman will, like the glance of the Medusa, turn a man to stone, or otherwise render him immobile and impotent [Briffault, 1959, pp. 240–41]. Furthermore, as Nemecek points out [1958, p. 26], all body orifices are fraught with magical significance in primitive beliefs. But the vaginal orifice has special significance because of its connection with the process of birth, and therefore death. The vaginal orifice is (in fantasy if not in reality) the threshold between life and non-life, and therefore lends itself equally well to optimistic or pessimistic fantasies. Insofar as the child receives a healthy and non-devouring love from his mother, he will regard the female genitalia as the source of life. But insofar as he fails to receive such love, or receives it only at the price of living solely for the satisfaction of maternal needs, he will regard the female genitalia as threatening his very existence. This threat may spring equally from his own insatiable desire for nurturance, security, and emotional quiescence, or from his fear that his mother will allow him to live only as a non-autonomous extension of herself. In this case, the vaginal orifice will have a seductive appeal which is not genital, but suicidal in nature, and will hence generate countercathexes which translate this seductiveness into fantasies of terrifying and irresistible monsters which devour, envelop, entangle, smother, and absorb.

This suggests an additional reason for the anxiety attached to defloration in so many cultures. My analysis would suggest that the connotation of maturity alone would generate some of this anxiety, and Abraham points out in support of this point that in Germany, "even grown up girls are referred to as 'it' as long as they remain unmarried" [1909, p. 164]. The fear of mature femininity is obviated by virginity. A girl who has not been deflowered is neuter.

To this interpretation may be added that of Nemecek, who argues that in primitive cultures "everything done for the *first* time is closely bound up with danger from magic."[32] He cites a variety of measures adopted to ward off evil spirits during defloration [Nemecek, 1958, pp. 33ff.; cf. also Freud, 1918b, p. 222].

More familiar to many, and not unrelated to my principal hypothesis, is Freud's theory that the taboo of virginity springs from fear of incurring the feminine rage which is induced at this final proof of her lack of a penis [Freud, 1918b, pp. 217–35]. It is worthy of note that Nemecek [1958, p. 51] believes concern over virginity to be peculiar to patriarchal societies, a view which would tend to integrate Freud's interpretation with the argument advanced here [cf. also Horney, 1932, pp. 349–50].

But we are now in a position to advance one further interpretation of the anxiety attached to defloration. So long as the hymen is intact the vaginal orifice is, at the fantasy level, closed [cf. Malinowski, 1948, p. 229]. This is perhaps the

[32] Thus the blighting effect of menstrual blood was of special potency if the woman was menstruating for the first time or for the first time following defloration [Licht, 1963, p. 367]. Nemecek goes on to say that this "led people to employ men of either higher or lower social status to initiate any new undertaking," and sees the *jus primae noctis* as subsumed under this general heading. This phenomenon, however, is certainly not limited to primitive peoples, since we find many examples in our own culture. High officials are required to cut tapes, lay cornerstones, and break earth, and it is even necessary for the president of the United States to throw the first pitch of the baseball season. Some of these acts, furthermore, are so similar to defloration as to suggest that the *jus primae noctis*, far from being merely one example of a general law, may be the prototype to which all others are associated. It is noteworthy, for example, that those ceremonies most closely resembling defloration all involve some invasion of earth. Since the earth is almost universally conceived as feminine, such activities as plowing and planting are everywhere regarded as the analogue of sexual intercourse. Breaking ground for a construction project of some kind is therefore a dangerous act, and the first spadeful must be dug by some person of consequence. But it would be difficult to find an act more closely representative of the *jus primae noctis* than the cutting of a ribbon by a high official as a prerequisite to the passage of vehicles along a highway or tunnel [cf. Abraham, 1923, pp. 83–85 for a discussion of the symbolism of roads and vehicles].

basis of the frequent use of keys and locks as symbols for the sexual act. The fear of the return to non-life is allayed by the presence of a threshold barrier [cf., e.g., Aeschylus: *The Choephori* 71–74]. Such a barrier, either in the form of actual virginity, or in the form of secondary virginal characteristics (such as youth, lack of pubes) will be particularly valued by persons experiencing maternal deprivation, or maternal affection with too great an admixture of envy and hatred, or to which too many sinister conditions are attached.

All of these theories help to illuminate the story of the wedding night of Admetus and Alcestis. Having failed to sacrifice to Artemis (i.e., to propitiate the virginal feelings of the bride) prior to the marriage, Admetus is terrified to find in his marriage chamber, in place of his bride, a room full of coiled serpents [Apollodorus: i. 9. 15]. The fantasy is reminiscent of Kenneth Elton, and the fear of mature femininity transparent.

Origins of the Cycle

I have described thus far what is essentially a self-repeating cycle of sex antagonism and narcissism. But although the problem requires a depth of historical understanding which is well beyond my grasp, it seems important at least to raise the question as to what might have set the cycle in motion, or, to put it more precisely, what might have caused the substitution of this cycle for some previous one.

Such a question requires subtler distinctions than the data for the most part allow. We can see the presence of half a dozen characteristics, and how they fit together into a pattern. It is more difficult to say what difference it would make if we ripped out one component and substituted another. The difficulty is compounded by the fact that each single component overlaps many other cultures, and its temporal boundaries are virtually impossible to establish. Sex segregation and antagonism, for example, characterize most of the Mediterranean world today, but not Greece in Homeric times; while a fairly marked tendency toward male narcissism exists over the entire time span and over most of the area, although never quite duplicating the intensity reached in fifth-century Athens. Indeed, Greece even today retains a certain primacy in the depth of the gulf between the sexes and the rigidity of masculine narcissism, and even provides a few signs of mothers controlling the household (despite extreme deference toward the husband) and furthering ambitions through sons [cf. Sanders, 1962, pp. 102, 129–31, 140, 191, 205ff., 254, 283–84; Friedl, 1964, pp. 36, 46–47, 63, 75–91; Clift, 1956, pp. 93–107; Lawson, 1964, p. 29]. Although whatever was dynamic in the pattern has long ago dropped out, something about it is of very long life.

Similarly, while the Homeric epics contain all the narcissism one would expect to find in a warrior culture, the sexual constellation seems to be lacking. Despite Licht's efforts to establish the contrary, homosexuality is, for example, trivial in the epics, although certainly present. It is the poets and tragedians who began to accentuate these homosexual themes. Licht is probably correct, however, in observing that homosexuality receded as foreign elements intruded upon Greek life during the Hellenistic period [Licht, 1963, pp. 136, 256, 449ff.]. Fear of the mature woman is also lacking in the epics, or any outstanding preoccupation with the nuclear family. All of these phenomena seem to have coalesced and hypertrophied somewhat prior to the fifth century.

A key symptom may be found in Thalia Feldman's observations regarding the Perseus myth. She observes that Homer never links Perseus and Gorgo—the latter was originally merely a bodiless head, an apotropaic mask [cf. also Walter, 1966]—but that the Perseus legend, judging from the artistic evidence, began in the eighth or seventh century, and suggests that changes in the myth as it evolved from the eighth to the sixth century reflected changes (unspecified) in the family structure [Feldman, 1965, pp. 485–88, 492–93].

There are several possible factors to which any such change

might be attributed. My first hypothesis—one which assumes a much earlier change point than that suggested by Feldman —was that the constellation derived its impetus from the gradual evolution of patriarchy [cf. Levy, n.d., p. 257], or a sudden transition from matriarchy to patriarchy. The tradition of a patriarchal conquest of a matriarchal society is an ancient one in classical scholarship—based on the evidence of early matrilineal, matrilocal, goddess-worshiping traditions being supplanted by their patriarchal counterparts [Murray, n.d., p. 56; Kitto, 1960, pp. 18–23; Briffault, 1959, pp. 84–90]. Indeed, some authors suggest an almost universal transition of this kind for civilized societies, and there is much supporting evidence [cf. Briffault, 1959; Campbell, 1959, pp. 315ff.; Neumann, 1955]. This is difficult to evaluate, however, since so much is based on mythology and tradition, and the *ontogenetic* experience of primeval matriarchy *is* universal, and may provide the source of much of this tradition. For the Greeks, at any rate, the evidence is real enough. Indeed, there seem to have been several invasions at various periods by patriarchal warriors, who, one can imagine, killed the indigenous males and took the females to wife. Since in all cases the women probably not only enjoyed a higher status in the older society, but also partook of a more advanced and sophisticated culture, one might expect to find here the ideal conditions for a brittle patriarchy, an anxious and hostile relationship between the sexes, and a transferring of libido by the wife from husband to child. The repetition of this experience several times over a millennium would gradually evolve the kind of cycle I have described.

While this hypothesis is not contradicted by any data, it receives little confirmation either. One can see the Dorian invasion as giving the final fillip to the process, and helping account for the differences between Homeric and classical times; but the invasion occurred some three hundred years before the major changes seem to have taken place. Furthermore, as Finley points out, it is never entirely clear when the Homeric epics are descriptive of the twelfth-century society to which they supposedly refer, and when they describe the tenth- or ninth-century society in which they actually evolved [Finley, 1959]. Insofar as they refer to the latter, the last known major invasion had already taken place, and while the feminine experience of being captured by male-slaughtering invaders never altogether disappeared from Greek life, it never again involved the entire Greek world. Although these ancient events may have lent something to the uneasy Greek marital relationship—the myths of the Lemnian women, of Zeus and Hera, and of Agamemnon and Clytemnestra certainly suggest it—they are insufficient in themselves to account for the apparent changes.

My second hypothesis centers around urbanization. As people gathered more into towns the role of the husband in the family changed—he absented himself more, his economic role became less visible (changes similar to those accompanying modern urbanization), and the wife became less mobile, more imprisoned within the household, thus upsetting some previous balance. It seems unlikely that this state of affairs applied to any large number of persons, however. More important perhaps was the breakdown of the extended family system and the increase in mobility mentioned earlier—both of these changes throwing an emotional burden on the nuclear family, which was unusually poorly equipped to carry it. Sex segregation is a manageable system only under conditions of strong kinship ties and residential stability. When ties of blood weakened, there was no strengthening of the marital bond to fill the gap, as often occurs in modern society with social mobility [cf. Young and Willmott, 1964]. When "blood became a weaker tie than party," the nuclear family tensions were simply accentuated [Thucydides: iii. 82; Gouldner, 1965, pp. 20, 61–62].

In Athens, where the pattern was, of course, most highly

developed, a third factor may have contributed—one closely related to the foregoing: the acceleration of social change reduced the authority of the older generation and engendered a high value on youth—a process which also contributed to the development of democracy [cf. Slater, 1963; Slater and Bennis, 1964; Gouldner, 1965, p. 73]. Certainly Athens was the most child-oriented civilized society known prior to the modern era [cf. Ehrenberg, 1951, p. 197; Ariès, 1962]. The decay of tradition removed another prop from the old family patriarchy and heightened existing pathology.

The brilliance of the Athenians is perhaps expressed in their ability to throw together a solution to this dilemma, out of the raw material which the pathology itself provided, i.e., out of homosexuality and misogyny. Pederasty universalized and defamilialized the socialization process, rescuing the male child from a disorganizing family situation and training him for the peculiarly diffuse and erratic life of Athenian democracy. The Athenians themselves were very conscious of this relationship between democracy and their homosexual attitudes [cf. Plato: *Symposium* 182; Thomson, 1950, p. 288].

This reconstruction is highly speculative, however, and treads on ground better left to the historian. Let us, therefore, return to the main task of identifying the familial configuration and showing its relationship to mythology. For before discussing the myths themselves it will be necessary to explore some of the symbols and unconscious ideas associated with familial relationships.

CHAPTER II

Symbols, the Serpent, and the Oral-Narcissistic Dilemma

Many and marvelous the things of fear
    Earth's breast doth bear;
And the sea's lap with many monsters teems,
And windy levin-bolts and meteor gleams
    Breed many deadly things—
Unknown and flying forms, with fear upon their wings,
    And in their tread is death;
And rushing whirlwinds, of whose blasting breath
    Man's tongue can tell.

But who can tell aright the fiercer thing,
The aweless soul, within man's breast inhabiting?
Who tell, how, passion-fraught and love-distraught,
The woman's eager, craving thought
Doth wed mankind to woe and ruin fell?
Yea, how the loveless love that doth possess
The woman, even as the lioness,
Doth rend and wrest apart, with eager strife,
The link of wedded life?
    [Aeschylus: *The Choephori* 585–601. Morshead trans.]

He who digs a pit will fall into it; and a serpent
will bite him who breaks through a wall.
                    [*Ecclesiastes* 10:8]

75

WHILE FREUD LONG AGO suggested that sexual organs were often represented in dreams through isomorphs [1900, pp. 350–66], in mythology the converse is true; for there are few objects in the physical environment which are not assigned explicit sexual meaning. Thus the Greeks, like many other peoples,[1] attached a feminine or maternal significance to earth and a masculine or paternal one to sky, sun, and rain. Such a view is facilitated by the analogue of generation: the earth, "fertilized" by sun and rain, conceives and bears fruit. Frazer discusses at length the homeopathic measures, such as having intercourse in a ploughed field, utilized by primitive peoples to increase through magic the fertility of the earth [1959, pp. 88ff.], and popular metaphors retain this idea [de Beauvoir, 1949, I, pp. 237ff.]. Contrariwise, menstrual blood is thought to make barren the earth. By extension, any human blood shed by another human acquires this power, particularly the blood of matricide. Thus Alcmaeon blighted and made barren the land by virtue of having slain his mother, who had cursed him and asked that the entire earth deny him shelter. But "though the whole earth was tainted with his crime, and had become uninhabitable for him, yet there was a spot of ground which was not under the eye of the sun at the time when the matricide was committed, and where therefore Alcmaeon yet might find a tranquil shelter . . . at the

[1] The Egyptian and Japanese pantheons are among the few that reverse this sex attribution, but the factors which determine such outcomes are obscure. Moon deities tend to become feminine through association with menstrual periodicity, but even here there are many exceptions, the moon often being seen as a kind of universal bridegroom [cf. Nemecek, 1958, p. 7; Briffault, 1959, pp. 252–53, 289–305, 320ff.]. The Egyptian reversal of the usual sky-male, earth-female pattern was only one of many sexual patterns which outraged the Greeks, who thought they did *everything* backward [cf. Herodotus: ii. 35].

mouth of the river Achelous, whose turbid stream was perpetually depositing new earth and forming additional islands" [Grote, n.d., p. 194; Apollodorus: iii. 7. 5; Pausanias: viii. 24. 8; Thucydides: ii. 102–3].[2] This was thus in every sense "virgin soil," and hence of neuter gender, devoid of the feminine principle. Furthermore, since this soil was not "known" by the sun (father), it was non-maternal, and did not partake of the maternal vengeance. In this myth we have another expression of the idea that men suffering from a disturbed relationship with the mother seek out and value virginity, which is freed of the menace they associate with the vaginal orifice.

This fear is complicated, however, by a more universal association between the womb and death. The earth served, in Greece as in our own society, both as womb and tomb—yielding forth fruits when sown and fertilized, but also insatiably devouring the dead [cf. Neumann, 1955, pp. 147–208]. The Greeks buried their dead in great jars, such as were also used for storing food—the opening of one of them by the great mother-goddess Pandora released many evils into the world—and their tomb-mounds were of the same circular shape as the *omphalos* or Earth-navel, itself originally a hero's tomb [Harrison, 1957, pp. 41–43, 169ff., 211, 238]. Tombs were thus not only final resting places but also sources of a kind of life, and were provided with attributes reminiscent of impregnation, pregnancy, and birth. Libations were poured onto them, and sexual symbols adorned them [Harrison, 1962, pp. 399ff.; cf. also Levy, pp. 54ff., 120, 123ff., 172–77].

Planting and burying are so closely related that the goddess of fertility is usually associated also with the realm of death. There is an ancient Brahmanic saying which expresses commonly held feelings about feminine powers: "woman is death" [quoted by Mauss and Hubert, 1961, p. 1090], and

---

[2] Graves argues a similar tradition for Orestes [1955, II, p. 70], and Harrison for Bellerophon [1957, p. 221].

this is made more concrete by the widespread use of the word "grave" for womb in the Middle East. Thus, when a child is born the "grave opens," and the taboo on a woman for forty days after childbirth is explained on the grounds that the woman's "grave" is still unclosed [Patai, 1959, pp. 156–57].

From the foregoing it is also apparent that chthonic, feminine powers tend to be dark and hidden. As Jane Harrison observes, "to the primitive Greek mind every bogey was earth-born" [1957, p. 235]. Death and birth share an element of mystery, and it is the woman's power over the latter process that causes her to be associated with the former. By the same token, the feminine, maternal quality attached to the earth is in part derived from the fact that caves and pools and other dark and mysterious places can be found in it.

Karen Horney argues that the non-visibility of the internal female organs has far-reaching psychological consequences— a woman cannot fully exhibit herself or understand by observation how she is made [Horney, 1924, pp. 52–53]. The fact that, with regard to the organs which principally differentiate the sexes, those of the female are mostly hidden and those of the male mostly manifest is not unrelated to the tendency for deities of the sky to be male and those of the earth female.

This equation of hidden with female and manifest with male is an important facet of the ritual of circumcision, which may be seen as designed to make the organ totally manifest and therefore totally male. This is implicit in some of Bettelheim's comments on the rite [1955a, p. 53], and sheds some further light on his interpretation of the Poro custom of females eating removed foreskins and males eating excised clitoridi and labia minora. Bettelheim notes the ambivalence usually associated with oral incorporation, the desire to destroy and the desire to possess being evenly balanced [*Ibid.*, pp. 200–1]. This ambivalence is also expressed in the fact that although, through eating the organs, each sex becomes magically bisexual, each is *left*, by the operation, more monosexual than before. The male has no "sheath," no "hiddenness," while the female has no "manifest" aspect, no protuberances.[3]

This equation may also influence the fondness of males for esoteric rites [*Ibid.*, pp. 227ff.]. To have something hidden is to have something female. As Bettelheim observes, "when men speak of the secret of women, they mean their sex apparatus and function" [*Ibid.*, p. 228]. Secret societies have certainly been immensely popular with males in all cultures and ages [cf. Simmel, 1950, pp. 345ff.], and undoubtedly reflect, as Bettelheim maintains, male envy of female organs and childbearing capacities. This is not merely a phenomenon of primitive cultures, as one can see from the frequency with which men's clubs in our own society exclude women altogether except for certain peripheral locations and at specified hours. Universities are particularly prone to this exclusion pattern, lending weight to the theory that intellectual creation is due to "men's disappointment at their inability to create human beings" [Bettelheim, *op. cit.*, p. 20. Note also his references to Groddeck, Landauer, and Chadwick]. But Bettelheim seems to imply that all formal social and political organization derives from this envy [see, e.g., Bettelheim, *op. cit.*, pp. 239–42], which is perhaps the basis of the popular feeling, expressed in sophisticated form by Simmel, that there is something fundamentally fraudulent at the core of organized social life [cf. Simmel, 1950, pp. 310–16]. Certainly only a very thin line separates the major fraternal orders in our own society from Chaga men, who pretend assiduously that after initiation they no longer defecate. The amused tolerance of the women, who have no need for fancy titles and bogus "secrets," is the same in both societies.

[3] That the uncircumcised penis is perceived, psychologically, as bisexual is indicated by a study by Bird [1958]. See also Daly [1950], Devereux [1950], and especially Nunberg [1947].

The Serpent

I must now turn, however, to one of the most ubiquitous and confusing of all mythological symbols, one which is notable in having both a manifest and a hidden aspect, and which therefore partakes of both male and female qualities. This is the serpent, from whose many symbolic connotations I will attempt to derive a unified and coherent meaning. It is a symbol which is almost universally represented in mythology and art—perhaps uniquely so among the objects of nature [cf. Aymar, 1956, p. 50].

The traditional psychoanalytic interpretation of the snake is a phallic one. Freud calls it the "most important symbol of the male organ" [1900, p. 357; cf. also Jones, 1959, p. 94], and the equation precedes Freud by more than a century [cf. Knight, 1786, *passim*]. The snake's predilection for penetrating into crevices or holes in the earth is a facet of this interpretation, and accords well with the remarks made above concerning earth. The contexts in which the serpent symbol is used also suggest a phallic, or at least sexual, meaning [Howey, 1956, pp. 42ff.], as do some of the real or imagined characteristics of snakes themselves: extending themselves, swelling (for cobras), attracting, and secreting a "magical" fluid [cf. Aymar, 1956, pp. 240–42, 256]. But there are many aspects of serpent symbolism which tend to jar this simple equation. The first is that phallic symbols are generally straight and rigid—the state of erection being almost as important in fantasy and religious ritual as the organ itself. Abraham seems dimly to recognize this problem when he suggests that the transformation of Moses' rod into a serpent "stands for the return of the erect penis to the flaccid state" [Abraham, 1909, p. 203]; but to generalize this penis-in-repose interpretation would bring confusion to phallic interpretations offered in the past. An additional complication arises when one considers the frequency with which phallic objects in fertility cults are represented with snakes coiled around them. Wright shows, for example, a bronze amulet (of a type still being sold in Naples at the time he wrote), consisting of a phallus encircled by a snake, with its mouth on the urethral orifice [Wright, 1866, pp. 65, 79; cf. also Flugel, 1924, pp. 162–63; Howey, 1956, p. 46]. Wright does not explain the use of this amulet, but the position of the snake suggests the possibility of its being a charm against the extraction of "vital fluids" by a succubus. In any case, it seems clear that the encircling snake is not masculine but feminine, and represents the same kinds of associations used by writers of popular erotic fiction who speak of "encircling arms" or "her arms entwined around his neck." (The "clinging vine" is still another serpentine perception of femininity.) Many of the feminine monsters referred to in the first chapter, especially the more salacious and vampiresque, were also serpentine [cf. Fontenrose, 1959, pp. 116–19].

Consider, for example, Ovid's rendering of the myth of Salmacis and Hermaphroditus. When Hermaphroditus jumps into her pool, the excited nymph follows him triumphantly:

> Surrounding him with arms, legs, lips, and hands
> As though she were a snake caught by an eagle,
> Who leaping from his claws wound her tall body
> Around his head, and lashed his wings with her
> Long tail, as though she were quick ivy tossing
> Her vines round the thick body of a tree,
> Or as the cuttlefish at deep sea's bottom
> Captures its enemy—so she held to him.
> The heir of Atlas struggled as he could
> Against the pleasure that the girl desired,
> But she clung to him as though their flesh were one,
> "Dear, naughty boy," she said, "to torture me;
> But you won't get away. O gods in heaven,
> Give me this blessing; clip him within my arms
> Like this forever." At which the gods agreed:
> They grew one body, one face, one pair of arms
> And legs, as one might graft branches upon

A tree, so two became nor boy nor girl,
Neither yet both within a single body.

When tamed Hermaphroditus learned his fate,
Knew that his bath had sent him to his doom,
To weakened members and a girlish voice,
He raised his hands and prayed, "O Father, Mother,
Hear your poor son who carried both your names:
Make all who swim these waters impotent,
Half men, half women."
                        [Ovid: *Metamorphoses* iv. 357–87. Gregory trans.]

This excerpt also expresses a fear of feminine envelopment
and of emasculation through sexual contact—themes we will
encounter again in our exploration of the serpent symbol.

Representations (on ancient medals, for example) in which
the snake-encircled phallus is replaced by an egg add another
complication, since the snake could connote either the fertilizing phallus or the female reproductive organs [cf. Knight,
1786, pp. 36, 171]. Leach points out that the Biblical serpent
is female in medieval representations, but concludes that it is
hermaphroditic [1965, p. 580]; while Fortune, applying a
phallic interpretation to a Maori myth (in which the serpent
is clearly male), is faced with the anomalous fact that the
Maori word for the serpent seems to refer to both male and
female sexual organs [1926, p. 241].

One could argue that the snake-and-phallus symbols are
homosexual—an argument supported by the ancient belief
that a man will become a woman or a homosexual if he wit-
nesses snakes coupling, as in the myth of Teiresias [Hyginus:
Fabulae 75; Apollodorus: iii. 6. 7 and Frazer's notes pp. 364–
65; Ovid: *Metamorphoses* iii. 324ff.]. But this is by no means
incompatible with the previous view: it is not unusual to find
condensed, in a single myth element, a means of defense
(homosexuality) against a fear, a precipitating cause (primal
scene) of the fear, and the return of the repressed fear itself
(i.e., of the seductive, possessive mother).

The foregoing at least suggests that the serpent symbol has something to do with sexual differentiation and the sexual act. This has misled many writers into assuming that myths and rituals involving serpents are concerned with phallic, oedipal, or genital issues. It is the principal weakness of psychoanalytic students of mythology that they so often mistake oral phenomena for oedipal ones, a result perhaps of their primary preoccupation with neurotic patients.[4] Greater understanding of schizophrenic ideation has shown that beneath apparently oedipal fantasies one often finds a totally oral orientation to the world. Rosberg and Karon [1958, pp. 221–25] show how the primal-scene fantasies of a schizophrenic patient are reinterpreted in oral terms, i.e., the devouring mother being fed by the father instead of feeding the patient, and Rosen [1953] has many similar examples. Thus it may be that the serpent is a phallus viewed in pre-phallic terms. What at one stage is a source of pleasure and a means of procreation, may at another be simply a proof of masculinity which might be lost, and at still another a source of nurturance or a threat to the integrity of the organism. To say that serpent = phallus, whether correct or not, tells us very little about its meaning.

What our analysis yields thus far, then, is little more than some suspicion that the symbol of the serpent is closely linked to sexuality and reproduction, that it is both male and female, and that it appears to have something to do with very primitive ideas about bodily integrity.

[4] It must be admitted, however, that Ferenczi, Rank, and, to a lesser extent, Freud himself, were aware that a more primitive oral interpretation often underlay a suggested oedipal one. Freud, however, left the question open and unanswered, like the problem of the "great maternal deities," and pursued his own interests [cf. Freud, 1913, p. 149]. Students of primitive and psychotic ideation such as Bettelheim, Rosen, Bateson, and Fairbairn have helped to remedy this defect in recent years. It is a tribute to Freud that he was able to perceive the oral stage as the primary one, despite his own relative neglect of it.

The Serpent as Life and Death

One way of clarifying the ambiguity surrounding the serpent symbol might be to examine the attributes which adhere to the snake in real life. Snakes are indeed remarkable for several reasons; their capacity to shed their skin has always attracted special attention, provoking fantasies of immortality and rebirth. Myths which assert that men once also had, or would have had, this ability but forfeited it to the serpent through some mischance are found in almost every part of the globe (including ancient Greece), particularly in Africa and Oceania [cf. Larousse, 1959, pp. 478ff.; Briffault, 1959, pp. 306–9]. In Greek the word *geras* means both old age and the slough of the snake, as does the Latin *senectus* [Rose, 1925, p. 142; Frazer, note on Apollodorus: iii. 12. 5].[5] The serpent's claim to have conquered death is reinforced by his hibernation pattern, and by his reflexive ability to inflict a mortal wound even when dead [Aymar, 1956, pp. 49, 273]. As a result, the serpent is viewed as possessing the secret of life, and becomes important in magical efforts to facilitate childbirth, heal the sick, or resuscitate the moribund [cf. Aymar, 1956, pp. 38–39; Briffault, 1959, p. 314; Apollodorus: iii. 3. 1 and Frazer's Appendix VII, pp. 363–70]. "The serpent, having the power of casting his skin, and apparently renewing his youth, became the symbol of life and vigour, and as such is always made an attendant on the mythological

[5] One is led to wonder whether this fascinating quality of the snake might not have contributed to the origin of circumcision. Bettelheim stresses the relationship of circumcision to fertility rites and ideas of renewal and rebirth. He quotes Nunberg as follows: "By the circumcision the glans penis is freed; it emerges like an infant from the mother's womb . . . a new penis is born which looks like a phallus in erection with retracted foreskin. . . . The initiated, the circumcised boy, is reborn without a foreskin . . ." [1955a, p. 53]. The Greek word *psolos*, which means both circumcised and tumescent, expresses this idea. [cf. Aristophanes: *The Birds* 507]. Circumcision is thus an attempt to obtain for the penis the reinvigoration experienced by the snake, through a bit of sympathetic magic.

deities presiding over health. It is also observed that animals of the serpent kind retain life more pertinaciously than any others except the Polypus . . ." [Knight, 1786, p. 36]. It is because of these imagined life-giving and life-renewing skills that the serpent is often phallic, just as it is also associated with the dying and reviving moon, with woman, the earth, childbirth, the womb, and fertility in general [Howey, 1956, pp. 42–43; Briffault, 1959, pp. 309–18; Harrison, 1962, pp. 297ff.]. Where serpents are not found, other skin-sloughing animals appear in the same role.

But by the same token, the serpent is intimately associated with death and the grave. Snakes appear on Greek portrayals of tombs, and there are instances in many mythologies of dead heroes adopting this shape [Harrison, 1957, pp. 327–30]. Among the Betsileo, the king assumes this form upon his death [Kardiner, 1939, p. 288]. The Greeks believed "that the backbone of a dead man when the marrow has decayed turns into a snake," a belief which Plutarch later attempted to rationalize by suggesting that " 'when part of the moisture of the marrow is evaporated and it becomes of a thicker consistency it produces serpents' " [Harrison, 1957, pp. 330–31]. Jane Harrison points out, in any case, that the dead Greek hero was always a snake, for the simple reason that the appearance of a snake near the tomb certified his status as a genuine immortal hero [1962, pp. 268–70].[6]

But it was not only the dead hero who appeared as a snake. Any angry soul might take this form. Jane Harrison argues convincingly that "very deep in the Greek mind lay the notion that the Erinys, the offended ghost, was a snake" [1957, p. 233]. Orestes sees himself as a serpent in avenging his father, and in turn fears the Erinys of Clytemnestra as a yawning dragon with attendant vipers [Aeschylus: *The Choephori* 549; Euripides: *Iphigenia in Tauris* 286]. Unavenged bloodshed may even generate a more or less random

---

[6] Immortal only in a chthonic sense, of course, not to be confused with godhood.

swarm of malevolent serpents [Aeschylus: *The Suppliant Maidens* 260ff.]. In general, then, snakes are closely linked to the realm of the dead.

It might seem as if our excursion thus far has led only to confusion and contradiction. Having first discovered that the serpent is both male and female, we now find that it symbolizes both life and death. These contradictions are more apparent than real, however, since we may conclude that the serpent is somehow involved in the issue of expressing or transcending sexual differentiation and the transition between life and death. These dichotomous distinctions which dominate our thinking are, at a more fundamental level, conjoined. Creation and destruction, male and female, death and fertility—each pair represents two aspects of an identical process [cf. Neumann, 1955a, p. 18]. Knight, for example, emphasizes the fusion of creative and destructive symbols in the representation of ancient deities [1786, pp. 135ff.]. He notes the intimate relation between the two in processes such as fermentation, and calls attention (rather obliquely) to the fact that in order for a new organization of matter and energy to be formed, an old one must always be dissolved, and others violated or disrupted in some way. The sudden appearance of worms in carrion epitomizes this. The snake may thus be regarded as a threshold symbol, or a symbol of change and transformation.

A similar view may be taken of the serpent's sexual ambiguity. Bettelheim stresses that the desire to possess the sexual apparatus of the opposite sex normally means in addition to, not in place of, one's own; and that it is intimately bound up with societal concerns about fertility [1955a, pp. 34, 144ff.]. Fertility is often expressed symbolically by bisexual figures, which may be another reason for the frequent appearance of the snake in fertility rituals.

According to Webster [*Dictionary*, pp. 2377–2378], snakes are distinguished by the fact "that the mouth is usually very distensible." It is further stated that they are "almost exclusively predaceous, generally *refusing all but living prey*, which consists of large insects, small mammals, birds, lizards, etc. *These they swallow whole, in some cases alive, in others after poisoning them, or strangling them in coils of the body . . ."* (italics mine). Thus the snake with its yawning jaws is primarily a devouring, enveloping, swallowing, strangling creature. It can not only penetrate but also incorporate, be both inside and outside, phallus and sheath, and its ability to shed its skin only underlines further this bisexual quality.

The Serpent as an Oral-Narcissistic Symbol

It cannot be denied, however, that the "female" quality is the more salient of the two. The snake appears far more often in mythology as a devouring than as a penetrating being, and when dragons appear in pairs, the female is almost always the more formidable of the two [Fontenrose, 1959, p. 255, *passim*]. This is perhaps a function of the priority of the maternal relationship in child development. Since the snake lives by devouring small beings, traditionally interpreted as symbolic either of phalli or children or both [Freud, 1900, pp. 357–58], it does indeed symbolize a "dangerous vagina" as Roheim suggests [Roheim, 1924, p. 408]. The "danger" arises, however, because the serpent, whether viewed as a genital or not, is orally defined, and the fear which it evokes is of being absorbed by the mother, or poisoned, or enveloped, or strangled—all common schizophrenic fantasies [Rosen, 1953, p. 99; Jung, 1957, pp. 277, 314; see also pp. 272–93, 330–36, 375–419, 475–82; Guntrip, 1952, pp. 86ff.].[7]

[7] Some of these techniques are analogous to those of the spider, which has also been interpreted as a symbol of the angry, castrating mother [Abraham, 1922, pp. 326ff.]. It would be difficult to find two other creatures who are at once feared and maligned and as useful to mankind as the snake and the spider (even in cultures where they were sacred, as the snake was in Greece). It may be that it is precisely that quality which makes them useful, i.e., their destruction of vermin, which also makes them feared as symbols of the evil aspect of the mother; for according to Freud, vermin = children in the unconscious [1900, p. 357]. The accusation that snakes are "slimy" is probably also due to their association with childbirth (water).

Guntrip, in his analysis of Fairbairn's theories of schizoid reactions, derives this fear of maternal engulfment from the love-hunger of the child. The child's need is so intense that he feels he will devour the object and lose it forever, or that his hunger will be reciprocated and he be gobbled up in turn—an outcome the possibility of which is made more vivid by his own wishes to merge and fuse and be incorporated by another. He has fantasies of being a vacuum cleaner, or "one big mouth," and to counteract all these threats to his own or another's bodily integrity he tries to keep aloof and detached [Guntrip, 1952, pp. 86ff.].

To this conflict between the desire to merge and the desire to be free and separate, I have applied the rather cumbersome title, "oral-narcissistic dilemma." It originates in a failure to negotiate successfully the transition from the infantile state of total narcissism and total dependence to one involving an awareness of the separate existence of others. As this awareness grows, one's sense of narcissistic integrity and one's dependency needs are simultaneously violated. The child who is comfortable in a strong but non-intrusive and relatively unconditional parental love can effect a new equilibrium, with a less inclusive definition of personal boundaries and a greater independence. Without these advantages both the need for dependence and the need for autonomy become too desperate, and the contradiction too absolute. Total fusion and stratospheric isolation become equally essential and equally terrifying.

The snake symbolizes both sides of this conflict, as well as the state of infantile omnipotence which precedes it. On the one hand it is the entangling, smothering, devouring mother who destroys the boundary between the child and the external world and returns him to a quiescent state of non-being. Only in a snake can one see an animal which has been swallowed whole, still visible as a lump inside the body of the devourer, but gradually disappearing as the snake digests it, breaking down its structure and boundaries and returning it to inert matter. This is the mirror-image of the pregnant woman, in whom one can correspondingly see the manifest signs of an organism forming out of an apparent nothingness. The serpent is thus the other half of the cyclical, dust-unto-dust, womb-tomb vision of the woman's procreative capacity —the child is swallowed up and disappears from whence he came.

At the same time, the snake represents the insatiable hunger of the child itself—the desire to gobble up the mother and keep her forever inside. "Once I said to her," a student wrote, describing his marital relationship, "that I sometimes wanted to swallow her. The image in my mind was of a snake swallowing an animal whole." This hunger may be projected outward, so that the dragons are seen as external. Grace Stuart quotes Riviere's description of the infant's response to acute hunger, ". . . a reaction in which the whole body is involved: screaming, twitching, twisting, kicking, convulsive breathing, evacuations. . . . The child is overwhelmed by choking and suffocating; its eyes are blinded with tears, its ears deafened, its throat sore; its bowels gripe, its evacuations burn it. The aggressive anxiety-reaction is far too strong a weapon in the hands of such a weak ego; it has become un-controllable and is threatening to destroy its owner" [Stuart, 1952, p. 44]. Stuart suggests that these uncontrollable feelings, projected, become "the swallowing monsters of folk-tale and nightmare" [Stuart, 1955, p. 143]. A similar projection is found in a curious neolithic shrine in Anatolia, in which the breasts of the mother-goddess are fashioned out of vulture skulls [Mellaart, 1963, p. 37]. Yet this hunger is not always projected: the popular myth—current wherever cows and snakes coexist—that snakes suck milk from the udders of cows, is a more direct expression of it [Aymar, 1956, pp. 101–2, 271]. The subtle thief is also widely believed to steal milk from women [Briffault, 1959, pp. 314–15]. When Orestes sees Clytemnestra as a devouring serpent [Euripides: *Iphigenia in Tauris* 286] he is only returning a compliment, for she dreams before he kills her that she has suckled a serpent which drew blood from her breast [Aeschylus: *The Choephori* 527ff.]. And Cleopatra, as she applies the asp to her breast, inverts the equation in a bit of gallows humor:

> Peace, peace!
> Dost thou not see my baby at my breast,
> That sucks the nurse asleep?
> [Shakespeare, *Antony and Cleopatra*, Act V, Scene 2]

Furthermore, children like Erichthonius, the legendary king of Athens, who are part or all serpent, are common in mythology [Hyginus: *Fabulae* 166; *Astronomica* ii. 13; Pausanias: i. 24. 7], as are children who change into serpents [Pausanias: vi. 20. 4–5]. Jane Harrison suggests that "snake and child to the primitive mind are not far asunder; the Greek peasant of today has his child quickly baptized, for till baptized he may at any moment disappear in the form of a snake" [1957, p. 133].

On the other hand, the snake also represents the other side of the ambivalence, the narcissistic desire to persist as a separate, intact, integral, boundary-maintaining organism. For it is only form and structure which are individual, matter and energy being common to all. The same is true of instincts and cultural pressures: it is only the ego, the peculiar organization of the personality which differentiates one person from another. In death this organization, both in its physical and psychological aspect, is dissolved into raw matter and energy, from which other and newer organizations will emerge. One way of viewing the "death instinct" of Freud is as a withdrawal of cathexis from this particular structure, an abandonment of the boundaries which hold it apart from other forms. This also involves a release from the responsibility and burden of maintaining intact and fostering the development of this particular organization. Struggling against this desire to "lose oneself" (i.e., one's structure) is the narcissistic need for continued apartness and ego-integrity, and this appears in the snake's attribute of immortality and rebirth. As noted before, both the shedding of the skin and the concept of the snake as the receptacle of the soul of the dead man express this theme. The fact that most snakes lay eggs may also contribute to a rebirth fantasy—the animal swallowed whole is seen as emerging, reborn, in the egg (quite in accord with the oral birth theories so prominent in mythology). In all these cases an apparent violation of ego-boundaries is transformed into ego-survival and boundary-maintenance.

Thus in mythology and literature, the serpent is associated not only with the waters of chaos—with disorder and nothingness [Fontenrose, 1959, pp. 217–66, 465–66], or with the unconscious [Neumann, 1954]; but also with narcissistic concern over self-maintenance and protection from ego-violation by others. Milton's Satan and Ovid's Envy [*Metamorphoses* ii. 768ff.] come immediately to mind, as well as Hawthorne's "Bosom Serpent" [Hawthorne, 1843]. It must be admitted, however, that this aspect of the serpent is defensive and secondary, while the threat of dissolution or fusion seems primary [cf. Dante, *Inferno*, Canto 25].

To summarize these reflections: the serpent represents the oral-narcissistic dilemma because it is the most common symbol of boundary-ambiguity. It appears in connection with the boundary between life and death, consciousness and unconsciousness, male and female, and so on. Devouring and being devoured are associated with it, dying and being born, and everything that has to do with the edges of the body or with changes in its shape (pregnancy). Thus the sexual organs receive serpentine associations primarily because copulation blurs the boundaries of the organism (a question I will elaborate in a later section), but actually all body orifices play some part in serpent symbolism.

Although they are probably found to some degree in all humans, these issues are matters of central importance to psychotics. Schizophrenics have particular difficulty in locating the boundaries of the self, and as Hall points out [1966, p. 11], they tend to experience anything occurring within uncomfortably close range as happening inside themselves. Limentani gives several examples of patients who could not distinguish themselves from the mother, and felt themselves to be extensions of her, or connected with her as are Siamese twins. The overt psychosis is precipitated by separation from the mother, and proceeds from a childhood situation in which the mother in fact treated the patient as a part of her. Limentani found these patients initially to be unaware of their wish to be united with the mother—consciously expressing desires to be independent but revealing at the same time a wish "to live according to the mother's pattern." They feared losing themselves utterly in any relationship in which they became at all involved, and saw the therapist as a "clinging vine," in contrast to neurotics who usually accuse the therapist of coldness and indifference [Limentani, 1956, pp. 231–35]. "The desire for symbiosis is matched by a fear of submergence implying loss of individuality and identity. The mother here becomes the great threat to the self"—hence the therapist must play a cautious role and allow both sides of the conflict to emerge. "Sometimes he appears to be on the side of separation and emerges into the consciousness of the patient as the great separator, the divider of the umbilical bond, the weaner. At other times he transforms the analytic situation into a great dark cave into which the patient can retreat" [Anthony, 1961, pp. 239–40]. The role is a difficult one when the ambivalence is so acute: ". . . any excellent care which met his most basic needs also tended to get too close to the child and resulted in fusion fantasies followed by panic and swift physical attack. At the same time too much distance from Ken also brought panic and fears of being abandoned . . . and this too was followed instantaneously by swift rage attacks" [Ekstein, *et al.*, 1959, p. 203]. In this case the patient, an eight-year-old boy characterized by a "wish for and dread of being contained in the 'mother box,' " acted out this ambivalence sequentially, "enclosing himself in a box, closet, or any dark place, only to burst out again using his feet vigorously." He played at being a phonograph record manipulated by the therapist, which he followed by wild, motoric outbursts; he crawled through subterranean passages and swarmed up trees; he was afraid of the toilet,[8] but engaged in water play all the time. He was particularly afraid of a stagnant pool, to which he was also drawn, and would "ask plaintively and despairingly of the therapist whether it could ever be cleared . . ." [Ekstein, *et al.*, 1959, pp. 192, 199–207, 213–15].

The desire for, and fear of, a return to the womb, plays the major part in the fantasies of shrinking which appear so frequently in folklore. *Alice in Wonderland* is a striking example, and it is noteworthy that most of the growing and shrinking in the story take place in the context of birth symbols—enclosed spaces with tiny exits, narrow passageways, water—and that Alice is in constant danger of being either smothered and crushed by her large size or overwhelmed by her diminutiveness. It is also characteristic of such fantasies (as well as those involving transformation) that they are brought about by eating something. Finally, when Alice achieves her greatest height she is accused of being a serpent, a psychologically just accusation, for although her voracity

---

8 As small children so often are, particularly around the age of two, when the question of autonomy is so prominent in the child's emotional life. At a somewhat later age the same boundary anxiety often expresses itself in the form of a growing dislike for foods of uneven or ambiguous consistency—stews and goulashes, pudding with lumps, cakes with nuts, and so on. The parent who tries to show the child that the mixture contains only foods that the child adores is thus missing the whole point, which is that separate identities must be maintained.

is carefully denied by the small amounts of food and drink she is said to consume each time, it is revealed by the great height to which she has grown [Carroll, *op. cit.*, pp. 3–61].

Similar fantasies appear in other children's books, most tellingly the Oz series of L. F. Baum, three-fourths of which contain adventures underground or underwater. In one story, *The Magic of Oz* (an exception to the above), a little girl and a one-legged old sailor go in search of a magic plant which grows on an island in the middle of a lake. The plant blooms continually, eternally, and everchangingly of whatever the beholder wishes, either fruit or blossom. The moment the pair set foot on the island, however, they take root in the earth and begin to shrink, as the ground gradually absorbs them through the roots in their feet [Baum, 1919]. Giving "earth" the maternal significance usually assigned to it, we have a fantasy in which "dust unto dust" or "the earth reclaims its own" is put on a rather immediate basis—the mother absorbing her children back into herself as a result of their immoderate and insatiable desires for nurturance. It is noteworthy that the island's magic does not affect the old sailor's wooden leg, or in general penetrate any except animal products (such as leather and wool), another way of expressing the connection between oral incorporativeness and susceptibility to absorption—only that which devours can be devoured. Wanting too much leads to being wanted too much.

As we shall see, Greek mythology is not devoid of such quicksand fantasies, or the related ones of being changed into plant life.

The Serpent as Umbilicus

I suggested earlier that the serpent was a kind of threshold symbol, and, indeed, he often appears as guardian of the threshold between the world of life and consciousness and the realm of death and the unconscious [cf. Campbell, 1956, pp. 77ff., 217ff., 245–46]. But what separates may also join, and the serpent also appears as the link between these worlds [cf. Aymar, 1956, p. 36]. This follows from the more general significance of the symbol as one of boundary ambiguity. Just as it symbolizes the sexual organs—the bond between male and female, or the processes of childbirth and death, so one also finds it marking the pathway to the supernatural. The serpent is assigned to tombs in part because he is oracular; and he is similarly found in oracular caves, at the entrance to the underworld, and in association with mysteries of all kinds.

This leads to a symbolic equation between the serpent and the umbilicus, so that the snake is seen as a bridge to the mother, to the womb, and hence to non-life, the unconscious, and the supernatural realm. In Dahomey, a "personal 'serpent,' equated with the umbilical cord, was the individual's vital principle. If this were well treated and propitiated, it would bring its owner wealth taken from other men who had neglected their 'serpents' " [Linton, 1959, p. 461]. Similar ideas about the umbilicus are found in many primitive societies. It is often buried in a secret place and treated as a kind of external soul.

In Greece, the serpent-umbilicus equation is made explicit by a number of religious practices, the most striking of which is the close association between the *omphalos*, the navel of Earth, and the serpent which guarded it and prophesied. Before the Pythoness, Apollo's priestess, sat on the stone *omphalos* to prophesy, one may imagine the Python itself to have rested, coiled, upon this stone.[9] It is frequently shown in such a position in vase paintings, sometimes in peaceful co-

[9] To interpret Apollo's slaying of the Python as cutting the umbilicus is consistent with the many anti-maternal elements in his career, as we shall see. The story of Alexander cutting the Gordian Knot can be similarly explained. One recalls that this act was seen as a prerequisite to the conquest of Asia, which is another way of saying that in order to conquer Asia he had to break his close emotional ties with Olympias and leave her behind him psychologically as well as physically. Knots were also viewed by the Greeks (as by many other peoples) as capable of magically delaying childbirth.

existence with the god [Rose, 1959, p. 138; Kerényi, 1960, p. 136; Fontenrose, 1959, p. 375]. The connection is further expressed in the fact that both "Delphi," Apollo's home, and "Delphyne," the more ancient title of the dragon, derive from a root meaning "womb." Originally, no doubt, the soul of a dead hero—the mantic snake—brought word from "beyond the grave," but also, thereby, from the great Mother Earth "who brings all things to life and rears and takes again into her womb" [Aeschylus: *The Choephori* 127; cf. also Harrison, 1957, p. 267]. *Omphalos* and tomb may in fact be equated in both shape and function [*Ibid.*, pp. 62, 325–30]. Fontenrose argues that the *omphalos* is the tomb of either Python or Dionysus [1959, pp. 374–75 and Addenda].

Although usually interpreted differently, the wool fillets with which the *omphalos* at Delphi was covered, dangling from the apex, may also have represented the umbilicus [Harrison, 1957, pp. 61, 319]. Just as the snake symbolized the bond between the hero and Mother Earth, so the fillets worn by suppliants and seers represented a similar tie—a kind of ancient "hot line." A vase painting reproduced by Jane Harrison shows a fillet coiled around a branch in an attitude which is palpably snake-like [*Ibid.*, p. 209].

Ferenczi [1921] discusses the symbol of the bridge as a comparable vinculum between life and death, or the world of reality and the womb. He speaks of "the regularity with which the symbolism of death and that of the maternal body are associated with each other in dreams and neuroses," and argues that "in the state of orgasm the whole personality (the ego) identifies itself . . . with the genitals, and (as in sleep and in certain stages of epileptic fits) demands a hallucinatory return to the mother's body; and that the male organ advancing towards the womb attains this aim partially, or more correctly 'symbolically,' and that only the genital secretion, the semen, attains this destiny in reality" [Ferenczi, 1939, pp. 202, 204]. This is a good example of an "oral" interpretation of a genital act, one in which phallus and umbilicus merge, since both may serve as a "bridge" to the womb. As such, the serpent may represent either indifferently, for the serpent is always an oral symbol, and at the oral level everything is reduced to questions of fusion and separation.[10]

Circumcision rites also express this association. In a Masai myth, the god gives the ancestor a knife which is to be used for circumcision and cutting the umbilical cord. Bettelheim stresses, as have many others, that one purpose of circumcision rites is to sever the ties binding the candidate to the mother [1955a, pp. 125–26, 224]. The fact that the foreskin is usually given to the mother to dispose of (often by eating) emphasizes this connection, as does the fact that the Masai boy walks backward to his mother's hut [*Ibid.*, pp. 159–60]. It is as if sexual maturity were only possible when the organs have been cut in some way analogous to the umbilical severance,[11] to free libido from the mother once and for all. Circumcision does this by cutting off that which is female; subincision does it by incorporation [*Ibid.*, p. 126].

It is because of the umbilical link to the womb that (a) the serpent is viewed as a source of knowledge (especially of the supernatural), and that (b) the acquisition of knowledge is so often defined in phallic terms.

In Greek mythology Melampus, Cassandra, Teiresias, Polyeidus, and many others achieve special gifts through en-

10 A fact which contributes mightily to the problems of symbolic interpretation of fantasy materials; only by the context can one arrive at a sense of the level. Orthodox psychoanalytic interpretations err frequently in assuming that because genital symbols are present they refer to genital or oedipal preoccupations. But at the oral level, copulation is merely another kind of feeding, or returning to the womb, or merging.

11 I once met an old Portuguese seaman who, having spent all his adult sexual life in brothels, was able to preserve intact some infantile sexual theories, one of which was that the penis was the stump of the umbilicus, clipped to size according to the generosity or niggardliness of the attending physician. The theory thus accounted for variation in penis size, providing a scapegoat for the old seaman, who felt himself to have been stinted.

counters with serpents, learning the language of animals, sexual knowledge, power over death, ability to foresee the future, and so on [Apollodorus: i. 9. 11 and note; iii. 3. 1, iii. 6. 7, and note on iii. 12. 5; Hyginus: *Fabulae* 75, 136]. In the myth of the Garden of Eden, the serpent is the source of all knowledge for Adam and Eve, and even exposes the crude mendacity of the Creator [*Genesis* 2:15—3:7; cf. also Milton, *Paradise Lost* ix, 550–816; Fromm, 1941, pp. 33–35]. Since the Eden myth, like that of Apollo and Python, celebrates the emergence and dominance of a repressive male-oriented religion, the originally benign and helpful snake is put in a somewhat bad light, but his primeval role as enlightener still shines through, just as does the prophetic Pythoness in the Delphic Oracle.

The serpent is wise and subtle because he has penetrated the "secrets of women," the sense of hiddenness and mystery which adheres, in the male mind, to the female reproductive organs. The womb, like the tomb, is a dark and secret place, associated with unknown and miraculous processes. The snake in myth is a bridge to this "beyond."

Abraham calls attention to the familiar oddity of the Hebrew language in which the word "know" is applied to the sexual act. The power of the father is established through sexual knowledge, achieved by means of a phallic "bridge" to the uteral cavity. The mystery of the female is viewed as having been mastered by the father through sexual intercourse. This is reflected, as Abraham notes, in the idea of the all-seeing Sun-god [cf. Abraham, 1913b, p. 176]. We still use somewhat phallic terminology to describe the acquisition of knowledge: we speak of "probing" and "penetrating" investigations, of "prying," "poking into," "digging," "delving," and so on. On the other hand, we also "dive into" the matter, "immerse" ourselves in knowledge, and generally use language which implies the transportation of the entire individual into the unknown [cf. Campbell, 1956, *passim*].

One of the outcomes of early scoptophilia is the acting out of fantasies of returning to the womb, by hiding in a totally darkened room, and so on [Abraham, 1913b, pp. 171ff.]. The desire for knowledge thus expresses both the wish to return to the womb ("know" here means "familiarize oneself with" or "know what it is like to") and the desire to obtain autonomy and separateness by mastering this mystery through adult understanding and genital sexuality (as the father is perceived as having done).

One of Abraham's patients wanted "to see with his own eyes his own birth out of his mother's body" [1913b, p. 219]. Knowledge here is closely bound to the issue of separation from and ultimate oneness with the mother. Thus while at one level the Garden of Eden myth may be concerned with the suppression of tree-worship and ancestor-worship by a patriarchal monotheistic cult [cf. Frazer, 1959, pp. 72ff.; Harrison, 1957, pp. 327ff.], at another level it reflects the oral-narcissistic dilemma. For while the consequence of the incident is separation and individuation, as Fromm stresses, the initial temptation, with which Fromm does not deal, expresses both sides of the ambivalence. The serpent does not merely offer freedom and separateness, he offers food. Just as in the schizophrenic fantasies which Guntrip describes [1952, pp. 86ff.], everything is lost through greed, through wanting too much. To keep the mother for always, and yet be free of her, and free of need for her, the child devours her, becomes omniscient, but loses her forever. At another level, the incorporation of parental knowledge, an act initially motivated as much by a desire to belong as by a desire to be separate and powerful, leads inexorably away from the infantile symbiotic dependence on the mother.

One might speculate that this tie between the oral-narcissistic dilemma and the search for knowledge had particular significance for the Greeks. For although the dilemma is universal, it becomes exacerbated in certain individuals in every society, and in some societies taken as a whole. In the previous chapter I described the maternal pattern which aggravated this conflict for the Greek male, and the desperate narcissistic flamboyance with which he so often countered his wish for fusion and annihilation. It seems likely that the striving toward rationality, toward consciousness and conceptual mastery of the universe, and the acute fear of being over-whelmed by impulse—by dark, irrational forces—was also re-lated to this constellation. However much the philosophers attempted to deny this heritage, the serpent was the oldest and most revered symbol in Athens. When the guardian snake of the Acropolis was said to have refused its honey-cake the Athenians believed the goddess herself to have aban-doned the city [Herodotus: viii. 41]. The mythical history of Athens revolves almost entirely around serpentine figures—the ancestral serpents, Cecrops and Erichthonius (ancient hero-kings of Athens), dominated the eastern pediment of the old Hecatompedon.[12] The generational perseveration of the oral-narcissistic conflict in the Greek socialization process finds its symbolic counterpart in the ritual of the royal fam-ily; for Zeus' daughter provided serpents as guardians for Erichthonius, and:

> This rite to the Erechthidae hence remains,
> Mid serpents wreathed in ductile gold to nurse
> their children.
>
> [Euripides: *Ion* 20–26]

The Serpent As Boundary Violator

If the serpent represents boundary ambiguity, and is seen as a link between bounded worlds, then we may also expect him to appear in the context of boundary-violation. It is in part because of concerns about the violation or permeability

---

[12] Jane Harrison observed that these serpents were dismissed as "decora-tive," by scholars sharing the Greek proclivity for denial [Harrison, 1906, pp. 47–48].

of psychological boundaries that the serpent plays so important a role in sexual fantasies.

For individuals in whom narcissistic anxieties are severe, the sexual act shatters the body image of both male and female. The boundary between Me and Not-Me crumbles, since the female is penetrated and part of the male disappears inside of another. In addition, psychological boundaries are obliterated through orgasm. The ego dissolves, inundated with impulse, and this may be experienced as a kind of death —as complete submersion in unconsciousness [cf. Neumann, 1954, p. 60]. At the oral level, ecstasy is feared as a bursting or disintegrating of the boundaries of the self [cf. Keiser, 1952, pp. 153ff.]. Finally, physiological changes do occur, particularly in the case of impregnation, and in oral fantasy these assume grotesque proportions. At this level all orifices are mouths, all sexual contact impregnating and boundary-shattering.

One would not go too far wrong in saying that the sexual fantasies associated with the oral-narcissistic conflict coincide with the actual sexual experiences of many simpler species. The "sexual" encounters of paramecia, for example, involve total fusion, each paramecium exchanging half of its total substance with the other. In multicellular organisms this fusion is delegated to a single cell, but human fantasy often recreates the more primitive process in the context and language of love [Rostand, 1961, 13–21]. The same may be said of species which dispense with males; species in which the male is merely a tiny parasite on the female or (more rarely) vice versa; species consisting of self-fecundating or mutually fecundating hermaphrodites; species in which impregnation occurs orally or through the skin surface; species in which the penis is permanently lost through intercourse; species in which one's gender is situationally determined, or alternates through stages of the life cycle; and, finally, species in which copulation is accompanied by considerable aggression: the

male mutilating the female or breaking into her body in a kind
of reverse Caesarean; the female devouring her mate altogether, insemination sometimes being provided by a decap-
itated and half-eaten male [*Ibid.*, pp. 27–29, 33–39, 42–43,
56, 71, 85–87, 90, 108–9]. Thus the oral-narcissistic sexual
orientation, while it profoundly distorts human sexuality,
nevertheless calls attention to an important fact which the
human sexual experience is largely able to ignore: that bi-
ologically, sexuality is fundamentally concerned with the
dissolution and rearrangement of boundaries. In some cosmog-
onies death and sexuality come into being at the same time
[Campbell, 1959, p. 177], as if to remind us that creation is
not possible without concomitant destruction.

Oral preoccupations lead to a definition of sexuality in
which destruction is uppermost, with sensual pleasure relegated to a poor third. A sexual encounter is experienced as
a serpent combat—an emotional swallowing contest, with:
". . . each principal seeking to get into his mouth the head
of his opponent." The serpent is at home in oral-narcissistic
fantasies because he ingurgitates his adversary or prey alive:
". . . the relentless jaws . . . steadily draw the fighting,
squirming thing inward. Gradually the food is swallowed,
with frequent pauses for breath and with halts to repress the
. . . fighting of the prey struggling inch by inch in the
throes of a living death." Rolker describes an incident in
which a snake eating a frog was half-swallowed by a competitor; when they were pulled apart by a zoo attendant the
disgorged snake was unharmed and completed his own meal
[Rolker, 1956, pp. 275–76].

But although this fundamentally oral view of sexuality is
identical for both sexes, the specific preoccupations differ in
accordance with sexual differentiation. The correlation is by
no means perfect, since the existence of the conflict presupposes an uncertain commitment to sexual specialization, but
one can at least say that there are distinguishable fears

which can be labeled "male" and "female." These are fears of absorption and penetration, respectively. Both represent the disturbance of a static equilibrium—one in which nothing is either gained or lost. Such an equilibrium does not exist in nature, but only as a narcissistic fantasy of paradisiacal aloofness and detachment. It is an extremely important concept in both primitive and "civilized" theories of bodily health and illness, however. "For sickness, according to a shamanistic theory, can be caused either by the entrance of an alien element into the body . . . or by the departure of the soul . . . and its imprisonment in one of the spirit regions" [Campbell, 1959, p. 260]. Both fears—the male fear of being drained and devoured and the female fear of being penetrated and poisoned—receive expression in the myths and actualities of serpentine life.

"It was thought by the ancients, and is still believed by the European peasantry, that during sexual conjunction the male serpent introduces its head into the mouth of the female, and that the latter gnaws and bites it off, thus becoming fecundated. The same idea appears to obtain in Polynesia, and is, no doubt, general among uncultured peoples" [Briffault, 1959, p. 315]. This notion, which establishes the nature of the serpent's role in sexual symbolism rather concisely, also summarizes the character of the male boundary fear. The serpent represents, among other things, the widespread notion of the "vagina dentata," and is often portrayed biting the penis [cf. the Minos in Michelangelo's "Last Judgment"]. "The serpent is not so much a phallic symbol, but the symbol of oral aggression against the phallus" [Ehrenzweig, 1949, pp. 112, 116].

The trivial realities upon which these grotesque fears are based are nothing more than ejaculation and detumescence, with the accompanying emotional quiescence. The oral-narcissistic conflict translates detumescence into castration—what once was is no longer (as exemplified by Beowulf's sword, which melts on contact with the mother of Grendel) —ejaculation into vampirism, and satiation into death. Concern over the loss of semen (hilariously but accurately portrayed in the film "Dr. Strangelove") is rife in Asian countries (see Chapter XII), where hunger and deprivation contribute to oral definitions of sexuality. But the sudden emotional quiescence is probably the most powerful factor in activating male fears, particularly in societies where masculine prestige is strongly dependent upon activity of some type. The Spanish refer to copulation as *la poca muerte* [Wahl, 1963, p. 188], an echo perhaps of the familiar *post coitum omne animal triste*, and Alexander is reputed to have said that only sleep and sexual intercourse made him conscious of his mortality [Plutarch: *Alexander* xxii. 3]. Horney asks whether love and death are "more closely bound up with one another for the male than for the female," since for the female a new life may result. She suggests a "secret longing for extinction," for a reunion with the mother, and quotes a poem by Schiller in which a young man dives into a whirlpool to win a woman —finding utter blackness and quiet beneath the surface turmoil, and, at the bottom, huge reptiles, "coil'd about the grim jaws of their hell" [Horney, 1932, pp. 348, 353].

For the "oral" female, however, the emergence of a "new life" inside of her hardly reduces her tendency to equate love and death. She will experience the foetus with as much joy as she would a rapidly growing intestinal parasite devouring her from within. The female fear, however, is not of an enveloping or draining quietude, but of an internal shattering. Root describes a patient who had "fantasies that the male excreted a poisonous revolting urinary mess into the female and that the penis, like a fetus, caused inner damage, as a cancer did." She countered these ideas and her numerous rape fantasies with the thought that her vagina could snap off her husband's penis—a good example of the mutually reinforcing nature of oral-narcissistic anxieties [Root, 1957, pp. 328–29].

A curious parallel to her initial fantasy is found in the story that Pasiphaë punished Minos for his infidelities by a magic spell which caused him to discharge, whenever he copulated with another woman, a swarm of serpents, scorpions, and millipedes which preyed upon her internal organs [Graves, 1955, I, p. 299].

The realistic kernel of these phantasms is impregnation—the fact that the male does penetrate the boundaries of the organism and put something inside which drastically alters the shape and intactness of the female body. The serpent becomes associated with this process because of his venom, which is equally potent and equally mysterious in its workings. Snakes are often referred to as "swollen with venom," although this is anatomically erroneous—an image clearly derived from tumescence.

A poem by Baudelaire captures this aspect of the serpent, and shows once again the perfect sexual complementarity of oral-narcissistic fantasies. The vindictive lover, hating his beloved's exuberant beauty, dreams of stealing into her room at night:

> Pour châtier ta chair joyeuse,
> Pour meurtrir ton sein pardonné,
> Et faire à ton flanc étonné
> Une blessure large et creuse,
> Et, vertigineuse douceur!
> A traverse ces lèvres nouvelles,
> Plus éclatantes et plus belles,
> T'infuser mon venin, ma soeur!
> [Baudelaire, "A Celle Qui Est Trop Gaie"]

Myths of impregnation by serpents and other reptiles are found in all parts of the world [cf. Briffault, 1959, pp. 314ff.], and my assumption that this symbolism is rooted in boundary-anxiety is reinforced by the fact that the serpent appears frequently in the context of defloration and menstruation. The belief that menstruation is caused by intercourse with a serpent is a common one; it attaches to the Garden of Eden myth and its Persian cousin [Briffault, *loc. cit.*].[13] In some cases the serpent is in jealous possession of the young maiden, inhabiting her body and ready to sting the penis of the man who deflowers her, unless he is possessed of some special power. This is sometimes the rationale for the *jus primae noctis* [Yates, 1930, pp. 169–70, 178]. It also illustrates again how the boundary-anxieties of males and females reinforce one another, each generating retaliatory fantasies corresponding to the fears of the opposite sex.

Freud called attention to this phenomenon in his study of the taboo of virginity [1918b], observing that feminine rage reactions often accompanied defloration, and that men had evolved many customs designed to counteract this anger. The term "violate," with its connotations of boundary and trespass, epitomizes the female version of the narcissistic definition of copulation.

Erikson points out that just as pre-adolescent boys tend to build towers with experimental play materials, and to be concerned with height, mobility, and downfall, girls construct static interior scenes which are peaceful until intruded upon. "The significantly larger number of open interiors and simple enclosures, combined with an emphasis, in unique details, on intrusion into the interiors, on an exclusive elaboration of doorways, and on the blocking-off of such doorways seems to mark *open* and *closed* as a feminine variable." Erikson points out, however, that high walls and closed gates rarely occur among undisturbed girls. Ordinarily the interiors are open, and the intruding element, which is always a male or an animal, causes excitement and amusement rather than panic [Erikson, 1963, pp. 331, 333–36]. It is well to remem-

[13] Briffault cites a European superstition that a hair plucked from a menstruating woman would turn into a serpent if buried, as would the hair of a witch. Japanese folklore abounds in tales of dragons' daughters whose hair turns to snakes at night. But in the ancient world, the hair of any woman might have this property as a result of jealousy [Briffault, 1959, pp. 312–13].

ber this point, since there is a tendency among psychoanalytic thinkers to generalize to all humans the boundary anxieties I have been discussing. Simone de Beauvoir also falls into this error: "*Et si l'on invoque la nature, on peut dire que naturellement toute femme est homosexuelle . . . toute adolescente redoute la pénétration, la domination masculine, elle éprouve à l'égard du corps de l'homme une certaine répulsion . . .*" [1949, II, p. 173].

The fear of penetration usually betokens other boundary fears, such as those found in a patient of Spiegel: she was afraid to take a bath at times, for fear she might dissolve into the water. Another patient was afraid of orgasm and of her own tender feelings, which she felt might cause her to fly into pieces. Still another told the therapist "that her 'teeth would be set on edge' when her husband would lovingly talk of becoming 'one with her' during intercourse" [Spiegel, 1959, pp. 101–3]. But it is primarily the fear of penetration which characterizes the snake fantasies of the hysterical Victorian ladies of early psychoanalytic literature. Abraham notes the frequency among narcissistic women of fantasies of immaculate conception, which he interprets as a way of saying "I can do it by myself" [1920, p. 354]. In both of two cases involving snake fantasies and phobias, discussed by Abraham, the snake is interpreted as representing the father's penis, but in both cases the father's embrace is feared as lethal [1912, pp. 159–62; 1913a, 164–65]. Abraham also comments on the association between snakes and death [1912, pp. 161–62].

Even in this sense, however, the snake as phallus is relatively infrequent in Greek myth, and it may be that the obstinacy with which psychoanalysts cling to this equation is based on a genuine cultural difference between Greece and Victorian Europe. It is assumed today that the fear of snakes[14] is found primarily among women (partly perhaps because

---

[14] It is sometimes argued that this fear is instinctive, on the grounds that chimpanzees display it, and humans who have never been injured by a snake [cf. Hebb, 1949, pp. 242–43], but the enormous variation in attitude toward the serpent prevents such a conclusion [cf. Aymar, 1956, pp. 74–80].

Victorian ladies were expected to be somewhat phobic), but this was certainly not true in ancient Greece. I have already related how Alexander's mother, Olympias, slept peacefully (I refer to the presumed reality, not the associated myth) beside a serpent; and Plutarch tells of wild Dionysian dances in which serpents wound themselves around the women and their spears and chaplets, "frightening *the men* out of their wits" [Plutarch: *Alexander* ii. 4-6; Harrison, 1957, pp. 397-98. Italics mine].

We would expect, from our analysis thus far, that in a given culture the sex experiencing the most acute pathogenic pressure from the mother would have the greatest fear of snakes. Yet we have also observed that each sex tends to inflict its anxieties on the other, so that the difference would be far from absolute.

One of the few instances of female ophidiophobia in ancient Greek folklore illustrates the importance of the maternal attitude. It occurs in Apuleius, but is nevertheless derived from what is almost certainly a Greek tale, and is probably very old [Flacelière, 1960, p. 194]. I refer to the episode in "Eros and Psyche" in which Psyche's sisters attempt to persuade her that her mysterious, unseen husband "who comes secretly gliding into your bed at night is an enormous snake, with widely gaping jaws, a body that could coil around you a dozen times and a neck swollen with deadly poison . . . when your nine months are nearly up he will eat you alive . . . his favorite food is a woman far gone in pregnancy" [Apuleius, *The Golden Ass*, pp. 103-4]. Since it is a woman's husband who is being portrayed as a snake one might assume that here, at least, we have an instance of the fear of penetration. But what are we to say of the gaping jaws and the coiling around and the eating alive? And why does this imaginary snake prefer pregnant women close to delivery? We are reminded that behind the adolescent husband of our heroine stands a jealous and implacable female—the Earth-Mother Aphrodite; she is angry and vindictive, like the plotting sisters, at being outshone by Psyche, and, with them, she is the source of all Psyche's troubles.

Perhaps in this fantasy of the snake is the fear that husband will turn into mother, a notion which, although realistically bizarre, is psychologically probable. For many a girl with a dependent and hostile relationship with her mother transfers this relationship to her husband, making the same ambivalent demands upon him as she made upon her mother as a child. As Freud remarked, every girl marries her father and then promptly transforms him into her mother [1931a, p. 258; 1933, p. 171]. We may thus interpret the episode in the following manner:

A young girl has been deprived and rejected by her mother, and wishes both to be free of the mother and to extract from her, infant-like, the warmth and nurturance she has missed. She imagines herself devouring her mother in her insatiable hunger. Then she dreams of a handsome husband who will rescue her from this dilemma. But even in fantasy the old conflict persists. Her hunger will give her a child as ravenous as herself, who will swallow her the moment it is born; it will transform the husband into the enveloping mother who will thwart her atrophied, struggling desires for autonomy and separateness. She fears losing herself in this relationship as she feared it in the old one. And, in fact, as the story of Eros and Psyche unfolds, we find her fears are justified. She makes too many demands upon her husband and is undone. Psyche begs him ceaselessly to let her see her sisters, so she can flaunt her good fortune; he yields, they frighten her with the snake story, and she peeks at him, discovering that it is indeed a handsome boy in bed with her rather than a serpentine mass of transference. But it is too late—she has hurt him and he leaves her. Psyche wanders from one mother-goddess to another, but they all refuse her, and she finally comes face to face with her angry mother-in-law, Aphrodite, who sets her a series of impossible tasks, including sending her to the underworld. She manages to perform them, however, and is re-

united with her husband, Eros. Thus she resolves the conflict
by returning to the source of it and fulfilling her apparently
insatiable needs (which she has thoughtlessly projected onto
the mother figure, perhaps with some psychological justice).
Note that while in the underworld Psyche must not permit
herself to accept any appetizing food or comforts, nor nurture any of those who seek help; she must maintain a cold,
narcissistic detachment—otherwise, as is always the case with
such tales, the visit will be permanent. For going to Tartarus
and back is the precise equivalent of the ultimate insatiable
need—the desire for the complete peace and security of the
womb, without being destroyed.

The Psyche tale is interesting for several additional reasons.
First, it epitomizes the source of marital difficulties for the female, reflecting, in somewhat glamorized form, the most mundane and familiar themes of clinical literature in our own day.
Second, it is an utterly matriarchal story, with three mother-
goddesses, two elder sisters, and a teen-aged husband. Only at
the very close does any sort of a father figure emerge, in the
form of Zeus, who, however, makes the decision which solves
the problem. The story thus suggests that only when a little
girl dares to risk transferring some of her dependency from
the mother to the less crucial and more distant father can she
hope for a satisfactory heterosexual adjustment. Third, it
illustrates, once again, the way in which a genital situation may
be redefined in oral terms. Finally, like so many folktales and
hero-myths, it expresses the idea that only when infantile
conflicts are overcome can adult gratifications be obtained.
Maternal dependency and oral-narcissistic anxieties must be
resolved or the ecstasies of mature sexuality will be corroded.
This theme appears prominently in tales of the "Beauty and
the Beast" or "Frog Prince" type, in which some kind of loving confrontation with a repellent animal is required in order
to transform it into an attractive prince or princess. Most
often the animal is some sort of serpent. The story of Prince

Alberic, who is tricked into swearing to kiss a hideous green serpent three times on the mouth, whereupon it becomes a beautiful fairy queen, exemplifies the type [Aymar, 1956, pp. 27–29]. Viewing the serpent as representative of the oral-narcissistic dilemma, one can interpret such tales as showing how this dilemma must be confronted before "genitality" is achieved. By the same reasoning we can predict that, in a given culture, ophidiophobia will be most pronounced in whichever sex experiences the greatest difficulty in relinquishing symbiotic dependence upon the mother.

The Serpent As Bisexual Integrity

I noted earlier that while the serpent was associated with death and fears of the dead, it also connoted immortality. In a similar fashion, the serpent appears as a homeopathic remedy for the fears of boundary violation which sexuality arouses in orally fixated individuals. The snake is often utilized as a bisexual symbol [cf. Neumann, 1954, pp. 10ff., 48–49], and bisexuality, like parthenogenesis, is an obvious solution to boundary fears. But while the parthenogenetic fantasy eliminates the male intruder, it does not resolve the more fundamental problem of sexual limitation. The oral-narcissistic conflict, it will be recalled, arises from a failure to cope with the loss of the infantile illusion of oneness with the world, of completeness and self-sufficiency.

Narcissistic concerns tend to focus on those parts of the body which vary most from person to person. The anatomical differentiation of the sexes is the most extreme form of variation, along with age (i.e., size) differences; and the discovery that one is equipped with the organs of only one sex, and that even these are small and inadequate as compared with those of adults, is perhaps the very first narcissistic wound. Bettelheim [1955a, *passim*] discusses the lengths to which members of some primitive societies are willing to go in an effort to remedy this defect. With the awareness of one's monosexuality must come an acceptance of one's incompleteness—childish fantasies of omnipotence cannot be sustained. A human being cannot reproduce himself without aid, but is dependent on another. But a being with the organs of both sexes is, on the contrary, self-sufficient. The problem is, as Bettelheim points out, particularly acute for males, who play such a brief role in procreation. Thus, above and beyond their fears of boundary-violation, the organs of each sex are a threat to the pride of narcissistic individuals of the opposite sex, and the "bisexual" nature of the snake is expressive of this preoccupation.

That this desire for bisexual unity is rooted in the very earliest period of psychic development is suggested by the frequency with which such bisexuality is associated with myths concerning existence in some sort of pre-dualistic paradise, and with androgynous gods who carry the attributes of infantile omnipotence [cf. Campbell, 1956, pp. 152–54; cf. also Galt, 1943; Licht, 1963, pp. 124–28]. Fantasies of having a twin or an animal companion may also have this meaning [Peller, 1959, p. 422]. These fantasies are not only bisexual but presexual, in the sense that they refer to a period prior to the child's awareness of sexual differences [cf. Peller, *op. cit.*, pp. 425ff.].

One of the most popular of these fantasies in Western culture is that of Aristophanes in Plato's *Symposium* [189–93], and it reveals the full ambivalence of the oral-narcissistic syndrome. As in all myths of androgynous self-sufficiency, there lurks here the notion of the One being formed of two united and inseparable parts, so that we may well ask whether the androgyne represents the utterly self-sufficient narcissistic ego or the self-contained unit of mother-and-child, joined in an inseparable bond by their joint concern with the satisfaction of the child's needs. The total omnipotence of the child is, after all, rooted in his total dependency, and in one sense the two sides of this autonomy-versus-engulfment conflict are not so far apart as they might seem.

In Aristophanes' fantasy, the two halves, following their division by Zeus (for it is the father in most cultures who separates the child from the mother and calls attention to specialized sex roles), "were on the point of dying from hunger and self-neglect, because they did not like to do anything apart" [Plato: *Symposium* 191]. It was to save them from this dilemma that Zeus instituted procreation through sexual intercourse. But this does not satisfy the desire for oneness, since "the intense yearning which each of them has towards the other does not appear to be the desire of lover's intercourse; but of something else which the soul of either evidently desires and cannot tell, and of which she has only a dark and doubtful presentiment. Suppose Hephaestus, with his instruments, to come to the pair who are lying side by side and to say to them 'What do you people want of one another?' they would be unable to explain. And suppose further, that when he saw their perplexity he said: 'Do you desire to be wholly one . . . ?' there is not a man of them who . . . would not acknowledge that this meeting and melting into one another, this becoming one instead of two, was the very expression of his ancient need" [*Ibid.*, 192].

It would be difficult to find a more direct statement of the pre-genital nature of this yearning than Aristophanes' statement that sexual intercourse fails to satisfy it, and that it is aimed not at growth and procreation but at a return to a previous state of existence. It abolishes dependency by surrendering to it utterly—an interesting resolution of the conflict. That the "previous state" is the mother-child dyadic unit is made clear by the description of the behavior of the divided beings following separation, which sounds very much like a modern clinical report of the apathy of mother-separated children [cf. Spitz, 1964; Bowlby, 1960].

The desire for bisexual self-sufficiency is merely another version of the wish to be reabsorbed into the mother with its attendant antithetical desire for autonomy. The conflict is beautifully expressed in the story of Salmacis and Hermaphroditus quoted above, in which this merging actually occurs, thus allowing the contrary feelings subsequently to appear. This interpretation also accords well with the prevalence, in puberty initiations and other *rites de passage*, of exchanges of clothes between the sexes. As Jane Harrison observes: "Manhood, among primitive peoples, seems to be envisaged as ceasing to be a woman . . . when he passes to manhood . . . (the) moment is one . . . of extreme peril; he at once emphasizes and disguises it. He wears woman's clothes" [Harrison, 1962, pp. 506–7].

The same effect may be achieved anatomically through an operation such as subincision, and it is noteworthy that one of the puberty rites Bettelheim discusses, the Kunapipi, centers around a large mythical snake. That subincision is indeed based on the motive assigned to it Bettelheim seems to have demonstrated. Even the name of the rite, Kunapipi, means both "Mother" or "Old Woman," subincision wound, and "uterus of the mother" [1955a, pp. 193–94]. The wound itself is variously called by terms meaning "vulva," "vagina," and "penis womb," while the blood from the wound is called "menstrual blood," "woman," or "milk" [*Ibid.*, pp. 176–77].

Kunapipi, the great fertility-mother, perpetually pregnant, is the foundation of the rites. She is seen as the creator of all beings, "in association with" Julunggul, the mythical snake. Because of this association, Berndt, upon whose monograph Bettelheim largely depends here, calls the snake "the symbolic Penis," but Bettelheim notes that although this is certainly a partial interpretation, the snake is usually described in myths as female, and suggests that "as a she-snake, it appears as a symbolization of the wish of men for female, and possibly also of the wish of women for male, sex characteristics and functions" [*Ibid.*, p. 196].

The sexual ambiguity of the snake symbol is well-exemplified by the myth. A female, Julunggul, is attracted and aroused by female functions, i.e., the menstrual blood and the afterbirth blood respectively of the two Wawilak sisters. When they run into their hut, Julunggul, male-like, puts her head into the hut and sprays them (and the baby) "with saliva from her throat to make them very slippery," but then swallows all three. The Wawilak sisters and the baby are all female, but it is the male novices at initiation who (so the women are told) are swallowed by the snake and reborn at the end of the ceremony. To further confuse the issue, the saliva of the snake is called by a word meaning semen [*Ibid.*, pp. 196–98].

Bettelheim observes, with regard to this symbolic intercourse episode, that it is "in coitus that the sexes merge most completely, psychologically and physiologically, and a man who desires to gain female sex functions might try to do so through intercourse" [*Ibid.*, p. 199]. But fundamentally, the swallowing of the females represents an attempt to acquire female functions through oral incorporation. "If the snake is the symbol of the male organ, it is the symbol of the incised penis that has incorporated into itself the incisure, the slit, the vulva, and is thus both male and female" [*Ibid.*, pp. 199–200]. However achieved, amalgamation is clearly the goal, as suggested by the fact that the entire mythical episode follows upon the birth of the child. The snake (i.e., the desire) is aroused by the smell of blood, particularly the afterbirth blood which represents the separation of the child from the mother, and secondarily by the menstrual blood which represents the separateness of man from woman. The snake is female because the desire is to be realized through the incorporation of female characteristics, as Bettelheim points out. Separation from the mother is thus negated through identification.

Asexuality and Maternal Appeasement

In maternally deprived persons one finds a number of desperation fantasies, all having the form "if I was (or was not) X, then mother would love me." Prominent among these is always the feeling that it is one's sex which is at fault. This, however, involves not the addition of organs but their replacement or removal, and thus may contradict, or is at least independent of, the wish for bisexuality. In the male, the desire for bisexual unity leads to such phenomena as subincision rituals, which attempt to master the loss of the mother through incorporation. The feeling that one would be loved if one's sex were changed leads to self-castration—a less primitive mode of coping with maternal loss. It is the result, after all, of a rudimentary reasoning process, which says, "Mother does not love me because of my maleness, therefore I will remove that which angers her." It makes a specific diagnosis and prescribes an appropriate, if drastic, therapy. For this reason, "castration, as an institution, appeared comparatively late in history among relatively sophisticated peoples" [Bettelheim, 1955a, p. 155]. Although it reflects anxiety about maternal love, it is peripheral to the oral-narcissistic conflict, and the serpent as a symbol is less often associated with it.

As Bettelheim points out, the great maternal deities such as Cybele, "required emasculation as the price of grace" [*Ibid.*, pp. 156–57; Frazer, 1906, pp. 163ff.]. Women who wished to dedicate themselves to the goddess had to cut off one or both breasts [Weigert-Vowinkel, 1938, p. 352], which is perhaps the origin of the story that the Amazons burned off the right breast to facilitate the drawing of their bows [Grote, pp. 159–61; Apollodorus: ii. 5. 9]. The female devotees of the goddess are secondary in the rituals, however, and seem to be a late development. Perhaps females experiencing maternal rejection of their femininity (a rejection that was culturally deviant) sought respite in a ritual originally oriented to the more modal tendency of mothers to reject the masculinity of their sons.

Since this maternal hostility seems to have been based on penis envy, the severed genitals were either presented to the goddess [Frazer, *op. cit.*, pp. 167ff.] or to women [Bettelheim, *op. cit.*, p. 157]. Bettelheim reports an Attis-type fantasy of a schizoid girl, provoked by the sight of a man urinating [*Ibid.*, pp. 157–58], and the following excerpts from the fantasy of a student, written as part of an autobiographical study, illustrate the same theme:

> [Hunting in the forest, I came] face to face with a monstrous female baboon. I knew she was about to attack. Flight was useless; she could easily catch me and tear me to pieces . . . I determined to take advantage of her maternal instincts and to react as a child, hoping she would accept me as an infant baboon until I had a chance to escape.
>
> I therefore approached and commenced to suckle at her breast. . . . She accepted me and we caressed and fondled each other. . . .
>
> I began to consider how I might escape . . . [by making] the initial physical separation . . . appear quite normal . . . I appeared to desire to urinate, and toward this end I moved off a few feet . . . though still within her reach, and opened my fly. At the sight of my penis, she became enraged, [and] . . . leaned over to bite it off. [He awakens.]

Bettelheim also puts forth many indications that circumcision is performed in part (since the custom has several determinants) as a sacrifice to the demands of women. The practice of presenting the foreskins, blood, or excised teeth to the mother attests to this, as does the custom of having the mother swallow the foreskin, and the suggestion of a maternal reward in the form of women's clothes [*op. cit.*, pp. 159–61, 213]. He calls attention to "revenge-like postcircumcision behavior" found in tribes such as the Kikuyu, among whom "the newly circumcised boys in groups of fifteen or twenty attack and rape *old women* and finally kill them" [*Ibid.*, p. 159. Italics mine]. In some tribes the women insist on circumcision as a prerequisite to intercourse or a genuine, lasting love relationship [*Ibid.*, p. 163]. In this they seem to be obeying a psychological law which says that positive feelings can only be released when the hostile side of the ambivalence that pervades human relationships has been discharged. The same law is at the bottom of the many fertility rites which include the purgation of evil influences through beating, ritual murder, and even promiscuous free-for-all fighting [cf. Harrison, 1957, pp. 100ff., 136]. Fertility, like love, can only emerge when destructive feelings have been expelled, since ambivalence inhibits the free expression of sexuality [cf. Frazer, 1959, pp. 519–45].

These placating rituals and fantasies, then, are secondary defensive responses evoked by situations in which maternal hostility is particularly acute. The individual becomes not bisexual but asexual, apparently operating on the unconscious assumption that the maternal demon, appeased by this desperate expedient, will leave the rest of the organism intact and autonomous. It is a narcissistic "solution," sacrificing the part to preserve the intactness of the remainder; and hence the lovers of the great Mother-goddesses who demand such sacrifice are invariably self-absorbed, narcissistic youths (Neumann, 1954, p. 50).

A Modern Example

I will conclude this discussion of the oral-narcissistic dilemma and the serpent symbol by showing its relation to a well-known contemporary case study—one which provided the subject matter for two books and a Hollywood film, "The Three Faces of Eve." The patient, Eve, who was studied in the early nineteen-fifties, was diagnosed as a case of multiple personality. The acute phase of her illness was precipitated by a miscarriage, and took the form of an attempt to strangle her daughter. Her first recollected fugue occurred in the context of sibling rivalry, and the two main themes of her anamnesis were sibling jealousy and an incident in which she was forced to touch the corpse of her grandmother. Her mother was the principal disciplinarian in the family, and apparently rather dour. The father was playful and amiable, but somewhat ineffectual and often absent [Thigpen and Cleckley, 1957, pp. 57ff., 134, 228–30, 246–48].

Eve had been frightened with a bogie rather reminiscent of the Eros and Psyche story:

"Mother . . . warned her of a horrible monster that lurked in the ditch, waiting to pounce on bad little girls who played along its banks. It was a monster with the head of a man and the scaly body of a snake, she added, and the creature had been known to crawl into houses in the dead of night and, like a python, crush the life out of children who'd been bad. . . . She became afraid even to cross the bridge over the ditch, because she was convinced that when she did she could see the baleful eyes of the monster glaring up at her out of the ditch's slimy, stagnant depths" [Lancaster, 1958, p. 13].

As in Psyche's sisters' fantasy, the monster is male, and is presented by one woman to another, perhaps with the same jealous motive.[15] There is again the warning that genital sexuality ("playing along the banks") will lead to calamity, and again this calamity takes the form of oral crisis. The "slimy ditch" is a typical fantasy characterization of the womb, and the fear of crossing the bridge expresses fear of her own wishes for fusion and quiescence. Ferenczi, for example, states that in bridge fantasies the bridge "spans a wide and perilous stream, from which all life takes its origin, into which man longs all his life to return" [Ferenczi, 1921, p. 353]. He presents a case of bridge-phobia, a young man whose mother, a midwife, "would not be parted from him

---

[15] While the baleful, glaring eyes of the monster may suggest a primal-scene experience [cf. Freud, 1918a, pp. 498ff.; esp. p. 505], it seems likely that one determinant is the uncanny appearance of the loved parent at the moment when she dredges up this monstrosity from her own unconscious. We do not know, of course, how much of the fantasy actually came from the mother. It is quite possible that Eve may have elaborated some of the details; for example, it might have been she rather than the mother who located the monster in the ditch [cf. Thigpen and Cleckley, 1957, p. 58].

even on the night of agony in which she gave birth to a girl-child." In adult life (partly through this experience, but more importantly through his mother's possessive attachment) he was terrified of female genitals and could not cross the Danube without a strong protector [*Ibid.*, p. 354]. Eve displays a comparable fear of males (she was frigid in all three personalities), but this fear does not seem to be the primary one. Since her mother would not permit her fully to cathect her father as love-object and protector, he could only be seen as a rival, and however much Eve may have resented the mother's interposition, she was too uncertain of her love to give up her dependence upon her. The horror experienced by Eve is not a fear of men per se, but a fear of losing, through an emotional attachment to a man, her mother's highly conditional love. The slimy ditch and strangling python reflect her inability to extricate herself from maternal entanglement as much as they do the dangers of men.

Eve's father, however, was not her only rival for her mother's love—siblings and sibling figures caused her a great deal of jealous anguish. Perhaps some of the horror attached to uterine symbols pertained to the womb as the source of present and future siblings. Ferenczi's phobic patient, for example, saw a sibling being born [1921, pp. 353–54].

The theme of the snake-as-devouring-child also occurs in Eve's story. As in the Psyche tale, Eve's hunger is projected onto her child, producing an Erichthonius in her dream world:

"There is a pool of stagnant green water in the center of the room. . . . I'm in the water with Bonnie, and Bonnie has the scaly body of a snake from the waist down . . ." [Lancaster, *op. cit.*, p. 61].

The term "stagnant" is particularly appropriate for an intrauterine fantasy, since it implies both death (motionlessness, decay) and birth (for it is in stagnant water that various forms of plant and animal life breed and grow).

Eve's boundary anxiety is disclosed by a second dream, one which is recurrent:

"I have dreamed that various parts of my body were turning into snakes. Each night more of me is consumed by reptiles . . . when I awake from dreaming it has taken me as long as an hour for me to convince myself my hands and feet were not snakes. . . . The dreams are frightening, the headaches terrifying, but the feeling of smothering is even worse" [*Ibid.*, p. 230]. Males also appear—usually in a protective role; but they are usually bitten by the snakes or thrown into a snake pit, and begin also to develop serpentine limbs [Thigpen and Cleckley, 1957, p. 208].[16]

This is an exceptionally clear expression of the oral-narcissistic conflict. She is "consumed by reptiles," i.e., reabsorbed into her mother's body, and hence experiences a frightful sense of smothering. She wishes to escape this fate and yet it is clear that the devouring serpent is not simply an enveloping maternal vagina but is within herself (she is turning into snakes), her own gnawing hunger for maternal love—for complete and eternal protection and nurturance. One speaks of people being "consumed with desire," and "eating themselves up" over something, or "eating their heart out"—this is the real, internal serpent.

The circumstances under which Eve's dissociation begins to dissolve reveal the primeval character of its inception. She suddenly recalls repressed incidents in her childhood when she attempts to retrieve a ball which her daughter has rolled under a porch:

"The dank smell of earth *the sun had never touched* filled

16 The dreams in part suggest, as does a picture drawn by the patient, a phallic interpretation, and it is clear that the idea of a strong, protective, tender, and seductive male was threatening to the brittle edifice Eve had built. Eve *was* in a sense dying, just as she felt she was, in that this series of accelerating snake dreams heralded the disintegration of her multiple-personality structure, the "death" of the fugue personalities, and the emergence of a single integrated ego.

her nostrils with a hauntingly familiar odor" [Lancaster, 1958, p. 230. Italics mine].

One is here reminded of Alcmaeon's refuge from maternal hostility in land which the sun had never seen [Thucydides: ii. 102–3], and of Hera's edict that Leto could not be delivered anywhere the sun shone [Hyginus: *Fabulae* 140]. The theme seems to involve a denial of parental sexuality—it is significant that in one version of the birth of Apollo Hera is unwilling to punish the island of Asteria (Delos) for giving refuge to Leto, on the grounds that Asteria had once rejected Zeus' advances [Callimachus: *Hymn to Delos* 244–48; Apollodorus: i. 4. 1]. In Eve's case it refers back to a time prior to awareness of parental intercourse, back to the period of infantile bliss in which no one existed for her but her mother and herself—the period prior to the conception and birth of siblings.

Finally, Eve's infantile "trauma" of being forced to touch her grandmother's corpse was disturbing only because it was associated with her central conflict (as is probably true of most such traumata—few events are inherently traumatic). A loving contact with death was frightening because of her own quest for non-life in the tomb of her mother's body. Describing the incident, Eve says:

"She looked all gray and muddy, like the man under the bridge . . . with a snake's body. . . . I thought he'd gotten grandma. . . . I was *afraid she might stick to me and never let me go*" [Lancaster, *op. cit.*, p. 234. Italics mine].

Eve's problems are focused with particular clarity on psychic boundaries and the ambiguity thereof. This is the reason for the omnipresence of the serpent in her fantasy life. For the serpent symbolizes this most primeval of all human conflicts:

> Even you, great Python of hillside and valley
> Who haunt the deepest shadows in men's hearts
> [Ovid: *Metamorphoses* i. 440–42. Gregory trans.]

Part Two

MYTHICAL DEFENSES
AGAINST
THE MATERNAL THREAT

CHAPTER III

Sexual Dominance: Zeus

JOCASTA: As to your mother's marriage bed,—
don't fear it.
Before this, in dreams too, as well as oracles,
many a man has lain with his own mother.
But he to whom such things are nothing bears
his life most easily.
[Sophocles: *Oedipus Tyrannus*
980–83. Grene trans.]

JANE HARRISON complains of the Olympian gods that they were so detached from their roots in the rich soil of popular religion and everyday magic that they became remote, two-dimensional, trivial, and cerebral [1962, 445–79]. Nevertheless they survived, and unless one is prepared to underwrite a theory of automatic lag (i.e., that any cultural item will persist *X* number of years even after it has ceased to be functional in any way), one must account for this persistence. It is at this point, I think, that social-psychological explanations are most helpful—one might argue that only some set of compelling psychological needs could maintain the existence of so bloodless a collection of images. Having lost so much of their original religious intensity and significance, the Olympians received a partial transfusion from the emotional concerns of the civilized Greek, who used them as a child uses play-therapy materials—forced to take into account their intrinsic character, but combining them in ways that expressed his inner preoccupations.

The gods and heroes discussed in this and in the following chapters of Part Two were selected because they illustrate these preoccupations, and develop a variety of "solutions" to the emotional dilemmas and interpersonal strains described in Part One. The mythical figures chosen are not all Olympian, nor do they exhaust or restrict themselves to any other category. I will try to show merely that the myths used are colored and shaped to varying degrees by the Greek family pattern and its emotional consequences. Each of the major male figures included, furthermore, tends to display a characteristic psychological technique for coping with these difficulties (although not without considerable overlap), and I shall try to analyze the ramifications of each of these mechanisms.

Commenting on the rites of passage of primitive societies, Joseph Campbell remarks that "a great number of the ritual trials and images correspond to those that appear automatically in dream the moment the psychoanalyzed patient begins to abandon his infantile fixations and to progress into the future" [Campbell, 1956, p. 10]. To illustrate this point he quotes Jung's report of a patient who, at the point when he "began to free himself from the bond of his mother complex," dreamed that "a serpent shot out from a moist cave and bit the dreamer in the region of the genitals" [*Ibid.*, p. 11; Jung, 1957, p. 413]. My discussion of the serpent symbol would suggest that central to this liberation from "infantile fixations" is resolution of the oral-narcissistic dilemma, represented in myth by the conquest of the serpent or dragon. Thus, three of the most important male figures in Greek mythology—Zeus, Apollo, and Heracles—initiate their careers by overcoming a serpent. These serpents, furthermore, are all of maternal origin.

It would be difficult, even in the huge trove of the world's mythologies, to find a figure more generally assumed to epitomize genital sexuality than Zeus. Indeed, there is a rather unequivocal Orphic myth which tells of his successful struggle with the oral-narcissistic dilemma and his attainment of genitality:

"When his mother, Rhea, foreseeing what trouble his lust would cause, forbade him to marry, he angrily threatened to violate her. Though she at once turned into a menacing serpent, this did not daunt Zeus, who became a male serpent and, twining about her in an indissoluble knot, made good his threat. It was then that he began his long series of adventures in love" [Graves, 1955, I, p. 53].

In part, this is a simple account, somewhat similar to Jung's example, of the process of abandoning a maternal fixation. The mother's own contribution to this conflict is also included, in that Rhea is possessive and forbids Zeus to marry. His response mirrors precisely the maternal ambivalence discussed in the first chapter, and her subsequent metamorphosis attempts to reactivate his infantile fears. Just as Athene protects her virginity through a borrowed maternal genital display (the Medusa's head), so Rhea attempts to ward off Zeus' threat by a comparable symbolic gesture. She is saying, in effect, "recall, when you were a helpless child I was an enveloping giant; my anger and my desire were alike uncanny and forbidding to you. Think now of your feelings then, and realize that to enter me is to return whence you came, and to find death."

Zeus, however, is unabashed, and proves his emergence from this infantile attitude by consummating the maternal rape. In this he is almost unique among Greek heroes, who, as we shall see, generally resolve the problem by some sort of killing or castration. While one finds occasional emulatory echoes in such incidents as Peleus' seduction of Thetis, Zeus seems distinctively set off by his bloodless and rather dashing response to maternal menace.

It is no coincidence that the chief god of the Greeks is portrayed as a sexual athlete. This quality is in fact his principal attribute in the more anthropomorphic accounts of Olympus. Other gods are shown as more wise, more just, more rational, more dignified, more beneficent, more charming, more ingenious, more awesome, more threatening, and more severe. But none is more promiscuous nor more prolific.

Now it might reasonably be objected that this trait is simply a consequence of the desire of many peoples to trace their lineage back to the chief of the gods, or to establish their local deities in the Greek pantheon. But granting the overwhelming importance of this motive, we must nonetheless realize that there are ways of dealing with it other than by creating the image of a great seducer. One can increase the number of legitimate progeny, as is often done; or one can de-emphasize the seduction aspect of these diverse paternities —a pattern sometimes followed with Heracles and other heroes, whose infidelities are at times treated simply as an adjunct and inevitable by-product of, or reward for, adventurous exploits. But the amorous adventures of Zeus are always seen as ends in themselves, and the purely sexual side of his procreative endeavors is always deliberately elaborated.

The desire for exalted ancestry is thus a necessary but not sufficient condition for the portrayal of Zeus which emerged in early Greek history. He might have appeared as a great king, with many wives and concubines; or the promiscuity once deemed necessary to express the conquest and integration of differing religions might later have been rationalized or muted in some way, or even delegated to some earlier god. Instead, it became the chief joy and theme of poets.

One reason for stressing the amorousness and potency of Zeus is that he represented the sexual dominance of the male over the great Earth-Mother goddesses, such as Hera, Leto, and Demeter. To overcome the awe that these goddesses were assumed to inspire, powerful desire and sexual aggres-

siveness were felt to be necessary. It is not without significance that Zeus is given the epithet "Lord of Hera" [e.g.,
Homer: *Iliad* vii. 411], as if his shaky marital dominance was
his major achievement.[1]

> Who else had power stern Hera's craft to stay,
> Her vengeful curse to loose?
> [Aeschylus: *The Suppliant Maidens* 586. Morshead trans.]

Zeus thus constitutes an explicit denial or reversal of the
feeling of helplessness, inadequacy, impotence, and terror
aroused in the Greek male by maternal ambivalence. He is
unawed even by Rhea, and equally capable of using his
sexuality as a weapon of hostility.

But as yet I have presented only one side of the picture.
Fantasy never succeeds in being purely and perfectly defensive. However much men may build a dream, saying "would
it were thus," at every point the reality of their doubts and
fears tends to seep back into the structure, and reveal the
purpose for which it was formed.

One sees this doubt first of all in the incident with Rhea.
In turning himself into a serpent and enveloping her Zeus is
in a sense identifying with his mother. He assumes her form
and her weapon (entanglement) in order to conquer her. The
entire incident seems to echo with great exactness the Kunapipi rite as analyzed by Bettelheim. It is, to begin with, an
initiation, and concerns not only the abandonment of the
infantile attachment to the mother, but also the working

---

[1] This equates his seduction of Hera with the slaying of heroes or
monsters. Hermes, for example, is called Argophontes, "slayer of Argus,"
and Bellerophon means "slayer of Bellerus." Gods and heroes took their
names from their chief source of narcissistic gratification—either their paternal lineage or some accomplishment. But there is another source for this
usage: "Lord of Hera" may originally have been, prior to the dominance of
the religion of Zeus, "Consort of Hera."

As Bettelheim points out [1955a, p. 158], the geographical area of mother-
goddess worship is also the area of the harem, showing that a preoccupation
tends to outlast any particular expression of it.

through of male envy and fear of the female reproductive apparatus. As in the case of subincision rites, this is achieved through the incorporation of female attributes, and represents an acquisition rather than an exchange of organs. Thus Zeus becomes female while remaining male (enveloping his mother he violates her); like the Australian initiates he seeks bisexuality, and here, as in the Kunapipi rite, the desire is symbolized by the serpent.

This is confirmed by the myth of the birth of Athene, to whom Zeus is mother as well as father [Apollodorus: i. 3. 6]. Dionysus is similarly born from Zeus [*Ibid.*, iii. 4. 3], and in one version Zeus and Hera compete in attempting to produce offspring unaided, the latter bearing both Hephaestus and the monster Typhon in this manner [Apollodorus: i. 3. 5; *Homeric Hymn to Apollo* 305–55; Hesiod: *Theogony* 924–29]. To have Zeus best Hera in this contest suggests the intensity of the fear of feminine superiority.

Zeus' relationship with Hera, moreover, is not one suggestive of comfortable patriarchal dominance: *"Ce maître souverain des hommes et des dieux n'a guère d'autorité dans son ménage . . ."* [Flacelière, 1960, p. 21]. In the *Iliad* he shows considerable apprehension of Hera's anger, as when Thetis pleads with him for Achilles:

> Deeply disturbed Zeus who gathers the clouds answered her: "This is a disastrous matter when you set me in conflict with Hera, and she troubles me with recriminations. Since even as things are, forever among the immortals she is at me and speaks of how I help the Trojans in battle. Even so, go back again now, go away, for fear she see us . . ." [Homer: *Iliad* i. 517–23. Lattimore trans.].

Later, he upbraids Hera for her vindictiveness, asking what Priam and his sons have done to merit her fury, and suggesting that her anger would be assuaged only if she were to "devour Priam raw, and Priam's sons and all the Trojans" [*Ibid.*,

iv. 35–36. Lang, Leaf, and Meyers trans.]. Yet despite the fact that Troy is his favorite city in all the world, he contents himself with extracting a promise from Hera to permit him to destroy one of her chosen cities if he should ever choose to do so [*Ibid.*, 39ff.].

Finally, when Athene and Hera attempt to subvert his plans, he threatens violence, and directs a stern rebuke to Athene:

> But with Hera have I not so great indignation nor wrath: seeing it ever is her wont to thwart me, whate'er I have decreed [*op. cit.*, viii. 407–8. Lang, Leaf, and Meyers trans.].[2]

Zeus' courtship of Hera is also revealing. Unable to win her directly, he resorts to a stratagem reminiscent of the baboon fantasy quoted in Chapter II. Like the frightened hunter, he decides "to take advantage of her maternal instincts," in this instance by assuming the disguise of a cuckoo suffering from the winter winds, which Hera warms at her bosom. He then resumes his true shape and ravishes her [Pausanias: ii. 17. 4]. Thus it is not through any masculine aggressiveness or sexual irresistibleness that Zeus becomes "Lord of Hera," but through a childlike appeal.

In one sense, Zeus' promiscuity itself reflects this self-doubt. Psychiatrists have much to say of the "Don Juan syndrome" and the various oedipal and homosexual tendencies which

---

[2] It is curious that Zeus and Apollo, the most important symbols of patriarchal dominance in the Greek pantheon, backed the losing side in the war. But Greek patriarchy was never really secure. Creusa's women are not in the least awed by Xuthus' power and threats in Euripides' *Ion* [666ff. and 76off.], but reveal his secret to their queen; and such fearless feminine loyalties are quite common in Greek tragedy. Perhaps Euripides best summarized the hollowness of Greek patriarchy in his *Hecuba* [88off.] when, with magnificent irony, he has the obtuse Agamemnon, just prior to his return to Argos, voice contemptuous incredulity at the idea that a woman could overcome a man. The fact that Euripides was not the most popular dramatist of his time is perhaps due to his tendency to expose too baldly the pathology of his culture.

give rise to it. But if this behavior pattern achieves anything, it is emotional distance from women—the avoidance of an involvement which might be feared as smothering or devouring. The poets express this fear both in the ephemeral nature of Zeus' extramarital relationships and in the tense and guarded cold war he maintains with Hera.

Finally, the myths which tell of potential or actual challenges to the power of Zeus, while perhaps essentially an attempt to allegorize the conflicts between religious or ethnic traditions, reflect, in their continued appeal and in the details of their telling, the prevalence of masculine self-doubt in Greek culture. One of the themes in these revolt-myths is the fear of the procreative powers of the mother—the fear that in her anger she will bear and foster powerful creatures and set them against the existing ruler. This is at the core of the Uranus-Cronus-Zeus legend, a fact obscured by the patriarchal twist of the early psychoanalysts [cf., e.g., Freud, 1900, pp. 256ff.]. Uranus himself is the child of Gaea, and fears his brother-children, especially the Hecatoncheires, whom he hides in the earth (i.e., keeps them unborn). But it is his mother-wife Gaea who plots vengeance, who makes the sickle, plans the castration, and induces Cronus to carry it out, the other sons being too fearful [Hesiod: *Theogony* 116–82]. Cronus in turn fears his children and swallows them, and it is his sister-wife Rhea who takes revenge on him through his son Zeus. But now Zeus, in his turn, fears the offspring of Metis and swallows her to avoid being overthrown [*Ibid.*, 886–900]. A similar apprehension of being supplanted by the children of Thetis causes him to avoid her and marry her to a mortal [Pindar: *Isthmian Odes* viii. 32ff.].

The relationship between Philip, Olympias, and Alexander provides an historical echo of these mythological families, which in turn capture the tendency of the Greek mother to get back at her husband through her children.

But Zeus must also deal with some actual revolts, and we are surprised to find that he is not entirely adequate in dealing with any of them. Two of the challenges come from Earth-born monsters, spawned specifically for the purpose by an angry Gaea, while the third comes from Hera herself. In the Giants' revolt he is saved by Heracles, in Hera's revolt by Thetis, and in one version of the Typhon myth by Hermes [Apollodorus: i. 6; Homer: *Iliad* i. 399ff.].

The Typhon struggle is interesting for several reasons. First, Typhon (or Typhoeus) is Gaea's youngest child, as Cronus had been when he castrated Uranus, and as Zeus was Rhea's [Hesiod: *Theogony* 137–38, 477–80, and 820–22]. Second, he was brought forth specifically to avenge the destruction of his brothers, the Giants. Third, he was the largest and most powerful of Earth's children, and almost came to reign. Fourth, like the Giants (not to mention the dreams of the patient, Eve), he was largely composed of serpents [Hesiod: *Theogony* 820–38; Apollodorus: i. 6. 1–3]. He thus personi-fies the feared generative power of the mother. But he also resembles, if indeed he is not identical with, the monster Typhaon, whom Hera produced unaided in a rage at Zeus. Hera prays to Gaea:

> "Grant that I may bear a child apart from Zeus, no wit lesser than him in strength—nay, let him be as much stronger than Zeus as all-seeing Zeus than Cronos." Thus she cried and lashed the earth with her strong hand. Then the life-giving earth was moved: and when Hera saw it she was glad in heart" [*Homeric Hymn to Apollo* 337–41].

The child is born "neither like the gods nor mortal men, fell, cruel Typhaon, to be a plague to men" [*Ibid.*, 349–52], and Hera gives it into the care of an appropriately gruesome baby-sitter—"bringing one evil thing to another such" [*Ibid.*, 353–54]—that same Python later slain by Apollo. Hera's vindictive intention is thus quite explicit, although Typhaon is never heard from again by this name, except as the mate of the serpent Echidna, i.e., as husband and father of other monsters [Hesiod: *Theogony* 306ff.].

But the fearsome Typhon is very much heard from, and although in Hesiod he is immediately defeated by Zeus after a close and violent struggle, in Apollodorus he wins the first several rounds. On his first appearance Zeus and the other Olympians take to the hills, save for Athene who is undaunted, and who shames Zeus into fighting. Zeus then wounds him with the same weapon that castrated Uranus, but Typhon wraps his many coils around Zeus, disarms him, and cuts his sinews with the sickle, so that he is immobile and impotent until he is rescued by Hermes, and Typhon is poisoned by the Fates [Apollodorus: i. 6. 3].

This story is fundamentally another version of the Zeus-Rhea incest, with the opposite outcome. Instead of a victorious assertion of masculinity, the male is smothered, castrated, and rendered impotent by maternal malevolence—ultimately to be rescued only by trickery, thievery, and fraud.

In the revolt of the gods, led by Hera, Zeus is also overcome, and again immobilized, this time by being tied. Thetis rescues him by sending one of the Hecatoncheires to untie him. Here Zeus is not only overcome, but humiliated, since the gods gather around to laugh at his impotence. Although he punishes Hera by hanging her by the wrists with anvils on her ankles, and subsequently maintains a kind of bullying dominance over her, it is always difficult to say which is more frightened of the other [Homer: *Iliad* i. 396–406 and xv. 18–25]. Zeus' control over Hera is never comfortable—it never *assumes* greater power but always seeks to have it accepted. Hera respects the force he can command, but not Zeus himself. In general their relationship is just what one would expect between an older sister and a younger brother with a quarrelsome history, at an age when the brother has become physically larger and stronger than his sibling. Zeus is never protective of Hera, for example.

The relationship of Thetis to the royal couple is an interesting one. In spite of (or because of) being rescued by her,

Zeus fears her. She rejects his advances, it is said, for Hera's sake [Hesiod: *Catalogues* 57; Apollodorus: iii. 13. 5], and this is an additional reason for his insistence that she marry a mortal. Yet Thetis not only successfully opposes Hera in the Trojan War, but also nurtures Hephaestus when he is rejected by Hera [*Homeric Hymn to Apollo* 316ff.], and protects Dionysus when he is persecuted by her [Apollodorus: iii. 5. 1]. This is one of several instances in Greek myth in which the chastity of one goddess is advanced as an explanation for the nonpunitiveness of another [cf. Callimachus: iv. 244–48].

In short, then, the portrayal of Zeus attempts to deny fear of the adult female by creating an image of a dominant, sexually potent male who is made chief of the gods. This image undergoes considerable erosion, however, as the very same doubts for which it was to provide quiescence re-emerge to alter it. Zeus repeatedly exhibits his fear and inadequacy toward maternal goddesses, as if the kinds of difficulties which the Greek male encountered in his sexual life puzzled not only the will but the imagination. Even in fantasy he could not devise a satisfactory mode of interaction with a mature woman.

Oedipus

It would scarcely do to pass by the topic of sexual confrontation between son and mother without mentioning Oedipus. I long assumed that the Oedipus myth grew out of a different emotional strand, and could not usefully be analyzed in terms of the familial processes discussed in Chapter I. This assumption was based more on psychoanalytic thinking about the myth, with its emphasis on father-son conflict and an unambivalent mother-son love, than on the myth itself as it is treated by post-Homeric authors. Had I given the matter any thought I might have noticed that: (1) the father-son conflict is but a tiny episode, while the prevailing situation is one of father-absence and mother-son marriage; (2) Jocasta

gives her son to the herdsman to be killed, so their relationship cannot be called devoid of a hostile component [Sopho-
cles: *Oedipus Tyrannus* 1173ff.]; (3) when Jocasta senses
the truth and rushes off to hang herself, Oedipus attributes
her distress to a narcissistic reaction [*Ibid.*, 1077ff.]; (4)
Laius was a pederast (some say the first), having once loved
and kidnaped Chrysippus, the son of Pelops [Hyginus:
Fabulae 85; Apollodorus: iii. 5. 5]; and (5) Laius rejected
Jocasta because of the oracle and refused her bed, so that she
was forced to seduce him when he was drunk [Euripides:
Phoenissae 21–22; Apollodorus: iii. 5. 7].

Stewart performs an interesting reconstruction of the myth,
one which is quite in accord with the ideas advanced in
Chapter I.³ He begins by asking why Oedipus, who commits
two outrages, is merely blinded and exiled, while Jocasta must
die for having committed only one. Combining some of the
facts just cited with nuances from Sophocles' drama, Stewart
argues that Laius' homosexuality is the crux of the matter—
that it brought down Hera's curse (some say it was Pelops')
and, because he acted upon the prophecy, Jocasta's wrath, Jocasta is "guilty" because she knows and is responsible—she saves
Oedipus in full knowledge that it will mean the death of
Laius, who has rejected and frustrated her. Stewart cites passages in the drama that suggest Jocasta both knew the truth
about the parricide and had immediately recognized Oedipus
[Stewart, 1961, pp. 424–27; see also Devereux, 1953; Kerényi,
1959, pp. 89–94; Licht, 1963, pp. 134–35, 458]. Whether
Stewart's thesis is altogether defensible or not, it calls attention to certain aspects of the myth which clearly reflect the
themes I have been discussing.

³ I am grateful to Elizabeth Lozoff for calling this paper to my attention.

▌ CHAPTER IV ▌

Masculine Antisepsis: Apollo

The door opened and what entered the room, fat and succulent, its sides voluptuously swelling, footless, pushing itself along on its entire underside, was the green dragon. Formal salutation. I asked him to come right in. He regretted that he could not do that, as he was too long. This meant that the door had to remain open, which was rather awkward. He smiled, half in embarrassment, half cunningly, and began: "Drawn hither by your longing, I come pushing myself along from afar off, and underneath am now scraped quite sore. But I am glad to do it. Gladly do I come, gladly do I offer myself to you" [Kafka, "The Green Dragon"].

Is it her singing that enchants us or is it not rather the solemn stillness enclosing her frail little voice? [Kafka, "Josephine the Singer, or the Mouse Folk"].

T HE MYTHS SURROUNDING APOLLO attempt simply to divest him of all suggestion of maternal enthrallment. He is the personification of anti-matriarchy, the epitome of the sky-god, a crusader against Earth deities. He is all sunlight, Olympian, manifest, rational. He opposes all that is mysterious, hidden, dark, and irrational. Or so, at least, the poets would have us believe. "Orthodoxy demanded that about Apollo there should be nothing 'earthy' and no deed or dream of darkness" [Harrison, 1962, p. 389].

Apollo's dematrification begins, naturally enough, with the

details of his birth. "He it was who escaped most completely from his earthly origin" [Levy, p. 277]. For, in keeping with the geophobia characteristic of Greek heroes, Apollo was born in a place of Not-Earth, an island in the sea, "a rock narrow, barren, and uninviting" [Grote, p. 71]—as dissociated as possible from fertile Mother Earth. Indeed, so unattractive was the isle of Delos that a mythical rationale was required to explain its selection as a birthplace for the god, and the island itself expresses its feeling of unworthiness: "I greatly fear in heart and spirit that as soon as he sees the light of the sun, he will scorn this island—for truly I have but a hard, rocky soil" [*Homeric Hymn to Apollo* 69ff.; cf. also Callimachus: iv. 11–13 and 240–43].

Now of course this is not to say that Delos was selected retroactively as Apollo's birthplace because of its barrenness, but rather that this attribute was particularly stressed in attempting to explain the tradition. It is highly unlikely that Delos is any more rocky than most Greek localities, but this aspect of its humbleness was emphasized because it allegorized Apollo's emancipation from maternal influence. Furthermore, in searching for a place to build his temple, Apollo chooses another earthless site, "rocky Pytho," a place so barren that his chosen priests are concerned how they will subsist [*Ibid.*, 183, 390 and 526–30].

We next find that Apollo, like many other heroes, was not suckled: "Leto did not give Apollo, bearer of the golden blade, her breast, but Themis duly poured nectar and ambrosia with her divine hands" [*Ibid.*, 123–25].[1] Furthermore, once having tasted the divine food, he burst his swaddling garment and began to walk and talk. In four days he called for bow and arrows and achieved manhood. His eagerness to liberate himself from childish dependency and maternal pro-

---

[1] Apollodorus uses an etymological argument to maintain that Achilles also was unsuckled [Apollodorus: iii. 13. 6]. Achilles' childhood appropriately alternates between all-male and all-female environments.

tection is also expressed by his having been a seven-months' child, and by his abrupt and more or less permanent departure from Delos [*Ibid.*, 127ff.; Hyginus: *Fabulae* 140].

Finally, while chronologically still an infant, Apollo slew the dragon Python. The jealous Hera had sent Python to prevent the birth of the god, but Poseidon having hidden Leto, the attempt failed, and Python returned to her lair on Parnassus. It is here that Apollo, tricked by the spring-nymph Telphusa, stumbled onto the serpent again and slew her with an arrow. Python lurked by

> a sweet flowing spring, and there with his strong bow the lord, the son of Zeus, killed the bloated, great she-dragon, a fierce monster wont to do great mischief to men upon earth. . . . Whosoever met the dragoness, the day of doom would sweep him away, until the lord Apollo, who deals death from afar, shot a strong arrow at her. Then she, rent with bitter pangs, lay drawing great gasps for breath and rolling about that place. An awful noise swelled up unspeakable as she writhed continually this way and that amid the wood: and so she left her life, breathing it forth in blood [*Homeric Hymn to Apollo* 300–4 and 356–62].

On this basis one could almost maintain that Apollo, like Macduff, is "not of woman born." Not only does he emancipate himself from the gentle bonds of the Good Mother, as represented by Leto, Themis, and Earth herself, and by the "golden cords" of the swaddling garment, but he also escapes and ultimately conquers the vindictive hatred of the Bad Mother, represented by his stepmother Hera and her reptilian hatchetwoman, Python. Apollo, like Zeus, initiates his career by mastering the oral-narcissistic dilemma.

Just as in the case of Zeus, however, a closer examination of the material spoils the pretty picture. One finds, first of all, that this radiant Phoebus, this arch-opponent of matriarchy, this lofty god who attempts to minimize the role of the woman in procreation [Aeschylus: *The Eumenides* 658ff.]

and who encourages matricide [Aeschylus: *The Choephori* 270ff.], showed some reluctance to leave his mother's womb: "Leto was racked nine days and nine nights with pangs beyond wont" [*Homeric Hymn to Apollo* 91–92]. Furthermore, the misogynist youth is born surrounded by women, for with Leto in her labor were "all the chiefest of the goddesses, Dione and Rhea and Ichnaea and Themis and loud-moaning Amphitrite and the other deathless goddesses save white-armed Hera" [*Ibid.*, 92–95].[2]

This intrauterine hesitation is of course attributed to envious Hera, who keeps Eilithyia, "goddess of sore travail," away from the scene; but this is simply a way of saying that the only safe place to be with a Bad Mother is inside her—that only in this way can one receive love and protection from her and satisfy her narcissistic demand that her child be a mere appendage of herself. Hera's commission to Python at the moment of Apollo's birth expresses the same thought, as does her edict that Leto would never give birth where the sun's rays penetrated. Both of these threats are circumvented by the awkward device of having Poseidon draw the waters of the sea over the island [Hyginus: *Fabulae* 140], so that Apollo is actually born under water (i.e., remains in the womb). This separation from the sun also belies his patri-

---

[2] This scene bears an interesting resemblance to the "disgruntled fairy" motif so common in European folklore, in which one fairy is not invited to the child's christening and repays the slight with a curse of some sort. The story of the "Sleeping Beauty" is the most well-known. One encounters echoes of it in the prophecies of the Moirai regarding Meleager [Hyginus: *Fabulae* 171], the first two of which are favorable, the third evil; and again in Hera's subversion of Zeus' prophecy concerning Heracles [Homer: *Iliad* xix, 95ff.].

The list of "chief" goddesses serves to remind us how much "choice" there is in mythmaking. Many figures are available for fantasy treatment, but only those who lend themselves to elaboration in terms of important cultural strains will be selected, the others falling into the background. Some choices, to be sure, are determined by the power and prominence of the worshipers (e.g., Hera, Athene), but most cannot be so explained.

archal bias and accords with his being amidst many women. Furthermore, at the moment of birth the rocky nature of Delos is suddenly forgotten by the author of the *Hymn to Apollo*, and he states that Leto "cast her arms about a palm tree and kneeled on the soft meadow while the earth laughed for joy beneath" [*Homeric Hymn to Apollo* 117–18].

We are forced to conclude that there is some tension about birth in Greek ideation, a tension also found in the myths of Hephaestus, Dionysus, and Heracles. This tension is in no way peculiar to Greek myth; on the contrary, it is found in the mythologies of all peoples, a point first made by Rank and later confirmed by modern anthropological findings [Rank, 1952; Kluckhohn, 1959, 276–77]. But it is rare to find such an elegant elaboration of the dependency-ambivalence which lies close to its root. The myth of Apollo seems to express an infinite process of doing and undoing, of affirmation and negation of the maternal bond. Our hero is premature yet his birth is delayed; his birthplace is a rock but he is born in soft earth; he is not nursed yet he is surrounded with nurses; he is born hidden from the sun yet he "leaped forth into light" at the moment of birth; he is cleansed of maternal contact yet wrapped in swaddling clothes, from which, however, he escapes, though only after being fed [*Homeric Hymn to Apollo*, 119ff.]. This process continues into his adult life, for while he vanquishes matriarchy he incorporates many of the attributes (such as prophecy) of the chthonic religion [Guthrie, 1955, pp. 199–204].[3] And although he is so loyal to the father that he imagines heredity to be transmitted only through the male [Aeschylus: *The Eumenides*, 657ff.], he and his sister are called Letoides, after their mother [Kerényi, 1960, p. 130]—not to mention his learning divination from

---

[3] This is a variant of the law that conquering nations typically absorb the cultural characteristics of the peoples they defeat, a pitfall into which crusaders throughout history have unimaginatively plunged. This process has been most carefully studied by Theodore Mills [1964, pp. 98–99].

goddesses behind his father's back [*Homeric Hymn to Hermes*, 550ff.], taking the name of another goddess, Phoebe, and using a priestess to utter his prophecies [Harrison, 1957, p. 394].

Even Apollo's rapid growth to manhood, which seems on the surface to connote rejection of the maternal attachment, has its reverse aspect. This theme of immediate maturation is a frequent one in the stories of gods and heroes in all mythologies and deserves a special word or two. As a son's fantasy it conveys the striving for liberation from dependency on the mother, but it also expresses oedipal feelings—the desire to be big and strong enough to compete with the father and satisfy the libidinal demands of the mother. But what would such a fantasy mean to a mother? Here we may draw upon the observations of Gerald Caplan concerning fantasies of pregnant women about their impending offspring. Caplan finds that the age of the child in the prospective mother's fantasy reveals her emotional orientation toward it, the best relationship being predicted for those women who daydream about the baby as a little baby—about nursing, bathing, dressing, or changing him [Caplan, 1955, p. 83]. In contrast to these women are those who daydream about the child going to college, taking specific courses, or engaging in specific occupations. "This woman, even before the baby has come, is already preparing to use the baby in furtherance of her own ambitions . . . things which she couldn't do in her life, she's going to do via the baby . . . this woman is already preparing . . . to react to the baby primarily in relation to her own needs and not in relation to . . . the baby's needs" [*Ibid.*, pp. 84–85].

McLuhan presents an interesting example of this kind of fantasy in his *Mechanical Bride*—a cod liver oil advertisement featuring a mother's "dream of *looking up* to my son . . . I see him one day as a man of stature . . . *I will help him grow in stature*, by giving him care which will add inches to his height, help him form straight, sturdy limbs, build a back *as erect as a great tree, and develop a mighty chest.* This dream I will make come true!" [McLuhan, 1951, pp. 76–77. Italics mine]. McLuhan interprets the ad as appealing to maternal dissatisfaction with the father and to the desire to create a superior son-substitute; which suggests that at least some aspects of the Greek family pattern are relevant to our own society.[4]

The theme of precipitous maturation usually appears when a maternal figure wishes for a strong protector and lacks a husband. Callirrhoë prays Zeus to make her sons full-grown in a day, that they might avenge their father's murder [Apollodorus: iii. 7. 6], and Apollo's first acts are the slaying of his mother's enemies, Python and the Giant Tityus [Apollodorus: i. 4. 1; Fontenrose, 1959, pp. 13–27]. Thus the son is to be pressed into immediate service as husband-substitute, savior, and protector.

In some myths, however, the other side of the ambivalence is expressed, and the son-savior is portrayed as immature—an infant in his mother's arms [Euripides: *Iphigenia in Tauris* 1249–1252], or at least an uninitiated youth [Apollonius Rhodius: ii. 701ff.; cf. also Fontenrose, 1959, pp. 16–21]. For the mother who wishes to make a husband of her son cannot, for the same reason, tolerate a mature male, and wishes to keep him childlike and sexless—a possession. Apollo is born to be "mother's helper," and as such the "down of manhood" can never appear on his "girlish cheeks" [Callimachus: ii. 37–38 and 103–4]. Only Leto can stroke his youthful locks, which are never to be shorn in initiation into manhood [Apollonius Rhodius: ii. 701ff.]. In keeping with the fact that boys from mother-dominant homes tend to dislike girls [Hoffman, 1961, p. 99], Apollo is notable for his homosexual

---

[4] Perhaps this particular one is important in all democratic and achievement-oriented societies [cf. McClelland, 1961, pp. 352–53; Slater and Bennis, 1964].

loves—Licht counts nineteen of them [1963, p. 193]—although his affairs with both sexes are rather unsuccessful. The male lovers are carbon copies of himself, perennially youthful and effeminate. The bulb of the flower which bloomed from the blood of his dead lover Hyacinthus, for example, was believed to be efficacious in delaying a boy's puberty [Kerényi, 1960, p. 140].

Earth and Sun Taboos

One further problem arises regarding Apollo's birth-mythology, one which promises to take us somewhat far afield. The attempt, however ambivalent and ineffectual, to separate Apollo from the Earth-Mother principle, is clearly understandable. The birth on the rocky isle is an analogue of the mistletoe, which, according to Frazer, "owes its mystic character partly to its not growing on the ground" [Frazer, 1959, p. 604]. Similarly, "a rowan that is found growing out of the top of another tree is esteemed 'exceedingly effective against witchcraft: since it does not grow on the ground witches have no power over it; if it is to have its full effect it must be cut on Ascension Day'" [Ibid., p. 605]. Rowan growing on a roof or in a rock-cleft has similar properties, and a man out in the dark should have some of this "flying-rowan" with him to avoid being "bewitched and . . . unable to stir from the spot" [Ibid.]. These plants are magic because they represent an assumed independence of maternal nurturance. They defend one against the fear of being (and the desire to be) swallowed up by the bad (poisoning, malevolent) mother, i.e., the witch. The Ascension Day requirement is an obvious device for strengthening the anti-matriarchal power of the plant, since this is the day which commemorates the departure of the Son from the Earth to join his Father in Heaven. The use of the plant to counteract the fear of being immobilized or "rooted" in the darkness shows the importance of the intrauterine fantasy in these beliefs, and the fact that the plant must be chewed betrays the necessity of counteracting one's own oral-dependent yearnings—the source of all the danger. The nectar and ambrosia fed to Apollo, and by virtue of which he bursts his swaddling garments, is of the same order, while the rocky-isle theme tends to make of Apollo himself a charm against such matriarchal powers as the witch-like Erinyes. The dolmens of megalithic times may also have been constructed on such assumptions [cf. Levy, p. 126]; Frazer notes the belief that witches being led to the stake would become invisible and escape if allowed, like Antaeus, to touch the ground [Frazer, 1959, pp. 580–81].

But what is one to make of the separation of this celestial god from the sun? Is this simply another contradiction of Apollo's patriarchal "image"? Frazer states that the prohibition against postpartum exposure of women and their offspring to the rays of the sun is found in all parts of the world [Frazer, 1959, p. 583]. At the most general level this seems to express the idea that paternal contact is destructive to the newborn. The prohibition may have some instinctual basis, since, as Briffault notes, "among carnivora the female takes great pains to conceal herself and her brood from the male, and drives him off lest he should eat the cubs" [1931, p. 18]. Again, reminiscent of Leto's wanderings: "the mammalian female is extremely particular, and even capricious, as to the choice of an abode, and is careful to select a well-concealed, dark and protected spot; she constantly changes it both before and after the birth of the young. . . . The male, who is prone to mistake the cubs for articles of food, is usually driven away" [*Ibid.*, p. 22]. Among humans such a separation serves the dual purpose of protecting the child against paternal jealousy and facilitating a withdrawal of cathexis from the father on the part of the mother, thus enabling her to concentrate her libidinal resources on the nurturance of the child. (The postpartum sex taboo is a good example of this kind of mechanism.) In the Delos myth the concentration of libido is symbolized by the multiplication of goddesses assisting at the birth.

In his discussion of sun taboos Frazer recounts an Acarnanian myth about a prince called Sunless who will die if he sees the sun. He lives in an underground palace, but each night crosses a river and visits his mistress in her castle. Eventually she, in her desire to keep him, tricks him into staying too long by cutting the throats of all the cocks in the neighborhood, and he is slain by the sun's rays on his homeward journey [Frazer, 1959, p. 584]. This is an intrauterine fantasy—the child can survive only by hiding in his mother's womb, and is destroyed by the father upon discovery. Yet the desire for growth and maturity is also dimly visible in this highly condensed myth. The child wishes to possess the mother in an adult, genital manner like the father, but she blocks this by infantilizing and castrating him (keeping him too long).

But there are other facets to the motif of sun-avoidance. Frazer argues that one "reason why divine personages may neither touch the ground nor see the sun, is . . . an apprehension that the divine being, thus drained of his ethereal virtue, might thereby be incapacitated for the future performance of . . . magical functions" [Ibid., p. 587]. Of the two, the earth taboo seems to be considerably more frequent and pronounced, a tendency which is in itself illuminating. I suggested that the magical efficacy attached to earth-free plants arises from the idea of independence from maternal nurturance. Similarly, "magical implements and remedies are believed to lose their virtue by contact with the ground" [Ibid., p. 581]. We might therefore hypothesize that a special magical power is associated with independence of parental sustenance and is lost through exposure to such support. This would explain the greater intensity of the earth taboo: since maternal nurturance is prior to and more complete than paternal nurturance, it is naturally more seductive and compelling. The intrauterine fantasy is simply the most extreme form of this attraction. At the other extreme is the avoidance of all contact with anyone for fear of arousing dependent responses, a fear which accounts for the widespread importance attached to isolated vigils as a means of preparation for exalted status, especially of a magical or religious nature. The same tendency toward generalization appears in the rule that the magical water of Andjra not only "should on no account be allowed to touch the ground," but also "should not be exposed to the sun *nor breathed upon by anybody*" [*Ibid.*, p. 582. Italics mine].

But what, one might ask, is so magical about emotional independence? Is not this emphasis on separateness simply a familiar prophylactic device for preventing magical contagion? Does some kind of *mana* actually inhere in independence, or am I simply misinterpreting, in an over-psychologized manner, methods of controlling the distribution of this force? Frazer merely states that "apparently holiness, magical virtue, taboo, or whatever we may call that mysterious quality which is supposed to pervade sacred or tabooed persons, is conceived by the primitive as a physical substance or fluid which can be drained away by contact with the earth" [*Ibid.*, p. 581]. Here the nature and origin of the "mysterious quality" are not specified, an omission which is characteristic of discussions of *mana* and taboo.

While this quarantine theory accounts adequately for the ideas regarding the *loss* of magical virtue, it does not explain why substances isolated from earth or sun should *obtain* magical qualities. The dependency theory seems to give a more adequate explanation for these phenomena.

Before arriving at a final conclusion, however, let us examine some of Frazer's further ideas on the subject. He states that the "two rules—not to touch the ground and not to see the sun—are observed either separately or conjointly by girls at puberty in many parts of the world" [*Ibid.*, p. 584]. These

prohibitions are invariably accompanied by a prolonged seclusion and some kind of fasting [*Ibid.*, pp. 584–86]. Such
customs seem to be designed to achieve, through a kind of
rigid ritual exaggeration, a relinquishing, on the part of the
young girl, of her childish attachments, and an acceptance
of adult status. She is separated, physically and symbolically,
from one or both parents, and from most of her other relatives and friends; and she must in addition tolerate considerable oral deprivation. Almost all students of puberty rites
have pointed to this function of relaxing the dependency ties
of childhood.

The earth and sun taboos, though crude in method, are
grounded in a psychological reality. In order for a girl to
achieve an adequate motherhood, she must to some degree
relinquish her libidinal attachments to her own mother and
father,[5] thus enabling her to fully cathect spouse and offspring. The belief that failure to uphold these prohibitions
will have a generally adverse impact on fertility is not without its grain of truth.

The appearance of the two taboos in the context of puberty customs thus seems to provide additional confirmation
of the dependency theory of *mana*. But why should a relationship between psychological independence and magical
virtue exist? Infantile dependence is, after all, what primarily
distinguishes humans from other mammals. Is this one of the
reasons why animals play such an important role in the
religious life of primitive peoples?

It was Freud who first pointed out that magical thinking
originates in the primary narcissism of the infant [Freud,
1913, 85ff.]. During this period, aided by his inability to
discriminate clearly between himself and the world around
him, the child lives in a hazy fairyland of omnipotence, with

---

[5] One must not make the error of assuming that there is a single parent-
figure of each sex in these societies. Often there are several "mothering" and
"fathering" persons. The relinquishing process, however, is the same.

his simple repertory of needs generally satisfied as they are expressed.[6] But in direct proportion to his becoming less dependent, he becomes more aware of how overwhelming his dependency actually is, and looks back nostalgically to his previous oblivion. Freud refers to the "narcissistic overestimation of subjective mental processes (such as the belief in the omnipotence of thoughts, the magical practices based upon this belief, the carefully proportioned distribution of magical powers or 'mana' among various outside persons and things), as well as . . . all those other figments of the imagination with which man, in the unrestricted narcissism of that stage of development, strove to withstand the inexorable laws of reality." He suggests that each person goes through a similar period of development and experiences a feeling of uncanniness when confronted with anything which reminds him of it [Freud, 1919, pp. 393–94]. Is it not likely that belief in the magical quality of persons and objects is also closely related to their ability to evoke in the beholder this reminiscence?

"We employ the term 'narcissism' in relation to little children, and it is to the excessive 'narcissism' of primitive man that we ascribe his belief in the omnipotence of his thoughts and his consequent attempts to influence the course of events in the outer world by magical practices" [Freud, 1917, p. 350]. In these attempts will he not seek materials which recall to him those feelings of oneness with and control over the world which characterized the period of primary narcissism? And will not those materials which seem to express, in their relationship to their environment, this narcissistic self-sufficiency be most highly valued by him as having a special magical potency and attractiveness?

We are now in a position to modify slightly my previous

6 Freud also suggests that the child, who is at this stage incapable of motor activity (it will be recalled how important the theme of forced immobility is in oral-narcissistic myths) satisfies its wishes by means of hallucinations [1913, pp. 83–84].

conclusion. It is not the lack of dependence in itself which makes the rowan magical, but the illusion of narcissistic self-sufficiency which this lack of dependence evokes: the image of a mature independence would have no such evocative power. The distinction may seem a trifle abstruse, but it helps to explain such inconsistencies as the fact that the mistletoe, while "independent" of the earth, is in a totally parasitic relation to the tree—a fact which would in this view *heighten*, rather than detract from, its magical virtue; for like the infant in the stage of primary narcissism, all its needs are being satisfied by another, without this dependence being manifest (cf. Bettelheim and Sylvester, 1960, p. 500). Indeed, in some instances, a material may become magical more because it expresses the identity of child and mother than because it symbolizes the illusory self-sufficiency. The virtue of an object lies in its capacity to liberate the vision of primary narcissism; secondary factors will determine which aspect of this ambiguous state is stressed.

This, then, is the origin and meaning of *mana*. *Mana* inheres in an object or person in direct proportion to the ability of that object or person to recapture the illusion of infantile narcissistic omnipotence.

Narcissism and Leadership

This definition has the advantage of illuminating some very obscure and puzzling facets of the relationship between leaders and followers in human groups of all sizes, from the dyad to the large modern society. Observers have often wondered at the strange divinity lavished on kings and queens by their insistent subjects. But from the point of view of the follower, the most important quality a leader must have is protective power, so that he may satisfy the follower's dependency needs. Since leaders are mortal, ways must be sought to exaggerate this power psychologically, and the most common method is to increase his "mana" in the sense used above:

in other words, to create a situation in which the leader approximates as much as possible, in his orientation to the world, the primary narcissism of the tiny infant.

Some individuals approach this orientation in their personality structure, requiring little or no "training" by their followers. Thus Freud describes the "narcissistic type" as follows: "There is no tension between ego and super-ego—indeed, starting from this type one would hardly have arrived at the notion of a super-ego; there is no preponderance of erotic needs; the main interest is focused on self-preservation; the type is independent and not easily overawed. . . . People of this type impress others as being 'personalities'; *it is on them that their fellow-men are specially likely to lean;* they readily assume the role of leader" [Freud, 1931b, p. 249. Italics mine]. The fatal charm of such persons lies in the illusion of independence they maintain—if others help them they perceive themselves not as receiving but as taking, by virtue of their cleverness at manipulating people. They do not in fact "need" specific others, since they are concerned only with their personal survival and self-aggrandizement. Nor does conscience ever make cowards of them, for they have none. This emotional obliviousness to others, this seeming independence and self-love, endows them with considerable *mana* as leaders.[7]

To be sure, there is some element of realism in the demand

---

[7] Rodrigué points out that autistic children, who are highly narcissistic, exert a similar appeal. They are often beautiful, graceful, and musically gifted (one thinks of Orpheus and the Pied Piper), and appear to be self-sufficient and inaccessible. Their charm is based upon this "blissful" indifference, which Freud suggested was also characteristic of many narcissistic women and members of the cat family [Rodrigué, 1957, pp. 178–79]. It is interesting that the treatment of autism requires the establishment of a normal dependency relationship with adults—a relationship which the autistic child dares not risk. An accurate sense of the conflict involved is perhaps best conveyed by the final scene in Henry James' *Turn of the Screw* [1930, pp. 120–34], in which the breaking down of the child's narcissistic aloofness is fatal.

for narcissism in leaders, since it helps ensure that the leader will not in turn continually seek direction from his followers. A comment by Konrad Lorenz illustrates this point: ". . . a swarm of small fish . . . never moves in a concerted way, but rather like an amoeba. If it extends one 'pseudopodium,' the fish in the latter notice that only few others follow them and soon turn back. Von Holst could make these fish behave in a beautifully concerted way *by removing the fore-brain of one fish which, thereby, became insensitive to whether the others followed it or not.* It just swam along independently and . . . became the leader" [Schaffner, 1957, pp. 104–5. Italics mine]. The experimenter has created a kind of piscine psychopath, who, experiencing no "need" for the swarm, is crowned by it.[8]

But not all individuals who find themselves in positions of leadership are characterized by a narcissistic personality, and most organized collectivities adopt customs designed to maximize this quality in their leaders. If leadership is an *achieved* status, narcissism can be assumed; but ascribed leaders, such as hereditary monarchs, must be trained from birth to adopt a lifelong attitude of primary narcissism. In the most extreme cases the king is simply kept in an infantile state by constant admiration, flattery, compulsory exhibitionism, and by refusing to permit him to satisfy any of his own needs without help. The phrase "your wish is my command" epitomizes the process of clothing the sovereign's utter personal dependency in the guise of omnipotence. When Freud uses the phrase "His Majesty the Baby" to describe the period of primary narcissism [1914, p. 48] he is ignoring the more interesting

[8] At the human level the relationship between leader and follower is more complicated, as Simmel observed [Wolff, 1950, pp. 181ff.]. To survive, the leader must in fact be aware of the needs of his followers, while maintaining at least the appearance of emotional independence.

The most profound portrayal of the dynamics of the leader-follower relationship is Kafka's "Josephine the Singer, or the Mouse Folk" [1961b, pp. 256–77].

aspect of the association, for it is not the sovereignty of baby-hood which should surprise us so much as the infantilism of majesty. The king who is not allowed even to dress him-self, and can gratify his personal wants only through the single permitted action of crying out to his servants, must be considered to have been placed in a condition of baby-hood.[9]

Freud viewed the elaborate measures adopted to increase in this manner the *mana* of the king as expressive of the ambiv-alence of the people toward him. He called attention to the taboos surrounding sacred kings and priests in primitive so-cieties (drawing largely on Frazer's *Taboo and the Perils of the Soul*), the most famous example of which was the West African king who "may not even quit his chair, in which he is obliged to sleep sitting, for if he lay down no wind would arise and navigation would be stopped" [Frazer, 1959, p. 146; Freud, 1913, p. 45]. He pointed out the contradictions, first, in "the same individual being both more free and more re-stricted," and second, in the fact that the ruler is attributed extraordinary magical powers over nature, yet must be care-fully protected against threatening dangers [Freud, *loc. cit.*, p. 48]. These contradictions are rooted in the combination of veneration and hate felt by subjects toward the rulers they have exalted, inasmuch as the taboo not only distinguishes the king and "exalts him above all common mortals," but also makes his life "a torment and an intolerable burden and re-duces him to a bondage far worse than that of his subjects" [*Ibid.*, p. 50].

Certainly this ambivalence is an extremely important factor affecting royal and priestly custom and ritual, but the primary motivation is to increase the king's *mana* by placing him in the role of the omnipotent baby. It is, after all, only a short step

[9] American baseball, always a rich source of pristine magic, also exhibits this pattern. Encouragement of the pitcher typically includes such phrases as "You're the babe!"

from saying, "he scarcely has to lift a finger to satisfy his every whim" to saying, "he scarcely has to lift a finger to affect the forces of nature." The unconscious thought, could it be verbalized, would be, "I know I can depend upon this person to protect and guide me, because he is omnipotent; and I know he is omnipotent because he has the same narcissistic orientation to the world that I had in the golden era when *I* was omnipotent."

The nature of the taboos makes this quite clear. Freud notes that "restrictions upon freedom of movement and upon diet" play the principal role [*Ibid.*, pp. 45–46]. These are issues which are primarily relevant to the earliest months of life for the helpless infant, or even to intrauterine life, in which he is almost completely immobilized, and truly "undifferentiated" from his environment, with all his needs "magically" satisfied. The immobility theme refers also to the incapacity of the tiny infant for locomotion.

The contradiction Freud points out between excess of freedom and excess of restriction echoes the paradoxical nature of infancy: the child's needs are satisfied but he is unable to satisfy them himself—he *may* do anything, but he *can* do nothing. The second contradiction—the necessity of guarding and protecting this "omnipotent" being—is also based on an infantile model and betrays the literalness of magical thinking. In order to recapture the sense of omnipotence one must also reconstruct the utter helplessness which is inseparable from it.

This interpretation accounts for the contrast between the degree of petty narcissism tolerated by an individual in his own interpersonal life, and what he not only tolerates but insists upon in relationships between nations. Public diplomatic exchanges between the major powers today are on a level of childlike petulance which would be ludicrous as interactions between adult persons, but are nonetheless accepted and discussed with complete seriousness by perfectly intelligent individuals. Of the same order is Flacelière's observation that while there are in Homer many relationships of enduring affection among mortals, the loves of the gods are shallow and impermanent, and that *"au lieu de cet 'accord de tous les sentiments entre mari et femme' dont Ulysse parle à Nausicaa, ce ne sont, dans ce ménage du roi et de la reine des dieux, que disputes, chamailleries, brouilles et même voies de fait!"* [Flacelière, 1960, pp. 20–21]. The Greeks demanded of their gods the same degree of narcissistic self-indulgence that men of all ages have demanded of their states [cf. also Jacobson, 1959, pp. 148–53].

" 'Twixt Heaven and Earth"

The narcissistic training of leaders seeks to increase their *mana* by attempting to imitate the desired condition of infantile omnipotence. The sun and earth taboos, to which we now return, seek to recapture this state of primary narcissism through symbolic representation. Just as this state antedates an awareness of both separation from and dependence upon the parent for nurturance, so primitive peoples endeavor to preserve intact the illusion of their rulers' narcissistic independence by preventing contact with either earth-mother or sun-father.

Such insulation also implies a denial of procreation—the covered and suspended monarch need not feel he owes his existence to beings with whom he has no contact. This is perhaps the basis of the association, appearing in several examples cited by Frazer, between immortality and the insulation from sun and earth. Thus the "wizened remains of the deathless Sibyl are said to have been preserved in a jar or urn which hung in a temple of Apollo at Cumae" [Frazer, 1959, p. 588]. Later aspirants for immortality received a similar fate, being enclosed, alive but shrunken, in bottles, jars, pillars, or baskets, and suspended inside churches, thus insulated from both sun and earth. For he who has not been born can never die.

Normally the dead are returned to one "parent" or another, usually the Mother Earth. Cremation is a more sophisticated conception, involving a division of the spoils between parents, an idea which is made quite explicit in the myth of Heracles' apotheosis. If one wishes never to die, one must therefore be insulated against the seductive appeal of parental protection, since it is by virtue of this appeal that one abandons the state of primary narcissism—that one comes into the world (psychologically speaking) and, consequently, goes out of it. In other words, human dependency is associated, quite rightly, with change and modifiability, and its absence with permanence and fixedness. The association captures the distinction between instinct and learning, translated by Freud, in his beautiful analogy of the Pompeian ruins, into that between the immutability of unconscious and the mutability of conscious ideas.

The king who is poised, then, like Frazer's golden bough,[10] between heaven and earth, possesses a maximum of *mana*, inasmuch as he is seen as in a condition of narcissistic independence. He is beyond the influence of humans: immortal, immutable, omnipotent. The sun-and-earth-avoidance themes surrounding the birth of Apollo (who we have, appropriately, left dangling like the king during this discussion) are simply another example of such insulation, probably arising from his role as a protector against malignant chthonic influence.

The Maternal Monster

It will be recalled that when Zeus was menaced by the maternal serpent he copulated with it. Apollo's bloody massacre

[10] Or like the infant Zeus, when hidden from Cronus by Hera and Amalthaea [Hyginus: *Fabulae* 139]. One is reminded of an identical suspension in the popular lullaby, "Rock-a-bye baby, on the tree-top," in which the period of primary narcissism comes to an abrupt end. That the mother should gloat over this rude awakening in the process of singing the child to sleep need not surprise us. Hostile lullabies are universal, reflecting the ambivalent nature of the request to sleep ("be rested and comforted" versus "be immobile, be dead").

of Python seems, in comparison, a rather compulsive and inelegant psychological resolution. It is by far the most common one in mythology, however, from Marduk to the Blackfoot Kut-o-yis [cf. Campbell, 1956, pp. 338–40; Fontenrose, 1959]. It expresses the unconscious feeling that the oral impulses represented by the monster are so powerful that they cannot be controlled and must be totally uprooted and destroyed. The rape of Rhea by Zeus is thus a highly sophisticated conception.

Python is very old, born from the mud of the flood—an indication both of her primitive, excrescent nature and her parthenogenetic origin [cf. Typhaon]. The oral context is announced by the description of the dragon as "fat" or "well-fed," and by the "beautifully flowing spring" which seduces the unwary into the neighborhood where the monster lurks. Apollo kills her with an arrow, and after she expires (with much commotion), he also punishes the spring-nymph, Telphusa, which seems a little excessive. Far from being "Apollonian," Apollo resembles the Puritan or anti-Communist in his anxious rooting out of maternal symbols.

Henry Alden Bunker argues, however, that the killing of mothers, mother figures, or maternal monsters in myths is simply a disguised form of incestuous intercourse, and that these myths are therefore nothing more than variants of the Oedipus myth [Bunker, 1944, 198ff.]. Since Apollo's destruction of Python would seem to fall under this jurisdiction, some appraisal of Bunker's position is in order.

Bunker, like Fromm, operates from a doctrinaire position which asserts that the myth is altogether different from what it seems to be, and requires us to disregard its most central aspect. But whereas Fromm demands that we pay no attention to the incest in *Oedipus Rex* [Fromm, 1951, pp. 201–2], Bunker demands that we ignore the lethal element in "mother-murder." But there are many perfectly straightforward oedipal myths which do not have this hostile admixture, and even if one accepts the necessity of disguise, we are still obligated to explain why it should take this particular form.

At the same time we need not ignore what Bunker can add to our understanding of the myth. Can we find, in the slaying of Python, sexual elements comparable to those Bunker detects in the myths of Bellerophon, Beowulf, and Bata? Certainly lacking are the elements of self-castration and paternal prohibition which form the principal basis for Bunker's equation of Orestes and Oedipus; and while one might argue that arrow-wounding has always had copulatory overtones, from Eros to Santa Teresa, it is difficult to see why an archer-god should be expected to consummate his deadly deed in any other manner. On the other hand, it must be admitted that the death throes of Python (see above) are even more suggestive of orgasm than the example given by Bunker [1944, p. 203]. We are thus left in a position where it is difficult either to accept or to ignore the relevance to the Python legend of Bunker's interpretation, and rather than simply let the matter drop we might briefly consider the possible implications of a sexualized "mother-murder."

In Chapter I it was pointed out that the mother's implicit sexual demands upon the child threatened him as much as did her hostile resentment. The "appropriate" fantasy response to such a double threat is an act of sexual violence, a sadistic oedipal rape.[11] On the one hand, it takes revenge upon the mother for her hostility and her impossible demands, and on the other it fulfills, with grim irony, the sexual needs she has displaced from husband to child. In addition, it salves the narcissistic wound created by the child's actual inability to satisfy these needs, his sense of weakness and inadequacy, his feeling of worthlessness when faced with his mother's moments of frustrated contempt and bitter resentment toward men. Kenneth Elton's seduction of little girls is a translation of

[11] Compare the primordial rape suggested by Zilboorg in opposition to Freud's primal-horde theory [Zilboorg, 1944, p. 282]. He finds in it the origin of the establishment of patriarchy throughout the world, and the basis of much mythology, but this is simply an unanalyzed root myth, like its Freudian predecessor.

this fantasy into reality.[12] From the helpless, confused, impotent, and scorned child he becomes the aggressive, potent, bullying ravisher.

Thus one should not be particularly surprised to find a sexual element in the slaughter of the maternal monster. In the case of Zeus and Rhea this sexual element predominates, with the hostile aspect muted. In the case of Apollo and Python it is the other way around, with sexuality playing at best a minor role.

There is one further instance in which the slaughter of maternal monsters, although not actually carried out, is at least discussed by Apollo. In *The Eumenides*, the Erinyes, roused to renewed fury by Clytemnestra's ghost, discover that Orestes has escaped them, and complain of Apollo's defiance of their ancient right. At this point Apollo enters, saying:

> Haste, tarry not! Out from the mystic shrine,
> Lest thy lot be to take into thy breast
> The winged bright dart that from my golden string
> Speeds hissing as a snake,—lest, pierced and thrilled
> With agony, thou shouldst spew forth again
> Black frothy heart's-blood, drawn from mortal men,
> Belching the gory clots sucked forth from wounds
> [Aeschylus: *The Eumenides* 180–84. Morshead trans.]

Even in this ensanguined outburst a sexual element may be observed, although it is certainly not in the least erotic. The speech fairly bristles with phallic boastfulness and sexual contempt, barely concealing the most profound dread of women. A short time earlier he refers to the Erinyes in an awestruck manner as:

> . . . these beldames old,
> Unto whose grim and wizened maidenhood
> Nor god nor man nor beast can e'er draw near
> [*Ibid.*, 68–70. Morshead trans.]

[12] In combination with other factors in his development, such as an intense rivalry with a little girl for his mother's affection.

His speech of expulsion attempts to dispel this feeling of awe by a swaggering display of virility, but his fear breaks through once more as he describes the consequences of his threatened aggression, and again as he consigns his opponents to "where there are sentences to beheading, gouging out of eyes, and cutting of throats; where *by destruction of the seed, the manhood of youth is ruined;* where men are mutilated, stoned to death, and where, *impaled beneath their spine,* they make moaning long and piteous" [Aeschylus: *The Eumenides* 185–90. Smyth trans. Italics mine]. It would be difficult to find anywhere a more complete compendium of techniques of real and symbolic emasculation compressed into so small a space.

Apollo's attacks on chthonic monsters thus incorporate the brittle narcissism of the Greek male, in constant struggle against inundation by oral-dependent longings and the dread of woman. It is this struggle, never distant in Greek fantasy, which underlies the several outbursts of vicious sadism attributed to Apollo. In commenting upon these (the flaying of Marsyas is the best example), Gertrude Levy observes that "his cruelties were always the result of wounded pride" [Levy, p. 278]. The Greeks could not envision a god so "Apollonian" that he would not fly into a tantrum at the slightest narcissistic nicking. Apollo's priggish and Draconian opposition to matriarchy in all its forms also betrays this weakness and self-doubt.

CHAPTER V

Matricide: Orestes

To mortal men peace giveth these good things:
Wealth, and the flowers of honey-throated song;
The flame that springs
On carven altars from fat sheep and kine,
Slain to the gods in heaven; and, all day long,
Games for glad youths, and flutes, and wreaths,
   and circling wine.
                [Bacchylides: ii. 7. Symonds trans.]

And as our vineyards, fallows, meads, and hedges,
Defective in their natures, grow to wildness,
Even so our houses and ourselves and children
Have lost, or do not learn for want of time,
The sciences that should become our country;
But grow like savages, as soldiers will
That nothing do but meditate on blood,
To swearing and stern looks, diffused attire
And every thing that seems unnatural.
                [Shakespeare, *Henry V*, Act V, scene 2]

Erxias, where is all this useless army gathering to go?
                [Archilochus of Paros.]

APOLLO'S CHARACTERISTICS display themselves most vividly in his support of his matricidal protégés, Orestes and Alcmaeon. It is Apollo who suggests the deed in both cases, and it is he who encourages and supports them in carrying it out, and defends them against the avenging Erinyes when it is done.

Orestes' matricide is the most fully elaborated. It has often been pointed out [cf., e.g., Bunker, 1944, p. 198; Friedman and Gassel, 1951, p. 424] that while Oedipus is the concern of only three surviving Greek tragedies, Orestes is in seven, and is treated by all three of the great dramatists. It could in fact be said that the Orestes myth was the most popular subject in Greek drama, and that the theme of matricide was one with which the Greeks were peculiarly preoccupied.

The Orestes legend has received many thorough and learned analyses, and it may seem tedious to travel the familiar ground once again. Yet aside from occasional rather frivolous interpretations by psychoanalytic writers,[1] it is usually treated as a kind of politico-religious allegory, dealing with the transition from matriarchy to patriarchy and from chthonic to Olympian religion. While this interpretation is undoubtedly correct, it does not entirely exhaust the significance of the myth. Social history may have provided much of the raw material for the Orestes legend, but it hardly accounts for its popular appeal. Athenian audiences had not experienced these ancient conflicts and transitions, but they currently lived amid sexual rancor and could each remember the emotional wrench of leaving the power sphere of the mother and moving into a male-dominated outside world. *This* transition to patriarchy was sustained by male and female alike, although in different ways.

The best illustration of this point is in *The Eumenides*, which is self-consciously directed toward dramatizing the great cultural upheaval associated with the Olympian ascendancy. What saves the trial of Orestes from the utter tedium of an historical pageant is the snarling spitefulness of the struggle between Apollo and the Erinyes—a struggle which is

[1] Perhaps the worst is by Friedman and Gassel [1951]. More interesting are those of Bunker [1944] and Melanie Klein [1963, pp. 23–54].

at once more personal and more universal. Beyond the great social and religious issues lies a simple and profound one—a battle between the sexes, filled with all the narcissistic petulance, the resentful envy, and the underlying queasy dread which always characterize such conflicts. Apollo's attempt to minimize the woman's role in procreation is breathtaking in its unreasonableness:

> Not the true parent is the woman's womb
> That bears the child; she doth but nurse the seed
> New-sown: the male is parent; she for him,
> As stranger for a stranger, hoards the germ
> Of life, unless the god its promise blight.
> [Aeschylus: *The Eumenides* 658–61.
> Morshead trans.]

This passage resembles the "Reuben and Rachel" song which school children sing—a song in which each sex tells the other how much more satisfactory the world would be in their absence. Yet Thomson quite correctly argues that this dispute over parental primacy is the crux of the entire *Oresteia* [1950, pp. 287–88]. It must be admitted, furthermore, that the victory of the male side does not seem to rest on male debating skill so much as on the frantic prejudice of the Athenians against women, which enabled them to sit through the above speech with a sober countenance.[2] Indeed, so poor is the reasoning of the "logical" sex that they are frequently forced to fall back upon religious expedients: thus Apollo's ultimate "proof" is that Athene was born from the head of Zeus without female intervention.

The immediate issue of this war between the sexes is

[2] "And when I say very few human societies have been as able to minimize the mother's role in childbearing, although the Rossel Islanders believe that the father lays an egg in the female, who is regarded as a purely passive receptacle, and the Montenegrins are reported to deny the mother any relationship to the child, this is still arresting, because it is apparent to the reader how much more difficult it is to deny the mother's parental role than the father's" [Mead, 1955, p. 35].

whether Clytemnestra's murder of Agamemnon or her own death at the hands of Orestes was the more heinous crime. A modern jury would have had difficulty in convicting Clytemnestra,[3] but the Greeks were terrified of the statuesque, passionate women they portrayed so effectively—Medea, Clytemnestra, Hecuba, Alcmene—and this fear obliged them to exaggerate and punish Clytemnestra's guilt.

A comparison between Clytemnestra and Medea is instructive, since Medea's crime is unrequited. Both women are able, long-suffering, resourceful, and purposeful, capable of great depth and intensity of feeling. The marriages of both were extremely costly—Clytemnestra losing her first husband and son (murdered by Agamemnon), Medea her father, brother, and homeland. Both are married to men who are consistently portrayed, even by the most sympathetic authors, as weak, vain, pompous, selfish, incompetent, and stupid. Both women are ultimately cruel to their children and turn on their erring husbands with savage and vindictive fury.

Why, then, is Medea spared and Clytemnestra murdered for her crimes? Clytemnestra kills only her husband and his concubine, and cannot bring herself to do away with her dangerous offspring; while Medea, with far less provocation, slaughters her brother, her children, two kings, and a princess, and attempts the life of Athens' most famous hero. Does the murder of one's husband, then, outweigh all of these crimes?

The answer is, of course, that it did. The marital bond was the weakest point in the Greek family, and the murderous hatred of a wife for her husband was felt to be the greatest potential danger and had therefore to be guarded against with the most rigid care and punished with the most compulsive severity.

Confirmation of this idea may be found in the horror with

[3] Especially in view of our intense feelings about child-murder. To the Greeks, however, the killing of a female child by her father could almost be considered venial, even without divine sanction.

which Greeks regarded the myth of the women of Lemnos, who murdered all their husbands and ruled the island by themselves. To modern readers this is an amusing fancy—one which, after all, ends happily with the pleasant sojourn of the Argonauts and subsequent repopulation of the island [Apollonius Rhodius: *Argonautica* i. 606–909]. Certainly it cannot compare in luridness with the cannibalistic and incestuous doings of Atreus and Thyestes, with the hideous deaths of Pentheus and Heracles, with the crimes and sufferings of Procne and Philomela, of Oedipus, Cronus, and a dozen others. But how the Greeks themselves felt about it may be judged from the following passage:

> But the summit and crown of all crimes is that which
>   in Lemnos befell;
> A woe and a mourning it is, a shame and a spitting
>   to tell;
> And he that in after time doth speak of his deadliest
>   thought,
> Doth say, *It is like to the deed that of old time in
> Lemnos was wrought*
>   [Aeschylus: *The Choephori* 631–34.
>   Morshead trans.]⁴

⁴ Herodotus also mentions the popularity of the expression "Lemnian deed" to refer to a heinous crime [vi. 138]. He appends to the old tale another, supposedly more modern, story of captured Athenian women raising their half-Athenian children to feel superior to the natives, and one is reminded again of the frequency with which this kind of situation must have arisen in ancient times. In the new tale it is the women and children who are murdered as a "preventive" measure, but one suspects this second incident may merely have been a bowdlerization of the original. The form in which the older story survives, meanwhile, provides motives which are suspiciously fifth century: The Lemnian women are visited with a bad smell by Aphrodite, whose worship they have neglected; their husbands, repelled, reject them and engage in extramarital raids on the mainland. In jealousy the legitimate wives kill not only their husbands but all the males on the island, fearing retaliation [Apollonius Rhodius: i. 607ff.; Apollodorus: i. 9. 17; Hyginus: *Fabulae* 15]. This cumbersome explanation probably masks what was once a simple tale of feminine heroism, as Nilsson suggests: The

Despite this fear and the blind prejudice to which it gives rise, the male contribution to the general unpleasantness is always made apparent. Agamemnon, in his narcissistic pursuits, inflicts so many injuries on Clytemnestra that she is driven to rage—a rage which spills over onto her children.[5] The usual chain is here interrupted, however, since Clytemnestra and Orestes, unlike the typical Greek mother and son, discharge the greater part of their hate directly onto the original objects.

One of the finest delineations of the Greek marital relationship is Euripides' *Iphigenia in Aulis*. It deals with the opening of the Trojan War in a manner that eloquently conveys the mood of patriotic insanity which overspreads all nations in wartime. When Menelaus asks Agamemnon if he will "not help Greece," the latter responds, in a rare moment of lucidity: "Some god has sent Greece mad and you with her" [Euripides: *op. cit.*, 412]. The drama presents a conflict between affection and ambition set in the context of a perfect

---

women were slaves captured in war, who ultimately revolted. But the later Athenians had no room in their thinking for such heroics—the mere idea caused a mortal funk. Since they could not identify with the heroines, they grafted onto the story their own gynophobic assumptions of male distaste and female jealousy, but the original plot shines through in the captured women who appear in all versions. Nilsson also suggests that the myth of the Danaides is the same story—a Judith and Holophernes tale on a mass scale. Once again: "The heroism of the [women] . . . had been forgotten in the Greek tradition. The Greek shuddered always in telling the story . . ." [Nilsson, 1932, pp. 64–67].

[5] This decathexis of the children is far from complete. The dramatists differ as to whether Clytemnestra's sorrow at the reported death of Orestes [Aeschylus: *The Choephori* 737ff.; Sophocles: *Electra* 765ff.] is as genuine as the anticipatory agony of Medea [Euripides: *Medea* 1021ff.], but there is, at least, ambivalence. And despite Electra's condemnation of her mother's utter iniquity and cruelty, Euripides has her blandly confident that Clytemnestra will come to her aid when she hears of Electra's confinement [Euripides: *Electra* 651ff.]. This assurance, which startles her fellow conspirators as well as the audience, forces her ultimately to admit her mother's love, and this is later verified by Clytemnestra's arrival and solicitude [*Ibid.*, 1102ff.]. There is perhaps no lovelier illustration of the degree to which maternal nurturance is taken for granted by resentful and accusing children.

frenzy of competing egoisms. Its theme is the progress of this contagious narcissistic mood until almost all the characters are swallowed up in it.

As the play opens, it is primarily the army as a whole and the lesser characters who are infected with the swagger-stick atmosphere. Agamemnon, despite the sardonic comments of Menelaus on his opportunism,[6] is still moved by feelings other than the desire for self-aggrandizement. He is even briefly able to reclaim Menelaus, and in a scene of rich comic irony, as the two unheroic brothers reflect upon their subservience to the rude mob surrounding them, they point stuffy self-righteous fingers at Calchas: "base, ambitious like every prophet born"; and at Odysseus: "It's his ambition, an evil and a cursed thing, piercing his very soul," and momentarily pretend to an enlightened modesty [*Ibid.*, 513–29].

But a new brand of foppery is now introduced in the form of maternal narcissism. Clytemnestra arrives in camp with Iphigenia and the infant Orestes, not without a certain amount of clucking and preening:

> Put him here, Iphigenia, at my feet,
> And stand beside me there yourself. The strangers
> Will envy me for my rich motherhood.
>   [*Ibid.*, 627–29. Stawell trans.]

Before long, however, she discovers that she has been hoaxed, and that her daughter is not to be married to Achilles, as she had been told, but sacrificed. At this point the aura of coxcombery is considerably enhanced by the entrance of Achilles, who immediately champions the cause of Clytemnestra and Iphigenia—not, to be sure, from any sensitivity to their feelings or plight, but rather from a kind of self-

6

> How suave you were, how friendly to each clown,
> Doors open to the world, so affable,
> Ready to talk with all, even when they would not!
> And so you bought your power. But power won,
> My lord was changed. He scarcely could be seen,
> His old friends friends no more [*op. cit.*, 338–45. Stawell trans.]

conscious chivalry. We find that Agamemnon has drawn on Achilles' personality as well as his own in concocting the story that Achilles was too proud to sail to Troy without having a child of Agamemnon's to wife [*Ibid.*, 100ff.]. For Achilles' main concern seems to be that Agamemnon has used his name in vain [*Ibid.*, 936–51], and he shows a continual preoccupation with issues of "face," appearances, and scandal:

> I speak not of my marriage: maids enough
> Woo me, pursue me, but Agamemnon's deed
> Is insult here. He should have asked my leave
> Before he took my name to lure the girl.
> [*Ibid.*, 959–62. Stawell trans.]

It is hard to imagine a more obtuse remark to a woman whose daughter's life is at issue. With an oafish vim reminiscent of fifth-century comic characterizations of Heracles, Achilles bustles self-importantly but ineffectually throughout the drama, until Iphigenia decides to immolate herself—a decision which he greets with obvious relief and thigh-slapping approval.

The only person motivated by anything other than vanity is Iphigenia herself. She is obviously attached to her father and greets him with a possessive affection which her mother tolerates indulgently [*Ibid.*, 631ff.]. She is concerned and sympathetic toward Agamemnon and treats the war as an irritating interruption of their loving relationship [*Ibid.*, 656–73]. Indeed, while her mother calls her proud [*Ibid.*, 995], we see no signs of it in the early part of the play. When she learns the awful truth her reaction is a simple horror at her father's rejection and her impending death.

> The sun is sweet!
> Why will you send me into the dark grave?
> I was the first to sit upon your knee,
> The first to call you father.
> [*Ibid.*, 1218ff. Stawell trans.]

And when he rejects her plea she cries to her mother:

> The daylight has died
> I have lost the light of the sun!
> [*Ibid.*, 1281–1282]

She scorns the vainglory of those around her:

> Life is sweet, is sweet!
> The dead have nothing. Those who wish to die
> Are out of reason. Life, the worst of lives,
> Is better than the proudest death
>   can be.
> [*Ibid.*, 1249ff.]

Yet ultimately she is infected by the bombast which fills the Greek camp. Her father having abandoned her, the army in arms against her, she rejects Achilles' offers of assistance and decides that a proud death is desirable after all. Through a desperate "identification with the aggressor" she eventually works herself into a chauvinistic delirium, creating an effect which would be comic but for what has gone before. She points to the soldiers ready to die for their "outraged country" and with the greedy narcissism of the dying cries:

> I, savior of Greece,
> Will win honor and my name shall be blessed.
> [*Ibid.*, 1383–1384. Walker trans.]

> Follow me now, the victor,
> Follow the taker of Troy!
> [*Ibid.*, 1474. Stawell trans.]

What is perhaps the most tragic is the lost opportunity to reverse the vicious circle of inter-sex hostility in the Greek family. Iphigenia's love for her father is one of the few instances of a benign father-daughter relationship in Greek mythology and drama. One cannot help feeling that such an Iphigenia would hold a great deal of promise as a benign wife and mother.

But Agamemnon's lust for glory and honor outbalances his fondness for his daughter, even though she is clearly the one person in his life who genuinely loves him.[7] One is not, however, surprised by this. Even the alleged anger of Artemis is itself a consequence of Agamemnon's vanity—he having boasted that he shot a deer more skillfully than could the goddess [Apollodorus: *Epitome* iii. 21; Sophocles: *Electra* 566–73]. In a speech of brutal insensitivity, unparalleled even among the Greeks, he patiently explains to his daughter that she must die in order that the soldiers' desire for adventure be not frustrated. He concludes his remarks with some ringing words of patriotism, to the effect that all is done for Greece, to "guard her freedom" and keep foreigners away [Euripides: *op. cit.*, 1258ff.]. This notion that "freedom" is best preserved by the military invasion of other countries has a strangely contemporary ring.

It is rather understandable that we next encounter Iphigenia as the bloody priestess of the Taurian Artemis, piously engaged in slaughtering passing strangers. I refer here to Euripides' rendering of that version of the myth in which Artemis substitutes a hind for Iphigenia at the moment of sacrifice and spirits her off to Tauris. The myth serves both to take some of the sting from Agamemnon's act and, more importantly, to provide an interpretation of the importation and adaptation of a barbarian religion.

But when the mythmaker wishes to clothe with flesh the clattering bones of religious intent, he draws upon the modal tensions of his society. Many might argue that the identity of Iphigenia the sacrificial victim and Iphigenia the priestess is based upon an earlier tradition of a dying and reviving goddess, à la Frazer, or bespeaks a conflict between two religions, as Graves maintains [Graves, 1955, II, pp. 78–79]. The implication is clear that a ritual or historical event which no longer

---

[7] Electra's retroactive protestations of love merely serve to justify her current hatreds.

has meaning undergoes change—is translated into a story of some sort. But what gives to the story itself sufficient meaning to preserve it intact? Must not any human story, in order to survive, contain some psychological potency? All may have forgotten the historical reason why Iphigenia the priestess is also Iphigenia the victim, but if one simply reads the myth as a human fantasy a new reason emerges immediately. I have already described the eleventh-hour identification with the aggressor displayed by Iphigenia in the Aulis drama. Here we see it carried one step further, in the form of a savage, if deflected, revenge. Sacrificed, she sacrifices; a trusting, naïve visitor, her victims are the same. And as she was killed in the service of Greek jingoism, in Tauris we find her in a position to collect this national debt [See Euripides: *Iphigenia in Tauris* 25–41 and 336–39; cf. also Herodotus: iv. 103].

Iphigenia in Tauris may be viewed, at one level, as a struggle between two alternative solutions to the cruel rejection experienced by the young girl, and the rage which this rejection engendered in her. Will she revenge herself according to the characteristic pattern of Greek women, attacking the male through his infant son? Or will she punish instead King Thoas, who stands in the relation of father to her in her new environment, and thus, though a surrogate, is nevertheless a more "direct" object of revenge than Orestes. For while the supernatural agency both in Aulis and Tauris is Artemis, it is Agamemnon in the former and Thoas in the latter who voice the human demand for blood.

In the end she deceives and betrays Thoas (just as Agamemnon had deceived and betrayed her), choosing to aid Orestes and return to Greece. Indeed, one is never given any obvious reason for expecting otherwise, since she expresses affection toward Orestes frequently, and clearly longs to return to her homeland. Had she sacrificed Orestes, it would have been "unwittingly."

But we are by now accustomed to the fictional device of

using "involuntary" to signify "unconscious," from figures
such as Oedipus and Deianeira, who subsequently behave as
if their involuntary acts had been voluntary. It is possible,
then, to view the unfolding of events, of "chance," as the
working out of this conflict within Iphigenia. Her recognition
of Orestes is at bottom an acceptance of him, a resolution of
her hostile feelings toward him. Without this implicit inner
struggle *Iphigenia in Tauris* would become a rather silly
melodrama.

As the play opens, Iphigenia has just had a dream which
she seems eager to interpret as an indication that Orestes is
dead:

> I seem'd,
> As I lay sleeping, from this land removed,
> To dwell at Argos, resting on my couch
> Mid the apartments of the virgin train.
> Sudden the firm earth shook: I fled, and stood
> Without; the battlements I saw, and all
> The rocking roof fall from its lofty height
> In ruins to the ground: of all the house,
> My father's house, one pillar, as I thought,
> Alone was left, which from its cornice waved
> A length of auburn locks, and human voice
> Assumed: the bloody office, which is mine
> To strangers here, respecting, I to death,
> Sprinkling the lustral drops, devoted it
> With many tears. My dream I thus expound:—
> Orestes, whom I hallow'd by my rites,
> Is dead: for sons are pillars of the house;
> They, whom my lustral lavers sprinkle, die.
> [Euripides: *Iphigenia in Tauris* 42–57.
> Potter trans.]

Only as sensitive a dramatist as Euripides could concoct a
dream so condensed as this to portray all the complex feelings
of an unhappy and bitter girl, betrayed by her father and
alone in a foreign land.

The first part of the dream expresses a simple wish—a yearning for home, for the uncomplicated, trustful peace of childhood, when the perfidy of men was unknown. How many Greek girls must have had such dreams! One is reminded of the wedding song of Theocritus, cited in Chapter I, and it is not difficult to imagine how much Athenian brides must have identified with Iphigenia when they dedicated their dolls to Artemis and went off to live with strangers.

But this nostalgic idyll is immediately disrupted by other thoughts and feelings—rage against Greece, rage against Agamemnon, rage against the childish vanity of military men. The dream becomes dark and violent—Argos is shattered, just as her life was shattered. This is a particularly fine piece of condensation, inasmuch as it compresses three separate thoughts into one dream element: (1) "My lovely childhood was suddenly devastated by a terrible upheaval (the war, Greece's madness, Aulis), I watched my dreams fall to pieces before my eyes"; (2) "My longing for home is undermined by my resentment of my family and my people for casting me out"; (3) "I will avenge myself by utterly annihilating my father's house, I will stand and watch with grim satisfaction as it crumbles to nothing before my eyes."

Finally, a third theme enters the dream, in the form of that cruel insight which was shared by so many Greek women: "sons are pillars of the house." She will wound Agamemnon by destroying his son, so that even his memory will be obliterated. For we must recall once again the importance of the son to the well-being of the father beyond the grave. If funeral repasts were not regularly offered by a descendant in the male line, "the dead ancestor fell to the rank of an unhappy and malevolent demon" [Fustel de Coulanges, 1956, pp. 48–49].

> For while they live, thou livest from the dead;
> Children are memory's voices, and preserve

The dead from wholly dying: as a net
Is ever by the buoyant corks upheld.
[Aeschylus: *The Choephori* 504-7.
Morshead trans.]

Glorying in her present power, Iphigenia prepares the hapless Orestes for the sacrifice, albeit (like Medea) not without some tears of regret for the infant child toward whom she had felt some fondness [Euripides: *Iphigenia in Tauris* 233-34]. Ultimately it is these affectionate feelings which prevail, but the dream itself betrays the whole familiar sequence of feminine unhappiness and oblique revenge.

Let us now return to Clytemnestra, in Aulis. What is the effect upon her of the "Greek madness"? Initially she seems a rather shallow figure, a bubbling, bustling Westchester matron, flattered by the status to be gained by Achilles' prospective match. She fails to perceive Agamemnon's agitation and brushes aside his attempt to get her to leave the "wedding" in his hands:

Now, by Hera, husband,
Do your man's work and leave the home to me.
[Euripides: *Iphigenia in Aulis* 739-40.
Stawell trans.]

But when she discovers the true state of affairs, a transformation takes place. If Iphigenia is ultimately infected by the narcissistic mania, Clytemnestra becomes a monument of opposition to it, stripping herself even of the vanity with which she entered the camp, as she begs Achilles for assistance:

O goddess-born!
You see a wretched woman at your knees!
All pride has left me. What should I care for now
Except my daughter?
[*Ibid.*, 899-902]

Her true stature is achieved, however, when she confronts the vacillating Agamemnon and pours out her hatred for him:

> By force, not of my will, didst thou wed me!
> Thou slewest Tantalus my sometime lord;
> Didst dash my living babe against the stones,
> Even from my breast with violence tearing him.
> > [*Ibid.*, 1149–1152. Way trans.]

Gone is her concern with feminine diversions as she contemplates the hideous consequences of the games of men. She points out the insanity of sacrificing his daughter for Helen and suggests Helen's own daughter Hermione as a more plausible victim. She contrasts her own fidelity with Helen's and insinuates that he is straining it to the breaking point. She then threatens him with the united hostility of his household:

> What will my heart be like, think you, at home
> When I look on my daughter's empty chair,
> And empty room, sitting there all alone. . . .
> What will your wages be when you come back?
> We who are left, we shall not want much urging
> To greet you with the welcome you deserve!
> > [*Ibid.*, 1173ff. Stawell trans.]

This speech represents the breakdown of feminine tolerance for the "secrets of men" [Bettelheim, 1955a, pp. 227ff.]. It is as if she were saying, along with all women who have been injured by war throughout the ages, "I will put up with your ceremonies, your puzzles, your contests, so long as you keep it to yourselves. I understand that you must construct situations of glory to cover up your emptiness, that you must destroy because you cannot create. But when your childish game of war strikes at the fruit of our wombs, it is not to be endured. Should our genuine and priceless creations be sacrificed to your artificial and puerile ones?" Military expeditions have always served to drive a wedge of resentment between the sexes, but the fact that it is a daughter rather than a son being sacrificed may also be important. Mothers in Greek drama often become rather carelessly chauvinistic where a

son's life is at issue [cf., e.g., Euripides: *Suppliants* 314ff.].
But sacrificing a *female* for male glory is crossing a sacred
boundary.

> If you come home,
> Will you dare kiss your girls? Or they dare come,
> That you may choose another for the knife?
> Have you once thought of this? Are you a man?
> Or nothing but a sceptre and a sword?
>   [*Ibid.*, 1191–1195. Stawell trans.]

But while Clytemnestra's point is well taken, Agamemnon
is nothing but a sceptre and a sword, and ten years must pass
before she can have her final word on this matter.

> At home there tarries like a lurking snake,
> Biding its time, a wrath unreconciled,
> A wily watcher, passionate to slake,
> In blood, resentment for a murdered child.
>   [Aeschylus: *Agamemnon* 154–55.
>   Morshead trans.]

Aeschylus' drama of the return of Agamemnon epitomizes
the Greek theme of the proud man destroyed by the angry
woman. One sees him arrive home in triumph, vaunting his
achievements with a vanity tempered only by superstitious
fears. Since Greek self-esteem was ever a house built on sand,
we are not surprised at the expression of these fears, but we
should not mistake their import. Agamemnon's pious philoso-
phizing and mock-modesty are no more than amulets to ward
off the jealousy of the gods—they represent no change of
character. A less narcissistic man would have been more cir-
cumspect in returning to his neglected kingdom after a ten-
year absence, particularly to a queen who had every reason
to hate him and was not devoid of energy and purpose. But
the infatuate general marches complacently into the trap,
ignoring the twice-offered covert warnings of the elders, and
with his captured concubine tactlessly in tow.

The cautions of the elders Agamemnon treats as an abstract issue, and after some boasting about his victory he smugly remarks:

> Few are they who have such inborn grace,
> As to look up with love, and envy not,
> When stands another on the height of weal.
> [Aeschylus: *op. cit.*, 832–33.
> Morshead trans.]

Nor does he become suspicious when Clytemnestra appears and gratuitously offers weak excuses for the absence of Orestes. Instead, his attention is altogether drawn to Clytemnestra's elaborate flatteries. These he in part accepts as his due, but affects a modest distaste for the red carpet which she has literally rolled out for his welcome:

> See too that not in fashion feminine
> Thou make a warrior's pathway delicate;
> Not unto me, as to some Eastern lord,
> Bowing thyself to earth, make homage loud.
> Strew not this purple that shall make each step
> An arrogance; such pomp beseems the gods,
> Not me. A mortal man to set his foot
> On these rich dyes? I hold such pride in fear,
> And bid thee honour me as man, not god.
> [*Ibid.*, 918–25]

Note what rich irony is generated by Agamemnon's timorous vanity. When he receives a warning he echoes the warning with a little homily, but he is not warned; now when he is flattered by Clytemnestra he rails against such flattery, yet is flattered. The crowning irony is his ultimate acceptance of the carpet after all this deprecation—like Caesar or Richard III refusing the crown. Once again he resolves his doubts magically, by reciting the very proverb whose significance he is blindly ignoring ("call none blest till peaceful death have crowned a life of weal"), and making a few more comments on the envy of the crowd. Finally he lets Clytemnestra coax him for a bit before yielding with a vengeance:

> Then, if thou wilt, let some one stoop to loose
> Swiftly these sandals, slaves beneath my foot;
> And stepping thus upon the sea's rich dye,
> I pray, *Let none among the gods look down*
> *With jealous eye on me.*
>
> [*Ibid.*, 944–47]

Whereupon, thoughtlessly committing Cassandra to his wife's tender care, he strides into the palace to his death.

That this is altogether a feminine triumph is made explicit by Aeschylus. It is Clytemnestra who comes out of the palace covered with blood and takes full responsibility for the murder. Scenes such as this, in which a vindictive woman makes a savage, gloating, exultant speech over the downfall of a man, are common in Greek drama [cf. Medea, Hecuba, Electra, Alcmene].

The method of killing seems to play upon fears of maternal entanglement:

> Even as the trammel hems the scaly shoal,
> I trapped him with inextricable toils,
> The ill abundance of a baffling robe;
> Then smote him, once, again—and at each wound
> He cried aloud, then as in death relaxed
> Each limb and sank to earth. . . .
>
> [*Ibid.*, 1381–1385]

Thus is the returning warrior enveloped, but, unlike the maternal monster-slayers, he cannot cut his way out, and is destroyed. In her ecstasy, Clytemnestra is transfigured, and becomes a kind of fertility goddess:

> Each dying breath
> Flung from his breast swift bubbling jets of gore,
> And the dark sprinklings of the rain of blood
> Fell upon me; and I was fain to feel

That dew—not sweeter is the rain of heaven
To cornland, when the green sheath teems with grain.
[*Ibid.*, 1388–1392]

Clytemnestra's lover, Aegisthus, with whom she plots the murder, is made clearly subordinate to Clytemnestra—her instrument and agent. All three dramatists portray him as weak and effeminate:

Thou womanish man [*Ibid.*, 1625].

Was then thy strength too slight to deal in murder? [*Ibid.*, 1643].

For he, the man, wears woman's heart [Aeschylus: *The Choephori* 304–5. Morshead trans.]

That abject dastard . . . who fights his battles with the help of women [Sophocles: *Electra* 300–2. Jebb trans.]

Everywhere in Argos thou wouldst hear such phrases as, "that woman's husband," never "that man's wife."
Yet 'tis shameful for the wife and not the man to rule the house [Euripides: *Electra* 930–33. Coleridge trans.]

But let me have a husband not girlish-faced like you . . . [*Ibid.*, 948–49. Vermeule trans.]

His role is analogous to that of the son used by the mother to destroy the father, and it seems reasonable to guess that the dramatists made unconscious use of this son-model in developing the character.

The stage is now set for the appearance of the actual son, Orestes. We have traced the psychological creation and development of two malignant "mothers"—Iphigenia, who was redeemed, and Clytemnestra, who flourished to destroy Agamemnon. Now let us examine the Orestean response to this maternal menace.

There are a number of peculiarities not present in our first two examples. Like Zeus and Apollo, Orestes is menaced by maternal serpent-monsters (the Erinyes). But in Orestes' case this occurs after he has killed his own mother, whose relationship with him, far from being the intense and over-involved attachment I have posited as more or less modal for Greek families, is virtually nonexistent. Furthermore, while in the case of Zeus the "good" and "bad" aspects of the mother were expressed through metamorphosis, and in the case of Apollo through the more usual fantasy device of separation into a good human and a bad monster (or step-mother or witch), for Orestes there are three maternal agents, even if one excludes the maternal role played by Iphigenia in the dramas already discussed. There is Clytemnestra herself, the unloving, father-killing mother. There are the Erinyes, the vindictive, devouring, castrating mothers. And finally, there is Electra, the protective and nurturant but also manipulating mother, who uses the child for her own ends.

The reader may feel, at this point, that I have gone wild with my equations, and that I am treating everyone in the plot who lays any claim to femininity as an aspect of the mother. This is perhaps not a problem as far as the Erinyes are concerned, since they are explicit extensions of Clytemnestra [Aeschylus: *The Eumenides* 115ff.]. But one might ask why we cannot simply treat Electra as the sister she actually is. The answer is that it is not I who insist upon this reassignment of roles; it is Electra herself:

> Alas for all my nursing of old days,
> so constant—all for nothing—which I gave you;
> my joy was in the trouble of it. For never
> were you your mother's love as much as mine.
> None was your nurse but I within that household.
>   [Sophocles: *Electra*, 1144–1148. Grene trans.][8]

[8] Orestes confirms the claim in another drama, by wishing for her when he believes his death is imminent:

"O, that a sister's hand might wrap these limbs!" [Euripides: *Iphigenia in Tauris* 627. Potter trans.]

The speech from which this quotation was drawn abounds in maternal remarks of this kind. Furthermore, it is Electra, in the Sophoclean version, who saves Orestes from death and sends him away to be reared in exile [cf. also Apollodorus: *Epitome* vi. 24].

It must be admitted that there is very little in either *The Choephori* or in Euripides' *Electra* to confirm this position (or to contradict it, for that matter), save perhaps for the fact that it is always Electra who pushes Orestes to do the deed and Orestes who hesitates and seeks advice and support. But in Euripides' *Orestes*, we once again encounter the maternal sister, nursing Orestes in his madness [*op. cit.*, 216ff.]. Perhaps it will suffice to say simply that if anyone represents the Good Mother in the Orestes saga, it is Electra.[9]

Certainly one can find in this myth most of the aspects of the mother-son syndrome described in Part One, from the strained marital relationship to the son's misogyny and madness (to which we will shortly turn). But why do these elements appear in so disconnected a fashion? Why is it Electra, for example, who uses Orestes as the tool of her revenge rather than Clytemnestra? If Clytemnestra can murder Agamemnon, why cannot Electra murder Clytemnestra?

To ask such a question is to ask too much of this mode of interpretation. We must not assume that the entire structure of the myth can be accounted for by some psychological process. The Orestes cycle has unique historical, cultural, and religious origins. We cannot say that each myth emerges full-blown from the family constellation—if we did, we would be hard put to account for the vast differences between them. Rather, I am attempting to show that elements of this constellation have crept into each myth—that each has been colored and molded by it.

I can best illustrate this process by considering the skeleton

9 In *The Choephori*, the old nurse also seems to play this role [*op. cit.*, 747ff.].

form of the myth and observing the subsequent elaboration of detail. The Orestes cycle, as presented by the Attic dramatists, is fundamentally concerned with the slaying of a mother by her son in revenge for the killing of his father. But this stark theme has a peculiarly Greek development and coda. One may ask, for example, why it is necessary to introduce Electra into the story, and why she comes ultimately to dominate it.

The earliest versions of the myth seem to concern little more than a battle over succession to the Argive throne, with women playing a secondary role. Electra is not even mentioned in the Homeric version, and it is Aegisthus rather than Clytemnestra who initiates the murder of Agamemnon. Orestes is not the infant son and matricide of later versions, but simply the exiled pretender, an early Bonnie Prince Charlie, who comes unaided to claim his throne. It is, as Gomme points out, "a very masculine tragedy" [Gomme, 1937, p. 93; cf. also Thomson, 1950, 247–48]. Homer is rather coy about the matricide, never saying that Orestes slew Clytemnestra, but nonetheless producing her corpse as soon as he has killed Aegisthus [Homer: *Odyssey* iii. 303ff., iv. 524ff. and xi. 405ff.].

But this simple tale of war and politics (Aegisthus was Agamemnon's cousin, a pretender to the throne disputed by their rabid fathers, Atreus and Thyestes) was later transformed into one in which the matricidal revenge was the central theme. Paradoxically (but not really surprisingly), it was the gynophobic Athenians who filled the story with women and made it a tale of family conflict. A people reared in such a culture would obviously be more impressed by the idea of a woman plotting against her husband than by anything else in the story. It would tap their fear of women and lead them to occupy themselves with the process of filial revenge. But given this fundamental concern, why was Electra introduced?

It is difficult to escape the conclusion that the Athenians

could not conceive of the possibility that a man could get the better of a woman without the assistance of another woman. Somehow the man must only be an instrument: the motive force must come from a woman. Furthermore, once having given Orestes a feminine "mover," it was inevitable that their relationship should begin to incorporate mother-son characteristics. One of these is the fear of envelopment and fusion, which is expressed particularly in Euripides' *Orestes*. When Orestes cries out that the Erinyes are pursuing him, Electra says, "I will not let thee go; but with arms twined round thee will prevent thy piteous tossing to and fro"; but Orestes is little comforted by this protection and screams: *"Let me go!* I know *you.* You're one of my Furies too! You're holding me down to hurl me into hell!" [Euripides: *op. cit.*, 262–65]. Later, on a less violent note, Electra longs aloud for a womb-like fusion with Orestes, in a kind of inverted reference to their common father and mother: "Oh might the self-same sword, if this may be, slay us, one coffin cedar-wrought receive!" To which Orestes rather unpoetically responds, with an uneasy fit of realism: "That would be an end most sweet; but surely thou seest we are too destitute of friends to be allowed to share one tomb" [*Ibid.*, 1051–1056].

It is interesting that Orestes identifies Electra with his mother's Erinyes at the moment when she offers encircling comfort and protection.[10] Such an association is inappropriate as regards Clytemnestra, who rejected and abandoned him, but Euripides is more interested in portraying the psychological and interpersonal realities of his time than in clinging to the unique probabilities of the myth. The fear of feminine envelopment is also manifested in other ways, such as the pre-

[10] One could argue that the identification takes place earlier, in line 255, when he speaks to his mother, Electra being the only real person in the room. It is significant that Orestes' attack occurs when he is telling Electra not to be like Clytemnestra [lines 251–52]. The very thought is enough to unhinge him—to start him talking to his dead mother and accusing Electra of being an Erinys—for it threatens his entire defensive structure.

occupation in the Orestan plays with the net, or sleeveless robe, used by Clytemnestra to swaddle Agamemnon; the contempt for women expressed by Orestes and Pylades; and the peculiar ambivalence which permits both Electra and Clytemnestra to be called masculine, the former as a compliment, the latter as a criticism [Euripides: *Orestes* 1204–1205; Aeschylus: *Agamemnon* 10–11 and *The Choephori* 630].

The most striking expressions of the oral-narcissistic conflict appear in Aeschylus' *The Choephori*, which is filled with references to devouring and encircling serpents and other oral themes. Orestes calls Agamemnon "our eagle-sire, whom to his death a fearful serpent brought, enwinding him in coils" [*op. cit.*, 246–49]. Later, in a long speech [*Ibid.*, 980–1006], he refers repeatedly to the "mesh which trapped his hands, enwound his feet!" and says of his mother:

> what venomed thing,
> Sea-snake or adder, had more power than she
> To poison with a touch the flesh unscarred?
> [*Ibid.*, 994–96. Morshead trans.]

Finally, when pursued by the Erinyes, he garnishes them with serpent forms [*Ibid.*, 1048ff.].

This maternal serpent is matched by the infant serpent of insatiable hunger, which appears in Clytemnestra's dream:

LEADER:　. . . her womb a serpent bare.
ORESTES:　What then the sum and issue of the tale?
LEADER:　Even as a swaddled child, she lull'd the thing.
ORESTES:　What suckling craved the creature, born full-fanged?
LEADER:　Yet in her dreams she proffered it the breast.
ORESTES:　How? did the hateful thing not bite her teat?
LEADER:　Yea, and sucked forth a blood-gout in the milk.
> [*Ibid.*, 527–33. Morshead trans.]

Orestes interprets the dream as referring to himself, an insight which comes to Clytemnestra only when he is about to kill her [*Ibid.*, 928]:

See, I divine it, and it coheres all in one piece. If this snake
came out of the same place whence I came, if she wrapped it
in robes, as she wrapped me, and if its jaws gaped wide
around the breast that suckled me, and if it stained the intimate milk with an outburst of blood, so that for fright and
pain she cried aloud, it follows then, that as she nursed this
hideous thing of prophecy, she must be cruelly murdered.

[*Ibid.*, 542–50. Lattimore trans.]

Thus, just as she fed, bathed, and swaddled her victim,
Agamemnon, so she fed, bathed, and swaddled her murderer,
Orestes. But at a more elementary level, this circularity expresses the emotional cycle inherent in the mother-child relationship: as she sows, so shall she reap, as she rejects, so shall
she be rejected, as she poisons, so shall she be poisoned. The
vicious oral sadism of the dream-Orestes reflects the maternal
deprivation he has experienced.

But it is not only Orestes who displays this insatiable and
vindictive hunger: it is a motif which dominates the entire
drama. As it opens, one finds that even the earth, and the dead
it contains (particularly Agamemnon), cries out for nourish-
ment. It is rather fitting that the play derives its name from
the libation-bearers, who seek thus to "soothe the ire of dead
men angered" [*Ibid.*, 13–15]. The earth must be appeased
in order that it shall not slake its thirst with the blood of the
living. As Electra pours Clytemnestra's libations on the
ground she says, "Lo! the earth drinks them, to my sire they
pass" [*Ibid.*, 164].

Similarly, all appeals made in the play are oral ones. When
Apollo wishes to impress upon Orestes the necessity for carrying out the matricide, he tells him that if he fails he will
receive no libations after he is dead—"no lustral bowl . . . no
spilth of wine" [*Ibid.*, 291ff.]. When Orestes seeks the aid
of his father's ghost he threatens him in a similar manner, saying that so long as he brings success to his children:

> So shall the rightful feasts that mortals pay
> Be set for thee; else, not for thee shall rise
> The scented reek of altars fed with flesh
> [*Ibid.*, 483–85. Morshead trans.]

Later, Clytemnestra makes her final plea for mercy by baring her breasts[11] to her son and crying:

> Stay, child, and fear to strike. O son, this breast
> Pillowed thine head full oft, while, drowsed with sleep,
> Thy toothless mouth drew mother's milk from me.
> [*Ibid.*, 896–98]

But Orestes reminds Clytemnestra that far from having been the nurturant mother she portrays, she had cast him out in his infancy [*Ibid.*, 900ff. and 913]. A child so starved of maternal affection is not inclined to be generous or forgiving: "Her children's soul is wolfish, born from hers, and softens not by prayers" [*Ibid.*, 420–22]. Euripides also captures this hunger in his *Orestes*. When Menelaus pleads with the hero for Hermione's life, Orestes can only respond repeatedly with, "What about me?" [*Orestes* 1613–1616].

Finally, the drama ends with a reminder that the entire saga was set off by an act of cannibalism, when Atreus, Agamemnon's father, served his brother Thyestes a stew composed of the latter's children [*Ibid.*, 1068ff.].

The Orestes myth, then, in its fifth-century form, has become a story of sex antagonism and mother-son conflict. This conflict is "solved" by the killing of Clytemnestra. And yet the story continues—the solution is ineffective, the feelings remain. When Menelaus asks him if the matricide did not slake his thirst for blood, Orestes replies: "I can never have my fill of killing whores" [Euripides: *Orestes* 1590], a sentiment frequently expressed by sex-killers, and one which reveals again

---

[11] This is the only tinge of maternal seductiveness in the drama. It appears also in Euripides [*Electra* 1206ff.], and is reminiscent of Helen's use of the same device to coax Menelaus from slaying her [Aristophanes: *Lysistrata* 155].

the importance of maternal seductiveness in generating pathology.

To understand this quenchlessness one must recognize the peculiar significance of the matricide. For while Bunker lumps together explicit matricide and any slaying of a she-monster, the two motifs are distinguishable in certain respects. The she-monster represents only the Bad Mother, or the oral-narcissistic conflict itself, and once it is dispatched the hero marries and lives happily ever after. The matricide, on the other hand, is trying to destroy the total mother—to extinguish all her passions simultaneously. He attempts to deal with his ambivalence toward her by abolishing the relationship altogether. This solution fails to provide a means of satisfying the positive, or at least dependent, feelings the hero has toward his mother. Hence, the matricide, unlike the monster-slayer, is afterwards troubled with longing and guilt. In Orestes' case these feelings are betrayed by his chronic dependence on feminine assistance (despite the misogynistic attitudes which he and Pylades affect), and by the Erinyes' persecution.

There are three extant plays which deal in a major way with Orestes' life after the matricide. In *Iphigenia in Tauris*, as I have mentioned, he is saved from death and enabled to accomplish his mission (i.e., stealing the statue of Artemis) by Iphigenia. In *Orestes*, he is protected and nursed by Electra, and it is her bold stratagem which rescues him from death at the hands of the Argives and forces Apollo's intervention, after Orestes and Pylades have exhausted their resources and are preparing themselves to die [Euripides: *Orestes* 1177ff.].[12] In *The Eumenides*, it is Athene who saves him from the Erinyes by casting her deciding vote in the trial and by paci-

---

[12] In characteristic Greek fashion, when Electra has offered this solution to the two hapless males, she is rewarded by being told she has the mind of a man [Euripides: *Orestes* 1204]. Socrates compliments the unfortunate wife of Ischomachus in the same way for one of her dutiful answers to her husband [Xenophon: *Oeconomicus* x. 1].

fying them when they threaten revenge. Apollo, his sponsor, instigator, and much-touted protector, is in fact unable to rescue his protégé.[13]

In other words, the mother-rejecting solution blindly ignores the intense, frustrated craving for maternal love and protection. An unrecognized force is all the more potent, and the repressed yearnings make themselves felt in Orestes' psychosis, as well as in his continued dependence on female figures. How to placate the maternal rage and bring back maternal love is the theme of the psychosis, while how to find nurturant substitutes is the theme of his overt interpersonal responses.

Unfortunately, there is no simple solution to ambivalence. A craving so intense leads, as we have seen, to fears of being utterly swallowed, and cannot, therefore, be permitted free expression. Thus far from selecting motherly figures to satisfy his dependent longings, Orestes chooses three notorious virgins: Electra, Iphigenia (priestess of Artemis), and Athene herself. We have seen that virgins are unconsciously experienced by men as less feminine, more neuter, and therefore less threatening to masculine narcissism than are sexually mature women. In *The Eumenides*, Apollo even goes so far as to say that Agamemnon would not have been dishonored had he been killed by an Amazon in battle, since the slayer would have been less feminine [*op. cit.*, 625ff.]. A "real woman" required of a man a more secure masculinity than Greeks of the classical period felt able to muster.

But there is still another twist to the Orestean nightmare. Nurturant virgins may be found, but can they make him proof against the fears which this very nurturance arouses? Iphigenia threatens his life, and Electra seems to turn into

[13] This is a consistent feature of Greek myth: males are supposedly more bold and clever, but are seldom able to manage without feminine help; male gods are more trusted and more often invoked, but seldom seem to be around when needed, or, if present, as in *The Eumenides*, able only to mitigate but not remove the threat.

Clytemnestra. And does not Athene herself wear the snake-festooned Medusa head upon her aegis? And what of the Erinyes themselves, the "Gorgon shapes" with snaky hair? Are they not also virgins?

Thus this avenue of escape is only an apparent one. Since the hungry serpent is inside, it seems to be everywhere. The maternally deprived child feels so impoverished that he cannot give, and because he cannot give, even the most simple and legitimate emotional demand placed upon him by another person will make him feel as if he were in danger of being gobbled up. Because his own needs are so insatiable he pictures everyone else as equally voracious. Orestes' fantasy of the less womanly but helpful virgin simply conjures up the image of a greedy, affection-starved "serpent" like himself. The following speech by the loveless Erinyes conveys this image of the devouring female, and divulges the Greek male's fear of being swallowed up through sexual intercourse:

> Yea, from thy living limbs I suck it out,
>   Red, clotted, gout by gout,—
> A draught abhorred of men and gods; but I
>   Will drain it, suck thee dry;
> Yea, I will waste thee living, nerve and vein.
>   [Aeschylus: *The Eumenides* 264–67.
>   Morshead trans.]

Or, to make it even clearer that the issue is one of emotional hunger:

> Not as a victim slain upon the shrine,
> But living shalt thou see thy flesh my food.
>   [*Ibid.*, 305–6]

In other words, the worst punishment a Greek male could conceive was being set upon by his exact counterpart in the opposite sex, a love-starved but man-hating female. But the Erinyes are "unconflicted" over the oral-narcissistic dilemma —they show no need to withdraw and keep separate, but satisfy both their demand for love and their resentful hatred by feeding upon others. Now this, it will by now be obvious to the reader, is precisely the kind of double-barreled pressure that unhappy Greek mothers placed upon their sons. No matter where the fancy turns to elude the conflict, it reappears, since it is internal. Its victim is like the fox ceaselessly trying to outdistance the dog's bell tied to his tail, in Pergaud's "Tragedy of Goupil."

Although the oral-narcissistic conflict itself cannot be solved, the particular set of fears represented by the Erinyes fantasy can be appeased by a counter-fantasy—the one encountered in Chapter II. If the male child feels set upon and threatened by omnivorous feminine sexual cravings, he is beforehand, and incapacitates himself, removing himself from the arena. Should he feel hated and pursued by virtue of his manhood, he unmans himself. This is the last, disastrous attempt at solution of the conflict; and it is in this sense that we should interpret the story that Orestes, during one of his mad intervals, bit off a finger to placate the Erinyes, which turned them white and restored his sanity [Pausanias: viii. 34. 1–3].[14]

The reason for the success of this stratagem becomes evident when one notes the intolerance of masculine narcissism manifested by the Erinyes themselves:

> And the proud thoughts of men, that flaunt themselves full high under the heavens, they waste away and dwindle in dishonour 'neath the earth at our sable-stoled assault and the vengeful rhythm of our feet.
> [Aeschylus: *The Eumenides* 368–71. Smyth trans.]

[14] No psychoanalytic symbolic substitutions are required to indicate that this "finger" was phallic, for the story is told to explain a conical stone marker on a tomb-mound. Now, there is no particular reason for a finger to appear on a tomb, but fertility symbols are common tomb ornaments, for the usual reason. As Jane Harrison puts it, "The chamber of death was crowned by the primitive symbol of life." Furthermore, the "Finger's Tomb," on which the story is based, is simply a Dactyl monument, and hence partakes of the Dactyls' phallic nature [Harrison, 1962, pp. 401–3].

This theme of the castrating female is also prominent in the descriptions of Clytemnestra's slaying of Agamemnon, and in the chorus' diatribe in *The Choephori* against the wickedness of womankind, Clytemnestra and the Lemnian women are compared with Scylla and Althaea: Scylla who cut off her father's immortal lock, and Althaea who burned the brand in which rested the life of her son [Aeschylus: *The Choephori* 602ff.].

But Orestes' conflict is never really solved. After years of madness (and the implementation of the various clumsy devices I have discussed) he finally achieves a modicum of peace and a relatively normal and successful life, but he dies in a fashion which reflects the persistence of the problem—not, as he had feared, by strangling in Athens [Aeschylus: *The Eumenides* 746], but by a snakebite in Arcadia [Apollodorus: *Epitome* vi. 28]—a serpent, serpent-slain.

The Greeks, nevertheless, were proud of Orestes. Indeed, if dramatic preoccupation be an index, he was their greatest hero. This pride shows most clearly when he is contrasted with a foreigner, as in the *Orestes*, when he is given a comic dialogue with a Phrygian eunuch [Euripides: *Orestes* 1506ff.]; or in *Iphigenia in Tauris*, when Iphigenia tells Thoas of Orestes' matricide, and Thoas exclaims: "O Phoebus! This hath no barbarian dared" [*op. cit.*, 1174]. The nature of his achievement is made clear in his speech to the Argives in *Orestes*:

> Pelasgians in ancient times, and later Danai, I helped you no less my father when I slew my mother; for if the murder of men by women is to be sanctioned, then the sooner you die, the better for you; otherwise you must needs become the slaves of women [*Orestes*, 932–37. Coleridge trans.].

Yet on the whole, Orestes is not a heroic figure in the Heraclean sense. He does not slay monsters or rescue maidens or liberate cities. His principal accomplishments are in the emotional and psychological arena, and even here success is not complete. Perhaps the primary reason that the Greeks held him in such affection and esteem was that the solution he adopted—total rejection of the mother and devotion to the father—was most peculiarly their own. None of the modes of response we are examining (with the possible exception of Apollo's, with which it is closely allied) will be quite so close to the classical Greek norm as this one; and there is no character in Greek mythology who seems to epitomize the fifth-century Athenian as fully as does the hero of Euripides' *Orestes*. Whatever kind of run-of-the-mill swashbuckler he may have been in earlier days, the dramatists molded Orestes in their own image, and with his tribulations the Athenians must have experienced an emotional empathy unmatched even in so powerful a repertory.

CHAPTER VI

Self-Emasculation: Hephaestus

JONATHAN: Ma-Ma-Mother says everyone must have a vo-
cation in life. . . .

ROSALIE: I don't think I've ever met anyone before who's
fed . . . uh . . . Venus'-flytraps.

JONATHAN: Ma-Ma-Mother says I'm va-very good at it.

MADAME ROSEPETTLE: . . . He tried to make me jealous but
there was nothing to be jealous of. His love was sterile!
He was a child. He was weak. He was impotent. He was
mine!

[Kopit, *Oh Dad, Poor Dad, Mama's Hung You in the Closet
and I'm Feelin' So Sad*, pp. 32, 71]

WHEN I TALK of Hephaestus' response as self-emasculation
I mean it neither in the sense of actual castration (as in the
case of Attis), nor in the sense of symbolic castration (as in
Orestes' case). While a psychoanalyst might interpret Hephaestus' lameness as symbolic castration, it would seem of less
significance than what might be called his "interpersonal" self-
castration. By this I mean his withdrawal from the lists of sexual
and marital rivalry, his role of clown—in a sense, his resignation
from manhood. Hephaestus conveys the interpersonal message:
"You have nothing to fear from me, nor is there anything
about me which should arouse your envy or resentment. I
am merely a poor lame clown, ready to serve you, and make
you laugh with jokes at my own expense." Thus, at the close

of the first book of the *Iliad*, we see him trying to keep peace between his parents, and pouring wine for the Olympians, while "Laughter unquenchable arose amid the blessed gods to see Hephaistos bustling through the palace" [Homer: *Iliad* i. 599–600]. In the vast drama of Greek mythology Hephaestus plays a relatively minor role: except for the conflicting stories of his birth, and for his frequent appearances as helpful servant and craftsman for gods and heroes, we see Hephaestus only as the victim of two falls from heaven and the butt of two bedroom farces.

Although I have included Hephaestus in a series describing mythical responses to the threatening mother, the role of clown seems more relevant to the father-son relationship—a method for gaining the affection of the forbidding father who brooks no rivalry.

When a little girl performs for the benefit of a paternal audience, hoping to gain the father's attention, his interest, his good humor, his affection, she may dance, sing, or dress herself in pretty clothes, and the father will no doubt be pleased and will admire this slightly seductive feminine display with warm benevolence. But what will a little boy do to match this performance? Shall he give a corresponding display of manly strength and athletic prowess? Will it produce the same affectionate reaction? Clearly it might; but even more clearly, it is less likely to, human vanity being what it is. For just as the daughter's performance contains an element of flattery, so the son's cannot avoid being inherently a little competitive—is he not, after all, striving to equal the father's masculinity and power, as he perceives it? Granting that the father may become threatened if the daughter's performance is too blatantly seductive, and may derive some gratification from the son's admiring emulation, on balance it requires more emotional maturity from him to respond as affectionately to the son's exhibition as he does to that of the daughter.

If the father lacks this maturity, or if for any reason the son feels uncertain of his tolerance and love, the only role left open to him if he wishes somehow to complement his sister's performance, is to play the role of buffoon and make his father laugh. If his sister does a graceful dance he will do a comic one.[1] Thus he will give the father pleasure without challenging him in any way.

Once this "self-castrated" definition of the situation is established, of course, much may be achieved. The Fool can insult the King. The clown in an ice follies, water show, or on a high wire, may actually demonstrate far more skill than any other performer, so long as he never "comes out of role" and says blatantly to the audience "I am a man." This is why dwarfed or deformed Fools were generally preferred—in a sense they *could* not come out of role altogether in a warrior society.

It seems from these observations that the clown role adopted by Hephaestus has to do primarily with the attempted solution of oedipal problems and is unrelated to the mother-son conflicts I have discussed. Such a view would receive support from the fact that, according to one tradition [Homer: *Iliad* i. 590ff.; Apollodorus: i. 3. 5], Hephaestus was lamed by Zeus, who threw him by the foot from Olympus so that he was crippled by the fall. In this same tradition, furthermore, the punishment resulted from his having come to the aid of his mother and defended her against Zeus' attack, thus abandoning the role of buffoon. Aside from this familial scene, his fall from heaven in itself associates him with such rivalrous oedipal figures as Talos, Icarus, Bellerophon, and the Miltonic Lucifer.

But this is not the whole story, since Hephaestus is also tossed from heaven by Hera and comes into conflict with her on at least one other occasion [Homer: *Iliad* xviii. 395ff.;

---

[1] Indeed, this sequence of feminine charm and male buffoonery has always formed the foundation of entertainment directed specifically to (non-homosexual) males, from the medieval caliph to the burlesque habitué.

Pausanias: i. 20. 3]. There are, in other words, indications of a maternal attitude which justifies my inclusion of Hephaestus in this series.

How are we to deal with this complexity? Should we accept one tradition and explain away the other? But both are found in the *Iliad*, and even if one argues some sort of historical conflict we are still obliged to account for their having been preserved side by side. Is there some sense in which the maternal and paternal conflict belong together? Is the self-emasculation response dependent upon a child being exposed to the vanity and invidiousness of both parents?

Heretofore I have tried to avoid too great a specificity in linking family strains and emotional responses in myth. To attempt to find dynamic determinants of symptom choice is at best a highly "artistic" process even with clinical data—to make such inferences from myth would seem the height of folly. Myths involve so many determinants that to seek anything beyond the very crudest approximation for a single level of analysis seems inappropriate. It is one thing to observe a psychological uniformity—a preoccupation with one type of emotional conflict which produces certain rough similarities in a variety of myths. It is quite another to endeavor to account for all of the remaining differences between these myths in psychological terms. The universality of the one argues psychological significance; the diversity of the other argues the importance of nonpsychological determinants. A myth is a little like a political platform: there is something in it for everyone; and for that reason one should not expect psychological consistency from a myth any more than one would expect value consistency from a political platform. Thus it would seem absurd to assume that one can account for "symptom choice" from hints in the myths themselves. Why Hephaestus should adopt the defense of the clown role, rather than killing his mother like Orestes, or raping her like Zeus, is a question which we must, in general, leave unanswered.

Once having pointed out the prohibitive difficulty of such a task, however, the temptation to essay it becomes irresistible. So with the full knowledge that we are on weak ground, let us see if there are not one or two discriminating generalizations which might be made regarding the relation between the Hephaestian response and others.

We might begin by noting that the buffoon role is not the only method of dealing with father-son rivalry in Greek mythology. It is not the way Zeus dealt with Cronus, nor Cronus with Uranus. The obvious difference which occurs to us is that for all their ambivalence, the mothers in the latter instances supported and encouraged their sons against their husbands, while Hera rejected her son the instant he was born. It would seem reasonable to assume that the self-abasing or buffoon response in real life is most likely to develop when both parents are intolerant of masculinity in a son. This rejection of masculine strivings by both parents is certainly present in the case of Hephaestus, and differentiates him from Dionysus and Heracles, who were persecuted by Hera, but lovingly supported and protected by Zeus.

But thus far I have actually said very little about Hera's relationship with Hephaestus. It is a reasonably complex one, with many contradictions, the first of which concerns his birth. For in Homer, Hephaestus appears to be the son of Zeus and Hera, while in Hesiod he is Hera's parthenogenous child, like Typhon [Homer: *Iliad* i. 577ff.; Hesiod: *Theogony* 927ff; *Homeric Hymn to Apollo* 305ff.]. Frazer points out, however, in relation to Apollodorus' comment on this discrepancy, that the term "father" in the *Iliad* "may refer to the god's general paternity in relation to gods and men" [Apollodorus: i. 3. 5 and note, p. 22]. In any case, Hesiod is quite explicit in attributing the parthenogenic birth to a quarrel between Zeus and Hera [*Theogony* 929].

Hephaestus, then, is in this tradition produced in anger. His very existence is due to parental strife, and to the bitter fantasy, common enough in neurotic women of every age [cf., e.g., Stein, 1960, pp. 95–96], but actually realized by the Queen of Heaven—giving birth without prior male assistance. The result is a highly narcissistic maternal attitude.[2] Hephaestus is an extension of Hera, a demonstration of her parity with Zeus, who bore Athene. But at the same time he is weak, ugly, and crippled, a living testimony to her organic and generative inferiority. He is both an expression of and an injury to Hera's maternal vanity:

> See now, apart from me [Zeus] has given birth to bright-eyed Athena who is foremost among all the blessed gods. But my son Hephaestus whom I bare was weakly among all the blessed gods and shrivelled of foot, a shame and a disgrace to me in heaven, whom I myself took in my hands and cast out so that he fell in the great sea [*Homeric Hymn to Apollo* 314–18].

She clinches this expression of motherly affection by remarking rather acidly that Thetis might have found better ways to help the gods than by rescuing him [*Ibid.*, 319–21].

Her attitude toward Hephaestus changes, however, as he becomes a skilled craftsman under Thetis' care. Now that he reflects glory upon her, she reinstates him on Olympus and their relationship becomes friendly [cf. Homer: *Iliad* i. 571ff.]. In Hesiod it is this positive side of the maternal narcissism which is stressed: ". . . she bare . . . a glorious son, Hephaestus, who excelled all the sons of Heaven in crafts" [*Theogony* 929b–929d]. In either case, the important issue is what contribution the child will make to the mother's amour propre. There is no question here, however, of achieving revenge upon the father through malevolence toward his

[2] Brody reports such an attitude in the fantasy of a little girl: "she would eat some special food and grow a baby herself—a boy baby, and she would take care of him until he got old enough to marry her . . . then she would have a girl baby, for which she had always declared a preference" [Brody, 1956, p. 382]. The goal is to reproduce herself—the male merely a means to that end.

son. Since Hephaestus is parthenogenous he escapes this burden, and although rejected he is not pursued.

Hephaestus' self-abasement is thus an appropriate response to his mother's narcissistic resentment of males—she cannot deflate him if he is already deflated—but it is therefore all the more inappropriate for dealing with her contrary desire for him to be a display piece and an agent for the expression of her masculine strivings. It is for this reason, after all, that she threw him down from Olympus.[3]

How, then, does Hephaestus become reconciled with Hera to the degree suggested by the benevolent relationship they appear to have, for the most part, in the *Iliad*? How does she come to view this object of shame as an adequate extension of herself? It seems clear that Hephaestus' occupation itself satisfies the needs which initially caused him to be scornfully discarded.[4] Since it is too dangerous for himself to serve as an object for maternal display, he can create objects which will function as substitutes in this regard.

But although these two mechanisms protect Hephaestus from Hera's ambivalent pressures it cannot protect him against his own. I have already mentioned how he defended Hera against Zeus, and how he was served by Zeus for his pains. Another tradition tells of an act of aggression toward Hera, brought on by an outburst of healthy skepticism concerning his parthenogenous birth, or in revenge for her early rejection of him [Pausanias: i. 20. 3]. Receiving from her son

[3] Once again Brody provides an analogue. She describes the case of a mother whose intolerance of male dominance and pride forced her son to behave like a clown, in "mock-obedience to her disparagement of his masculinity." As a result, however, the mother's narcissism was offended and she sought treatment for the boy [Brody, 1956, pp. 391–92].

[4] The etiological sequence of this interpretation should not be construed to imply any historical order. Hephaestus' smith and craftsman attributes probably existed long before he became Hera's offspring or became associated with the fall-from-heaven theme. The psychological factors described here simply constitute the glue which knitted these elements together—which made people feel they somehow "belonged" together.

a golden throne, she sat in it, only to discover that she had been imprisoned by the contrivance, and was released only when she swore to the truth of the birth story or, in another version, promised Aphrodite to her son. A device which binds and immobilizes is a fitting mode of revenge for a son crippled and bound by his mother's ambivalence.

Hephaestus' mixed feelings toward Hera are expressed in words as well as in actions. In Book i of the *Iliad*, in an effort "to do kindness to his dear mother," he counsels her to observe caution with Zeus, and is gentle and protective toward her [Homer: *Iliad* i. 571ff.]. In Book xviii, on the other hand, he reveals quite different feelings when he praises Thetis for saving him "when I suffered much at the time of my great fall through the will of my own brazen-faced mother, who wanted to hide me, for being lame" [Homer: *Iliad* xviii. 394-97. Lattimore trans.]. The fact that the codifiers of the *Iliad* preserved both of these passages, which seem to be based on different traditions, suggests that such contradictory attitudes seemed somehow natural to them.

But the most serious reflection of Hera's feelings toward her son is his tendency toward self-abasement in his sexual relationships. Outside of some minor marriage announcements there are only two myths dealing with Hephaestus' erotic life: his unsuccessful attempt to ravish Athene and his cuckolding by Aphrodite. It would be difficult to imagine anything more ardently self-destructive than to make a crude sexual attempt on a notorious virgin, or to marry a goddess as flagrantly promiscuous as Aphrodite and then advertise the inevitable betrayal to all Olympus.

The first incident is described by Apollodorus as follows:

> Athena came to Hephaestus, desirous of fashioning arms. But he, being forsaken by Aphrodite, fell in love with Athena, and began to pursue her, but she fled. When he got near her with much ado (for he was lame), he attempted to embrace her; but she, being a chaste virgin, would not submit to him,

and he dropped his seed on the leg of the goddess. In disgust, she wiped off the seed with wool and threw it on the ground; and as she fled and the seed fell on the ground, Erichthonius was produced [Apollodorus: iii. 14. 6].

In a note on this passage, Frazer points out the importance of false etymology in the creation of myths (Erichthonius is derived from "wool-earth"). Even more important was the need to retain Athene as the mother of the Athenian kings without forfeiting her acquired virgin status [cf. Grote, p. 77]. But these factors do not entirely account for the construction of this bizarre tale. A hypothetical mythmaker faced with this theological need and furnished with this bit of etymology would still have considerable leeway for his imagination, which would be influenced by the modal anxieties of his culture, and by what would make psychological sense for the principal characters of his drama.

The story of Aphrodite's infidelity is an even greater exercise in self-humiliation. Having discovered the existence of her affair with Ares, Hephaestus forges a net with which to catch the lovers *in flagrante delicto*. Having succeeded in trapping the pair, he shouts:

> Father Zeus, and ye other blessed gods, that live forever, come hither, that ye may see a mirthful thing and a cruel, for that Aphrodite, daughter of Zeus, ever dishonours me by reason of my lameness, and sets her heart on Ares the destroyer, because he is fair and straight of limb, but as for me, feeble was I born [Homer: *Odyssey* viii. 266ff. Butcher and Lang trans.].

Thus he brings all the gods to laugh at his plight, and exposes himself to future cuckoldings by displaying to his fellow gods the enticing sight of his errant wife in a compromising position. Like a Dostoyevskian hero, he seems to revel in his humiliation.

Since most of us have been habituated to the Victorian

literary convention of husbands letting fly with firearms in such situations, Hephaestus' mode of revenge seems almost feminine—reminiscent of Clytemnestra. Like Agamemnon, Ares braves the dangers of war only to be trapped when he re-enters the world of women. But Ares is only subjected to ridicule and injured pride: "Lo, how Hephaestus, slow as he is, hath overtaken Ares, albeit he is swiftest of the gods" [Homer: *Odyssey* viii. 330–31]. Just as Samson, the powerful, was rendered impotent by a female, so Ares, the fleet, is rendered immobile, and sexual intercourse is made to appear slightly dangerous.

Thus even this comic episode reveals characteristic Greek apprehensions. As usual, the situation is narcissistically defined, the elements of love, rivalry, jealousy, and hate being replaced by bodily display, injured pride, public ridicule, and public admiration. Sexual intercourse is viewed as safe only for women, since the man, whether he wins or loses the sexual competition, exposes himself to possible humiliation. Even the most virile and aggressive of men runs the risk of being made to look ridiculous. But although Aphrodite is also enmeshed and exposed, her plight elicits no mockery; it only arouses admiration and desire.

Ares

Hera is generally credited with another son, perhaps the most famous of her rather undistinguished brood (which also includes, in various versions and varying combinations, Hebe, Eris, and Eileithyia; none of Hera's children really stimulated the imagination of mythmakers). This son, moreover, the rough and quarrelsome Ares, seems to represent everything that Hephaestus is not allowed to be: he is uncrippled, virile, and aggressive. How can these qualities be reconciled with my analysis of Hephaestus?

Ares' masculine strivings, however, do not go unpunished.

We have seen him subjected to ridicule, and he is usually defeated in battle, twice by Athene alone [Hesiod: *Shield of Heracles* 357ff. and 450ff.; Homer: *Iliad* v. 385ff., 840ff., and xxi. 400ff.]. Furthermore, he is hated by the gods, even by his father and mother. In the *Iliad*, when Ares fights beside Hector, he so arouses the rage of his mother that she goes to Zeus to ask "wilt thou at all be wroth with me if I smite Ares and chase him from the battle in sorry plight?" [Homer: *Iliad* v. 762–63]. To which Zeus readily responds, "set upon him Athene driver of the spoil, who most is wont to bring sore pain upon him" [*Ibid.*, v. 765–66]. When Athene has speared him he runs screaming to his father, complaining bitterly of parental favoritism for Athene:

> With thee are we all at variance, because thou didst beget that reckless maiden and baleful, whose thought is ever of iniquitous deeds. For all the other gods that are in Olympus hearken to thee, and we are subject every one; only her thou chastenest not, neither in deed nor word, but settest her on, because this pestilent one is thine own offspring . . . my swift feet bare me away; else had I long endured anguish there amid the grisly heaps of dead, or else had lived strengthless from the smitings of the spear [*Ibid.*, 875–87. Lang, Leaf, and Meyers trans.]

But this petulant speech, more appropriate to a squabble between ten-year-olds, is not received sympathetically by Zeus:

> Nay, thou renegade, sit not by me and whine. Most hateful to me art thou of all gods that dwell in Olympus; thou ever lovest strife and wars and battles. Truly thy mother's spirit is intolerable, unyielding, even Hera's; her can I scarcely rule with words. Therefore I deem that by her prompting thou art in this plight [*Ibid.*, 889–94].

Yet when Athene is gloating over Ares after her second victory, she seems to suggest that it was his mother's curse that actually brought him low; but Hera is not appeased even then, goading Athene to attack Aphrodite for helping Ares off the field of battle [Homer: *Iliad* xxi. 410–26].[5]

Hera's Heroes

Although her relationships with Zeus, with her sons, and with her stepsons, suggest a generalized hostility to males, there are other heroes who are generally considered as protégés of Hera, operating under her protection and favor. In the *Iliad*, for example, it is said of Agamemnon and Achilles that Hera "loved both alike and had care for them" [Homer: *Iliad* i. 195–96], and her support of Jason is even more explicit.

Yet Hera's attitude toward her favorites was not altogether unambivalent, nor her support of lasting efficaciousness. On the contrary, it was almost a kiss of death, since Achilles and Agamemnon both were cut down in their prime, while Jason died a broken and ruined man. Once they had accomplished her purposes she seemed to have no further use for them—unlike the abiding affection of Athene for Odysseus.

When we examine Hera's motives for favoring these men we find ourselves on the familiar ground of personal narcissism. Agamemnon and Achilles are assisted in order that Troy be destroyed, to avenge the insult of the lost beauty contest on Mt. Ida. Jason is supported to punish Pelias for having insulted Hera on a number of occasions [Apollodorus: i. 9. 8–9]. But Hera is easily offended, particularly by masculine assurance or pride—witness her reckless fury in the *Iliad* at Hector's mild boasting [Homer: *Iliad* viii. 185–207]. Thus the very heroes who achieve her ends become, through their victoriousness, an abomination to her, and she abandons them to their fate.

[5] It is striking how much more bellicose and vindictive the goddesses are than their male counterparts in this episode. While Ares is continually characterized as bloodthirsty, it is Athene, Hera, and Artemis who do most to earn this epithet. The males try to avoid or withdraw from battle, while the females egg them, and each other, on [Homer: *Iliad* xxi. 415–501].

Agamemnon and Jason are most strongly associated with Hera's worship. Both achieve their goals (and Hera's) only after organizing huge and unwieldy forces to aid them. Both give relatively undistinguished performances on their expeditions, and both require a great deal of supernatural assistance. Both return home in triumph only to be ultimately destroyed (spiritually or actually) by their wives, whose aforementioned similarity may be further extended to include Hera herself, whom they certainly resemble in many respects, and to whose heart they were more truly dear than either of their husbands.

On the other hand, one should not exaggerate the personal similarities between the two men, for while Euripides' portrayal of Jason is not unlike the portrait of Agamemnon that emerges from Homer and the tragedians, the most extensive characterization of the Argonaut displays a very different figure—an anxious, timid, dependent, helpless, and rather depressive young man, placed, for some strange reason, in charge of a group comprising the principal heroes of Greece. As Rieu points out in the introduction to his translation of the *Argonautica*, "the term that Apollonius most often applies to him is *amechanos*, 'without resource' " [p. 15]. Hera, on the other hand, is in the more familiar role of "a self-important, pompous, and vindictive woman, whose interest in Jason is inspired far more by her desire to bring King Pelias to book than by the slight service that Jason had rendered her" [*Ibid.*, p. 19]. This view is confirmed by the order and emphasis Hera herself gives to these two motives [*Ibid.*, iii. 62 ff.].

In any case, Jason is persistent in his dependence upon feminine help. Although aided occasionally by men, at every really crucial juncture—when it is a matter of life and death, or of the success or failure of the mission—it is a woman who saves the day: Hera, Athene, Aphrodite, Thetis and the Nereids, Medea, Chalciope, Circe, Arete, the Hesperides. Yet, like Orestes, he is correspondingly unwilling to recognize this dependence, or even to acknowledge that women have an important role in life in comparison with the trivial achievements of his band of heroes. At one point, with a lack of insight which is wildly comic, Jason cries, "oh, how bleak the prospect is, with our one hope of seeing home again in women's hands!" [*Ibid.*, 485–86]. Although almost all of their divine support comes from Hera, Athene, and Aphrodite, the Argonauts persist in devoting the overwhelming majority of their sacrifices to Apollo, who does nothing whatever for them. A particularly droll example occurs shortly after Athene, with a good deal of hustle, has brought the Argo through the clashing rocks and wearily departed for Olympus; the Argonauts behold Apollo loftily flying north, and are so impressed by this useless vision that they spend two days dedicating an island to him [*Ibid.*, ii. 597–713].

Jason also displays the usual Greek fear of mature or passionate women. It is perhaps natural that he should be frightened of the grim Hecate, who appears festooned with serpents and accompanied by underworld hounds [*Ibid.*, iii. 1214ff.], but he seems to be equally terrified of his lovesick bride, especially when she displays any intensity of feeling [*Ibid.*, iv. 350–94]. So inhibiting is this dread that after the lovers have journeyed all over the world together, Medea is still a virgin—an oversight which necessitates a hasty eleventh-hour remedy to avoid having Medea returned to her father [*Ibid.*, iv. 384ff. and 1095–1169].

But leaving aside the personal traits of the characters in this particular narrative, it is possible to view the entire myth of the Argo expedition as a dramatization of the attempt to master the oral-narcissistic dilemma. Consider, for example, the Symplegades, the rocks which clashed together to destroy travelers attempting to enter the Black Sea, until Jason's safe passage kept them harmlessly and permanently apart. As Joseph Campbell has pointed out, such "thresholds" are common in hero-myths, particularly those involving the harrowing of Hell [cf. Campbell, 1956, *passim*].[6] But why is the world of the dead so often reached only by passing through a narrow and dangerous passage? Whether one treats this other world as the unconscious or as some supernatural sphere, the importance of images of death and rebirth, by re-entry into and re-exit from the womb, has become a banality of myth interpretation. The "clashing rocks" hence become the vagina dentata, one of many expressions in this myth of the fear of the maternal genitalia.

Beyond the threshold, says Campbell, "the hero journeys through a world of unfamiliar yet strangely intimate forces" [*op. cit.*, p. 246], a phrase reminiscent of Freud's discussion of the ambiguous German word *heimlich*, meaning both "familiar" and "strange," as well as "uncanny" [Freud, 1919]. Quoting Grimm, Freud shows how the former meaning is elaborated into its opposite:

"From the idea of 'homelike,' 'belonging to the house,' a further idea is developed of something withdrawn from the eyes of others, something concealed, secret . . ." [*Ibid.*, p. 376].

"Heimlich places in the human body, pudenda . . ." [*Ibid.*].

"Heimlich . . . as withdrawn from knowledge, uncon-scious. . . . *The notion of something hidden and dangerous . . . is still further developed so that 'heimlich' comes to have the meaning usually ascribed to 'unheimlich' "* [*Ibid.*, p. 377].

Later, he himself observes: "It often happens that male patients declare that they feel there is something uncanny about the female genital organs. This *unheimlich* place, how-ever, is the entrance to the former heim [home] of all human beings, to the place where everyone dwelt once upon a time and in the beginning. There is a humorous saying: 'Love is home-sickness'; and whenever a man dreams of a place or a country and says to himself, still in the dream, 'this place is

[6] The following discussion draws heavily upon Campbell's book.

familiar to me, I have been there before,' we may interpret the place as being his mother's genitals or her body. In this case, too, the *unheimlich* is what was once *heimisch*, home-like, familiar; the prefix 'un' is the token of repression" [*Ibid.*, pp. 398–99].

This is why Jason is not relieved to have passed the Symplegades successfully. On the contrary, he now berates himself for having undertaken the journey, and confesses that he is "obsessed by fears and intolerable anxiety" [Apollonius, *Argonautica*, ii. 607–37].

The technique for mastering these fears is the same employed by Zeus—a symbolic act of oedipal rape. But this seems impossible to the weak and helpless child, and Jason is downcast when he hears of the task set for him by the king, namely, to harness his two fire-breathing bulls and plow a four-acre field. "Plowing" Mother Earth is a paternal prerogative, and the phallic power of the father, here represented by the bulls, cannot even be confronted, much less mastered and utilized. Furthermore, the large field is "too much" for the little boy, just as the maternal genital is too much for his inadequate organ. When it is said that the task "seemed so impossible to all of them that for a while they stood there without a sound or word, looking at one another in impotent despair" [*Ibid.*, iii. 502–4], the translator's choice of words is eminently appropriate.

Jason's impotence, however, is cured by Medea's magic, for on the day of the trial her elixir makes a new man of him:

> Next, Jason sprinkled his own body and was imbued with miraculous, indomitable might. As his hands increased in power, his very fingers twitched. Like a war-horse eager for battle, pawing the ground, neighing, pricking its ears and tossing up its head in pride, he exulted in the strength of his limbs. Time and again he leapt high in the air this away and that, brandishing his shield of bronze and ashen spear" [*Ibid.*, iii. 1259–1265].

From this display of phallic enthusiasm and the equine simile one is to understand that Jason has already acquired the power of the father, and that the yoking of the bulls will follow as a matter of course.

But the violation of Mother Earth reactivates other fears in the form of the serpent's teeth which must be sown. These may be interpreted in a number of ways, but most importantly they represent children, as they are, after all, sown, and emerge as armed men. The threat posed by them is the same as for Uranus and Cronus—the fear of the mother's capacity to produce rivalrous offspring. The method of handling this threat is to get them fighting among themselves.

This task accomplished, Jason must still face the monstrous serpent which guards the fleece. The conflict is not yet solved. Once again Jason is helpless to deal with the problem, but is saved by Medea, who puts the serpent to sleep with some sort of archaic barbiturate. Jason is now ready to return from the land of nightmares.

There is another version of the story, unfortunately lost to us except for a single vase painting. This painting, reproduced by Campbell, shows Jason emerging from the jaws of a huge toothy serpent, with a helpful Athene standing by [Campbell, *op. cit.*, p. 247].[7] It is interpreted by both Campbell and Jane Harrison as expressing Jason's rebirth from the belly of the serpent [*Ibid.*, pp. xv and 90ff.; Harrison, 1962, pp. 35–36], and this seems reasonable, although he seems more dead than alive as his arms and head hang limply from the dragon's jaws. But whether he is now being devoured or has been devoured and is now re-emerging, the fear of such devouring seems to be an important theme of the Jason story.

[7] The painting bears a remarkable resemblance to the famous picture of the Aztec serpent-god Quetzalcoatl devouring a man. The only difference is that Quetzalcoatl's victim has only his legs showing, while it is the top half of Jason's body which is in daylight. Presumably this is an indication that the former is going in while the latter is coming out.

CHAPTER VII

Identification with the Aggressor: Dionysus

I. THE RITUAL

And if the Babe is born a Boy
He's given to a Woman Old,
Who nails him down upon a rock,
Catches his shrieks in cups of gold.

She binds iron thorns around his head,
She pierces both his hands and feet,
She cuts his heart out at his side
To make it feel both cold and heat.

Her fingers number every Nerve
Just as a Miser counts his gold;
She lives upon his shrieks and cries,
And she grows young as he grows old.

Till he becomes a bleeding youth,
And she becomes a Virgin bright;
Then he rends up his Manacles
And binds her down for his delight.

He plants himself in all her Nerves,
Just as a Husbandman his mould;
And she becomes his dwelling place
And Garden fruitful seventy fold.

[Blake, "The Mental Traveller"]

IN HER DISCUSSION of Greek mystery cults Gertrude Levy remarks that "in the ritual of Dionysus the Son eclipsed the Mother" [Levy, p. 292]. I may perhaps be forgiven if I attach to this statement a significance somewhat alien to the context in which it was uttered, for it was not only in the realm of ritual that this eclipse took place. What is unique about the Dionysian solution is that the maternal threat is welcomed, and boundary-loss actively pursued. Instead of seeking distance from or mastery over the mother, the Dionysian position incorporates her.

One can scarcely pick up a volume on Greek mythology and religion without encountering an expression of puzzlement when the topic of Dionysus is first broached. There is a quality of dissonance about the god, some incompleteness which resists interpretation. Although perhaps all gods in all religions are fusions of opposites, here the fusion has not altogether been achieved. No other religious figure so often arouses the fantasy that some important bit of evidence has been lost to us, which, if discovered, would illuminate him completely.

This chaotic quality is manifested in the god's many names and shapes and in his motley entourage. As Jane Harrison points out, "he is Bacchos, Baccheus, Iacchos, Bassareus, Bromios, Euios, Sabazios, Zagreus, Thyoneus, Lenaios, Eleuthereus, and the list by no means exhausts his titles" [Harrison, 1957, p. 413]. All of the major Greek gods were in part amalgamations of local divinities, and all boasted, as a result, some subsidiary appellations and theriomorphic antecedents. But in Dionysus the process of integration seems less complete, so that diversity and hence metamorphosis remain as *attributes* of the god when the mold of early Greek religion is hardened by civilization. "Apollo the artists represent in

paintings and sculpture as ever ageless and young, but Dionysus they depict in many guises and forms; and they attribute
to Apollo in general a uniformity, orderliness, and unadulter-
ated seriousness, but to Dionysus a certain variability. . . ."
[Plutarch: "The E at Delphi" 389b]. Very little effort seems
to have been made to "tighten up" or rationalize this strange
deity. While he is exalted and spiritualized by Orphic mystics,
he loses little of his conglomerate and morphologically unstable character. Perhaps his ecstatic nature requires this: as
Miss Harrison observes, "it is only in the case of Dionysus
that we catch the god at the moment of his making, at the
moment when the group ecstasy of the worshipper projects
him" [1963, p. 98].

Fortunately, my task does not require me to attempt a general interpretation of Dionysus. For our more limited purposes only the following problems seem important:

(1) The transformation of a bearded, phallic god into a
youthful, effeminate god, from whom the phallic element has
been separated and externalized;

(2) The significance of the mythical Dionysian entourage,
and the emotional function of the religion for women;

(3) The "tacking-on" of the myth of maternal persecution
to material which seems rather irrelevant to the mother-son
syndrome, and the peculiar nature of the Dionysian response.

The first two problems are best considered together, since
they are intimately related and involve Dionysian ritual as
well as mythology.

Guthrie opens a discussion of Dionysus with the remark
that: "it is useless to try to account for his nature by an
origin in one single functional type, such as that of the
vegetation-god, however many characteristics of that type
he may display. Always there is something more" [Guthrie,
1955, p. 145]. With this statement I must heartily agree, and
it will still be true when the present exploration is concluded.
But we may chip away a little at the area of indeterminacy,

first by recognizing that the Dionysian religion was a proto-universal one, bridging class lines as well as geographical divisions; and as such, it meant different things to different groups. For the rural lower classes Dionysus may have been a simple vegetation-god or fertility god, one reinterpreted by the more well-to-do urban classes in terms of their own cultural strains.[1] On the one hand, a good case can be made for arguing that Dionysian religion in civilized Greece took a form which was centrally directed toward the expression and attempted resolution of modal familial conflicts, while on the other hand, it would be equally correct to say that each of the elements serving this function originally had nothing whatever to do with it. Of diverse and scattered origin, they became relevant to the family structure only through the manner in which they were combined, and each retained its original meanings in other contexts. Dodds' suggestion that the Peloponnesian War brought with it a major revival of orgiastic religion, and that it was this revival that aroused Euripides' interest in the topic, seems compelling to me, and utterly understandable in terms of the exacerbation of sex antagonism caused by the war [Dodds, 1960, pp. xxiii–xxv].

An example of the redefinition of existing elements may be found in the use of the phallus in Bacchic ritual. In more than

[1] Guthrie provides support for this view when he points to rural Dionysian festivals as "occasions so far as one can see for communal drinking and village merrymaking, in which the phallic element was present," but lacking the element of wild seizure associated with the "nocturnal mountain revels" [*op. cit.*, p. 178]. This frenzied aspect would have its greatest appeal among the more emotionally and physically incarcerated urban women seeking release from the frustrations of their confined everyday lives. While urban women did not create, and may not even have participated in these revels in their more extreme form, they exerted a special fascination for them. The entire issue of the origin of Bacchic frenzy is too difficult and obscure to consider here, except to say that I find it difficult to accept the idea that it could be traced to some simple and primitive culture. Such manifestations are more usually found in societies which are at least socially complex—on the verge of urbanization, or involved in some sort of cultural collision or decay [cf. Dodds, 1960, pp. xvff.].

one time and place Dionysus was an ithyphallic deity, like
Pan, Hermes, and Priapus [cf. also Kerényi, 1960, pp. 272–73],
and this fertility principle is retained in the Satyrs and Sileni
of his entourage. Now in such a context, the use in ritual of
the *liknon,* a shovel-shaped basket, filled with fruit and a
sacred phallus, seems ordinary and uncomplicated—a symbol
of fertility amid other such symbols [cf. Harrison, 1957, pp.
517–26; Nilsson, 1957, pp. 33ff., 66ff.]. But how much additional significance a disembodied phallus must have held for
the deprived and resentful Greek matron. The ambivalence
which was so disturbing to the phallic narcissism of her male
offspring is beautifully integrated in the *liknon* ritual. The
phallus is in many ways a focus for her feelings. Deprived by
her neglectful husband, she tends to make a separation between the organ which gratifies and its possessor who does
not. The *liknon* ceremony realizes this separation. Second,
she wishes to possess the organ in its own right, as a symbol of
the favored status of males in Greek society—to incorporate
it and make it her own. The ceremony realizes this possession.
Third, she wishes to attack her depriving husband and tear
his organ from him, thus reciprocating his deprivation and
destroying the basis of his superior status. The ceremony may
be fantasied as a celebration of this attack.

But what is one to make of the fact that in some representations of Dionysian ritual a child appears in the *liknon* (which
served as a cradle as well as a harvest basket in ancient times)
in place of the phallus? In terms of simple fertility ritual there
is of course no problem—human produce has always been associated with agricultural and animal fecundity, and it is not
much of a step from the instrument of conception to the
fruit thereof. The *liknon* is simply "a cornucopia that for
human fruit becomes a cradle" [Harrison, *op. cit.,* p. 526]. If
there is some additional appeal in this it must lie in the significance of the infant in the ceremony, rather than in its mere
presence.

Freud might have attributed this significance to the replacement itself, since "the feminine situation is . . . only established when the wish for the penis is replaced by the wish for a child—the child taking the place of the penis in accordance with the old symbolic equation" [Freud, 1933, pp. 164–65]. But although penis envy was assuredly conspicuous enough among Greek women to warrant application of Freud's somewhat prejudiced theory that the girl's desire for a penis is more primary than her desire for a child, we do not know whether phallus and child were used in the same ceremony, or, if so, in what way. While it may be true, as Nilsson says [1957, pp. 110–11], that children were not initiated into the older mysteries—that the sentimental love of children only became a popular theme during the Hellenistic period—this does not mean that the child was not important as a symbol prior to this time. Perhaps one reason why this sentimentalizing tendency fastened onto Dionysian religion as much as it did was precisely because it had always been preoccupied, however unsentimentally, with the theme of birth and childhood, to an extent found in the worship of no other Greek god [cf. Nilsson, 1957, p. 111]. This emphasis is certainly strong in *The Bacchae,* although the god is full-grown in the action itself [but cf. Guthrie, 1955, p. 161]. Even in Homer, reference is made to the nurses of Dionysus, and in the incident involving Lycurgus the god seems to be a child [Homer: *Iliad* vi. 130ff.]. This is often denied [cf. Harrison, 1957, p. 401], but it is not clear, from the passage itself, on what grounds, since it states that the god was frightened by the attack on his nurses and plunged into the sea, "where Thetis received him cowering in her bosom" [cf. Nilsson, 1927, pp. 493–94; Harrison, 1962, pp. 39–40]. One suspects that the desire to interpret this as the behavior of an adult god is due to the fact that it fits more nicely the traditional view that the lordly Homer was contemptuous of Dionysus and his unseemly rites [cf. Guthrie, 1955, p. 165].

Jane Harrison reminds us that "Dionysus was represented in ritual as slain and dismembered," and suggests that "there was some sort of resurrection of the god, a new birth as a little child" [Harrison, 1957, p. 401]. Now, resurrection is certainly an important aspect of fertility ritual, as Frazer so painstakingly pointed out, and its representation provides grist for the homeopathic magic mill. To ensure the advent of spring one need merely reassure oneself with analogues of seasonal change: the sun and the phallus set only to rise again, the snake sloughs his skin and becomes young, the living god is slain but a child-god is born anew—suddenly bustled into the foreground from his hiding place backstage, after the fashion of Medea's rejuvenation mummery with Pelias.

With the advance of civilization the concern with fertility gradually shifts to a preoccupation with personal immortality, but the symbols of one serve equally well for the other— restoration, resurrection, and abundance counteract loss and destruction. Nilsson, for example, claims that the phallus in Dionysiac ritual in the Roman Age was significant less as a symbol of fertility than as an antidote to death, and the fre quency of its appearance in mortuary art is well-known [Nilsson, 1957, pp. 44–45; cf. also Frazer, 1906, pp. 279–80].

It would seem, therefore, that part of the appeal of Dionysian ritual to Greek women lay in the presentation of either child or phallus with other symbols of abundance and ceremonies of rebirth, restoration, and resurrection. Over and above any intrinsic beauty or edification in the ritual, Bacchic ceremonies must have served as something of a tranquilizer. Whatever wish fulfillments may have been represented in the Dionysian rites, it was important for the Greek matron to be reassured that her destructive impulses toward child and phallus would have no consequences in reality.[2] It was pos-

---

[2] We have no functional equivalent in our own society, testifying perhaps to the higher status of women therein. For children, however, such an equivalent does exist in the form of animated cartoons of the "Tom and Jerry" genre, in which the protagonists are subjected to a fantastic variety of tortures: explosions, electrocutions, falls, flattenings, and so forth, without suf-

sible for her, in a somewhat literal sense, to eat her cake and have it, too; to rend her child and resurrect it, to destroy the penis and have it reappear in full bloom from its coyly ineffectual hiding place in a veiled *liknon* [cf. Nilsson, 1957, pp. 66–76].

We are admittedly on somewhat infirm ground here inasmuch as we know so little of what the Dionysian ritual consisted, and can only infer from scattered references. On the one hand, there are these rather late representations involving the *liknon*, all of which seem mild enough. On the other hand, there are both early and late references to wild orgies with dismembered animals and "red and bleeding feasts" [Harrison, 1957, p. 481], which seem to bear little relation to the *liknon* ceremonies. One is further hampered by the fact that the Dionysian myths, rather than symbolizing the ritual, as in the case of some myths, actually purport at times to describe it. This is a unique and confusing aspect of the religion —that not only the god but also his worshipers are the subject of myth. Can one really assume, then, as Jane Harrison does [*Ibid.*, p. 401], that the sedate *liknon* ritual and the mountain orgies are contained in the same ceremony?

The answer probably lies in Jane Harrison's careful phrasing, that "Dionysus was *represented* in ritual as slain and dismembered" [*Ibid.*, p. 401. Italics mine]. In civilized times and places the more lurid phase of the ritual was obviously given milder form than that which we find in *The Bacchae*. But the tearing and eating of animals or humans is such an intrinsic part of Dionysian thought that it seems reasonable to assume that it found some kind of symbolic expression in all Bacchic ceremonies [cf. Harrison, 1962, pp. 22–23]. There is

---

fering any permanent damage. It is interesting that these scenes always occur in a domestic setting, and that the instruments of torture are usually household appliances—for it is just this complicated array of household goods which serves to dam up the child's normal exploratory and aggressive impulses.

some indication, furthermore, that the more pure form survived in some areas, or at least was generally believed to exist. Jane Harrison quotes Plutarch, Clement, and Arnobius to this effect:

" 'There are certain festivals . . . and sacrificial ceremonies as well as unlucky and gloomy days, in which take place eatings of raw flesh and rendings asunder. . . .' "

" 'The Bacchoi hold orgies in honour of a mad Dionysos, they celebrate a divine madness by the Eating of Raw Flesh, the final accomplishment of their rite is the distribution of the flesh of the butchered victims, they are crowned with snakes. . . .' "

" 'You twine snakes about you, and to show yourselves full of the divinity and majesty of the god, you demolish with gory mouths the entrails of goats bleating for mercy' " [1957, pp. 483–84].

One can only with great difficulty, if at all, distinguish among the many sources of meaning for a given rite: what it symbolizes to contemporary participants, what it may have been derived from, how it will be rationalized or allegorized or archetyped by latter-day mystics, what it will smell of to hostile critics. Is one to assume that the *omophagia* is always a ritual representation of the slaying and eating of a child, in fact of Dionysus himself? Is this its most "primitive" meaning, or is it simply its special Greek meaning?

Many have argued for the first of these two possibilities. Jane Harrison sees "behind" the Cretan ritual of tearing and eating a bull the "dreadful suspicion" of "an orgy still more hideous, the sacrifice of a human child" [*op. cit.*, pp. 482, 488], and Guthrie suggests that "it may even be that once in primitive Thrace or Phrygia the victim was a human child, and that some memory of this horror had lingered on" [Guthrie, 1955, p. 166; cf. also Dodds, 1960, pp. xviii–xix].

I cannot accept this view. In the first place one cannot help noticing, in the excited little shudders with which this scandal is conveyed to us and in the tendency to assign it to a remote time and place, the characteristic bias of the classicist. Jane Harrison mentions that a fifth-century vase painting, "too revolting for needless reproduction here, represents a Thracian tearing with his teeth a slain child, while the god Dionysos, or rather perhaps we should say Zagreus, stands by approving" [*op. cit.*, p. 488]. Wherever and whenever this act is seen as having taken place, it was of very considerable interest to someone in civilized fifth-century Greece. Today we are shocked by child-exposure, but not even the most ardent representative of the "deportation" school of Greek scholarship would deny the existence of such exposure during the classical age [cf. Blümner, pp. 81–82; Rose, 1925, pp. 114ff.]. If infanticide was an everyday matter, the rending and eating of a child was probably no more disturbing than gunfighting is to a modern American—not something one actually participates in, but an appropriate topic for representation [cf. Nilsson, 1927, p. 509].

A more serious flaw in the vestige-of-human-sacrifice argument is the assumption that human sacrifice is more "primitive" than animal sacrifice. But the goal of cannibalistic sacrifice is, as Miss Harrison herself points out, the absorption of the qualities of the incorporated being, and while anyone can easily perceive desirable characteristics in animals—strength, ferocity, cunning, fertility, speed, agility—the idea that there might be virtues in a human infant is an extremely sophisticated conception [cf. Harrison, 1962, p. 110; 1957, pp. 486–87]. Primitive mythologies are populated largely with animal figures, and it is usually only at the dawn of civilization that theriomorphic deities begin to yield precedence to anthropomorphic ones. Everything we know of primitive religion argues that animal sacrifice precedes human sacrifice, rather than the other way around. It is only when a society has begun to develop a stable agriculture, a complex political hierarchy, and a trace of urban life that humans begin to outweigh animals in value; and it is just at such periods that human sacrifice is most highly developed (e.g., the Aztecs, the West African kingdoms in their prime, and the early Mediterranean civilizations). While the rending and eating of a human child will at some point become a thing too harsh for a civilized society to tolerate, it seems unlikely that the animals which preceded it will now be returned to favor as a proper substitute. Having achieved the complex and mystical notion that there is more power and virtue in humans than in animals, but having become too fastidious for all the bloodshed, the more natural progression would be toward bloodless and symbolic substitutes—rituals and pantomimes with actors and artifacts, such as characterized many of the Greek mystery cults, as well as most surviving religions today.

The foregoing is a prelude to the thesis I would like to put forward here, that it is precisely the rending and eating of a *human* child, by *women*, which is the most characteristically Greek idea in the entire mélange of Dionysian ritual and lore. Whether or not any single Hellene ever sank his or her teeth into a child's flesh in anything but playful affection is of no consequence to this argument, which is simply this: in the supermarket of imported rites and myths, what really excited the Greeks was everything that related to eating children. Greek mythology as it has come down to us certainly shows an extraordinary preoccupation with this theme. I would therefore argue that the infanticide and cannibalism lay "behind" the *omophagia*, not in a chronological but in a psychological sense: that from the bloody animal feasts they wandered in fantasy to the slaughter of children, and felt that somehow this was the "true" meaning of the rite.

The initial stimulus is a rite with a male horde rending and devouring a live animal to incorporate its virtues—a rite probably found in many places. In some, the religion developed to the point where the slain animal represented a deity, and as the deity became humanized a human may actually have been substituted. It was, in any case, symbolically substituted in Greek thought.

But now another modification occurs—the male horde is transformed by degrees into a female horde. The first step may be seen in the Orphic idea that the Titans who tore Dionysus to pieces and ate him were instigated by Hera. The ultimate transformation is found in the stories of Agave and the daughters of Minyas, where it is women who rend, and in the latter case devour, their own sons—instigated, however, by the youthful Dionysus.

What complicates the understanding of such phenomena is the cultural variability in a major civilization. Not only will there be cultural islands in which the foreign rite might preserve its original significance, but also, among urban peoples, it may hold a special emotional appeal for various subgroups in the population. Furthermore, although I have argued that the mother-son relationship in the Greek family was the most stressful one, it was not the only source of strain, and one can of course assume the usual range of individual family differences. Consequently, along with the additions and transformations, the original rituals and their attendant myths were preserved, thus forming the strange confederation that has come down to us as Dionysian religion.

Plutarch argues that the *omophagia* was not in honor of any god, but was performed with a view to the riddance of evil spirits, as were the human sacrifices "of ancient days" [Plutarch: "The Obsolescence of Oracles" 14]. These evil spirits, I would suggest, were internal, and their propitiation and appeasement refer to the fact that one must express such murderous impulses in some harmless form in order to keep them from erupting in their original raw and ugly state. Since even among such virtuosi of impulse control as the modern English-speaking peoples such crude mechanisms are not uncommon, it is not surprising to find them among the rather impetuous peoples of the ancient Aegean world, the tenuousness of whose efforts at self-restraint is perhaps reflected in the prevalence of unruly and rebellious hordes in their mythology (Giants, Titans, Sileni, Satyrs, Maenads, Centaurs, and so forth). Furthermore, when Plutarch equates these rites with human sacrifice, it is in terms of their function—both serve to discharge the hostile affect, therefore both are "propitiating."

Once again I would interpret Plutarch's reference to past human sacrifice as a psychological rather than historical statement. Since, at some point in the dim past of the individual, impulses like these were not under any internal control, it is easy to fantasy that what is now symbolic was once actual. But normally, the power to carry out impulses fortunately develops only with the ability to control them, so that the notion of "bad old days" is as much a figment as is that of "good old days." This tendency to reify early fantasy experiences is always difficult to resist, and one can hardly criticize Plutarch for confusing ontogeny and phylogeny when Freud and Jung were guilty of the same error.

Infanticidal impulses originate partly in sibling jealousy—a more or less universal experience that we would expect to be greatly augmented by a disturbed mother-child relationship. But death wishes constitute a problem only under two conditions: when they are seen as containing an immanent power to fulfill themselves, and when they are coupled with more affectionate feelings toward the object in question. Infanticidal wishes held a special resonance for the Greeks precisely because such wishes sometimes came true in the form of child-exposure. The mere existence of the practice and its importance in mythology provided this resonance. The feelings aroused when exposure was an immediate family experience would be heightened to a degree unimaginable to the inhabitant of a society in which infant mortality, even of an accidental nature, is an unusual event.

Vague references made to a past age of infant sacrifice should thus be translated as referring to the dark uncertainty of Greek childhood, when wishes were dangerous and infants were, or might be, destroyed. Although we do not know how common exposure was in reality, it was undoubtedly as important a component of the fantasy life of Greek children as are the orphan fantasies of modern children. Furthermore, when it did occur, it was usually a younger sibling who was exposed, especially if a girl [Rose, 1925, pp. 114–15].[3]

Infanticidal impulses were also important in the myths of madness, as we saw in Chapter I. It seems reasonable to assume that the kinds of behavior which are popularly believed to emerge in a psychotic condition are those which are felt to require the greatest effort to control under normal circumstances. For the Greeks, infanticide was clearly one of these.

Still another expression of this concern may be found in the rules regarding impurities in the sanctuary of Bromios (a Theban title applied to Dionysus). The two most severe impurities (one could not enter the sanctuary for forty days following either one) were those resulting from miscarrying or exposing a child [Nilsson, 1957, pp. 134–35].[4] This obsessional dread of infanticide occurs in precisely the setting which serves to reduce this fear, as if proximity to the actual fact of child-slaying would overload the emotional circuits of the institution.

Although infanticidal impulses were a problem for both sexes, it seems clear that in the Dionysian religion the major emphasis was on the murderous impulses of the mother toward her son. The earlier stories of male hordes did not

[3] This also meant that a disproportionate number of Greek families had boys without sisters to moderate the maternal impact (especially older sisters).

[4] Since this item comes from a second century A.D. inscription at Smyrna, it may seem inappropriate to offer it as relevant data, but there is good reason to believe that the rules were of ancient origin.

completely recede, since they found a responsive chord in male feelings and fears, but were always subsidiary to this dominant theme.[5]

Thus far we have observed two components of the Greek family pattern expressed in Dionysian religion: feminine ambivalence toward the phallus and toward the child. The first appears in the feminization and infantilization of the god, together with the preservation of the impersonal phallus and the phallic entourage of semihuman and equally impersonal Satyrs and Sileni, thus providing a dissociation between genital excitement and the complex feelings which distorted and interfered with it. The second appears in the *omophagia* and the myths of the rending and destruction of the child-god, together with his restitution and rebirth (reassuring the mother that her impulses were not irremediable).

With this ambivalence appears the serpent: it is rare to find either a description or a representation of a Maenad without a serpentine stole or snood; and the purification ceremonies of newborn and nonexposed children were typically concluded by presenting the infant with a cuttlefish or squid [Rose, 1925, p. 116]. This was a form of homeopathic magic; the monsters would ward off the evil eye—like the Gorgon and serpents embroidered on Ion's cradle blanket [Euripides: *Ion* 1413–1431]—as well as the mother's entangling behavior. The ambivalence is also depicted behaviorally: "his frenzied women votaries, in the passionate abandonment of his service, take young beasts in their arms and with maternal tenderness give them the breast—the same women who with scarcely

---

[5] To the extent that I pursue these subsidiary issues I will be discussing matters that are less and less specifically Greek, and more and more characteristic of human existence. The strains in ancient Greek culture are present in reduced degree in every culture, and vice versa—it is only a certain intensity and concentration that calls our attention to them. So long as we remain at the summit of the Greek family syndrome we are in a good position to talk of relationships with other aspects of Greek culture, but as we descend to the lower slopes, we are less and less able to differentiate this society from its neighbors'.

conceivable savagery tear the limbs from the young creatures and fasten their teeth on them" [Guthrie, 1955, p. 146].

One often hears modern women speak of the therapeutic value of "getting out of the house," and "getting away from the children," as if there was some tendency for malignant sentiments to accumulate in a constricted interpersonal situation, requiring some sort of external discharge. Hence it is not surprising, in view of the confined status of urban women in Greece, that the theme of liberation-versus-restraint was so prominent in Dionysian lore. This liberation is a double one: both physical and emotional. In Euripides' *The Bacchae,* Pentheus endeavors to restrain the womenfolk, to shackle Dionysus, and to control his own impulses, but fails in all three. As Guthrie remarks, "the greatest gift of Dionysos was the sense of utter freedom, and in Greece it was the women, with their normally confined and straitened lives, to whom the temptation of release made the strongest appeal. Dionysos . . . 'pricks them to leave their looms and shuttles.' . . . Nothing is lacking which can serve to increase the sense of exaltation and of shedding the self of everyday existence" [Guthrie, 1955, p. 148; cf. also Dodds, 1960, p. xxvi]. The liberation factor is also of interest because of the ambivalence it betrays with regard to emotional separateness. On the one hand the women achieved a greater independence from spouses and children, while on the other they experienced a loss of identity and autonomy through their emotional fusion and oneness with the god.[6]

Before becoming too enamored of this notion, however, we

[6] It is perhaps this same ambivalence over boundary-violation which is responsible for the tendency for some women [in an unpublished study by Robert Kastenbaum] to visualize death as a sweet-faced young man, rather than the more common image of an older, sterner figure. This Dionysian youth may be a corollary of what Abraham calls "The Bride of Death Ceremonial," significantly associated with a dread of snakes [cf. Abraham, 1912, pp. 157–63]. For an interesting study of the fantasy of death as a lover, see Greenberger [1961].

should confront the difficult issue of determining the extent to which accounts of Bacchic orgies are mythical. The problem is raised succinctly by Miss Harrison:

"The husbands and brothers of the women of historical days would not, we are told, have allowed their women to rave upon the mountains; it is unthinkable taken in conjunction with the strict oriental seclusion of the Periclean woman. That any woman might at any moment assume the liberty of a Maenad is certainly unlikely, but much is borne even by husbands and brothers when sanctioned by religious tradition." She observes that the orgies were no more popular among the men of Macedonia in Alexander's time, but were permitted out of superstitious fear (a fear no doubt bolstered by the mythological tales of the consequences of resistance to Bacchic worship). She points out that several of the reforms of Solon and Epimenides are directed against feminine "excesses," in particular those associated with religious ceremonies [Harrison, 1957, pp. 397–400].

In a similar vein, she suggests that while the word "maenad" ultimately came to refer to mythical beings, it is reasonable to assume—in part from the word itself, which means "one possessed"—that originally it was used merely to designate the raving worshipers [Ibid., pp. 395–96].

In any case, the Attic women who held biennial orgies[7] on Parnassus were real enough for Pausanias to talk to them [Pausanias: x. 4. 2–3 and x. 32. 7; Harrison, 1957, pp. 391–93]; with this evidence, it is mere prejudice to argue that accounts of Dionysian rites have nothing to do with Athens. What seems most likely is that the Athenian men did oppose, and ultimately placed constraints upon, Bacchic worship (perhaps, as Miss Harrison suggests, the elaborate Athenian restrictions on women actually originated in such opposition), but that the original rites—possession, *omophagia*, and all—were

---

[7] What social forces maintained such an awkward interval remains a mystery.

as typically characterized, and survived, in muted and bowd-
lerized form, into the classical period. Indeed, Guthrie argues
[1955, p. 179] that there was no break in "this less respectable, more fearful side of the worship" from archaic times
down to the first century B.C., and offers supporting evidence
[cf. also Lawson, 1964, pp. 222–32].

That the sexes should battle over Dionysian religion befits
its sex-antagonistic origins. The feminization of the god over
time, his sexual transformation in myths, and his birth from a
male all express tension between the sexes. Just as Greek men
could not tolerate mature women, Greek women could not
tolerate mature men, and just as the males converted Artemis
and Athene into virgin goddesses, so the females rejected Zeus
for Dionysus.[8] Hostility toward dominant persons of the opposite sex was so compelling that it even superseded the dependency orientation upon which religious feelings are so
largely based. Non-adult figures were accepted as deities even
though they seemed to be less protective. For both sexes this
deficiency was partly offset by same-sex deities of a more
parental cast: Zeus for men, Hera and Demeter for women.
But opposite-sexed deities aroused so much ambivalence that
it seemed necessary to infantilize them to a certain extent—
to take the curse, as it were, off their sexual identification.

The sexes differed, however, in expression of this ambivalence. For men there was a tendency to dissociate the contradictory feelings. Mature goddesses, like Hera, became
villainous, while virgin goddesses evoked more positive feelings. For women the ambivalence was contained in the single
figure of Dionysus.

I have devoted this attention to Dionysian religion only because in it myth and ritual are virtually inseparable. While the
myth of Attis and Cybele may serve as an explanation of *why*
the priests of Cybele castrated themselves, the priests themselves

---

[8] Thus Kerényi calls Dionysus a second Zeus, "a Zeus of women" [1960,
p. 251].

do not appear in myth, nor do other worshipers. In the mythology of Dionysus, however, the congregation plays a major role.

The salience of the Bacchic entourage has complex determinants. I have already discussed the use of the Satyr to express the depersonalized sexuality formerly attached to the god himself. One may also say, in a general way, that the importance of the entourage in myth is a direct expression of the importance of the *process* of Bacchic worship as compared with other forms: the profound emphasis on the production of religious enthusiasm through group activity. But over and above these factors stands the powerful suspicion that the need for mythical attendants reflects some special complexities in the worshiper's identification with the god.

The deities of literate civilizations tend to evoke in their devotees an attitude compounded of filial reverence or submission on the one hand, and identification or fusion with an ideal self or cosmic entity on the other. In some cases these attitudes are dissociated: the filial orientation is directed toward one deity or group of deities, the identification is directed toward another, or toward a hero figure of some kind. In the Greek world, with its profusion of deities, this was a relatively simple matter. Women could identify exclusively with Kore and Demeter, men with Heracles, "at whose shrine no woman sacrificed; by whose name no woman took oath" [Engle, 1945, pp. 357–58]. In monotheistic societies this has often created some difficulties, as is apparent in the religious struggles of the Old Testament, the triumph of Christianity, and the greater popularity, in Protestant countries, of folktales with feminine protagonists.

Dionysus, however, is a somewhat complicated case. His rejuvenation made possible an emotional response to the god, but his feminization and the retention of some of his archaic and theriomorphic aspects made him also the passive object of the oral-destructive drives of his devotees. As a Magical

Thing to be torn and devoured, he frustrated the more "civilized" need for an object of identification, and the mythical entourage was elaborated and preserved because it compensated for this lack.

When we turn to the more familiar province of Dionysian mythology, we notice first that Hera's persecution of Dionysus is attributed to jealousy aroused by the infidelity of Zeus [Apollodorus: iii. 4. 3]. That the sins of the father should be vented upon the son has aroused no one's interest, partly because classical scholars have always agreed that the clothing of Greek mythical ideas in the form of a boudoir farce should be viewed as an unfortunate accident. Guthrie, for example, dismisses the jealousy theme as "superficial" and attributes Hera's anger as due to the antagonism between the cults, since "Hera is patron of marriage, whereas Dionysos by the license which his cult bestows on women is a subverter of the marriage tie" [Guthrie, 1955, p. 159]. Be that as it may, one cannot intelligently maintain that a theme so constantly iterated in its mythology has no significance for Greek culture.

Hera's hostility toward her stepchild receives three separate expressions: her attempt to destroy him in the womb, her attempt to destroy him at birth, and her successful effort to drive him mad upon his reaching maturity. I shall discuss each in turn.

CHAPTER VIII

Identification with the Aggressor: Dionysus

II. THE ATTACK IN THE WOMB

Zeus loved Semele and bedded with her unknown to Hera. Now Zeus had agreed to do for her whatever she asked, and deceived by Hera she asked that he would come to her as he came when he was wooing Hera. Unable to refuse, Zeus came to her bridal chamber in a chariot, with lightnings and thunderings, and launched a thunderbolt. But Semele expired of fright,[1] and Zeus, snatching the six-month abortive child from the fire, sewed it in his thigh [Apollodorus: iii. 4. 3].

THE USE OF SURROGATE FIGURES (stepmothers, mothers-in-law, witches, and monsters) to symbolize negative qualities of the real mother is a familiar phenomenon in the analysis of fantasy. It might be fruitful, therefore, to approach this incident with the assumption that Hera represents a negative aspect of Semele, and that the dialogue between them is

[1] Originally the manner of death was more direct: Semele was consumed by the lightning itself—thus destroyed phallically, as in oral-narcissistic fantasies [cf. Euripides: *The Bacchae* 242ff.].

essentially an internal one.[2] On this basis I would conclude that the Semele incident describes how certain of the Greek mother's needs bring disaster upon her, and produce a negative orientation to her child.

These needs, as one might expect, are narcissistic. Sexuality is subordinated to the desire for self-glorification, and her narcissistic definition of the situation causes her to experience the sexual act as a shattering, disintegrating violation, in which she will be penetrated and destroyed. Furthermore, it appears to her that procreation is something solely for the benefit of fathers and children—something for which women are exploited and mutilated. The easiest method of attacking this coalition is through a persecution of the weakest member, and this is expressed in Hera's subsequent pursuit of Dionysus.

An interesting echo of this view may be found in the bloody and terror-ridden landscape of Aztec mythology. Neumann recounts the belief that the souls of women who have died in childbirth become demonic spiders dangling from the heavens. Not only do they escort the sun to its daily death in the west, but also will swallow up mankind when the end of the world approaches [Neumann, 1955, pp. 184–85]. These spiders are "hostile particularly to men." Procreation is thus defined as in the Semele-Dionysus myth. It is not surprising that the vengeful, infanticidal mother is so pervasive in Dionysian mythology when its principal origin tale contains this symbolic matricide.

But I have described this incident as an expression of maternal hostility as well as a reason for it, and the myth proves indeed to be a complex one of revenge and counter-revenge. For while Semele is destroyed by Zeus and Dionysus, Dionysus is almost destroyed by Hera's wiles, and Zeus in turn revenges himself by outdoing Hera in her own feminine specialty, and giving birth to a child all by himself.

[2] In at least one tradition Hera *is* the mother of Dionysus [Smith, 1957, p. 457].

It is probably inutile to think in temporal terms at all—to talk of the sequence as beginning somewhere and ending somewhere. Each act is a revenge for each other act, and one is simply confronted here, as elsewhere, with an endless cycle of sex antagonism. The hostile assumptions and definitions of one sex are dependent upon those of the other. While I will later argue that the many tales of Dionysus driving women mad constitute an identification with and revenge against Hera (who had driven Dionysus mad), Kerényi can see the persecution of Dionysus as a *consequence* of his having "seduced the women into madness" [1960, p. 262], and one view is certainly as valid as the other. When we remember that the result of this madness was often the killing and dismembering of sons, the cyclical character of the revenge process becomes even more clear. Kerényi also suggests that "the death of Semele—the prototype of Dionysiac women—must originally have been the punishment for what her immortal son had to suffer . . . from his female companions" [*Ibid.*, p. 263].

One must also recognize the identity of Zeus and Dionysus in the Semele myth. In one version Semele is impregnated by drinking a potion prepared by Zeus from the heart of Dionysus, who had already been torn to pieces by the Titans [Hyginus: *Fabulae* 167].[3] "Heart" probably means phallus here, as Kerényi suggests [1960, p. 257], for the Orphic stories speak of one organ being saved by a goddess and hidden in a covered basket, which recalls the covered phallus in the *liknon* ritual. Kerényi points out that the *Kradiaios Dionysos* carried in the *liknon* has a double meaning, since it can be derived both from *kradia* (heart) and *krade* (fig-tree or figwood object), and thus may have referred initially to the

---

[3] Conflicting chronologies are produced whenever latter-day synthesizers attempt to amalgamate two alien myths. I discuss the Semele story before the Titan tale only because Dionysus is unborn in the former and newborn in the latter.

figwood phallus used in Dionysian processions and said to have been made by Dionysus himself [*Ibid.*, pp. 255–56, 259].[4] This suggests that Semele was impregnated, not by Zeus, but by Dionysus himself. One of the mysteries of Dionysus, then, was that he was his own father, self-created and reborn. The father may thus be attacked and punished through the son because the father *is* the son, in the sense that both represent maleness and the pain and wronging of women. It is not Zeus or Dionysus upon whom revenge must be wreaked, but men in general.

That a child should be the recipient of this onslaught requires one further comment. Clearly, it is not simply the child's vulnerability and accessibility that brings this about, for fantasy is not bound by the practical limitations that cause scapegoating in everyday life. A more important consideration is the fact that it is through children that the male is most easily injured. As men have been lamenting for centuries, his immortality is out of his own control. Not only must a woman bear his child, but he cannot know for certain whether the child she bears is his own. This dependence continues, furthermore, after the child is born, in the overwhelmingly more important role played by the mother in the first few years of life.

It is perhaps this vulnerability of the male in the sphere of worldly immortality which gives rise to the concept of the "external soul," so prominent in magic and mythology [cf. Frazer, 1959, pp. 594–604]. In the most typical story of this kind a paternal and villainous figure of some sort—king, ogre, magician, or Jinni, has his soul hidden in some external object, where it seems quite safe until the secret of its whereabouts is betrayed to a young hero by the daughter, wife, or captive concubine of the villain. The hero then destroys the

---

[4] The use of the figwood phallus in ritual was later explained by a tale concerning Dionysus' trip to the underworld to rescue his mother [see Kerényi, 1960, p. 259; and Frazer's notes on Apollodorus iii. 5. 3]. This myth will be discussed in Chapter X.

external soul and the villain dies. In the Greek tale of Meleager, however, it is the hero who has the external soul and his mother who destroys him.

These tales express what is primarily a masculine concern.[5] A woman holds her immortality within herself; who impregnates her is of little importance in this respect. She need not guess whether something of herself continues on in a new organism—she can see the child emerge from her own body. Thus if one translates "soul" in these stories as "that part of me which will live on after I die," the woman initially holds

[5] Occasionally the subject of an external-soul tale is a woman, although I do not believe this occurs in the two cultures discussed in this chapter. But however rare the exceptions, they require a more inclusive conceptualization. One can say, first of all, that women who are narcissistically over-identified with their children approximate the situation of the male. Bibring, *et al.*, describe the difficulty such a woman has in changing from "being a single, circumscribed, self-contained organism . . . to reproducing herself and her love-object in a child who will from then on remain an object outside herself" [1961, p. 17]. A more general interpretation would then be that anyone who has invested most of his or her libido in a real or potential child (or other external object) can be said to possess an "external soul"—feeling indifferent about his or her own person, but vulnerable with regard to the well-being of the other. It is perhaps for this reason that the subjects of such tales are so often elderly, and so often betrayed by youth. Frenkel-Brunswik relates a revealingly benign external-soul tale—the spontaneous fantasy of a twelve-year-old girl. In it a giant finds and raises a little girl who grows up to be beautiful. A prince comes and offers to rescue her, but she tells him this can only be done by finding the giant's heart. Thus far the story resembles the most typical mythical versions. But instead of destroying the heart the prince feeds it to the giant, who "becomes kind" and lets the girl go [Frenkel-Brunswik, 1963, p. 394]. In this more generous rendition one can see clearly what the other myths are about. The father must decathect his child so she can marry and live happily ever after. The prince restores the invested libido to the giant so that he can love someone else (or no one) and relinquish his hold on the girl. The external-soul myth is thus a representation of narcissistic love and its consequences for both subject and object. Since children are the most common objects of this kind of love—extensions of the parental self—they figure importantly, if symbolically, in the myths. In the Celtic dragon myth, for example, the mermaid who has an external soul covets the fisherman's child—indeed the entire myth is founded upon his pledge to give her his firstborn [Campbell and Henderson, 1911, pp. 34ff., 80–82].

her "soul" within herself. It is only the man whose "soul" always resides outside of himself.

This interpretation receives some support from the nature of the external soul's location, which is typically some rather standard womb symbol, or several combined: inside of an egg, or a casket, or the body of some beast, a bird, or fish, or at the bottom of some remote body of water, or perhaps all of these—one inside of the other [*Ibid.*, pp. 594–98]. It is always remote, hidden, and ultimately unsafe, and whoever possesses it holds the life of the man within his hands. But this vulnerability occurs only when the whereabouts of the soul is revealed, usually through an act of betrayal by a woman. Having persuaded the magician or Jinni to confide his secret to her, she tells the hero, who finds the soul and destroys it. It does not seem unreasonable to interpret this theme as saying that a man confides his hopes of self-perpetuation to a woman, and that if she betrays him these hopes will be extinguished, along with his life and his genes.

Now it may be objected that our selection of soul-holders has been biased, and that in many cases it resides, not in a womb-like place, but in a phallic object: a bird, a branch, a sprig of mistletoe, a jewel, a lizard, shark, or crocodile.[6] And in some cases the external soul is attached to the body, usually in the hair, as in the case of Samson, or in a single hair or lock, as in the case of Nisus and Pterelaus, Greek kings who were betrayed to enemies by their daughters, Scylla and Comaetho. Stories of men whose strength lies in their hair and who are betrayed by women are found in every part of the world [Frazer, 1959, pp. 595–96, 598–99].

In such cases the "external soul" clearly signifies the geni-

---

[6] Some of these, such as the reptiles and fish, are ambiguous symbols, as we have seen. The phallic significance of jewel, bird, and mistletoe requires little comment here. The first appears in colloquialisms ("family jewels," "schmuck"), the second in the winged phalli of ancient fertility cults [see Knight, 1786; Wright, 1866]. Mistletoe was believed to be the genitals of the oak.

tals of the male, and the betrayal, as numberless interpreters
have pointed out, a symbolic castration. The difference between the two types is hardly compelling, since in both cases
the soul is in the hands of a woman and her betrayal leads to
its destruction. Cutting off the genitals is depriving the male
of immortality just as surely as, and rather more permanently
than, rejecting his seed. Indeed, the soul in some cases rests
in an object which suggests both phallus and womb. Thus
the brand of Meleager is kept in his mother's box after being
removed from her hearth, while the soul of the Jinni, in the
tale of Sayf-al-Muluk, was placed in the crop of a sparrow
which was then shut up in a box: "the box I set in a casket,
and enclosing this in seven other caskets and seven chests, laid
the whole in a alabastrine coffer, which I buried within the
marge of yon earth-circling sea" [*The Book of the Thousand
Nights and a Night*, Burton trans., 1885, Vol. VII, p. 350].
The soul is thus inside the penis, which is in turn, in the
confused anatomy characteristic of unconscious ideas, inside
the womb—which may in part account for the frequency
with which multiple enclosures appear in these tales.[7]

Once again, however, this interpretation is not intended to
be complete. At least one further interpretive principle is
necessary, just to account for the differences between these
two types; and even if we look only at what is common to
all of the tales we will find other important motifs, such
as the attempts of the heroes and heroines to free themselves

[7] Like all myth elements, however, this one is overdetermined. The box-
within-box-within-box (or trout-within-crow-within-deer) idea is primarily
a device for combatting the anxiety of vulnerability through obsessive elaboration. It also suggests the idea of lineage—one box or animal "begetting" the
next. These two meanings, furthermore, are related: it is when one sees not
only one's children, but one's grandchildren and great-grandchildren that
one feels fully secure—an idea that appears repeatedly in the Bible.

In one story [Frazer, 1959, p. 596], the soul is a jewel in a bird's head in
a hare's head in a seven-headed Hydra's head. The Hydra's ability to regen-
erate its heads when cut off provides additional insurance against mortality
and castration anxiety.

from incestuous attachments. These efforts are usually more or less successful in the magician tales, but Meleager dies a victim of his maternal bondage, while Scylla's venture in adult love fails miserably. In any case, the issue is not unique to the external-soul stories, but appears in most folk tales involving family relations. The focus of the external-soul tale seems to be sex antagonism and biological continuity, and one would expect to find such stories most highly developed in societies where these traits are prominent.

Variant Types of External-Soul Myth

We might even find here a basis for differentiating between the two types of external-soul tale, hypothesizing that in the magician tales the concern with progeneration is more important than the sex antagonism, while in the magic lock tales the reverse is true. Two variables would serve as criteria here: (a) the extent to which the destruction of the soul looks like castration, rather than merely the killing of seed; (b) the extent to which it is the hero who is killed through the female's acts, instead of a villain figure.

The external-soul myth conveys the notion that an individual's narcissism—generally a man's—can be centered in an object external to himself, and that while this protects him from certain kinds of wounds and slights, it makes him in some ways more vulnerable. Since the greatest narcissistic wound is total extinction, the desire for immortality is at the center of all external-soul tales, and their manifest content expresses this. But narcissism in all forms is exacerbated by sexual antagonism, making it more likely that other, related concerns will be grafted onto the longing for immortality. Castration anxiety and doubts about sexual adequacy will influence the nature and structure of the myths.

If we compare two cultures prominently involved in the production of external-soul myths—classical Greece and medieval Islam—obsession with progeneration is a constant; variation in sex antagonism alone determines whether immortality or castration is thematically predominant. For the Greeks, as we have seen: "Everyone . . . had an interest in leaving a son after him, convinced that his immortal happiness depended upon it" [Fustel de Coulanges, p. 49]. Celibacy was "both for himself and for his ancestors . . . a sort of damnation" [*Ibid.*, p. 50; cf. also Lysias: "Eratosthenes" 33–34 and "Simon" 6–7; Pindar: *Olympian* x. 85–91; Plato: *Symposium* 208–9].

Patai notes a similar emphasis in the Middle East, from Biblical times to the present. Not only was a man's position during his lifetime dependent upon the number of his sons, but "not to leave his seed behind meant a death almost as personal as his own bodily demise" [Patai, 1959, pp. 71, 92, 253ff.].

Sex antagonism, on the other hand, while sharp in both cultures, seems to have had a more destructive impact upon the Greeks.[8] Both cultures were patriarchal and secluded their women, but the Middle Eastern patriarchy seems somehow more successful and less phobic than the Greek version. Males in both cultures were vain and narcissistic, but while the Greek male was often totally unable to relate sexually to a mature female, the Arab male was deeply involved in mature heterosexual attachments—intensely and ecstatically involved. The Middle Eastern system nonetheless developed a pathology of its own. For while capable of deep love for a woman, the Arab male seemed to find it impossible to trust her, and was continually racked by jealous doubts. Sexual inequality is always a two-edged sword, and there is much to suggest that it cut the Middle Eastern male—often and deeply.

---

[8] In all of the comparisons which follow I will be discussing characteristics for which there are large areas of overlap between the two cultures, and small but noticeable points of difference. There is probably some danger, in bringing the latter to light, of exaggerating them.

This distinction expresses itself in the external-soul tales. For the Middle Eastern male the fear was that the woman would betray him and "destroy" his seed. For the Greek male the fear was that she would destroy him as well, and in some cases this more primitive fear is so overwhelming that the other recedes into the background. A man is unlikely to be as acutely aware of his fear of foreign countries if he is also afraid to leave his house.

Let us now examine the two types of story in more detail, beginning with the "pure" Arabian Ifrit tale, and then tracing the embellishments generated by Greek pathology. In doing so I am not, of course, implying any chronological sequence, for while both types are undoubtedly of very early origin, the Arabian versions that are available to us are later than the Greek by perhaps two thousand years. This sequence is not a temporal but a synthetic one.

At the same time, the essential features of the Arab preoccupation—which one finds in the more urban and sophisticated *The Thousand Nights and a Night*—are all present in Biblical times. Patai, for example, notes the enormous emphasis on fertility in the book of Genesis, and then comments that "it is a peculiar feature of the patriarchal story that in the midst of all this pressure for fecundity three out of the four traditional mothers of the Hebrew nation were barren for long periods before, by the special grace of God, they were able to conceive and thus ensure the future of the promised seed" [Patai, 1959, p. 73]. From our perspective, of course, it is not peculiar at all. In what other way could a woman in so extreme a patriarchal society revenge herself upon her husband for the thankless role she played in it? One can imagine the resentful reluctance to feed these endless aspirations of men, despite fondness for the spouse and the dependence of the woman's own status and comfort on these aspirations. Conflict must have raged within her, particularly if she was competing with other wives and concubines, and it is small wonder that magic had often to be employed to tip the emotional balance away from masochistic sabotage and toward expedient submission.

But Patai makes another observation which is important for our understanding of the Arabian external-soul tale. He notes that "sterility is felt to be such a misfortune, such a crushing blow, that the religious Middle Eastern mind is involuntarily driven by it to soul-searching, to self-examination, and to the inevitable conclusion that some heinous sin must have brought it about" [*Ibid.*, p. 80]. This sin, it turns out, is adultery, or some comparable sexual transgression, and the barrenness caused by it is seen either as magical contamination or as divine retaliation. Anyone sterile is automatically suspected of adultery.

For a man, then, the barrenness of his wife is directly equated with his being cuckolded [*Ibid.*, p. 82], and one begins to suspect that the two concerns are really one and the same. Both sterility and adultery on the part of the wife challenge the man's sexual adequacy. Both, furthermore, endanger his biological immortality, for even if his wife does bear a child, it may not be his.[9]

The Arabian Jinni Tale

The Thousand Nights and a Night is rich in both preoccupations. The tale of Sayf-al-Muluk, from which I quoted the procedure whereby a Jinni safeguarded his soul, begins with the childlessness of a great king, and ends with the marriage of his son. As the story opens, the king is weeping and sitting on the floor, to the great terror of his nobles, who fear that such self-abasement may soon be externalized. The cause of his grief is made very clear:

[9] Similar assumptions underlie Gusii ideas of the supernatural consequences of adultery, which impinge upon the husband (causing him to become ill) or the child (causing illness or, to the unborn child, miscarriage), rather than upon the wife herself [B. Whiting, 1963, pp. 118–19].

Every one of these is happy and rejoiceth in his children, whilst I, I have no child, and to-morrow I die and leave my reign and throne and lands and hoards, and strangers will take them and *none will bear me in memory nor will there remain any mention of me in the world* [*op. cit.*, Vol. VII, p. 314. Italics mine].

O Wazir, I weep not for monies nor horses nor kingdoms nor aught else, but that I am become an old man, yea, very old nigh upon an hundred and fourscore years of age, and I have not been blessed with a child, male or female: so, when I die, they will bury me and *my trace will be effaced and my name cut off;* the stranger will take my throne and reign and none will ever make mention of my being [*Ibid.*, p. 316. Italics mine].

The wazir, who is in similar straits, decides to seek the help of Solomon, who provides the two with a magical formula to make their wives fertile. This formula requires the old king and his wazir to slay two serpents and give them to their wives to eat—fertility is thus made dependent upon prior resolution of the oral conflicts. The formula is in any case successful—sons being born to both king and wazir—and the overjoyed king feasts the entire populace, frees all prisoners, and declares a moratorium on taxes. All is not yet solved, however, since in later years the young prince, Sayf-al-Muluk, abandons his homosexual attachment to the wazir's son only to fall in love with a picture of a daughter of the Jann. The rest of the tale involves his adventures in search of this lady, who ultimately becomes his bride.

It is in the course of this journey that he encounters the Ifrit's prisoner, Daulat Khatun, whom he saves by destroying the Ifrit's external soul. In doing so he almost loses his own life and his future bride when the Ifrit's father wishes to take revenge. Ultimately, however, the prince achieves his goal: he marries the daughter of the Jann and simultaneously marries Daulat Khatun to his friend, the wazir's son.

Now there are one or two rather strange details in this story. We are somewhat unused to a hero rescuing a maiden he does not marry, and might suspect that in some earlier version of the tale the prisoner and the prince's bride were one and the same. Great care is now taken, however, to separate them, so that when Daulat Khatun speaks of the daughter of the Jann as her sister, we are obliged to hear a dull anecdote explaining that they are not blood sisters but only "milk sisters" [cf. Patai, *op. cit.*, p. 196]. Sayf-al-Muluk not only does not marry the rescued maiden, but in their travels together they sleep with a sword between them, like Tristan and Isolde.

The reason for this peculiarity is explained by another oddity. Daulat Khatun, after the manner of young ladies in patriarchal societies, loudly affirms her virginity, despite the fact that she was carried off naked by the Ifrit and has been his prisoner for an extensive period of time.

> When he is here, he eateth and drinketh and kisseth and huggeth me, but doth naught else with me, and I am a pure virgin, even as Allah Almighty created me [*The Book of the Thousand Nights and a Night*, Burton trans., VII, p. 349].

Our skepticism is no whit eased when the slaying of the Ifrit is later justified on the grounds that he was in the habit of carrying off young women and debauching them [*Ibid.*, Vol. VII, pp. 1ff.]. Apparently the Arab obsession with virginity [cf. Patai, 1959, pp. 66–70] does not allow even a secondary heroine to be deflowered before her marriage, and a primary heroine must not even be suspected of such a thing. An earlier and simpler tale, devoid of the two colorless secondary characters, was probably adjusted to meet this awkward problem, and the heroine displaced to the remote regions of the Jann, far above any suspicion of even involuntary defloration. One might wonder how Daulat Khatun was able to produce the traditional bloodstained "tokens of virginity," but such thoughts will never tarnish the prince's bride.

Sayf-al-Muluk's adventures are thus infused with the same fear of biological extinction voiced explicitly by his father—the anxiety itself projected onto the hapless Ifrit. And if the connections still seem somewhat uncertain, there is no difficulty in finding similar examples to elucidate them, in one of which, as we shall soon see, the external-soul emerges from its hiding place in a bizarre but revealing guise.

The beginning of a tale usually betrays the main psychological or emotional problem with which it is concerned.[10] If it says at the outset that it is about three brothers, or three sisters, one can be sure that sibling rivalry will be the prevailing issue. If it revolves around twelve sons and one daughter, then sex-role identification for the girl is the problem to be unraveled. Confronted with a poor woodcutter, hungry children, and their stepmother, one can expect to find oral deprivation and its consequences elaborated throughout the drama. My analysis of Sayf-al-Muluk is based on the same principle. May we not, then, make this assumption for *The Book of the Thousand Nights and a Night* as a whole? What caused the King Shahryar to marry a maiden each night and have her beheaded in the morning, until Shahrazad beguiled him with her repertory of folk tales?

The answer is given in the question. Such a device is employed only by a man who wants to guarantee fidelity—who wants to ensure that no other man has shared or will share his bride. Now many motives could engender such a concern: oedipal strivings, latent homosexuality, sibling rivalry—and all of these are important in the *Nights*. But they are secondary to the fanatical obsession with progeneration. Short of King Shahryar's ultimate (and self-defeating) device, the harem is the most extreme expression of this obsession, and points up

10 Often in the form of a trivial and easily forgotten detail, as Peller observes [1959, pp. 417, 420–21].

the fact that sexual fidelity per se is not at issue—rulers were relatively indifferent to the sexual activities in which their wives and concubines might indulge with their eunuchs and each other, since these activities could not result in pregnancy.

A glance at the events leading up to Shahryar's "final solution" will illuminate this argument. The story opens with King Shahryar's younger brother, the Shah Zaman, preparing to visit him. Returning to the palace for something forgotten, Shah Zaman finds "the Queen, his wife, asleep on his own carpet-bed, embracing with both arms a black cook of loathsome aspect and foul with kitchen grease and grime" [*The Book of the Thousand Nights and a Night, op. cit.*, Vol. I, p. 4]. After hacking the pair to pieces, he proceeds on his journey, deep in melancholy. But soon after arriving at his brother's palace, he recovers his health and spirits somewhat upon discovering that King Shahryar is being treated no better:

> But the Queen, who was left alone, presently cried out in a loud voice, "Here to me, O my lord Saeed!" and then sprang with a drop-leap from one of the trees a big slobbering blackamoor with rolling eyes which showed the whites, a truly hideous sight. He walked boldly up to her and threw his arms around her neck while she embraced him as warmly; then he bussed her and winding his legs around hers, as a button-loop clasps a button, he threw her and enjoyed her [*Ibid.*, p. 6].

Shah Zaman now reflects that since "there is no woman but who cuckoldeth her husband, then the curse of Allah upon one and all and upon the fools who lean against them for support or who put the reins of conduct in their hands" [*Ibid.*, p. 7]. Much cheered, he eats a hearty meal and informs his brother of their identical misfortunes. The two then propose to wander over the earth to find someone "to whom the like calamity has happened; and if we find none then will death be more welcome to us than life" [*Ibid.*, p. 10].

Thus far we are struck by the extent to which these misfortunes are narcissistically and invidiously defined. It is not the loss of love which is uppermost but the humiliation and disgrace, and one can be cheered by finding a companion in misfortune. The ultimate disaster is having this humiliation reserved for oneself alone. But let us continue the story.

Before traveling very far the two brothers are startled by a huge Jinni who rises out of the sea carrying a crystal coffer on his head. Putting the remnants of their royal dignity aside, the two brothers swarm up a tree, and from this post observe the following tableau:

> [The Jinni] set down the coffer on its bottom and out of it drew a casket, with seven padlocks of steel, which he unlocked with seven keys of steel he took from beside his thigh, and out of it a young lady to come was seen, white-skinned and of winsomest mien, of stature fine and thin, and bright as though a moon of the fourteenth night she had been, or the sun raining lively sheen [*Ibid.*, pp. 10–11].

Then follows a scene of the purest farce. The Jinni (or Ifrit) reveals to us that he kidnaped this young lady (who is not a Jinniyah) on her bride night, that he dotes on her, that she is of noble lineage, that it was of utmost importance to him that he take her maidenhead, and that he believes himself to be the only being to have enjoyed her. He then announces that he wishes to sleep and puts his head on her lap. She, however, spies the two brothers, and immediately slips away from the Ifrit and insists that they come down and copulate with her. After some conversation, in which the brothers protest that their fear of the Ifrit renders them unfit for the task, and each tries to persuade the other to accept priority, the woman all the while threatening to arouse the Ifrit upon them if they defer any longer, they finally do her bidding. She then takes from them their seal rings, which she adds to a string of others, belonging to "five hundred and seventy men who have all futtered me upon the horns of this foul, this foolish, this filthy Ifrit." Commenting upon the Jinni's attempts to guard her chastity she adds: "what so woman willeth the same she fulfilleth however man nilleth" [*Ibid.*, pp. 12–13].

The brothers are highly impressed that the Ifrit, so much more powerful than they, is in an even worse plight, and decide to seek revenge on women's malice, which "hath no mate in might." Shahryar then slays his entire harem and begins his three-year regimen of decimating the virgins of the city with his one-day marriages.

This is not the end of infidelities in the *Nights*, however. In the stories of the first twenty nights alone there are six additional adulteries, four real and two imagined. Of these, three involve Negro slaves, one a Turk (probably a late addition, according to Burton), and one a woman betraying an Ifrit with a man. In only one is the lover of the same ethnic background as the husband, and even here his social status is considerably lower. In three of the real and one of the imagined adulteries, the woman is killed upon being found out, usually hacked to death immediately by the husband. In the remaining real case, she is transformed into a mule, while in the final (imaginary) case she is beaten by her husband with such ferocity that she bears the scars for the rest of her life, although the pair are later reconciled.

It is clear, then, that the Arab entrusts his "external soul" to women only of necessity and with the most overpowering trepidation and suspicion. He takes every precaution to exclude all other males from the sanctuary but is ever troubled with obsessive fantasies that his efforts have failed. This is the most obvious meaning of the container-within-container aspect of the external-soul tale—each container represents some further precaution: the veils, the secluded harem, harem guards, harem walls, spies, and so on. This is brought out very clearly in the story of the cuckolded Jinni, who keeps his bride in a casket within a coffer, locked with seven steel padlocks and hidden at the bottom of the sea.

A concern with masculine potency may be responsible for the frequency with which Negroes appear as the object of adulterous feminine passion. In a footnote to the first of these incidents Burton argues that Arab men take care to keep Negroes away from their wives because the latter are believed to be tempted by the large genitals of Negro men, and by other physical attributes tending toward increased sexual gratification. Burton, who seems to have shared their preoccupations, claimed that Arab men were below the European average in penis size [*Ibid.*, p. 6]. All of this is reminiscent of the prevailing group fantasies of our own tormented Southland. The puritanical relish with which these adulteries are revealed resembles the lip-smacking horror of the embellished rape stories which lynch mobs use to massage themselves into their highly sexualized rages.

Fears of sexual inadequacy are not the only source for the fascination with Negro adulterers, however. Generally they are also slaves or otherwise of very low status, thus increasing the narcissistic humiliation and the insistent invidiousness of Arab sexual relations. But there is still a third reason, related to the other two. Should such an infidelity bear fruit, the offspring would tend to provide a visible proof of the adultery. The Arabs were first and foremost breeders of animals, and their views of human relationships were strongly colored by this fact. The Negro adulterers are never described as handsome or strapping, but always as physically repellent, dirty, and diseased. This not only serves to intensify the husband's humiliation, but also accentuates the blow delivered to his hopes for progeny of whom he can be proud.

It is perhaps for this reason that women, who hold such inferior status in Arab society, seem to have a virtual monop-

oly on magical powers in the *Nights*. Only women can transform people into animals, can make and break spells, enchant
cities, battle successfully with Ifrits (directly, as well as in the
manner of the lady in the casket), and so on. Is not this
"magic" the ability to give birth, and to determine in secret
whose child it will be? In one story, for example, a man's
wife, discovered in bed with a Negro slave, transforms her
husband into a dog by sprinkling a little water over him and
muttering spells [*The Book of the Thousand Nights and a
Night, op. cit.*, p. 36]. Is this not a way of expressing the
power that women have to determine the biological future of
the male—the replica of himself that he expects in his heir
shockingly transformed to something indisputably alien and
undesirable? It is thus a variant of the changeling myth—both
emphasizing the feared shock of a long-postponed revelation.
The woman is a magician because she can keep a man in the
dark for so long, "transform" his child into someone else's, or
into a monster, without his being aware of it.

This is why the enchantments and transformations can only
be broken by women. The husband changed into a dog
is freed by another woman, who then changes the wife into
a mule. This is characteristic of such tales. Generally the
other woman is a young virgin, reflecting the notion that the
pain and loss inflicted by a barren or faithless wife (and, as
Patai shows, these are essentially equated in the Middle Eastern mind) can only be cured by starting anew with a young,
fruitful, and innocent one. The reality to which it corresponds is the practice of taking a concubine when the wife
proves unfertile. This is illustrated in the First Shaykh's
Story [*Ibid.*, pp. 27–31]. A man takes a concubine after living
thirty years with a barren wife, and has a son by her. The
wife transforms both into cattle and the concubine is
butchered. The son is saved and disenchanted, however, by
a young virgin, who then changes the wife into a gazelle. The

young virgin marries the son, thus illustrating her true role as guarantor of biological continuation. Great pains are also taken to emphasize her virginal modesty: as in the previous story, when the animal is brought in to her she veils herself and protests to her father that he cheapens her honor by bringing in strange men to her—it is in this way that the enchantment is made known. Chastity is thus the antidotal magic that solves all such problems.

This perceived power of women to make or break a man's narcissistic dreams also helps explain the lack of sympathy often exhibited for kidnaped brides, like the Ifrit's prisoner in the sunken casket. Although one might feel that her manifold cuckolding of the Ifrit is an apt revenge for his having captured and imprisoned her—and might admire her ingenuity in finding a way to retaliate in her state of utter helplessness—she is viewed with alarm and an almost superstitious awe by the two kings, who are impressed less by her plight than by her power.

Nothing could better display the ambiguous and ambivalent nature of the patriarchal enslavement and seclusion of women. To an outsider, the striking aspect of both the Arab folktale and the Arab reality is the lack of choice held by the woman in all matters pertaining to marriage and sexual relationships. No notice is paid to her preferences, and even if carried off against her will she is expected to remain faithful. Furthermore, a virtual prisoner, her opportunities were at all times severely circumscribed.

Yet from the viewpoint of the Arab male, the really impressive fact is that the woman can choose and does choose—possessing a fearful power to decide whom she will love and whose child she will bear. All the restrictions and precautions he imposes upon her are simply his impotent gestures toward curtailing this awesome power. Do what they will, the external soul can be found and destroyed if a woman really wishes to do so, for it is always a woman who knows the secret and must betray it if the soul is to be destroyed. "This wretched Jinni wotteth not that Destiny may not be averted nor hindered by aught, and that whatso woman willeth the same she fulfilleth however man nilleth. . . . For wonderful is he and right worthy of our praise, who from wiles of female wits kept him safe and kept him sound" [*Ibid.*, pp. 12-13].

This power is dramatized in the *Nights* by presenting the choice as a completely capricious one, even at times perverse. A woman married to a rich and handsome prince prefers a wretched, diseased slave, despite the fact that she is a powerful sorceress. Nor is it simply to injure her husband that she makes this choice, as would most certainly be the case if the tale were Greek. The love for the slave, although presented in the most unsympathetic fashion imaginable, is deep and lasting, involving intense devotion and self-sacrifice.

I will return later to this interesting concession by the Arab male to what he obviously views as the most despicable kind of woman, since it lies at the heart of the difference between Arab and Greek misogyny. Let us first examine the origin of this fantasy about the feminine ability to make perverse choices—to set the lowly above the exalted.

The most obvious interpretation is that it is based on the unpredictability of mother love, as contrasted to the rigid tradition of inheritance by the eldest son. Patai points out the preoccupation with sibling rivalry in the Middle East, and suggests, citing both the Old Testament and modern ethnographic studies, that it is in part due to a deliberate tendency on the part of parents to provoke it [1959, pp. 215-20]. In the Bible, however (in which the rivalry of brothers is the single most prominent family motif), this rivalry is always in relation to the patriarchal father, who tends to maintain a stubborn preference for his last-born. Since women are so assiduously shoved into the background in the Old Testament, it is difficult to ascertain what part women played in this preference. I can merely point out that: (1) a mother will generally be seen by an older child as favoring a younger one, whether she does or not, because the dependency of the infant calls forth more frequent and clear-cut demonstrations of love and nurturance; (2) in any case, a mother is never obliged to favor the heir and often will not —as heir he belongs to the father, not to her, and will inherit whatever resentments the father has provoked; (3) there is a tradition, in the Middle East, of this status reversal in the family, one on which Christianity, with its Prodigal Son and its last-shall-be-first philosophy, is founded; (4) the *Nights* are permeated with tales of a woman rejecting a rich, legitimate, and exalted spouse for a poor, illicit, and lowly lover. Considered all together, it seems likely that part of this fear of feminine betrayal comes from a maternal source.

One factor that accentuated the fear of feminine whim was the fact that a man generally married a bride about whom he knew nothing. This was mitigated if a man married his father's brother's daughter, since the couple would then have grown up in the same home. For this and a number of other reasons, summarized succinctly by Patai [1959, pp. 27–31], patrilateral parallel-cousin marriage has always been the most favored form of marriage in the Middle East. Proverbs express the practical economic advantage of such marriages, their general success, and the fact that the husband knows what he is getting for a wife [*Ibid.*, pp. 29–30]. In the *Nights*, the greatest lovers are often parallel cousins, and the term "father's brother's daughter," which means "wife" to the Arab, is used as a term of endearment by unrelated spouses.

It is therefore somewhat surprising to see how often even these marriages turn out badly in the *Nights*—how, despite the great love and affection apparently existing between the couple, the wife turns out to be unfaithful, or a sorceress, or both. Nothing reveals the persistent gnawing doubt, and the fear of the "might of women's malice,"[11] as do these tales in which a parallel-cousin marriage takes a turn of this kind. It is like saying, "even a childhood playmate may be untrustworthy and dangerous."

An excellent example is the story of the Ensorcelled Prince [*The Book of the Thousand Nights and a Night, op. cit.*, pp. 69ff.]. The prince begins by saying that his cousin, whom he married, "loved me with such abounding love that whenever I was absent she ate not and she drank not until she saw me again." After five years, however, he discovers that her feeling for him has abated somewhat ("I loathe thee and I loathe thy whole body, and my soul turneth in disgust from cohabiting with thee") and is now directed toward another, who lives, it seems, in a mud hut amid the rubbish heaps outside the city, "a hideous negro slave with his upper lip like the cover of a pot, and his lower like an open pot. . . . He was to boot a leper and a paralytic, lying upon a strew of sugar-cane trash and wrapped in . . . the foulest rags and tatters." Considerable detail is added to increase the humiliation: the wife abases herself, the slave curses her, and gives her the leavings of his dinner to eat (rat bones and beer dregs from the slop pot). When she climbs in bed with the slave the prince starts to administer the usual remedy, but makes a botch of it and only succeeds in paralyzing, silencing, and weakening the slave so that he is "unable to do her love-service." In true talionic revenge, the wife turns the prince to stone from the waist down, and enchants the entire city, turning the citizens

---

[11] This malice was a very concrete phenomenon among harem women, who display incredible sadism toward men in the *Nights*, often purely for amusement [see, e.g., Vol. I, pp. 286–87, 324–28]. The emotional dilemma of the Arab male arises from his seeking a genuine love relationship with a woman he has callously imprisoned in his mistrust of women. This is reflected in the magician tales: the magician reveals his secret because of his blind love for his captive, despite the most obvious signs that she will take full advantage of it, and he is heartbroken when she does.

to fish, and so forth. Daily, for a period of years, she scourges her husband and nurses her paramour until tricked by a wandering hero into disenchanting the prince and his city.

One might wonder how the Arab male maintains his romantic absorption in women in the face of such mistrust. Why does he not flee in horror like the Greek male, and reserve his deeper sexual and emotional attachments for men? Certainly homosexuality has never been uncommon in the Middle East (it is a frequent theme in the *Nights*), but sex antagonism seems more often to be handled within the context of a determined heterosexuality. This is illustrated by the reaction of males in the two cultures to the genitalia of women:

"Then she stripped off her outer gear and she threw open her chemise from the neck downwards and showed her parts genital and all the rondure of her hips. When Badr-al-Din saw the glorious sight his desires were roused . . ." [*Ibid.*, p. 222]. Badr-al-Din's reaction is typical of masculine appreciation of women in the *Nights* [cf. also Vol. VIII, pp. 91–93], and in marked contrast to Greek Medusa fears—best exemplified by the myth of Alcestis and Admetus (see Chapter I).

One source of this difference might be that the Arab bride, although just as youthful as the Greek one, was less likely—because of the prevalence of parallel-cousin marriage—to find herself in the home of a stranger. This allowed her to feel somewhat more comfortable in the marital relationship, despite the physical restrictions to which she was subject. And since this custom also reduced male anxieties, she was likely to receive more gratification from her husband. The self-perpetuating cycle was hence somewhat less pathological than that of the Greeks.

The form taken by family pathology in the Middle East may also be understood in this way. Since the mother was less desperate in her marital relationship, her tensions did not compel her to behave in a destructive manner to all her male

children. Aware that she could be loved, she felt able to love
in return, and could "choose" (not necessarily in a conscious
sense) which son to love and which to reject, as opposed to
the Greek mother who was driven to hate and depend upon
all her male children, willy-nilly. Since the Arab mother did
have her share of destructive resentment, this "choice" was of
rather vital importance to the sons, and hence the peculiar
violence of sibling rivalry in Middle Eastern culture.[12] Family
pathology in the Middle East, in other words, was more selective—only certain sons had to pay the price of patriarchal
despotism over women.

This difference bears a mythological parallel. The Arab
villainess has magical powers and clear, though unacceptable,
life goals. The Greek villainess is less likely to have such
powers and more likely to be a devouring monster, if immortal, or a raging, impulsive termagant if mortal. There is
more *id* and less *ego* in the Greek villainess—she is driven by
mad desires and insatiable needs, and cannot really manage her
life. The female bogies are *compelled* to devour and destroy—
they cannot help themselves; and this is a true reflection of
the Bad Mother in Hellas. The magical powers of the Arab
villainess simply reflect the superior ability of the Arab
woman to choose, to select, to love whom she pleased and
hate whom she pleased, to control herself and her environment. The villainess of the *Nights* is on the whole capable,
while the Greek villainess more often is not, at least where
her own interests are at stake. The closest the Greeks can
come to inventing a villainess of the Arab type is Medea, and
even she, although a sorceress, is far more self-destructive
and out of control than her Arab counterparts. This, of
course, makes her more rather than less frightening; the
arbitrary and capricious quality of the Arab villainess is eerie,
but one feels she could always be bribed; while the Greek

[12] Rivalry among sisters is no more prominent in the *Nights* than in any
other collection of folklore.

bogie or tormented mortal is unable to respond to any kind
of rational appeal. This difference seems to be a reflection of
the stronger ego of the Arab mother.[13]

One might even speculate that the Greek family pattern
was simply a decadent or corroded form of the Middle Eastern one, a form in which the emphasis on human fertility—a
saving grace and part of the raison d'être of exaggerated
patriarchies—had atrophied, leaving a rather meaningless structural shell behind it, unmitigated, for some reason, by parallel-cousin marriage. The most striking characteristic of the
Greek terrain was, as Kitto notes [1960, pp. 29–30], its
variability, which lent itself in very early times to a complex
and versatile economy. Can we not imagine that one of the
many invaders of early times was a tribe of pastoral nomads,
who conquered and imposed their family structure upon the
natives with whom they intermarried—that their descendants
involuntarily perpetuated this structure in response to the
psychological pressures it persistently generated, despite its
irrelevance to their more diversified economy? This is historical reconstruction of the crudest kind, however, and one
can only guess at the complex processes that translate one
family system into another.

Scylla and Nisus

This brings us back to the Nisus and Pterelaus tales, which
are of particular interest because they seem intermediate between the more classic external-soul story and that of Meleager. Up to the moment of betrayal, they resemble the Arab
stories rather closely, except that the betrayed and the be-
trayer are father and daughter rather than villain and captured

[13] Both cultures recognize the "primeval matriarchy" of early childhood,
the Greeks in the myths of Lemnos, the Amazons, and powerful goddesses;
the Arabs in innumerable strange lands ruled by queens, private courts of
teasing women, and so on. The faraway "land of women" is an important
memory in patriarchal societies.

concubine, thus exhibiting in undisguised form the cross-sex parent-child hostility which so dominates Greek fantasy. The most characteristically Greek feature, however, is the reaction of the conquering hero to his devoted feminine fifth column:

> Now Nisus perished through his daughter's treachery. For he had a purple hair on the middle of his head, and an oracle ran that when it was pulled out he should die; and his daughter Scylla fell in love with Minos and pulled out the hair. But when Minos had made himself master of Megara, he tied the damsel by the feet to the stern of the ship and drowned her [Apollodorus: iii. 15. 8. For the virtually identical Pterelaus tale see ii. 4. 7].

While some say that Minos had Scylla killed [Pausanias: ii. 34. 7], and others that he did not execute but only abandoned her [Ovid: *Metamorphoses* viii. 6ff.; Hyginus: *Fabulae* 198], all agree that Minos reacted with great revulsion, just as if he were not interested in conquering cities and seducing pretty women. Identification with the plight of the lovelorn Scylla [cf. Ovid: *loc. cit.*] was so impossible in the fifth century that Aeschylus drops the love theme entirely and suggests that the princess was bribed with a necklace [*The Choephori*, 612–22].

Thus while the Nisus tale resembles the Arabian type in its preoccupation both with feminine control over masculine immortality and with the attempt of the woman to free herself from an oedipal attachment to the father, it differs in three respects: (1) it is more direct in its concern with hatred between parent and opposite-sexed child; (2) the feminine attack is more blatantly castrating; and (3) the crude attempt of the female to achieve mature sexuality and freedom from oedipal fixation is a total failure, foundering on the infantilism of the Greek male. In a sense, the Nisus story may be viewed as an ironic commentary on the plight of the Greek woman—tearing herself with pangs of doubt and distress from her ambivalent and unresolved attachment to an ephemeral father, only to find herself in worse straits with her squeamish husband.

One missing link in the interpretation of the Nisus tale is the manner in which the male concern with immortality became attached to a father-daughter relationship in the first place. It is not enough to say that family preoccupations were "tacked on" to an external-soul myth—we need to understand how this specific preoccupation could become associated with this particular myth. One can see how a wife's infidelity could deprive a man of his own progeny, or a mother's possessiveness and hostility destroy his potency;[14] but how can a daughter constitute a threat of this kind? Whatever incestuous reservations a father might have about his daughter's love for a stranger, it can hardly affect his concern for immortality, except in a positive direction. Is the father-daughter pair chosen, like the parallel cousins, because it is putatively the safest, and hence reveals the futility of all protective measures; or is there some other basis? A possible answer to this puzzle is supplied by Fustel de Coulanges, who calls attention to the fact that in Greece, as in much of the ancient world, if a man had no son his daughter was forced by law to marry her nearest male relative (who was also his heir *pro tem*), even if both parties had to divorce their spouses in order to do so. Furthermore, the son born of this required union became, in law and custom, her *father's* son, and followed his worship and performed his funeral rites. When he came of age it was the son and not his mother or biological father who inherited the patrimony of his grandfather [Fustel de Coulanges, *op. cit.*, pp. 76–77]. Thus the daughter, in order to satisfy her father's need for progeny and immortality, might be forced to abandon her own children and con-

---

[14] Frazer cites a modern Greek magic-lock story involving a son destroyed by his mother [1959, p. 596].

tract a new marriage with an unwilling husband—a marriage from which she gained absolutely nothing, but in fact ultimately lost another child. It would not be surprising if tension were to arise between father and daughter around this issue, or if she were tempted to refuse him this son and elope with a stranger or her original husband.

Meleager

With Meleager the pathology is still deeper, perhaps because the myth concerns the mother-son relationship. Meleager not only fails to shed his attachment to his mother, but dies of it directly. It is interesting to follow the course of this tale from its rather simple beginnings to its full flowering in the later mythographers.

In the Homeric version [*Iliad* ix. 529–99] there is no mention of the brand or of Meleager's death (presumably omitted out of tact, since the story is being told to Achilles as an inducement to battle), but only of the mutual hostility between mother and son (Althaea curses him and prays to the Erinyes and other chthonic powers for his destruction). Later sources elaborate the incipient sex antagonism in the tale, muting the role of the perfectly feminine Cleopatra and heightening that of Atalanta [cf. Bacchylides: v. 93–152; Aeschylus: *The Choephori* 604–11; Hyginus: *Fabulae* 174, 185].

The version given by Apollodorus [i. 8. 2] is as follows:

Althaea had also a son Meleager, by Oeneus, though they say that he was begotten by Ares. It is said that, when he was seven days old, the Fates came and declared that Meleager should die when the brand burning on the hearth was burnt out. On hearing that, Althaea snatched up the brand and deposited it in a chest. Meleager grew up to be an invulnerable and gallant man, but came by his end in the following way. In sacrificing the first fruits of the annual crops of the country to all the gods Oeneus forgot Artemis alone. But she in her wrath sent a boar of extraordinary size and strength, which prevented the land from being sown and destroyed the cattle and the people that fell in with it. To attack this boar Oeneus called together all the noblest men of Greece, and promised that to him who should kill the beast he would give the skin as a prize. . . . When Cepheus and Ancaeus and some others disdained to go a-hunting with a woman, Meleager compelled them to follow the chase with her, for he desired to have a child also by Atalanta, though he had to wife Cleopatra, daughter of Idas and Marpessa. . . . Atalanta was the first to shoot the boar in the back with an arrow . . . but Meleager killed it by a stab in the flank, and on receiving the skin gave it to Atalanta. Nevertheless the sons of Thestius, thinking scorn that a woman should get the prize in the face of men, took the skin from her, alleging that it belonged to them by right of birth if Meleager did not choose to take it. But Meleager in a rage slew the sons of Thestius and gave the skin to Atalanta. However, from grief at the slaughter of her brothers Althaea kindled the brand, and Meleager immediately expired.

Althaea's response may seem strange to us, since we are accustomed to seeing sororal loyalty subordinated to mother love. But such lateral emphasis is pronounced in any unilineal descent system. Although her son may serve at a personal, emotional level as a narcissistic extension of herself, in terms of objective social criteria of status, his successes or failures redound to his father's credit or dismay, while hers are tied to her own father and brothers.

Ovid—who, for all his embellishments, seldom strays far from the psychological core of a myth—stresses this contrast in the tortured soliloquy of Althaea in the *Metamorphoses:*

> Should I stand still *while happy Oeneus*
> *Takes pleasure in the glory of his son—*
> And this while sons of Thestius fall dead?
> Shall he be careless, proud of his success,
> And, *big with pride,* rule over Calydon?

> No, that is not my will: let him go down,
> *Down with his father's hopes, his wealth, his throne.*
> [*loc. cit.:* viii. 486–98. Gregory trans.
> Italics mine.]

Thus far we have simply an intensification of the Arabian theme of male vulnerability through feminine betrayal. This is expressed in three ways: first, through Althaea's adultery, by which she frustrates Oeneus' immortality; second, by the burning of the brand, a symbolic castration; third, by the destruction of Meleager, wherewith she destroys Oeneus' sociological child just as she previously "destroyed" his biological one. Meleager is the "brand" of Oeneus, the external symbol of his power and status, as Ovid so dramatically points out.

But the theme of sex antagonism is further elaborated. It is the man-hating virgin huntress, Artemis, who sends the boar in the first place, to gore, castrate, and disembowel the flower of Greek youth; and the warlike and masculine heroine of the story, Atalanta, is a carbon copy of the goddess. Like Artemis, she is a virgin huntress, and punishes the attentions of would-be suitors with cruel death. Furthermore, her own history reveals the origin of this attitude, for it is said [Apollodorus: iii. 9.2] that her father had wished for a boy, and had exposed her on a mountain top, where she was suckled by a bear which the goddess sent to her aid. In her refusal to marry, in her competitions with men (beating them at racing and at wrestling), and in her general masculine demeanor, Atalanta both complies with this wish and expresses her resentment of it.

Sex antagonism also appears in the conflict between Atalanta and Ancaeus, the boastful hunter who initially disdains to hunt with a woman. When the lanky virgin draws first blood from the boar, Ancaeus and his fellow men are put to shame, and angered at having been shown up as cautious and clumsy. In Ovid's rendering [*Metamorphoses* viii. 380–402],

Ancaeus then makes a long speech about teaching everyone how to hunt and demonstrating how vastly superior a man's strength is to a woman's. He not only taunts Atalanta with the inadequacy of her arrows, but also sneers at Artemis, and promises to kill the boar with his heavy axe. This phallic vanity leads to the usual outcome, however, for the boar dodges and gores him to death.

Meleager is a hero because he upholds the honor of men, and kills the boar before Atalanta can. He is also a hero because he defeats the goddess Artemis by destroying her tusked executioner. Ultimately, like other heroes, he is destroyed by a woman—in this case, without disguise, his own mother. The mother-son theme is peculiarly Greek, as is the fusion of seduction and hatred in the symbolism of the burning brand. It is perhaps unnecessary to elaborate on the hostile side of this ambivalence; nor is it exceptionally difficult to see its sexual aspect, inasmuch as Meleager comes into the world with his externalized and vulnerable phallus burning cheerily inside the maternal hearth. One might be tempted to argue that the entire episode is simply a picturesque way of saying that Meleager was consumed with oedipal passion from the day he was born. If it is a son's fantasy, however, it is an accusatory one, since the fire and the power to ignite it are hers. Meleager is consumed by Althaea's passion, from which his own is derived.

One might think of the Fates as saying to Althaea, "your sexual arousal of your son will destroy him if you do not inhibit it." In a sense she heeds the advice, but note that the brand is now hidden in her chest, and if we become too mechanical in our symbolic interpretations we can easily fall into the error of assuming that one symbol of incestuous intercourse has merely been substituted for another. Alternatively, one might see both fire and chest as ways of expressing Althaea's desire to reverse Meleager's birth, to destroy him and take him back into her womb—a hungry, devouring unwillingness to part from anything or tolerate an autonomous being, especially a male. But one must also take into account the fact that a fire is *not* a chest, and the substitution has extremely serious consequences for our hero. While fire is destructive, a chest is protective.

When Meleager becomes enamored of another woman, however, to the extent of insulting and eventually killing Althaea's brothers, her narcissism is doubly wounded, and the sublimation breaks down. The desire both to possess him and to destroy him can no longer be contained, and are fused in a single act. She plunges the brand into the flames, and Meleager perishes, with symptoms that bear a suspicious resemblance to those of a perforated ulcer [Pausanias: x. 31. 3–4; Ovid: *Metamorphoses* viii. 515ff.].

The Meleager myth portrays a futile masculine effort to achieve freedom from maternal involvement. Meleager must prove and establish his manliness in hunting and daring exploits, and when he chooses a woman it must be one as unlike his mother as possible, one who lives a life completely undomestic and masculine—woodsy, vagrant, and free:

> Her lovely face seemed boyish for a virgin
> And yet was far too girlish for a boy,
> And when the Calydonian hero saw her,
> Love at first sight had turned his heart to fire.
> [*Ibid.*, viii. 322–25. Gregory trans.]

The demands of his uncles threaten Meleager's liberation, however, since they reaffirm his attachment to his mother. For Meleager, all love is mother love and "turns his heart to fire" in a very literal sense.

It is interesting to compare this view of Meleager with the one in Homer. Here there is no hypermasculine reaction-formation, no preference for boyish virgins. Meleager is quietly married to an ordinary woman named Cleopatra, and his maternal dependence is expressed very simply in his reluctance to get out of bed and fight the army led by his uncles.

Conclusion

I began this discussion of the external-soul myth with the suggestion that the destruction of the external soul symbolized masculine fear of the power of the female to prevent or destroy the progeny of the male. Let us now return to Zeus, Hera, and Dionysus and examine the outcome of the Semele incident with this in mind. Hera's attempt to destroy the unborn Dionysus is a manifest attack on Zeus, and an effort to undermine the extension of his godhood—these motives are usually made explicit in the telling of the tale. Zeus himself is too powerful, but through his divine offspring the core of his narcissism may be wounded, and his cavalier treatment of his spouse avenged. But now observe how Zeus counters this attack: "snatching the six-month abortive child from the fire, (he) sewed it in his thigh." As in the Meleager story, the child is rescued from the devouring fire of feminine passion. But unlike Meleager, Dionysus is separated from women altogether, and is reborn from a male. This, then, is the ultimate denial of the external-soul problem—the child is no longer external and vulnerable because Zeus manages to dispense with the woman altogether, and bears his own child. The external soul has been internalized.

CHAPTER IX

Identification with
the Aggressor: Dionysus

III. THE ATTACK ON THE NEONATE

As RANK [1952] first pointed out so dramatically, attempts to destroy infant gods and heroes are not uncommon in the mythologies of Europe and the Mediterranean civilizations, nor indeed, of the entire world. It is more rare, however, for the agent of destruction to be a woman, and even more unusual for the destruction to be successful, as it is in the Orphic story of the birth and death of Zagreus (one of the many primitive gods absorbed by Dionysus). In this myth, Zeus copulated with Persephone in serpent-form, as he had earlier done with his mother Rhea, and as he was later to do with Semele [Nonnos: *Dionysiaca* vii. 328–33]. From this union sprang the horned god Zagreus-Dionysus, who briefly occupied the throne of Zeus. But jealous Hera instigated the Titans to attack, rend, and devour the infant child as he innocently regarded himself in a mirror. This they did, all but his "heart" which was rescued by Athene, and, as we have seen, formed the basis for his rebirth (Kerényi, 1960, pp. 252–56; Nonnos: vi. 169–210; Diodorus Siculus: iii. 62 |.

Thus far we are on familiar ground. A serpent-cursed child is partially rescued by a boyish virgin, who retrieves his phallic pride from its terror-stricken deflation by the destructive mother. It is a tribute to the pervasiveness of this conflict that it could thus Hellenize and feminize a ritual and myth which in its original totemistic form—i.e., sans Hera, Persephone, and Athene—was unimaginably remote from such concerns. The tale is in the end similar to that of Meleager—a vulnerable boy with a devouring mother who almost destroys his masculinity, which is only salvaged by the love of a not-too-feminine woman who is sexually undemanding.

An additional word or two might be said about the equation between heart and phallus, which was discussed in Chapter VIII. In that instance the equation was a manifest one, but since rescue of or attacks upon the heart as an isolated organ are rather common in mythology one might ask whether such an equation should generally be made, or at least, what the organs have in common symbolically and why one should be substituted for the other. Since myths do not in general reveal such fastidiousness there seems to be no particular reason for assuming a "displacement upward" on grounds of prudery, but such an unvarnished substitution does imply some kind of defensive process. Note that the displacement is not only "upward" but also "inward," and this is perhaps the key to the matter: we may be dealing here with a kind of external-soul-in-reverse.

The Theme of the Attacked Heart

The external-soul tales do not really resolve the question they pose: whether it is safer to carry one's narcissistic libidinal cash on one's person or to put it in a bank somewhere. In some tales it is deposited in a womb and invested in a child, in others it is retained in the phallus itself, but both methods come to grief. I have already suggested that the latter approach is the more infantile and anxious of the two, and it would seem to follow from this that walling up the "soul" within the heart, taking it from the outside and sealing it up inside, is the most regressive of all.

Now it might be objected that it is more "natural" for the heart to be the vessel of the soul and the symbol of the individual's emotional vulnerability. In this context, however, "natural" must be distilled into "elementary," for most adults do invest their libido in objects, and when one sees a psychotic person or one totally absorbed in a painful disease he is called narcissistic, and it is said that his libido is withdrawn from love-objects and concentrated in the ego. Freud asserts: "so long as he suffers he ceases to love. . . . The sick man withdraws his libidinal cathexes back upon his own ego, and sends them forth again when he recovers. 'Concentrated is his soul,' says W. Busch, of the poet suffering from toothache, 'in his jaw-tooth's aching hole' " [Freud, 1914, p. 39]. The heart-penis-seed dimension thus expresses increasing trust—increasing willingness to cathect objects outside oneself.

But why the penis, and why the heart? Why does such a fundamental concern express itself in genital terms? Primarily because it is only through procreation that one avoids the ultimate narcissistic wound, death. The individual is confronted with a dilemma—in order to satisfy his most cherished narcissistic wish (to live forever) he must relinquish some of his narcissism and invest libido in others. In Briffault's memorable words: "Mankind cannot have both; men must choose between the moon and the banana" [1959, p. 211]. The myth of Dionysus' self-procreation through the preservation of his heart is thus a fantasy of circumventing this dilemma: he does not cathect any objects yet still achieves immortality, without committing his penis or his seed to the tender mercies of a woman [cf. Mead, 1955, p. 58]; in fact, as we have seen, he virtually manages without the aid of a woman at all since his ultimate birth is from the thigh of Zeus.

When I say that the Meleager and Nisus tales are more regressed than the Jinni tales, I am recognizing the reluctance expressed therein to entrust the phallus to a woman—in particular, to relinquish the sexual secretion. This is in itself a narcissistic withdrawal of libidinal cathexis—the libido is instead invested, as Freud says, "in the organ which engages his attention" [Freud, 1914, p. 40]. But instead of being a diseased or painful organ, it is that organ which represents the narcissistic dilemma itself—whether to give of oneself and thus survive oneself, or to hold back and protect oneself. For the male, the penis must always, for this reason, be a major focus of narcissistic concern.

In the soul-in-phallus myth the male has drawn his libido back upon himself, but upon that part which is most outside of himself, most often entrusted to another, and therefore most vulnerable. The soul-in-heart myth goes one step further —the libido is withdrawn from the penis and walled up safely inside, where it cannot be reached. Yet this libido retains associative remnants of its former residence, and myths involving the-heart-attacked-by-a-woman are best interpreted by viewing the heart as a hidden and guarded penis, narcissistically invested.

Ferenczi talks of "the phallus as a miniature of the total ego," and argues that "this duplication of the ego is for the narcissistic ego the fundamental prerequisite of love" [1938, p. 16; cf. also Kerényi, 1956, pp. 182–83]. He also points up the narcissistic barriers to procreation and the struggle to overcome them:

". . . The acts preparatory to coitus likewise have as their function the bringing about of an identification with the sexual partner through intimate contact and embraces. Kissing, stroking, biting, embracing *serve to efface the boundaries between the egos of the sexual partners,* so that during the sex act the man, for example, since he has as it were introjected the organ of the woman, need no longer have the feeling of having *entrusted to a strange and therefore hazardous environment his most precious organ.* . . . The carefully guarded

member certainly will not get lost, seeing that it remains with
a being with whom the ego has identified itself" [Ferenczi,
op. cit., p. 17. Italics mine].

Ferenczi maintains that there is in men a strong identification not only with the penis but with the sexual secretion as
well, which bears the individual's narcissistic dreams of immortality. He therefore feels there is an unconscious need to
"safeguard the security and welfare of this secretory product
inside the body of the woman" [*Ibid.,* p. 18]. Thus there are
three interrelated identifications made by the male in normal
coitus: "Identification of the whole organism with the genital,
identification with the partner, and identification with the
sexual secretion" [*Ibid.*].[1] The difficulty experienced by the
Greek male in achieving the second identification, and the narcissistic exaggeration of the first and last, burdened his heterosexual life with anxiety.

A number of fantasy "solutions" to this problem appear in
Greek culture. One solution is to divest the organ and the
secretion of their narcissistic importance, hence the popularity
of myths (such as those of Danaë, Erichthonius, and Minos)
in which conception takes place by unusual means [Apollo-
dorus: ii. 4. 1; iii. 14. 6 and iii. 15. 1 and note]; and the tendency to displace the narcissistic cathexis of the penis onto the
entire body, noted in the first chapter. Another "solution" is
an overcompensatory identification with the female, expressed
in the effeminacy of Dionysus. A final solution is the avoidance of heterosexuality altogether—hiding the phallus in
fantasy inside the heart, where the hated female cannot get
at it at all. As is typical of neurotic solutions, all of these may
occur together, since all of them are unsuccessful in eliminating the tension which the conflict creates.

---

[1] This occurs in the context of his rather exotic theory that the strivings
of all organisms are regressive—aiming for return to the womb, to the sea, to
quiescence; Edens from which they have been expelled by a series of traumata.

Myths of the attacked heart have male heroes, and the woman who attacks the heart may be identified as the mother. She either appears explicitly as such, or as an obvious surrogate (stepmother, mother-in-law), or is linked to the mother by a common malevolent attitude toward the hero. The fantasy is a self-protective one, and pertains to a castrating image of the mother. Since it is his masculinity which arouses her ire, the hero is moved both to protect it and to get rid of it. All of his narcissistic libido is drawn to it by this ambivalence, and when the anxiety becomes extreme he wishes to draw the overcathected penis into himself, along with the feelings associated with it. In a sense, the heart fantasy solves both contradictory needs: the penis *is* better protected but it is also got rid of, for it is of the essence of a penis that it is external and properly placed. To put the penis inside is to have an inside organ, which is to have a vagina. It is also to identify with the mother, and to mother oneself; to be the Good Mother and the protected infant at once.[2]

We are so used to thinking of the heart as the seat of the soul, or of the emotions, that the foregoing may seem a little gratuitous. Yet it should be remembered that it is largely in Western societies that it plays this role, which is reserved in other cultures for the liver or the stomach. Even in our society the heart figures most prominently in questions of narcissistic injury: we do not refer to a bereaved individual as having a broken heart, but rather to one who has been rejected by a lover. Then we use such terms as "hurt," "wounded," "cut to the heart," or "bleeding heart." The heart is viewed as the center or point of origin for narcissistic libido, with the penis as a kind of frontier outpost for the normal male. When love-objects are too rejecting or threatening, or when internal disruption occurs, the libido, in Freud's theory, flows back onto some such outpost—that part of the body in which the internal disruption is localized, or which is associated with the ex-

[2] I am indebted to Dori Slater for this observation.

ternal rejection. In the case of the castrating mother, the hypochondriacal concern of the male child is focused on the penis, and if the anxiety becomes sufficiently intense there will be a further withdrawal—a desire to relocate the exposed libidinal outpost in the "capital," as it were; to unite all of the narcissistic libido in one desperate last stand.

But this imaginary strategy is always unsuccessful as a device for relieving anxiety, for it leads with apparent inevitability to the terrifying fantasy that the Malignant Mother will find the hidden penis-heart and tear it out. This is the ultimate narcissistic wound; for not only is the hero finally and irrevocably unmanned, but also finally and irrevocably annihilated. Or so it would seem.

Examples of the Attacked Heart

Let us now consider some examples of the attacked-heart fantasy, first from literary sources, then from mythology and folklore. In Blake's "The Mental Traveller" (see Chapter VII) the image of the devouring, Malignant Mother, feeding and thriving upon her son's pain, is drawn with exceptional vividness, and in the crucifixion verse we see the ultimate fear realized:

> She cuts his heart out at his side
> To make it feel both cold and heat.
>
> Her fingers number every Nerve . . .

It is in the failure of a structure that one most easily perceives its function, and in this grim fantasy the anxieties underlying the hiding and withdrawal are illuminated. The feeling is one of exposure, of hypersensitivity, of vulnerability. The little boy feels he cannot get away from the mother because she is all around him, inside him, playing on him, overstimulating him. He attempts withdrawal but fails, for he is "hooked" in a symbiotic relationship with her. He cannot escape but he cannot tolerate the intensity of her feelings toward him, nor of those she arouses in him. He is inundated with chaotic, disorganizing emotions. He cannot gain enough distance and separateness from her to integrate his own personality, yet cannot safely and comfortably slip into a parasitic dependence on her. He does both and neither, and feels himself a helpless and suffering victim, swept hither and yon by cataclysmic forces over which he has no control.

Blake's fantasy makes apparent the seductive as well as the destructive side of the mother's ambivalent response to the male child. The little boy hides his penis because devouring includes arousing as well as destroying it. But she discovers the subterfuge and undoes it, making the narcissistic libido again subject to both "cold" (her rejection) and "heat" (her desire). She both castrates him (cutting the "heart" out) and arouses him ("her fingers number every Nerve"). That this arousal is not simple sadism is made clear by the subsequent verse in which he becomes a man, she a young virgin, and he conquers and ravishes her. For this is the essential part of the mother's disturbed relationship to the son. She is disappointed in men, and he is her hope as well as her revenge. She wishes for a man who would be strong and gratifying and protective, but since her experiences with men have been quite the reverse, she hates and fears them. They seem alien and inimical, and she can only tolerate one who is not too much of a man. A little boy fulfills this need, and since he is her own, and a part of her, he seems less strange, less threatening. But he is small and impotent and cannot satisfy any of her sexual or dependency needs, and this enrages her and seems further proof of the iniquity of men. Blake's fantasy provides a solution to this problem, for she finally succeeds in rousing the child to manhood while she becomes young again and a virgin; that is, she has a chance to start over again with a male of her own construction. She happily relinquishes her power position to become an innocent and yielding girl with a powerful male she feels she can trust.

Our second example comes from a poem by Baudelaire called "Benediction" [1936, pp. 258–65]. It concerns a young poet and prophet, innocently religious, though treated with contempt by all and vindictively hated by mother and wife. When he is born, his mother screams at God:

> Upon his helpless form, whereby Thou humblest me,
> I shall divert Thy hatred in one raging flood;
> And I shall twist so well this miserable tree
> That it shall not put forth one pestilential bud!

As in the Blake poem, stress is placed on the helplessness of the child and the mother's need to arouse and distress him. The actual attack on the heart, however, comes from his wife, who shouts "in public places" her desire to exploit his love, to make him worship her as an idol while she laughs at him:

> And, when my pleasure in these impious farces fails,
> My dainty, terrible hands shall tear his breast apart,
> And these long nails of mine, so like to harpies' nails,
> Shall dig till they have dug a tunnel to his heart.
>
> Then, like a young bird, caught and fluttering to be freed,
> ('Twill make a tasty morsel for my favourite hound)
> I'll wrench his heart out, warm and bleeding—let it bleed!—
> And drop it, with contempt and loathing, to the ground.

The entire passage is indeed so similar to the Blake fantasy that little more need be said about it, except to note the special emphasis on narcissistic concerns: ridicule in public places, degradation and disdain, the wife's fantasy of being idolized. The poem also stresses the ability of the boy to keep himself to himself—to preserve a tranquil and detached mien.

I have suggested that the attack on the heart represents the ultimate narcissistic wound—a totally tragic fantasy. On closer examination, however, one finds that this unhappy dream contains within itself the most optimistic and buoyant of rebirth fantasies. Dionysus himself is the most distinguished example of this phenomenon, which ultimately becomes the keystone of Dionysiac religion. But one also finds it in the two poems. In "The Mental Traveller" the child survives the attack and becomes a man, while at the very end he is reborn as a babe and the entire sequence renewed. In "Benediction" the destructive fantasy of the wife is followed by a rapt portrait of the husband lost in ecstatic dreams of a blissful afterlife. Thus at one level the fantasy of the attacked heart expresses the idea that through self-destruction the little boy can rid himself of the persecutions of the mother and recreate himself along more satisfactory lines.

Closely related to this fantasy of rebirth is that of propitiation, not only of the mother's hostility but also of her sexual demands. There is a feeling that the hero can escape death only by appeasing these needs, but that only his self-destruction will in fact appease them. Rebirth is thus the only means to existence at all. It is clear to him that he cannot provide what she wants, that what she wants has something to do with his being male, and that his inability to provide it has something to do with his being too small. Perhaps he even senses that in some manner he is being put in the place of his father. It is not necessary for him to know that the only baby he can give his mother is himself; he can still sense that it will take all of him to sate her, and hope that in response to this self-sacrifice she will permit him to live again.[3] Some such notion would explain the frequency with which the attacked-heart fantasy is associated with a sexual act, a conception, and a rebirth. It is as if to say: "my mother is hungry and angry. She is dissatisfied and I cannot please her. If I give myself to her to devour perhaps her passion (a word which nicely fuses the two emotions involved) will be slaked. After she has

---

[3] This conception is thus more infantile than the self-castration of the priests of Cybele; in the latter case the focus of the mother's anger and hunger is understood. To sacrifice the part for the whole is a sophisticated adult device—for the child, part and whole are not sufficiently distinguished.

swallowed me she will give birth to me again, and I will be better this time and she will be satisfied."

Such a definition of the mother-son relationship would suggest the necessity of analogous propitiation in fertility rituals. If the earth is seen as a mother, any culture in which this emotional constellation is prominent will assume that she requires such propitiation. Whether it entails the sacrifice of a whole child, or its heart, or merely a phallus, will depend upon the intensity of this constellation in the culture. The devouring passion of the mother should be represented by the serpent.

Erich Neumann provides two examples of rituals involving propitiation of the Terrible Mother with hearts and phalli to assure the fertility of the earth, and in both instances the serpent is prominently involved as the recipient of these sacrifices. Thus: "All Aztec policies were subordinated to the wars that were waged for the purpose of taking prisoners to be sacrificed in the cult of the Snake Woman, who yielded fertility only when satiated by terrible blood sacrifices. . . . The characteristic Aztec form of sacrifice was to tear the heart out of the living body and offer it up to the sun; this gave assurance of the fructifying rain that made the earth fertile" [Neumann, 1955, p. 186]. Although offering the heart to the sun seems to contradict the interpretation suggested here, Neumann argues that the solar emphasis is merely a patriarchal overlay, superimposed upon the Earth-Mother cult. Why the cutting out of the heart was maintained during this transition, however, remains a question to be investigated. Neumann associates the Aztec mythology and ritual with the castrating or dismembering of the son by the "Terrible Mother," but also suggests that "in incest with his mother, the hero begets himself." Further, "as son of the snake-mantled mother, he is entwined in snakes, his scepter is a snake; his drum is a snakeskin," just as Dionysus is a snake, and Zeus must always become a snake in order to beget him [Ibid., 1955, pp. 185–186, 192, 198, 199; Kerényi, 1960, pp.

252–53; Nonnos: *Dionysiaca* vi. 155–205 and vii. 319–43].

Neumann sees "an identity between the cutting out of the heart and birth" [*op. cit.*, p. 200], thus linking the castration and rebirth interpretations. "The dying prisoner was the generative feminine earth principle, the woman dying in childbirth; in dying he engendered his heart. . . . The husking of the corn, the heart, is castration, mutilation, and sacrifice of the essential male part; but at the same time it is birth and a life-giving deed . . ." [*Ibid.*, pp. 202–3].

Neumann's second example is the Greek Thesmophoria:

"Blood sacrifice and dismemberment belong to the fertility ritual of the Great Mother. Both fecundate the womb of the earth, as can be seen from a number of rites in which the pieces of the victim—whether man or animal—are solemnly spread over the fields. The Greek Thesmophoria, in which little pigs, symbolizing the *children* of the earth sow, and *phallic symbols* are thrown into *a ravine supposed to be swarming with snakes*, also belongs to this context" [*Ibid.*, p. 189. Italics mine].

One may interpret this ritual of propitiating the serpent as essentially a projection of male fears and female resentment. In the ritual of the Thesmophoria, for example, the women who perform it are projecting onto the Earth-Mother their own modal conflict, saying, in effect, "she will conceive and bring forth only when her hatred and fierce hunger have been sated with the blood and organs of the offending male."[4] The latent thought behind the male-oriented Aztec sacrifice is identical.

There is even a hint of this propitiation ceremony in Baudelaire's "Benediction." Millay's translation, which has the poet's heart fed to a "favourite hound" (partly for rhyming purposes) does not quite capture the mythic character of

---

[4] It needs no special cultural neurosis to generate the idea that phalli might help fertilize, but their use in these rites was reinforced by the overtones of blood sacrifice.

the phrase "*pour rassasier ma bête favorite*," but a woman with nails "*pareils des ongles des harpies*" may surely be assumed to have a more sinister domestic familiar.

Bata

My final example of an attacked-heart fantasy—drawn, like the story of Zagreus and the Titans, from ancient folklore[5]— is the Egyptian tale of "The Two Brothers," which is usually dated from the thirteenth century B.C.

The story begins with a Potiphar's-wife episode. Bata, the hero, lives with his elder brother, Anpu, and the latter's wife. Failing to seduce Bata, the wife accuses him to Anpu, who tries to slay him. But Bata escapes and flees to the Valley of the Cedar. Before leaving he holds a conversation with Anpu across a crocodile-infested stream (which Ra has made to obstruct Anpu's pursuit). He tells Anpu the true state of affairs and then cuts off his own phallus and throws it in the river, where it is devoured by a shad. Anpu is remorseful but cannot cross the stream because of the crocodiles.

Bata then tells Anpu that he is going to cast a spell on his heart so that he can place it in a flower of the cedar tree. When the tree is cut down he will die but can be revived by placing the heart in a jug of water. Anpu will know of this by

[5] Both stories also have many points in common with the myths surrounding Osiris, especially his dismemberment by Set and the irretrievable loss of his phallus to the fish of the Nile [Plutarch: *Isis and Osiris* 358]. The connections between Osiris and Dionysus were noted in ancient times [*Ibid.*, 364], but in many respects Bata seems closer to both gods than they are to each other.

My reservation of this famous tale for the last has been deliberate, an attempt to recapture some of the sense of confirmation I experienced upon first reading it. For the entire interpretive scheme was formulated when I knew nothing of "The Two Brothers," other than that it contained the motif of the externalized heart. To find united in one story the entire sequence of ideas, which had been pieced together from several different sources, provided a reassurance which is rare to those who wander in the morass of myth interpretation.

certain signs and must come and save him. Bata then departs for the Valley of the Cedar. There he lives alone, hunting during the day and sleeping beneath his heart during the night. The gods are disturbed at his bachelorhood, however, and, after the officious fashion of married folk of every era, they put their heads together and find a wife for him—in this instance one who is custom-made. She, however, reveals her divine origin by proving contrary, avaricious, and having a beautiful body, and eventually leaves her impotent husband for the Pharaoh. For some reason she is not content with this improvement in her social and sexual fortunes, but insists that the Pharaoh destroy Bata by cutting down the cedar in which his heart lies.[6] The doting Pharaoh carries out her wish, and Bata is temporarily deceased.

After four years of searching, Anpu, clued by magic signs of Bata's demise, finds the heart and Bata is revived. Bata then swallows his heart and enthusiastically informs his weary brother of his latest scheme, which is to take the form of a bull and go to the Pharaoh's court to seek out his wife. This is done and Bata's wife promptly has the bull slaughtered. But two drops of blood from his neck fall by the doorway of the palace and become two huge cedar trees. Once again the dull-witted Bata compulsively informs his erstwhile spouse of his identity, and she has the trees cut down. But while this is being done a splinter flies into her mouth and she conceives. The child is, of course, Bata himself, who, when he comes of

[6] The moral to be drawn from all these external-soul tales would seem to be that if one cannot keep his mouth shut he might just as well carry his soul around with him. None of those engaging in soul externalization seems to be able to resist confiding to someone its location and the way to destroy it. This is of course necessary if the story is to move along, but it also expresses the lonely emptiness of a life of complete emotional safety. Danger is life, and the only complete security is in death, just as the only complete cure for castration-anxiety is castration. Bata seems to approach this solution when he unmans himself and hangs his heart on the Egyptian equivalent of the weeping willow tree, but even he apparently cannot live without some kind of intimacy.

age and succeeds to the throne, has his mother put to death
[Budge, 1914, pp. 196–207; Fontenrose, 1959, pp. 191–192;
Pritchard, 1955, pp. 23–25].

All of the elements of the attacked-heart story are here
combined. The castrating but seductive mother appears both
as Anpu's wife and as the wife of Bata himself. Their maternal
aspect is not left to the psychoanalytic imagination of the
reader—Bata's own wife actually becomes his mother, and one
is told explicitly that Anpu's wife may be so viewed. When
she first tries to seduce Bata he protests, "You are like a
mother to me, and your husband is like a father to me! Because—being older than I—he was the one who brought me
up." [Pritchard, 1955, p. 24]. When she tells her version to
her husband, however, she puts these words in her own
mouth: "But I wouldn't listen to him: 'Aren't I your mother?
—for your elder brother is like a father to you!' " [*Ibid.*].
And Bata prefaces the relation of his side of the story to Anpu
by saying, "You are like a father to me, and your wife is like
a mother to me! Isn't it so?" [*Ibid.*, p. 25].

Bata is, in fact, an oedipal hero, although characteristic defenses are used to deny these tendencies. Temporal reversal
is the first, for one notes that instead of the usual oedipal
sequence of growth, patricide, incest, and castration, the
castration comes first, then the marriage which will later become incestuous, then the death of the Pharaoh, who has now
become Bata's father, and finally his growth to manhood after
having become a child. This trick does take the edge off the
raw oedipal fantasy, but we are not altogether fooled. Whether
a man marries his mother or becomes his wife's child amounts
in the end to the same thing; for in the latter case he
simply becomes incestuous retroactively. Bunker similarly
remarks [1944, p. 205], quoting Roheim, that the castration
avows the very crime which Bata denies.

Bata's relationship with Anpu reveals another reversal, for

far from being competitive and hostile he is a model son in every respect. He helps Anpu in his work and carries out every order with perfect obedience and alacrity, and at the end of the story Bata dies after a twenty-year reign and Anpu succeeds him. It is as if to say, "how can you imagine that I want to take your place? Look! In my fond daydream you will take mine!" The ludicrousness of Bata (who has died three times, been reborn, and led two complete lives) being succeeded by the much older Anpu discloses the intensity of this need to deny competitiveness. The oedipal wish in this case is completely to possess and thereby completely free oneself from the mother and yet somehow retain paternal protection.

Projection is also used to accomplish this goal. Instead of taking his mother-wife away from the Pharaoh, his father the Pharaoh takes her away from him.[7] Similarly projective is the Potiphar's-wife theme, in which oedipal guilt is projected onto the woman. This is not entirely successful, however, for subsequent events reveal traces of Bata's own guilt. It is difficult to see, for example, why he feels called upon to castrate himself and go into exile if he is not in fact guilty. When the gods ask Bata why he dwells alone in the Valley of the Cedar, they point out that Anpu's wife has been slain and that Bata has "made an adequate answer to the attack" which Anpu made upon him. And when Bata is justifying himself to his brother he says, "Behold, thou art ready to remember against me *one bad deed of mine* but thou dost not remember my good deeds . . ." [Budge, 1914, pp. 200–1. Italics mine]. Once again it is not only the mother who is seductive and devouring, but also the child. This is expressed in the fact that

[7] In part this is simply the child's perception of the matter—as he becomes older he becomes more aware of his father and of the fact that his mother in some respects belongs more to her husband than to him. This is experienced as a loss and a taking away, relative to the earlier perception of his mother as existing solely for him and the satisfaction of his needs.

Bata was conceived in serpent form [Fontenrose, 1959, p. 192].

But myths universally show a preference for injured innocence over insight, and despite occasional hints of the ways in which the hero's own feelings collude in the production of these various disasters, the principal emphasis is on the Bad Mother and her machinations. She is out to seduce him, to incorporate him, to isolate and alienate him, to castrate and obliterate him, to betray and abandon him, and these evil intentions are the well-spring of action in the story.

The attack on the heart itself takes a form (chopping down the tree) which shows very clearly its connection with castration. Furthermore, Bata's actual castration and the hiding of the heart in the tree are conjoined in the story, as if to show that the separation of the penis and of the heart from the body are one and the same.

The story's emphasis on rebirth hardly needs comment. Bata is reborn again and again, always in forms which reveal his phallic narcissistic ambitions: he is a great bull, two giant trees, and King of Egypt. The theme of propitiation is also present in Bata's constant willingness to reveal his identity to his wife, and in his final gesture of allowing her to swallow him.

Central to the entire tale is the external-soul dilemma, discussed at the beginning of this chapter. Uncertainty over its optimum solution is expressed in the many different ways of combining seed, phallus, and heart as libidinal receptacles. When the phallus becomes overinvested with narcissistic libido Bata cuts it off, but its incorporation by a shad is reminiscent of external-soul myths in which the soul is hidden inside a fish. Fundamentally, the self-castration necessitates a contraction of libido into the heart, but no sooner does this occur than he extrudes his heart. But maternal rejection and castration again occur, and the heart again becomes the principal focus of narcissistic libido. No sooner is Bata revived by

Anpu, however, than the phallic emphasis reappears in the bull and the two trees.[8] When these, too, are destroyed, the threefold symbol reappears in the form of the splinter, which is at once the heart of the tree, the phallus which enters his mother-wife's body, and the seed which becomes a child. But the child is himself, showing his unwillingness to entrust his seed to another. All through the story Bata seems to struggle to make this short-run narcissistic sacrifice for the long-run gain (i.e., immortality). But he never quite dares, and in the end can only have a child by fleeing in terror to his mother's womb. Emotionally sterile, Bata can produce nothing but himself, and is succeeded not by a son but by a father-surrogate. It is with a shortage of seed, in fact, that his troubles begin: Anpu sends him back from the fields for more, and it is his desire and ability to carry a great quantity of it that leads Anpu's wife to admire his strength and desire him [Pritchard, 1955, p. 24; Budge, 1914, pp. 197–98]. Since Anpu is also childless one might suspect that it is the image of youth and fertility which the large burden of seed suggests to Anpu's wife rather than strength in itself. In any case the consequences are disastrous and fecundity remains subordinated to rebirth throughout the rest of the tale: a victory of moon over banana in Briffault's polarity.

One might therefore distinguish "The Two Brothers" from other external-soul stories by saying that the desire for biological immortality does not develop out of a prior resolution of more primitive infantile conflicts, but is merely part of a desperate casting about for alternative hiding places for narcissistic libido. The story does not say: "Am I safe and mature enough to entrust my libido to another," but rather, "nothing and no one is safe, not even myself; where can I hide it?" Its

[8] Note that from the blood of the castrated Bata spring not one but *two* phalli, substituting abundance and superfluity for scarcity and loss, and providing the kind of security which comes from not having all of one's narcissistic eggs in one basket.

mood is best captured by Kafka's story, "The Burrow" [Kafka 1952, pp. 256–304], in which a little animal obsesses endlessly about the relative safety of different systems of distributing his food stores, hiding the entrance to his burrow, or arranging his network of passages. His attempt to decide upon the relative safety of centralization and diffusion is particularly reminiscent of poor Bata's dilemma.

"The Two Brothers" is the story of a frantic man trying to avoid being inundated by feelings in a world out of control.[9] In this sense Bata resembles Dionysus: both perform very few acts relative to the many things (mostly persecutory) which are done to them. Insofar as they do act it is not upon the world but upon themselves: their solutions to life's problems are autoplastic rather than alloplastic. Bata is more extreme, but even Dionysus provides a sharp contrast to, let us say, Heracles, who while perhaps the most persecuted figure in Greek mythology aside from Dionysus himself, is full of feats and accomplishments. Dionysus' only alloplastic maneuver is to induce others to commit self-destructive acts, and when not engaged in this "activity" he often seems utterly impotent. Even Nonnos, who seems determined to mold Dionysus into an epic hero, is unable to transcend this fundamental defect; with the result that the god usually appears cowardly and foolish because of the contrast between his divine power on the one hand, and his puny acts on the other.

The passivity of Dionysus may in part be associated with the fact that so many of the myths take place in his childhood, but he is at all ages unable to cope with Hera, and reacts to any threatening gesture she makes with panic or paralysis, or both. Thus in the initial slaying of Zagreus by the Titans he fights successfully for his life "until Hera with jealous throat bellowed harshly through the air. . . . Then

---

[9] The preparation of a Mexican intoxicant is alternatively designated as "castrating" or "cutting the heart from" the plant that possesses it [Neumann, 1955, p. 301].

the bold bull collapsed: the murderers each eager for his turn with the knife chopt piecemeal the bull-shaped Dionysos" [Nonnos: *Dionysiaca* vi. 200–5]; and in his adult adventures he displays a similar fragility. Dionysian myths in fact follow a consistent pattern, in which the god is first attacked and seems helpless and impotent, but ultimately shows his power in some magical way, usually by visiting his persecutors with madness. This sequence occurs in his encounters with Lycurgus, Pentheus, the Tyrrhenian pirates, Perseus, and in many of the tedious adventures narrated in the *Dionysiaca*. Defeat followed by ultimate triumph is hardly unusual in heroic adventures, but Dionysus is unique (at least prior to the blundering "private eye" or secret agent of modern American myth, who must be beaten up at least once during every caper) in the frequency with which he is defeated, bound, imprisoned, routed, and even destroyed; and in the number of times he must be rescued. It is almost as if the defeats and persecutions were the important part of the story—they are often dwelled upon more fully than his triumphs, and even the latter focus more on the disintegration of his enemies than on the mastery of the god. There is a masochistic sensuality about these tales—a voluptuous savoring of degradation and disintegration, such as one often encounters in modern literature (e.g., Dostoyevski, Mann, Gide, Williams, Nabokov), and which one generally associates with certain kinds of male homosexuality. Such a mood is of course an essential part of the ecstatic nature of the cult—self-control, self-consciousness, and narcissistic caution must be abandoned, logical distinctions and differentiations must be ignored. Even the boundaries between the sexes are to be dissolved, men becoming passive objects to be castrated or otherwise dismembered, women becoming active, roving hunters, savagely attacking and destroying their animal or human prey. This was perhaps one of the central psychological functions of the Dionysian cult—it provided the ultimate fantasy solution to the torment which sex antagonism occasioned in Greek life by eliminating the exaggerated differentiation imposed by culturally defined sex roles.

Another facet of Dionysus' passivity is stressed by Nonnos,[10] and recalls the discussion of maternal narcissism in Chapter I. This is the extent to which he is a pawn in the struggle between Hera and Semele. Semele appears as almost a precise duplicate of Hera in her arrogance and narcissism, and, perhaps bearing in mind that it was this trait which brought about her electrocution in the first place, Nonnos presents her in Olympus perpetually boasting about "my son, the god." Even at the moment of destruction she vaunts her superiority over her sisters at having Zeus for a husband and Hera for a rival and ridicules their mates and offspring [Nonnos: *Dionysiaca* viii. 375–88]. Later, she sneers at Hera and Ares, Leto and Apollo, Maia and Hermes, Hephaestus, and Heracles, comparing them all unfavorably to herself and her son [*Ibid.*, ix. 208–42]. Finally, when Ino leaps into the sea after being persecuted by Hera for hiding the infant Dionysus, Semele mocks her son's aunt and benefactor in similar fashion, making invidious comparisons between Athamas and Zeus, between Dionysus and the luckless Melicertes [*Ibid.*, x. 129–36]. In Nonnos, Dionysus knows no mother love, but is merely a tool which can be manipulated to enhance maternal prestige and fulfill maternal ambitions.

[10] Nonnos of course writes much too late to provide any sort of empirical support for my interpretations, for although, as Rose points out in his introduction to the Loeb edition [pp. x–xi], later writers like Nonnos often use local legends that are of greater antiquity than those used in the classical period, much of the concrete detail in the *Dionysiaca* is simply added by the author. At best, Nonnos' intense commitment to Dionysian religion suggests a personal familial experience resembling the modal cultural one of the earlier period, and his fantasies therefore might merit our interest, even if we assign no real weight to them in forming our interpretations.

CHAPTER X

Identification with
the Aggressor: Dionysus

IV. THE ATTACK ON THE MATURE GOD

THERE IS A SUBSTANTIAL TRADITION regarding Dionysus, to the effect that "when he grew to manhood Hera recognized him as Zeus's son, despite the effeminacy to which his education had reduced him, and drove him mad . . ." [Graves, 1955, I, p. 104; see Apollodorus: iii. 5. 1; Euripides: *The Cyclops* 3]. To this madness are generally attributed his wanderings, in latter-day attempts to synthesize the many and disparate aspects of the god. Greeks of the classical period, having inherited this "crazed god," associated for centuries with orgiastic rituals originating in long-forgotten conditions, sought to rationalize what seemed to them his bizarre characteristics and behavior. The solution they found was quite naturally based upon their own cultural surroundings—if a man was effeminate and berserk his mother must have made him that way, and if a god was in similar straits a jealous mother-goddess must be responsible.

"The male experiences this force that violates him not as something of his own, but as something 'other,' alien, and therefore feminine . . . whether he is transformed into an animal . . . whether he is . . . castrated; or whether, dressed as a woman and identified with the Feminine . . . he fulfills the function of the Feminine" [Neumann, 1955, p. 304].

Neumann sees all intoxication, all ecstasy and madness, as feminine, in line with the traditional Jungian equation of masculinity with consciousness. The Greeks apparently had a similar view, and however oversimplified the Jungian position may be, it does fit the constellation of traits that one finds in Dionysian religion. As Neumann shows, Dionysian characteristics are normally found in association with a maternal goddess of the more terrible variety. Madness, darkness, the serpent, and the sea are typically feminine attributes in mythology. It is a goddess who floods the poor mortal with emotion, just as the awesome Mayan snake-goddess Ixchel threatens to inundate the world with water [Neumann, 1955, pp. 187, 207, 300–2].[1] Dionysus having become detached from the mother-goddess with whom he was originally worshiped, it was necessary to imagine him as having "caught" his psychotogenic tendencies from Hera.

This parallelism reveals Dionysus' characteristic "mechanism" for coping with maternal malevolence—what psychoanalytic theory calls "identification with the aggressor." It is epitomized in two traditions—that of Dionysus' effeminacy and that of his capacity for inducing madness.

Dionysus' Feminine Identification

Dionysus' incorporation of feminine attributes begins with his sire. I have already noted how Zeus turned himself into a serpent like his mother in order to ravish her, and how he competed successfully with Hera in producing offspring unaided. Zeus, however, is in no way feminized by these incidents—there even seems to be some underlying feeling that his manhood is incomplete until feminine abilities are also ac-

---

[1] Compare the connection between Dionysus and the flood-dragon suggested by Fontenrose [1959, p. 420].

quired. This is the burden of Bettelheim's interpretation of puberty initiation practices such as subincision, which gives men a "male womb" or "penis womb" [1955a, pp. 109–14, 177–78]. Dionysus' birth from the thigh of Zeus [Euripides: *The Bacchae* 524ff.] reflects another idea behind such rites, namely, that to become a real man one must be reborn from a man. Bettelheim gives examples in which rebirth is directly pantomimed, even to anal imitation of postpartum purificatory procedures [1955a, pp. 109–14, 214–23].[2]

Yet not every society has elaborate puberty rites with genital mutilations. As Whiting and his associates have shown, they tend to appear in those societies in which the father plays a minor role and the mother an overwhelming one in the early life of the male child. The relationship is particularly marked in the case of prolonged exclusive mother-son sleeping arrangements (i.e., the father sleeps apart) and a long (i.e., more than a year) postpartum taboo on marital intercourse. Whiting reasons that such customs intensify the libidinal and dependent attachment of the son to the mother, and require a comparably extreme ritual to dramatize the boy's detachment from the mother, home, and femininity, and his new commitment to a life among males. The puberty rituals, with their tortures, seclusion from women, tests of strength and endurance, and genital operations (perhaps to

---

[2] All of this was fully understood by Jane Harrison (anticipating Bettelheim by almost fifty years), who points out the reference to "male womb" in *The Bacchae* [526–27] and relates it unhesitatingly to puberty ritual and the transfer of young boys from the world of women to that of men. Most exciting of all is her disappointed statement that "nowhere have I been able to find among savage tribes any mimic birth from the father," which is today an ethnographic commonplace [Harrison, 1962, pp. 34–38].

Bettelheim suggests that the rebirth theme is most marked where ignorance regarding the male role in procreation is greatest. The same masculine envy creates, in less naïve societies, an exaggerated view of the role of semen. He quotes the Henrys' description of the Pilagá belief that "the man's ejaculation projects a complete homunculus into the woman, and . . . it merely grows in her until it is big enough to come out" [Bettelheim, 1955a, p. 111; cf. Aeschylus: *The Eumenides*, 658ff.; Mead, 1955, p. 35].

incorporate what is being lost), are viewed as filling this need [Whiting, Kluckhohn, and Anthony, 1958; Burton and Whiting, 1961; Stephens, 1962].[3]

Greek mythology includes several echoes of such rites, as many authors have pointed out. Yet each case has undergone its own peculiar transformations, so that the differences between them are as illuminating as their common origin. Both Dionysus and Achilles, for example, are disguised as girls in their youth in order to protect them. But note how Nonnos is inspired by the effeminate nature of the god to elaborate this incident:

> Oft he would show himself like a young girl in saffron robes and take on the feigned shape of a woman; to mislead the mind of spiteful Hera, he moulded his lips to speak in a girlish voice, tied a scented veil on his hair. He put on all a woman's many coloured garments: fastened a maiden's vest about his chest and the firm circle of his bosom, and fitted a purple girdle over his hips like a band of maidenhood [Nonnos: *Dionysiaca* xiv. 159–67].

This episode is not in itself a departure from the puberty-rite tradition. Transvestism is one way of attempting to achieve freedom from feminine domination. The men try to show that they can be women as well—wear their clothes, acquire their organs, give birth—and hence do not need them any longer [cf. Harrison, 1962, pp. 505–7]. Thus Bettelheim describes examples of the wearing of women's clothes both by the initiates themselves, and by the adult males who spon-

---

[3] Burton and Whiting suggest that the tough, delinquent, compulsively anti-feminine lower-class gang in our own society serves the same function for the lower-class boy who grows up in a fatherless or at least mother-centered household. This problem is particularly marked, as so many have noted, in the lower-class Negro family. One might even wonder if in some grotesque way the civil rights movement has not performed a function similar to the puberty rite, with Negroes seeking admission to the larger society being beaten up, tortured, or otherwise "hazed" by males representing the dominant white society.

sor them and who are called "mother" by them [1955a, pp. 211–14]. These are "male mothers" like Zeus, or the young man who aped the birth-pangs of Dionysus' bride, Ariadne, at her festivals [Kerényi, 1960, p. 271]. They facilitate a libidinal transfer from mothers to fathers by acting like the former and encouraging object-loss identification.

The theme of the transvestite initiate is found again in the story of Achilles, who is disguised as a girl by Thetis and hidden in the women's quarters in an attempt to forestall his inevitable death [Apollodorus: iii. 13. 8]. This, too, may be seen as a survival, representing both the early feminizing experience and the escape through identification. But Achilles *does* join the male group and goes off to war, while Dionysus remains effeminate. Both myths have "forgotten" their original significance, but that of Dionysus has become elaborated to an extent that actually seems to controvert it. Achilles is presented with masculine and feminine trinkets and correctly chooses the former (although his behavior at Troy is an early demonstration of the hollowness of such psychometric techniques). Dionysus never loses his femininity, and even Nonnos' latter-day attempt to make a heroic figure out of him only serves to intensify it.

One interesting difference in the myths themselves is that while Achilles was hidden *by* his mother, Dionysus' disguise was to protect him *from* Hera. Once again, where one finds elaboration one finds maternal malevolence. We also find a breakdown in one of the major devices used to ensure masculinity—rebirth from the father. Zeus steals the attributes of womanhood from Semele, and Dionysus is "not of woman born." Yet he is not valorous, nor does he join the male group. On the contrary, his struggle with women and femininity continues endlessly. What began as simple hermaphroditism in the god—expressive of his completeness and fertility—was gradually translated into a psychopathological defense. Dionysus no longer *includes* femininity but merely

takes refuge in it. Nor is this effeminacy any longer a mechanism for escaping from the feminine world into the masculine one, as in the intermediate case of Achilles. Dionysus is
eternally frozen in his defensive posture by the shared fears
of the classical period. He neither escapes from his infant
dependence on woman, nor becomes manly, nor wards off
maternal malignance, nor relinquishes his absorption with it.
The original vigorous hermaphrodite dwindles into a simple
homosexual god of the most anthropomorphic type. This is
expressed in some of the secondary names assigned to Dionysus, such as "Pseudanor," "gynnis," and "arsenothelys"
[Kerényi, 1960, p. 273], and extends, as Kerényi points out,
to Dionysus' male attendants in late representations:

> As the god's tutor, Silenos became very unlike the Silenoi
> who were the lovers of the nymphs: he is an aged, effeminate
> figure with a thick stomach and almost womanly breasts, or
> he is clad in a long gown—which, by the way, is also the char-
> acteristic apparel of the full-grown Dionysos. It seems as if
> the only male being in the scene is the nurseling. Although
> born of Zeus—this fact receives exaggerated emphasis—and, in
> a way, the continuation of his father alone, he appears only in
> association with women: at this period of his life, with moth-
> erly, breast-giving, tending women [Ibid., p. 258].

—women whose nurturance seems largely restricted, however,
to these static tableaux.

A final example of Dionysus' femininity is the Prosymnos
episode. It is related that Dionysus made a journey to the underworld in search of his mother, Semele, to bring her back
from the dead and make her immortal. To do so he plunged
into a bottomless pool in the dismal swamp of Lerna. But not
knowing the path to the underworld he first inquired it of a
guide, Prosymnos, who promised to tell him on condition that
the god submit to intercourse with him. "Only if he did this
could he reach his mother and bring her back" [Ibid., p. 259].
Dionysus' journey was successful and he made his mother im-

mortal, naming her Thyone ("the ecstatically raging"). But when he returned from his mission to keep his bargain with Prosymnos he found that the pathfinder had died. He therefore erected a phallus carved of figwood on the dead man's grave and fulfilled his promise in effigy [see Frazer's footnote to Apollodorus: iii. 5.3].

Once again we have an extremely complex set of factors producing a single, rather trivial, myth. As Frazer points out, the myth serves in part to explain the wooden phalli which were so important in Dionysian ritual, as well as the nocturnal death-and-resurrection rites which were celebrated annually at Lerna (associated with both Dionysus and Demeter). But these raw materials, while essential to the myth, are not sufficient in themselves to produce the theme of homosexual submission. The mystical notion that death can be overcome by surrendering to it may also be seen in the Prosymnos episode, as well as the idea that a successful afterlife is dependent upon learning a kind of map of the underworld, such as the Egyptian Book of the Dead, the labyrinthine codes of megalithic Europe, and the sand drawings of Malekula [Levy, pp. 116–64]. There is also, as Kerényi observes, a faint reminiscence of Trickster, who also plays the part of woman at times, and whose sexuality "knows no bounds, he does not even observe the boundaries of sex" [1956, p. 188]: Kerényi points out that Dionysian ecstasies similarly abolished sexual boundaries. But what provides the final link among these diverse elements is the homosexual defense against the "Terrible Mother." To appease Death life must be sacrificed, and the hungry Earth requires similar gestures, as we have seen. The Angry Mother demands of her ambivalently-regarded male offspring a sacrifice of masculinity. In this episode of the Lernean swamp these aspects are fused. For it is to bring back his mother (i.e., her love) that this feminine submission is required. Her "ecstatic raging" is linked with a symbolic castration. There was a certain grain of truth in the medieval belief that sex reversal in poultry was caused by witches [Scott, 1958, p. 128].

Identification with the Aggressor

Dionysus' unique solution, however, is less his defensive femininity than his psychotogenic powers. Just as he is driven mad by a woman, so he himself has the power to madden other women, a power which he seems to exercise on every possible occasion. This mythical madness is, of course, an unsympathetic rendering of Dionysian ecstasy, but the fact that the most typical act of the deranged women is to murder their sons betrays other motivational sources.

Dionysus' characteristic attribute of boundary-violator is symbolized by the Orphic myth of his serpent birth—a myth whose great antiquity is alleged by Kerényi [cf. also Euripides: *The Bacchae* 100ff.]. Demeter is said to have hidden Persephone in a cave in Sicily, guarded by two serpents. While the maiden was engaged in weaving, however, Zeus came to her in the shape of a serpent and copulated with her, Dionysus being the fruit of this union [Kerényi, 1960, pp. 252–53]. His ability to shatter cognitive boundaries is thus intrinsic, and does not depend upon any external power. He is in fact born with it—it is the child itself which drives the mother mad by its very existence. Just as the child has twice violated the physical boundaries of the mother by its conception and birth, so it drives her to raving infanticide by its having ceased to be a psychological part of her. In the child-murdering myths of Dionysus one can easily discern some of the underlying ideation of the postpartum psychosis.

> But when they find the frowning Babe,
> Terror strikes thro' the region wide:
> They cry "The Babe! the Babe is Born!"
> And flee away on Every side.
>   [Blake, "The Mental Traveller"]

Guthrie argues (against an historical interpretation) that the stories of persecution and revenge in Dionysian mythology are merely an expression of the pattern of the ritual itself —the resistance and ultimate submission to an ecstatic state: "No man can submit without a struggle to the experience of having his distinctively human faculty of reason, and all that connects him with the normal world, overwhelmed and submerged by those animal elements which, normally dormant or at least in subjection, are released and made dominant by the irresistible surge of Dionysiac power" [Guthrie, 1955, p. 172]. Except for the unfairness of foisting the unique intensity of human affect onto the placid animal, this interpretation seems eminently reasonable, although it is equally plausible that historical resistances to the spread of the Dionysiac revival provided some of the raw material. Yet, as Guthrie notes, the stories of persecution "have one almost universal feature, namely that the god's vengeance takes the form of visiting with madness the women of the land where he has been spurned. This usually leads to their tearing a victim to pieces, either the king who has been the god's opponent, or, when the women themselves have been the offenders, one of their own children. The two motives are combined in the Pentheus story . . ." [*Ibid.*, pp. 165–66]. These elements do not follow automatically from either the historical or the ritual interpretation, which could combine to generate a number of alternative myths. The additional determinants are Greek sex antagonism and the family pattern. The former assures that the acts of aggression shall almost always take place between males and females, the latter that mothers shall so often murder sons.

Frazer points out that collective female frenzies are not limited to Dionysian mythology. In a footnote to the Loeb *Apollodorus* he quotes Ivor Evans as relating that Jakun women in Malaya "were frequently seized by a kind of madness—presumably some form of hysteria—and that they ran off singing into the jungle, each woman by herself, and stopped there for several days and nights, finally returning almost naked, or with their clothes all torn to shreds" [*op. cit.*, Vol. I, p. 147].

Even more closely related is an example from India:

> A great company of Baiga women were filled with one of those "inspirations" that descend from time to time on primitive tribes. They dressed up as men, adorned themselves with men's ornaments and tied turbans on their heads. Carrying spears and bows and arrows, they went out as an army. When they came to a village, they beat all the men, and drove them to take shelter in their houses. Then they caught a pig, cut off its ears and tail and gave them to the headman. They took the pig and marched home. Then the women of the village they had visited took the ears and tail from the headman and themselves formed an army and marched to the next village. There they repeated the process with another pig. Meanwhile the women of the original village captured a man and made him their servant. They made him kill the pig and roast it. Then they had a great feast and ended all with the Karma.
>
> "We men were very frightened," says Dhan Singh. "For the women had spears and they were mad. Who knew what they would do?" [Elwin, 1939, pp. 238–39; quoted by Stephens, 1963, p. 303].

It seems rather likely that the men overestimated the involuntary aspect of the women's behavior, both there and in Greece. One suspects that the women rather looked forward to these outbreaks as a welcome relief from everyday drudgery and a disadvantaged social position [cf. Dundas, 1913, pp. 494–95]. Lack of communication and understanding between the sexes would facilitate such naïveté.

In Euripides' *The Bacchae* we find the theme of the Maenad horde closely tied to sex antagonism and narcissism. For in one respect, Pentheus is entirely consistent from the beginning of the drama to his death: whether railing against the Bacchic movement or primping in his woman's costume, he is activated primarily by vanity. Nor does Dionysus offer us any motivational variety. As William Arrowsmith comments in the introduction to his translation of the drama, ". . . each is deeply jealous of his own personal honor and ruthless in enmity. . . . For Dionysus, the motives of humiliation and revenge are crucial. . . . Thus, point for point, each of Pentheus' threats, insults, and outrages is revenged with ironic and ferocious precision. . . ." [1960, pp. 534–35]. Indeed, Dionysus' petulance and bravado are at times so extreme as to detract somewhat from the intensity of the play [Euripides: *The Bacchae* 604–59, 850–61, and 1330ff.].[4]

Teiresias, living up to his reputation for wisdom, is well-attuned to the motivational monotony of the protagonists:

> Think:
> you are pleased when men stand outside your doors
> and the city glorifies the name of Pentheus.
> And so the god: he too delights in glory.
> 　　　　　[Euripides: *The Bacchae* 319–21.
> 　　　　　Arrowsmith trans.]

This pervasive narcissism does not exist in a vacuum, however, but is closely tied to sex antagonism. Agave's wild boasting, when she imagines she has killed a lion with her bare hands, is directed against men, who hunt with nets and spears and armor. She taunts them with her achievement and asks her father to admire her bravery—to glory in her kill as if she were his son. Pentheus' most profound insult to Dionysus is to cut off his feminine curls. He rails continually against the women of Thebes for abandoning their traditional role of domesticity, and feels humiliated by their participation in Bacchic rites [*Ibid.*, 215ff., 493, 778–86, 1202–1211, 1233–1243]. When the Bacchae are disturbed in their revels by

---

[4] I am assuming the various reconstructions of the lacuna to be accurate, although some of the speeches which follow it serve on their own to support the argument.

male voyeurs they begin rending steers and flaying bulls, following which there is a literal battle of the sexes:

Then the villagers,
furious at what the women did, took to arms. And *there*, sire,
was something terrible to see. For the men's spears were
pointed and sharp, and yet drew no blood, whereas the wands
the women threw inflicted wounds. And then the men *ran*,
routed by women!

[*Ibid.*, 758–64]

Upon hearing this story Pentheus is so angered he vows to bathe the woods of Cithaeron in the blood of women. Almost immediately, however, Dionysus takes advantage of Pentheus' own voyeurism to seduce him into spying on the Maenads himself.[5] Pentheus' sneers at the god's effeminacy are now requited as Dionysus dresses him in women's clothes for the event, despite Pentheus' repeated protestations that this seeming relinquishment of manhood would humiliate him beyond endurance. As soon as he is garbed, however, Pentheus becomes totally absorbed in the performance, mincing about coquettishly and asking if he does not, thus attired, resemble his mother or his aunt. Paradoxically, he feels himself at this moment imbued with superhuman strength [*Ibid.*, 796–950].

Ambivalence, however, is inherent in sex antagonism. Hos-

[5] Gilbert Murray's theory that Dionysus simply hypnotized Pentheus into saying what the god wanted him to is not only naïve but utterly misses the significance of the entire drama. Pentheus' fascination with Dionysus is apparent from their first encounter, when he comments on his attractiveness and accuses him of trying to make him curious [*The Bacchae* 451–59 and 475]. Dodds, whose psychological perceptiveness is worthy of Euripides' own, points out that "Pentheus speaks of Bacchism as if it were a physical infection transmissible by contact . . . something in him knows already the fascination and the mortal peril which the new rites hold for him." And again, "the god wins because he has an ally in the enemy's camp: the persecutor is betrayed by what he would persecute—the Dionysiac longing in himself." Pentheus is a "dark puritan whose passion is compounded of horror and unconscious desire" [Dodds, 1960, pp. 114, 172, 97–98].

tility toward the other sex, wishing to do without that sex, fearing its contamination, yet imitating it, are all part of the same syndrome. The Bacchae, in their isolated haunts, become hunters—cross-culturally the most exclusively masculine of all subsistence activities [cf. Stephens, 1963, pp. 282–83]. The women of Lemnos dress in their slain husbands' armor. And men, in the secret rites of their fraternal associations, dress as women. Conjoined with hatred and fear is fascination and curiosity—as with any form of group segregation. The Athenians were notorious for their misogyny, yet left us a legacy of female-centered literature and mythology almost unmatched among vanished cultures in its richness and profusion.

To some extent this is simply a response to the artificiality of the separation. Part of the chronic tension and the brittle veneer of tough masculinity in lower-class gangs in our own culture (of which Pentheus, despite his exalted status, could easily be a member) is due to the fact that sexual identification cannot be established by group identification alone—ultimately it must be defined by sexual behavior. A man apart from women is not altogether a man, and must continually "prove" his identity negatively—by stressing what he is not. When Pentheus finally abandons this elaborate defensive structure and expresses all at once the feminine side of his nature, he experiences an enormous surge of energy—suddenly released from its neurotic tasks—and imagines he can move mountains.

The Bacchae expresses the folly of exaggerated repressions. Dionysus represents not so much irrationality as the liberation of natural emotions from the tyrannies of ideology and culture.[6] When Teiresias accuses Pentheus of madness, and warns

[6] Dodds seems correct in interpreting *The Bacchae* as an object-lesson in the power of impulse to destroy those who ignore it. History has repeated the lesson frequently—Nazism is the most striking of the many contemporary examples—but it has never been learned. The greatness of the play lies in the fact that although presumably directed toward contemporary issues,

him that power is not all of life [*Ibid.*, 310-27] he is not merely hurling a *tu quoque*. For it is the insanity of the social structure that generates the insanity in the Bacchic rites—the two are complementary. Dionysian religion is the "return of the repressed" for the full range of neurotic defenses embedded in Greek culture. Every pre-school-age boy may wish to spy on his mother, dress up in her clothes, be carried by her and nurtured like a baby [*Ibid.*, 955-58 and 966-69], but it is the exaggerated constraints of the culture which cause such desires to erupt full-blown in a grown man. Dionysian ecstasy fused together what the rest of Greek culture strove so obsessively and superstitiously to keep separate. Narcissism and sex segregation both express a fear of boundary-loss, aroused by the mother's psychological invasion of the child when she attempts to maintain her own internal stability by discharging unmanageable affects into her relationships with her children.[7]

The nature of these affects is also dramatized in *The Bacchae*. Phallic competitiveness, for example, is evident in the wands that are more penetrating than the men's spears, and in

---

it anticipates (and mocks) the course of Western civilization during the centuries that have elapsed since it was written. Pentheus' adventures with Dionysus—misperceiving his own impulses, mistaking them for something else, trying unsuccessfully to bind them, then being seduced, overwhelmed, and destroyed by them—are chronically re-enacted.

The increasing derogation of emotion in the fifth century—reaching a climax in the fulminations of Socrates and Plato—corresponds directly with the feminization of Dionysus during the same period. The ideal male becomes unable to evince any feelings except anger and pride, other emotions being relegated to women and foreigners—like the Phrygian in Euripides' *Orestes*, who plays the role usually assigned to the Negro in old Hollywood comedies, and for roughly the same reasons [Dodds, 1960, pp. xlii-xlviii, 128, 133-34, 191].

[7] In *The Bacchae* emphasis is placed on the fact that the very women who suckle fawns and cubs have abandoned their own children at home. This expresses the fact that the emotional needs of the Greek mother blocked her ability to nurture, without abating the desire to do so. Symbolically, as Dodds points out, by suckling animals women became foster mothers of Dionysus himself [1960, p. 163].

Agave's insistence that the sonless Cadmus treat her like a victorious boy:

> Now, Father,
> yours can be the proudest boast of living men. For you are
> now the father of the bravest daughters in the world. All of
> your daughters are brave, but I above the rest. I have left my
> shuttle at the loom; I raised my sight to higher things—to
> hunting animals with my bare hands.
>
> [*Ibid.*, 1233–1237]

One also sees an echo of the weak marital bond, for Echion, Pentheus' father, is conspicuous by his absence. To some extent Cadmus plays the paternal role in the drama, and Agave's response to his failure to reward the above speech is revealing:

> How scowling and crabbed is old age
> in men. I hope my son takes after his mother and wins, as she
> has done, the laurels of the chase . . .
>
> [*Ibid.*, 1251–1253]

Once again the mother whose vanity is wounded tries to use her son to fulfill her frustrated aspirations. But here the resentment is also expressed, for in Agave's slaying of Pentheus, Cadmus' biological immortality is destroyed. How similar to an Arab lamentation is this speech of Cadmus:

> All our house
> the god as utterly destroyed and, with it, me. For I have no
> sons left, no male heir; and I have lived only to see this boy,
> this branch of your own body, most horribly and foully
> killed.
>
> [*Ibid.*, 1304–1307]

Pentheus is thus brought down like Meleager, to exterminate the paternal line, although in fact Pentheus is not a son of Cadmus at all.[8] Agave compounds this anomaly when she asks

---

[8] Euripides is careful to establish an affectionate paternal bond, however, through Cadmus' reminiscences [*The Bacchae* 1316–1322; cf. Dodds, 1960, p. 233], and it is Cadmus, not Agave, who makes the first lamentation.

why Pentheus should pay for her crime [*Ibid.*, 1301]. It would seem more logical to ask the reverse, but Euripides is tapping deeper currents here than mere descent rules and myths of blasphemy. It is Agave's passion that destroys Pentheus; and it is Cadmus, the father, toward whom this passion is in part directed, and who is injured by it, regardless of the particularities of kinship. Thus is the myth tailored to Greek familial preoccupations.

The deracination of Cadmus' lineage shades into the more Meleager-like theme of castration when one sees Pentheus first feminized and then attacked by the Maenads:

> Then Agave cried out: "Maenads, make a circle about the trunk and grip it with your hands. Unless we take this climbing beast, he will reveal the secrets of the god." With that, thousands of hands tore the fir tree from the earth, and down, down from his high perch fell Pentheus, tumbling to the ground, sobbing and screaming as he fell, for he knew his end was near.
>
> [*Ibid.*, 1106–1113]

Pentheus' attempts to reason with this feminine Jack-the-Giant-Killer are unavailing:[9]

> . . . she was foaming at the mouth, and her crazed eyes rolling with frenzy. She was mad, stark mad, possessed by Bacchus. Ignoring his cries of pity, she seized his left arm at the wrist; then, planting her foot upon his chest, she pulled, wrenching away the arm at the shoulder—not by her own strength, for the god had put inhuman power in her hands. Ino, meanwhile, on the other side, was scratching off his flesh. Then Autonoë and the whole horde of Bacchae swarmed upon him. Shouts everywhere, he screaming with what little

---

[9] If Cadmus is more successful [*The Bacchae* 1264ff.; cf. also Dodds, 1960, pp. 229–30], it is simply because he is a better therapist, using precisely the same method as would a modern psychiatrist with an acute psychotic episode—focusing, narrowing, and funneling attention on concrete objects in the immediate environment.

breath was left, they shrieking in triumph. One tore off an
arm, another a foot still warm in its shoe. His ribs were
clawed clean of flesh and every hand was smeared with blood
as they played ball with scraps of Pentheus' body.

                              The pitiful
remains lie scattered, one piece among the sharp rocks, others
lying lost among the leaves in the depths of the forest. His
mother, picking up his head, impaled it on her wand.

                                  [*Ibid.*, 1122–1141]

Pentheus and Dionysus thus represent two modes of responding to the same phenomenon—Pentheus the strident male
who tries directly to combat maternal malevolence and is
destroyed by it—Dionysus the subtle, defensive, female-
identifying male who defeats the mother by overtly placating
her and then besting her at her own game of psychological
invasion and disruption.

Some Modern Parallels

One could fill a volume with cases of disturbed children who
bear resemblances to some aspect of the Dionysian myths. For
this tedious exercise let me substitute a brief discussion of
two examples, to give some idea of the flavor of the correspondences without either exhausting them or establishing
their limitations. No two children are alike, nor any two
myths, nor is any myth just like any case history, and it
seems pointless to elaborate this truism.

    We begin with the case of Harry, in Bettelheim's *Truants
From Life* [1955b, pp. 389ff.]. At first glance there seems to
be little relationship between Dionysus and this aggressive
little seven-year-old (who runs away, steals, sets fire to his
sister's hair, and tries to kill his mother with a butcher knife)
beyond an ambivalent mother-son relationship. Harry's mother
was a deprived woman whose father and husband were both
alcoholics. Her marriage eventually dissolved and both parents

remarried, Harry going to live with his father, who had some affection for him. The mother, whose experiences with men had been generally unrewarding, was distressed with Harry's exploits but seemed also to take pride in them, insisting that he narrate and act them out for visitors—even his attempt to stab her. His two younger sisters were viewed as good children and held up as examples, while he was defined as bad, smart, and indestructible (the latter in relation to his predilection for death-defying feats). The father was submissive to his wife when sober, but would beat her, smash furniture, and often rape her when drunk.

The intense sex antagonism prevailing in Harry's home led to familiar responses: exaggerated narcissism, anti-feminism conjoined with transvestism, and fear of castration:

> For months after coming to the School he would provokingly display his genitals; pointing his erect penis aggressively at others, he would shout at the top of his voice, "Look at my beautiful prick!"
>
> At the same time, he often would anxiously and aggressively ask women to show him their penises. . . . His confusion . . . could be traced back to his feelings about his mother, which he revealed in such statements as, "My mother has no tits; she's a man."
>
> After Harry had been with us for some time, he revealed how closely his truancy was related to his fear of being castrated. He built a snow man and threatened to punish it by tearing off its genitals because the snow man had supposedly run away. . . . Harry's castration anxieties were so great that he made self-destructive efforts at mastery by inflicting on himself what he feared others would do to him. He stated, for example, that he was going to eat his own genitals . . . in order to make his genitals secure from external dangers.[10]
>
> His fear and hatred of mother figures . . . were illustrated by his actual attempt to kill his mother, and later by similar

[10] Compare the discussions in Chapters VIII and IX about the relative safety of internal and external locations for the "soul."

attacks against his female counselors. . . . One day, while taking a bath, he suddenly grabbed his penis with one hand and made sawing gestures at its base with the other. In extreme agitation, he asked his counselor, "Do you think any mother would do this to her little boy?" . . .

. . . since his mother preferred his sisters, to receive her love he wanted very much to be a girl. This went so far that, even much later, he now and then would claim half seriously to be a girl, and would dress up in girls' clothes, which he carefully arranged so that they hid his otherwise chronically displayed genitals. Shortly afterward, he would have to overstress his masculinity by loudly asserting that he hated all females, and by committing aggressive acts against them. . . .

. . . He would suddenly and unpredictably switch from a feminine, passive, or submissive attitude . . . to uncontrolled, aggressive and destructive behavior, which readily reminded one of an intoxicated person [Bettelheim, *op. cit.*, 397–99].

Perhaps some of the central emotional themes of *The Bacchae*—including the alternation, in both Pentheus and Dionysus, of submissiveness and effeminacy with megalomanic fantasies of power, the sexual confusion, the vengeful, castrating, mannish mother, the boastfulness, the self-destructiveness, the uncontrollable affects—can be understood in relation to the foregoing material. It also suggests that Dionysus' transformation from a phallic to an effeminate god may be a less drastic one than is usually assumed.

My second example comes from a case reported by Ilse Hellman [1960, pp. 359–77]. Hellman describes a symbiotic relationship between an eleven-year-old male patient and his mother, expressed largely in maternal hypochondriasis. She quotes Winnicott regarding the boundary-blurring aspect of this syndrome, exemplified by a little boy who told the doctor, "my Mum complains of pains in my tummy." Such hypochondriacal fears were, in the case of Eric's mother, related to the fact that she had not wanted the child, had tried to abort him, had hated him from birth, and had had physical battles with him constantly. As to the father, who was competent in his role as provider, but extremely passive in the home, her "need to denigrate him, to deny his masculinity, and to treat him as a powerless, useless being was intense" [*Ibid.*, pp. 361, 363].

Eric feared being poisoned by his mother, and this fear proved to be not altogether unwarranted since she often gave him food of doubtful quality and then became extremely anxious, questioning him about his digestion, possible pains, and so forth; "and whenever her anxiety became too great to tolerate the uncertainty any longer she gave him one of her many tablets to counteract the fantasied harm she had done. Eric unfailingly took these tablets. He shared all her magic beliefs, wore articles of her clothing for extra safety, and they took the same tablets to prevent what they anticipated would be the same illness. He even took tablets which were given to her for menstrual pains. . . . Their fantasies of bodily unity became clearest in the simultaneous experience of pain" [*Ibid.*, pp. 366–67].

But Eric's mother was by no means alone in her hostility. Eric was described as "ruthless" toward her and full of sadistic fantasies. One was that he was "a surgeon who deceived his patients in the hospital, promising them cure, but in fact making them suffer the most horrible pain by severing their limbs, skinning them, etc., so that they could never recover." He also had sadistic intercourse fantasies and an intense fear of castration, expressed in "sudden abdominal pains and anxiety about a possible appendectomy" [*Ibid.*, p. 367].

Hellman notes that Eric could talk easily about his aggression, but not about the sexual side of his fantasies. It was later discovered from his mother that she obtained her only sexual gratification from love-play with Eric:

> She was frigid with her husband and fought against his attempts to have intercourse with her, either by feigning illness or by having the boy in their room. However, she could reach

an orgasm by tightly holding and *stimulating Eric into complete helplessness*. Such scenes began with fights with the excited, struggling boy until he finally was *overwhelmed by his excitement and by her physical superiority* [Ibid., p. 368. Italics mine].

In this transfer of the mother's libidinal interest from husband to son, in her simultaneous fierce hostility toward the boy as a representative of maledom, and in Eric's consequent grandiosity we can see a simple exaggeration of the Greek pattern. In the strong boundary confusion, the identification with the malevolent mother, the transvestism, and most particularly in the unsuccessful struggle against overwhelming impulses, the broad outlines of the Dionysus-Pentheus constellation begin also to emerge.

Sex antagonism is omnipresent in the case study. Eric sees his father as utterly benign, women as dangerous. His mother has a "horror of being penetrated," and a "fantasy of robbing her father's penis" [*Ibid.*, pp. 364, 368]. Pregnancy was "experienced as 'proof that she had lost the battle,' as she put it. Her husband had won, had pushed something into her against her will, and she felt compelled to try to do away with it" [*Ibid.*, p. 371]. She was overcome by jealousy when she saw her husband happily holding Eric, and felt compelled to interfere [*Ibid.*, p. 372]. And when Eric reached puberty and asked her about his first emission she said, " 'This is nothing special. All men and women have this' " [*Ibid.*, p. 374].

The mother's anxiety about boundary-maintenance, together with her hostile and envious feelings toward men, generated even more boundary-anxiety in Eric. His response to it is again reminiscent of *The Bacchae:* a "dread of being overwhelmed by uncontrollable powers" would lead to "megalomanic mechanisms," such as a "weather machine" through which he would control the elements (of which he was very much afraid). Like Harry, Eric coupled his fears of castration with physical attacks on his mother, which she felt unable to cope with after he became four years old. He had "nightmares in which he was facing a bleeding woman with her head cut off," and attacked his female therapist with a knife, hurting her "accidentally" [*Ibid.*, pp. 363, 369–70].

Not only was Eric continually overstimulated by the mother, but this overstimulation was combined with considerable physical restraint. She was angered by his first movements when she was pregnant because she could not control them, and she kept him strapped unusually often as a small child [*Ibid.*, pp. 371–72].[11] Thus he was continually faced with impulse-arousal and no opportunity for motor discharge. "Moreover, the anxiety over loss of control was heightened by the fact that the only way open for discharge was through rages" [*Ibid.*, p. 372].

Dionysian mythology, then, expresses conflict between the sexes and two of its consequences: the Angry Mother's invasion of the male child, and a rather complex but not unusual mechanism for coping with this attack. It is largely an autoplastic "solution," involving self-castration, self-destruction, and identification with the tormenter. On the other hand, the result of this identification is to bring about a kind of revenge after all. *Because* the mother has not permitted clear boundaries to develop between them, a self-injury becomes an injury to her also—their symbiosis can be used against her, and if he intoxicates himself, he intoxicates her also. The theme of rebirth expresses this, too—by getting inside her he can disrupt her from within, as the hero so often does when swallowed by a serpent or sea-monster [cf. Campbell, 1956, pp. 90–95, 207–8, 247–48; Radin, 1956, p. 105].

Yet this conquest is self-defeating for the same reason that

[11] Like Hera, Eric's mother is moved to attack him at three stages: in the womb, when movement is felt; at birth, when he separates physically from her; and as he matures threatening emotional separation as well. All are experienced as disruptive to her psychic boundaries, and she responds in kind.

it is possible: since they are not fully separated from one another, her defeat defeats him as well—when Dionysus drives a woman mad she kills her son, not herself. This expresses the real futility of the Dionysian response—where there is no separation there can be neither victory nor resolution.

Yet nothing comes closer to a rational comprehension of the Greek cultural sickness than this ecstatic and morbid mythology, which, in its appreciation of the intense affects determining the nature of Greek experience, reveals the Apollonian myths for the self-deluding, uninsightful sham that they are. And perhaps most important of its many truths is the vicious circularity of the process: from male to female to male again, and from parent to child to parent again, in the seemingly unending chain that makes cultural patterns of such long life.

> And none can touch that frowning form,
> Except it be a Woman Old;
> She nails him down upon the Rock,
> And all is done as I have told.
>   [Blake, "The Mental Traveller"]

CHAPTER XI

Maternal De-Sexualization:
Perseus

In the middle of the wood was a Red Witch.
Max half expected her. He never expected
To find a witch's house so dirty and foolish,
A witch with a wide bosom yellow as butter,
Or a witch combing so many obscene things
From her black hair into her scarlet lap . . .
"Littlest and last Van Vrooman, do you come too?"
She knew him, it appeared, would know him better,
The scarlet hulk of hell with a fat bosom,
Pirouetting at the bottom of the forest.
Certainly Max had come, but he was going,
Unequal contests never being commanded
On young knights only armed in innocency.
"When I am a grown man I will come here
And cut your head off!"
　　　[John Crowe Ransom, "First Travels of Max"]

W HEN YOU ENTER A GROVE peopled with ancient trees, higher than the ordinary, and whose boughs are so closely interwoven that the sky cannot be seen, the stately shadows of the wood, the privacy of the place, and the awful gloom cannot but strike you, as with the presence of a deity, or when we see some cave at the foot of a mountain penetrating the rocks, not made by human hands, but hollowed out to great depths by nature; it fills the mind with a religious fear; we venerate the fountain-heads of great rivers; the sudden eruption of a vast body of water from the secret places of the earth, obtains an altar; we adore likewise the springs of warm baths, and either the opaque quality or immense depths, hath made some lakes sacred" [Seneca: 41st Letter to Lucilius. Quoted by Jung, 1957, pp. 83–84].

Religious awe may certainly be generated by natural phenomena of other kinds, and one has no way of knowing why Seneca chose only vaginal and uterine symbols to illustrate such awe. But the legend of Perseus is concerned with the specific awe which Seneca's examples suggest—the child's sense of uncanniness when confronted with maternal sexuality and fecundity.[1] The themes of feminine awesomeness, of frozen staring, of confinement, of impotence, of flight, suggest a peculiarly Greek primal-scene fantasy—one which focuses almost exclusively on the *mother's* sexuality. As usual, the mother is malevolently defined, but the malevolence is not personalized as in the more literary examples. It seems to be inherent in the sexuality itself. The myth is thus one of confrontation rather than relationship—of moment rather than pattern.

Perseus' response is commensurately impersonal. Like other heroes he attacks and kills the representative of the Evil Mother, but in this case the emphasis is placed on what we might call, with only partial inappropriateness, castration. To do so is not to make some automatic equation: decapitation = castration; nor am I entirely influenced by the fact that Perseus uses the same weapon as did Cronus in castrating Uranus, and Typhoeus in rendering Zeus impotent.[2] Castration is used here in the more general sense of "unsex-

[1] Actually the Greeks called all the sexual parts *aidoion*—inspirer of holy awe [Taylor, 1965, 146–47].

[2] The name "Perseus" means "the Cutter" [Feldman, 1965, p. 492].

ing": the mother and her sexual aspect are separated. This separation appears in several forms in the Perseus myth. In the Cronus myth the child separates mother and father by castrating the latter. But the legend of Perseus scarcely contains any father at all—each paternal candidate is kept at bay, save for the ubiquitous Zeus, and even his liaison is a brief and rather ethereal one. The mother's sexuality is detached from her involvement with the father, and confronts the child as a direct and immediate force. The emotional goal of both acts of "castration" is the same: to restore the mother to the son as a nurturing, nonsexual being who gives all and asks nothing. The variations arise from the contexts in which the acts occur.

Before going further, however, let me summarize the essential components of the myth:

An oracle told Acrisius, King of Argos, when he inquired how he should get male children, that his daughter Danaë would give birth to a son who would kill him. He therefore shut her up in an underground brazen chamber guarded by a nurse. This sexual seclusion was no more successful than such efforts usually are, however, and in time Danaë was delivered of a son. There are two versions of how this impregnation was effected. In one, the father was Acrisius' twin brother Proetus, with whom Acrisius was in constant conflict (it was even said that they had quarreled in the womb). When they fought over Argos Acrisius was initially victorious, but ultimately was forced to yield Tiryns to his brother [Apollodorus: ii. 2. 1 and ii. 4. 1].

The second and more popular version makes Zeus the father, taking the shape of a stream of gold which poured through the roof of the chamber into Danaë's lap.[3] Acrisius

___

[3] Licht shrewdly interprets the shower of gold as a poetic symbol for a bribe, since it was indeed by way of gold properly distributed to servants and go-betweens that access to carefully guarded females was obtained [Licht, 1963, pp. 63–64].

not unreasonably refused to believe this improbable tale and locked up mother and infant in a chest and threw them into the sea. Washed ashore on the island of Seriphus, they encountered another pair of brothers: Dictys, the fisherman who found them, and Polydectes, the king of the island, in whose house Perseus was reared. Polydectes attempted (successfully, in some versions) to force marriage upon Danaë but was prevented by Perseus, who had now somehow grown to manhood. To circumvent Perseus, Polydectes pretended to be a suitor for the daughter of Oenomaus and asked for contributions from his subjects for the necessary gift. Perseus, being without assets, was unable to produce his quota of horses for the gift, whereupon Polydectes took him up on his boast that he feared nothing, not even the Gorgon's head, and asked him to fetch it.

Perseus now received considerable assistance from supernatural sources. From Hermes he obtained a sickle with which to perform the deed, and from Athene a brazen shield. With their aid he made his way to the Graeae, three swan-shaped sisters who had been aged crones from birth, and who had only one eye and one tooth among them. These Perseus stole and agreed to return only on condition of being told the way to the three nymphs, who gave him winged sandals, the cap of Hades (which rendered him invisible), and a wallet in which to carry the severed head. He then flew to the Gorgons, whom he found asleep in their cave by the ocean. They had great boar's tusks, scaly heads swarming with serpents (in lieu of hair), brazen hands, and wings of gold; and whoever beheld them was turned to stone. But Perseus used Athene's shield as a mirror, and with the gray-eyed goddess guiding his arm he cut off Medusa's head and put it in his wallet. The other sisters awoke and with "ravening jaws" pursued him "unapproachable and unspeakable, longing to seize him," while he fled in terror. "Two serpents hung down at their girdles with heads curved forward: their tongues were flickering, and their teeth gnashing with fury, and their eyes glaring fiercely" [Pindar: *Pythian Odes* xii; Hesiod: *Shield of Heracles* 229-37]. But the cap of invisibility protected him, and he flew to Ethiopia (or to Joppa).[4]

There were several new beings engendered by Perseus' encounter with Medusa. From her severed neck sprang the warrior Chrysaor and the winged horse Pegasus. Furthermore, as Perseus flew over the Libyan desert, some drops of the Gorgon's blood fell on the sand, breeding a race of venomous serpents [Apollodorus: ii. 4. 2-3; Pausanias: iv. 35. 9; Apollonius Rhodius: iv. 1513ff.].

On reaching Ethiopia Perseus discovered Andromeda, the king's daughter, tied to a rock, a sea-serpent's prey. Cassiopeia, the queen, had boasted herself more beautiful than the Nereids, and Poseidon, at their behest, had sent a flood and the monster as punishment. The oracle of Ammon had predicted deliverance if King Cepheus exposed his daughter to the monster, and this he had finally done. Perseus fell in love with the girl immediately and extracted a promise from her parents that she would marry him if he slew the monster. When the monster had been slain, however, it was revealed that Cepheus' brother Phineus was already betrothed to Andromeda, and a battle ensued in which Perseus used the Gorgon head to turn Phineus and his followers to stone.

Returning to Seriphus, Perseus learned that Dictys and Danaë had been forced to take refuge from Polydectes in a temple. The hero proceeded to the palace and again made use of the Medusa head to vanquish his enemies. Dictys was made king, the magic implements restored to Hermes and the nymphs, and the Gorgon head placed in the middle of Athene's shield.

Perseus, Andromeda, and Danaë now returned to Argos to find that Acrisius had fled to Larissa on word of their advent.

---

[4] Porphyry's description of a Cretan initiation serves to remind us that the Medusa episode may portray a similar rite [Harrison, 1962, p. 57].

There Perseus soon came to participate in funeral games, and accidentally slew his grandfather with a wayward discus, thus fulfilling the oracle. Ashamed to reign in Argos, Perseus exchanged kingdoms with Proetus' son, Megapenthes, and ruled over Tiryns for the remainder of his life. He had several sons and a daughter by Andromeda, and founded Mycenae [Apollodorus: ii. 4. 3–5].

An indistinct tradition of a conflict between Perseus and Dionysus also exists—even that he slew the god and threw him into the Lernean lake, entrance to the underworld. Other versions have Dionysus victorious [Fontenrose, 1959, p. 388]. The significance of this conflict is undoubtedly complex, and probably derives from the historical portion of the Perseus myth (i.e., that there was a king named Perseus who was the son of his mother's uncle, who fought relatives for his throne, who successfully or unsuccessfully resisted the worship of Dionysus, and who founded a dynasty). Nothing in my conceptual framework is dissonant with this conflict, since Dionysus and Perseus display antithetical responses to the maternal threat, just as do Dionysus and Apollo. But whereas Apollo opposes a narcissistic and antiseptic detachment to Dionysus' pursuit of mystical fusion, maternal identification, and bisexuality,[5] the contrast between Dionysus and Perseus lies on the dimension of activity-passivity. Dionysus represents an essentially masochistic solution, Perseus a sadistic one, and in their decisive battle each merely manifests his own response.

The Threat

Perseus is in effect fatherless, and from the variant versions of the story one gains the impression that potential fathers

[5] The conventional rational-irrational antithesis—always difficult to maintain in the absence of anything that could be mistaken for rationalism in the worship of Apollo—can be derived from this polarization of the oral-narcissistic conflict.

have gradually been excised from it. The myth consequently reveals a psychological dilemma: on the one hand the boy wishes to possess his mother exclusively, but on the other he is terrified of the intensity of her sexual needs and his inability to gratify them. He wishes her only as a nurturing, undemanding mother, but recognizes that the price of possession is that he be adult and potent. In real life the only way this can be achieved is by identifying with the father and learning how to be a man, at the same time relinquishing childish dependence upon the mother. The irony of this solution is, of course, that in so doing the primary motive for the entire enterprise is lost as well: sexual maturity and adult mastery become ends in themselves, new sexual objects are sought, and the oedipal wish is relegated to a diffuse romantic nostalgia which tinges fantasy life and erotic experiences.

Environmental factors influence the course of this development, however. If the boy has many caretakers (as in many primitive societies) the phenomenon is correspondingly diluted, while an isolated nuclear family system will intensify it. The mother's desires will also have a profound effect—she may derive her greatest satisfaction from having an infant, in which case the boy will not be motivated to mature at all, or she may want a substitute husband and hence push him toward adulthood. But of greatest importance is the role of the father; if he is absent or inadequate the boy has no leverage for becoming a mature male. Yet it is under just these conditions that his oedipal wishes will be most intense, fanned by his mother's frustration and need. Hence the more he needs a father the less he can tolerate one, and the more he desires his mother the more he will be terrified of being sexually overwhelmed and devoured by her.

It is presumably for this reason that fathers tend to be absent or peripheral in the histories of monster-killers. This is not to say that the myth of Perseus was necessarily created by males with fathers who were absent or who neglected their families, but only that the myth reflects the concerns of the little boy who faces a sexualized encounter with his mother, unbuffered by any adult male presence. The experience itself may be more or less universal, although as a sustained dilemma it depends upon intrafamilial pathology.

The myth of Perseus shows a trend toward the elimination of sexual partners for Danaë. In what is probably the form closest to historical tradition, Perseus is the son of Proetus, and after she is expelled from Argos, Danaë is married to Polydectes. To explain Danaë's impregnation in the absence of her uncle, recourse is made to Zeus (always ready in the wings) and to the device of the golden rain; while to remove Polydectes as a mate one is asked to believe that the passion which this worthy held for Danaë somehow only made itself felt after she had been in the palace for ten or fifteen years, by which time Perseus had become a barrier to its consummation. Through these mechanisms Danaë is unsexed. Just as the beheading of the Gorgon is a symbolic device for separating motherhood from sexuality, so in the molding of the myth itself does this "castration" take place. From a woman who had at least two royal lovers, one of them incestuous, and outwitted her harem guards, Danaë is systematically divested of all eroticism, and becomes a passive, colorless, and more or less virginal figure who contributes little to the story besides her son, and who is left at the end without a mate, alone with her son and his spouse.

Indeed, guarding Danaë's chastity becomes the focal point of the entire myth, leading, in the final version, to both her divine impregnation and the slaying of the Gorgon. The anxious desire of the son to purify his mother of sexuality is also seen in the fact that even Zeus is not allowed actually to touch her, but must impregnate from a distance.

Separating sex from motherhood by separating mother and father is logically sound but psychologically unsound, since this sexuality thereby confronts the child all the more directly. Thus it is a hostile impulse toward a father figure (the predicted slaying of Acrisius by Perseus) which sets the story in motion; and although otherwise they play a relatively passive role in the drama, it is the father figures who unleash the terrible feminine forces: Polydectes who forces Perseus to confront the Medusa, Poseidon who sends the sea-monster [Apollodorus: ii. 4. 3].[6]

We can better understand the special characteristics of the Perseus myth by contrasting it with a more classic oedipal fantasy, the tale of "Jack and the Beanstalk." In this story it is only the paternal figure who is menacing, and the problem for the male child is one of rivalry and mastery. The story begins with the oedipal wish already realized: the father is dead, the boy is living alone with his mother. But immediately the small print in this Devil's pact is made apparent: the little boy is inadequate to play husband to his mother. They are starving and he compounds their difficulty by foolishly trading their principal source of livelihood, a cow, for a few worthless beans. This exchange has two other meanings, however. In part it expresses a cynical view of the oedipal wish: how stupid he is to want to exchange a mother who will take care of him for a wife he must care for. It also represents the sacrifice he must make to realize the wish: giving up his childlike dependence upon his mother in exchange for sexual potency; and this exchange is indeed made—the seeds turn into a gigantic phallic object which reaches to the sky. Initially, the mother contemptuously rejects his sexuality, throwing the seeds out the window. This generates the compensatory fantasy of phallic amplitude and the attempt to draw upon the father's store of virility. Jack climbs the stalk and encounters the parental pair in more archaic form, at a

[6] The behavior of Acrisius also illustrates the notion that the son's difficulty with the mother may arise in part from the mother's difficulty with her father—an idea I discussed at length in the chapter on Orestes. Despite Danaë's attachment to him, when the chips are down Acrisius cares more for his own welfare than for hers.

stage when he is tiny in relation to them. His need to borrow paternal potency through incorporation is projected onto the father, who becomes an ogre seeking to devour him. With the help of the giantess, however, he steals various magical objects and flees. The ogre pursues him down the beanstalk, which he chops down, and the ogre dies. Jack and his mother become rich by means of the hen that lays golden eggs.

"Jack and the Beanstalk" is a beautifully condensed fantasy, and this very partial analysis does not begin to exhaust its meanings. But with all its eat-your-cake-and-have-it contradictions and complexities, the concern over adequacy, the need to borrow strength from the father, and the fundamentally oral nature of the oedipal wish seem to stand out with particular clarity. The "castration" at the end, for example, is applied to both himself and his father. Having called his father from the dead and extracted his adult secrets from him, he now sends him back; but at the same time he divests himself of his phallic attributes. The hen with the golden eggs might seem to connote potency, but if one returns to the reality level with which the tale begins and ends one can see that it serves primarily to enable Jack to possess his mother as a child—to be cared for and provided for without having to assume an adult role. As soon as he solves the oral problem he is quite happy to dispense with sexuality (as represented by the beanstalk) altogether and settle happily into childhood again.

If one compares this tale with the Perseus legend the most striking difference lies in the respective roles of the two parents. In "Jack and the Beanstalk" all of the power and all of the menace are concentrated in the father, while in the Perseus legend these reside in the mother. Jack must confront the ogre and gain power from him, while Perseus must confront the Medusa and gain power from her. Jack must draw from a man the strength to be a man in relation to a woman; Perseus must draw from a woman the strength to confront other men. Jack wins his mother, while Perseus' victory is merely that of the dog in the manger—he keeps his mother from any other alliance.

One might infer from this that "Jack and the Beanstalk" arose in a society in which the father's presence and salience in the nuclear family were generally assured, and the mother therefore a benign and non-frightening figure. The father's absence in the tale is a virtual rather than an actual condition: a wish rather than a deficiency. The Perseus myth, on the other hand, reflects a social system in which the father is peripheral in the home, and in which emotional power is seen as residing in the mother. It is she who must be confronted, and when Perseus wishes to vanquish his enemies the only way he can think to do it is by exposing them to the same maternal bogie which so terrifies him. Like the boys of many primitive societies who live in the women's quarters until puberty [cf. Burton and Whiting, 1961], he has no paternal model of mastery, and assuming the male role is full of difficulties.

There is, indeed, a deeply comic quality in Perseus' exploits with the Medusa head: one cannot help but smile at the child's fantasy that a view of the maternal genitalia would be as devastating to a group of grown men (including the rapacious Polydectes) as it is to him. The entire legend begs for parody, yet to my knowledge there was scarcely any attempt on the part of the classic dramatists to subject Perseus to the kind of comic treatment accorded Heracles and Dionysus. The Greeks seem generally to have been rather humorless and touchy on the subject of threatening females.

Such a statement depends, of course, on the validity of my view that the Medusa head *is* a symbol of maternal genitalia. If the reader has stayed with me this far, the basis for the equation is probably apparent, but a little review might be useful.

In Chapter I we explored the fantasy life and childhood experiences of the sexual psychopath Kenneth Elton, and observed an explicit and conscious terror of mature female genitalia, and in particular of pubic hair. I cited his dream, in which hair was equated with menacing snakes. I quoted Ferenczi's observation that the Medusa head seemed to symbolize female genitalia for his patients but rejected his view, shared with Freud, that the many snakes necessarily symbolized, in an overcompensatory way, the absence of the penis. I noted that Athene wore the Medusa head on her aegis to protect her virginity, as if such a display were somehow inherently repellent.

But under what conditions can a visual stimulus which is ordinarily aphrodisiac produce a repulsion so reliable as to guarantee a goddess' virginity? First of all, it must in some way represent the *mother's* genitals,[7] and will only have meaning and impact in a society in which maternal libido is directed toward sons rather than husbands, with an admixture of hostility.

But why is the *head* used as such a symbol? Freud's interpretation employs the concept of "displacement upwards" —the prudish substitution of a "higher" (more cerebral) body part for a "lower" one. If we are to be consistent, however, we cannot rest with this, but must again ask, why this one symbol rather than another? Why the head rather than the chest, navel, throat, or mouth?

One possible answer is historical: when the myths of Perseus and Medusa were fused [Feldman, 1965, pp. 485ff.], the instinctual fear attached to the representation of a bodiless head (see Chapter I) was conjoined with the cultural dread of the maternal genitals, and the one lent itself as a symbol for the other. The snakes were probably added at the point at which this fusion of meanings began (although this occurred well prior to the eighth century, when Feldman says the myth first assumed its present form), for originally the Gorgon head was merely shaggy [Feldman, 1965, p. 487]. The name Gorgo is derived from throat sounds (gorge, gargle,

[7] The birth of Chrysaor and Pegasus from the severed neck of the Medusa corroborates this maternal interpretation.

gurgle), and hence can be associated with either strangulation or being swallowed up [Feldman, 1965, p. 493].

This idea is helpful but insufficient—some further link seems required to cement the connection. Perhaps the importance of the face as a vehicle for the expression of emotion provides such a link. The human face (or its representation) is the first complex stimulus to which an infant can respond—the use of masks in drama to convey feeling states reflects this significance. It is the mother's emotion toward the child which gives the genital display its awesome impact, after all. Fusing the two symbols thus maximizes their power.

The display of female genitalia is itself a common apotropaic device. Freud discusses this in his paper on the Medusa's head [1922, pp. 105–6], and points out that it was thought to be a means of frightening away the Devil. Wright argues [1866, p. 42] that apotropaic amulets representing nude females exposing their genitals "in the most unequivocal manner" [*Ibid.*, p. 36] are almost universal, but also comments on the peculiar frequency of *Shelah-na-Gig* monuments in Ireland, and contrasts this "singular fact" with the use of the phallus on Roman churches for the same purpose [*Ibid.*, pp. 32–39].

This raises the problem, also confronted by Freud [*op. cit.*, p. 106], that the male organ is also used apotropaically, with equal or greater frequency.[8] Furthermore, it is perfectly clear

---

[8] Both devices survive to this day in our own culture, although their significance is no longer understood. Wright points out [1866, pp. 48–49] that the lucky horseshoe, which in rural areas is nailed over the barn door, originated in the widespread old-world practice of drawing or nailing up over the door the vulva of a cow, mare, or female camel to avert the evil eye; and the rabbit's foot is probably a similarly displaced fertility charm of phallic origin. The phallic hand, originally apotropaic, is still current throughout the Western, and especially the Mediterranean, world as a gesture of scorn. It is my impression that the concept of the evil eye and the measures for averting it are most pronounced in sex-antagonistic cultures, providing still further basis for the use of sexual display gestures as a means of defying and frightening evil and invidious forces.

that not all of the *Shelah-na-Gig* figures are intended to frighten, for while some have fearsome, grimacing faces, grotesque and full of teeth, others appear benign. In part, male and female organs are apotropaic simply because they are symbols of fertility. That either should assume a frightening aspect as well would seem due to the cultural factors which augment incestuous bonds and sex antagonism [cf. Licht, 1963, pp. 367–70, 501].

Freud argued that the apotropaism of the erect male organ was based on a different principle [*op. cit.*, p. 106]—a kind of complementary defiance to the female threat. I suspect, however, that this is true only in cultures such as that of Greece, where the female threat predominates. The derivation of the word "fascinate" from the Roman *fascinum* (meaning phallus, especially a phallic amulet),[9] and the use of the amulet so designated to perpetrate as well as to defend against magical influence, suggest that the numinous aspect of the phallus need not be attributable only to its significance in fertility ritual [Wright, pp. 28–29].

Freud also seems in error when he interprets "turning to stone" as a symbolic erection, a defense against the fear of castration [*op. cit.*, p. 105]. While the idea of erection may be present in the "stiff with terror" response, the immobility is much more suggestive of impotence, and this interpretation fits better the many examples of paralysis and turning to stone which we have already encountered. Furthermore, the unusual emphasis on mobility and flight as attributes of the hero who struggles against the menacing mother argues for the view that the enstonement is not a compensatory comfort, but a feared outcome. While Freud focuses on stiffness, one can just as well stress the numb or anesthetic aspect of turning

[9] It is interesting how the old meaning still clings to this common word. While it has many substitutes in most contexts, it is always used in situations which concern involuntary, frozen, or hypnotic staring, and is almost obligatory in connection with snakes.

to stone. Certainly the purpose of Athene's aegis was to render potential ravishers impotent rather than to provide reassuring erections.

At the same time, to reject a symbolic equation simply because its opposite is also (and more tellingly) true is generally pointless and, in the long run, wasteful. A symbol as specific as turning to stone needs all of its attributes explained, not merely those most dramatic and most central to the myth's principal themes. The child's response to a confrontation with parental sexuality will involve an ambivalent mixture of feelings: sexual excitement, fear, "fascination," curiosity, inadequacy, awe. The symbol of turning to stone captures not only the response of the moment—the frozen, hypnotic staring—and the conjoined feelings, but also the more long-range adjustment to these: impotence, frigidity, anesthesia. We know, from clinical studies, how frequently these outcomes are associated with early incestuous arousal.

It may be objected that the primal scene, the parental genitalia, and parental seductiveness are overwhelming to a child only in a society like our own, in which clothing, separate rooms, dolls without genitalia, and a variety of other cultural factors contrive to make such exposure so rare as to exaggerate its effect when it occurs. To an extent this is true, just as an extended family system dilutes incestuous attachments. While even very primitive societies usually make some effort to secure a modicum of privacy for parental intercourse, and have some device for covering the genitals of at least one sex (usually, as in Greece, the female), the child in many primitive societies can certainly view parental sexuality in a far more matter-of-fact manner than can an American child.

But this is beside the point. In the first place, these qualifications apply very little to the cultures under consideration here. Greek women in the classical period were as exaggeratedly clothed, relative to the climate, as a Victorian Englishwoman, and in well-to-do Athenian homes the children slept apart in the women's quarters, while the parents apparently slept in the men's quarters when together [cf. Lysias: "On the Murder of Eratosthenes" 9ff.]. Second, it is not the *existence* of parental sexuality which the child finds frightening, but the fact that it is directed toward the child itself—that it occurs in the context of need and resentment, and is mixed with hostility and contempt.

Freud's dubious interpretation thus provides a necessary degree of complexity to this schema. Since we have found the Greek mother's approach to the child to be highly ambivalent, we might expect the child's response to be correspondingly contradictory. The symbol of turning into stone expresses this duality, and we will find it again in the symbols associated with the slaying of the Medusa.

Let us return to the theme of the dangers of looking. One of the many indications that, for the Greeks, the vulva had the magical power not merely to neutralize but also to frighten evil spirits is that the device was used against men as well as bogies. The intrepid Bellerophon—a figure closely related to Perseus—was routed by it, as we shall see, and the use of the Gorgon's head and other snaky objects on the shield of Heracles and the aegis of Zeus suggests the probability that direct or indirect representations of maternal genitalia may commonly have been placed on shields to ward off swordpoints, just as Athene used the Medusa head to discourage less unkind thrusts. The association is not an idle one—for did not Caenis, upon being ravished by Poseidon, wish to become an invulnerable man, safe not only from sexual penetration, but from the sword as well [Ovid: *Metamorphoses* xii. 524ff.; Apollodorus: *Epitome* i. 22]? The thought seems to be that the sight of the maternal genitalia on the shield will render the sword of one's opponent weak and impotent, just as it might affect his phallus.

A similar interpretation has been made by the English

anthropologist, Leach [1954], of some superficially abstract designs on the shields of warriors in the Trobriand Islands. Leach argues that the design represents a flying witch, and suggests that it is placed on the shield "because of the poison-ous emanations that are believed to be emitted by the vulva and anus of such witches." He points out the exaggerated emphasis given to these orifices in the figure (they are indeed the most easily identifiable part of the design); and he shows a number of other correspondences between the design and beliefs about the witches. Since war magic, intended to give the shields the power to ward off spears, was an important part of military preparation, Leach's interpretation is ex-tremely plausible. The Gorgon on Agamemnon's shield, then, derived its psychological power not merely from innate fear of the severed head, but also from these more cultural factors [Homer: *Iliad* ii. 32ff.].

The Response

The legend of Perseus is the prototype of the "Superman" genre familiar to twentieth-century comic book devotees: an apparently weak or helpless individual has or obtains super-human powers with which he defeats his many enemies and amazes the crowd. The most significant and dramatic power, however, is the ability to fly. In psychoanalytic thinking, flight is seen as having phallic connotations, and the bird is a penis symbol—partly because the slang word for copulate in Ger-man is *vögeln*, but more importantly, because of the func-tional association between flight and erection. Freud suggests that the latter seems impressive because it involves "an ap-parent suspension of the laws of gravity," and remarks that "we shall not be surprised when we hear that some dreamer or other is very proud of his powers of flight." He also notes the frequency of the winged phallus in the Mediterranean civilizations [1900, pp. 394, 583n.; for examples and discussion of winged phalli see Knight, 1786, pp. 13, 35, 63; and Wright, 1866, pp. 11, 15, 75].[10]

One might suspect from these considerations that for the male, at least, flight does not represent sexuality as such, but sexuality warped by narcissism. The goal is not pleasure, but accomplishment: copulation is defined as conquest, erection as achievement, woman as the enemy, lack of desire as failure. The winged phallus probably found its greatest use, for example, as a magical cure for impotence.[11] But one need not go so far afield to appreciate the meaning of Perseus' flight. If the sight of the maternal genitalia produces immobility and impotence, then the hero who succeeds in countervailing this threat must be mobile and potent. Instead of being frozen into stone with terror, he becomes winged, like the phallic amulet. The ability to fly also contrasts sharply with Perseus' own initial immobility, when he was imprisoned with his mother underground, or confined with her in the tiny ark on the ocean.

It is not without significance that Perseus is alone with his mother in these two enclosed spaces, both of which (interment and the floating ark) are traditionally associated with the intrauterine state.[12] It suggests a desire to deny the mother a pre-maternal existence, a sexual life. She is born along with her child, as it were, and hence belongs only to him and has

10 And who does not remember Boccaccio's charming story (Fifth Day, Fourth story) of Caterina, who wished to hear the nightingale sing?

11 In our own society it is international policy rather than religion through which the sexual pathology of the population is funneled, and hence these concerns find their expression in the language of rocketry. The desire for phallic superiority is manifest in discussions about which nation has the biggest rocket, or the one with the greatest "thrust." Most revealing of all in its peculiar inversion of usual exit-entry thinking is the fact that a rocket which escapes the earth's atmosphere more or less on course is said to have made a "beautiful insertion."

12 Of all the heroes cast into the water in arks at birth (Sargon, Moses, Karna, Oedipus, Tristan, Romulus, Siegfried) Perseus is the only one who takes his mother along [Rank, 1952, *passim*].

no independent existence or outside ties. It is thus a possessive, oedipal fantasy, but one which also conveys the seclusion of harem life and the sense of inferiority which it assigns to women and children. This is another of the myth's many psychological dilemmas: having mother as a child means being weak and despised and powerless, but gaining power and stature means being alone. The solution is to attempt to possess the mother as an adult, but, as in "Jack and the Beanstalk," this entails initially giving her up and struggling in isolation (a very partial isolation in both myths, however, since a great deal of feminine help is forthcoming).

A similar ambivalence appears in movement toward and away from the mother. Achieving flight (erection) is not only a counter-fantasy to feelings of awe and impotence, but also expresses the child's eroticism—his desire to possess the mother sexually as an adult. Perseus approaches and attacks the mother (as Medusa), but at the same time flees in terror from her (as the Gorgon sisters). Neumann points out [1954, pp. 214–15] that in Greek art the most frequently portrayed aspect of the Perseus legend is not the killing of Medusa, but the terrified flight from the pursuing sisters. As in any fully developed myth, all possible contradictory feelings are included.

Neumann also observes that despite all the help and gifts Perseus receives, he is "barely man enough" to kill the Medusa [*Ibid.*, 215]. One is reminded of Pelops, who required not only winged horses and chariot but also a bribed charioteer to overcome a paternal opponent. But the Perseus legend is far more extreme, with two gods aiding him, a superfluity of magic implements, a sleeping enemy at whom he cannot even look, and a goddess guiding his hand to actually commit the act. Has there ever been so helpless and dependent a hero?

Certain antiseptic elements are also predictably present in this enterprise. Since fathers can only be enemies, and since mothers are the main objects of terror, it is necessary to have youthful gods as helpers. The virginal, masculine, anti-matriarchal Athene is de rigueur for hero myths, but the inclusion of Hermes is more unusual. Hermes represents not a paternal helper but a mirror-image of the hero—phallic, winged, and fatherless—as Apollo was to Orestes.

The second element of antisepsis is the use of Athene's shield-mirror to dilute the impact of the Gorgon head.[13] The Perseus myth never strays far from the theme of looking—of an ambivalent scoptophilia. The mother's genitals are frightening, yet fascinating—the child does not wish to look or be caught looking, but still wants to see. The notion here is that what is directly viewed can "look back"; that between the eye and its object there is an interaction; that the aggressive act of looking can produce an equally aggressive retaliation (witness all the lethal punishments for peeping at naked goddesses). To see without being seen or frightened is the desire, and it is expressed both in the use of the mirror to kill Medusa and in the cap of invisibility with which Perseus makes his escape. It is as if showing any sexual interest in the mother was a dangerous commitment, one which would encourage her own insatiable sexuality.

This brings me to the final and crucial expression of ambivalence in the Perseus myth: the act of murder itself. In the chapter on Apollo I attempted to come to grips with Bunker's interpretation of all mother-murder myths as disguised incest fantasies. I concluded that while the sexual themes to which Bunker points should not be ignored, neither should the more obvious lethal ones. Since the mother's attitude toward

[13] Neumann [1954, p. 216] suggests that "the power of the Great Mother is too overwhelming for any consciousness to tackle direct." The Medusa-slaying myth thus describes the mythmaking process itself: the representation. in metaphorical terms, and concerning persons and events remote from the speaker, of feelings and thoughts which would be overwhelming if considered as concrete realities [cf. Slater, 1961].

the child in the Greek family pattern is both seductive and vindictive, it seems appropriate that this ambivalence should be reciprocated in the fantasy of a sexualized murder.

But what sexual elements *are* there in the slaying of Medusa? We have no penetrating sword or arrow here with which to make traditional phallic equations, but only a beheading. Indeed, were it not for the birth of Chrysaor and Pegasus, the case for a sexual interpretation would be rather flimsy. But murders as such do not yield progeny, and whenever the latter appear one can reasonably assume some sort of sexual admixture. Certain contextual elements lend additional weight to this view. The fact that Perseus attacks Medusa while she is sleeping accords with infantile sexual theories in which sleeping and copulating are equated, and the preparation for the event bears some resemblance to Greek wedding rituals: the gifts, the leading into the chamber, the unveiling of the bride, and so on [Blümner, pp. 140–41; Ehrenberg, 1951, pp. 193–94]. We know that the moment when the bridegroom first beheld the bride held some tension for Greek males, exemplified in the myth of Alcestis and Admetus [Apollodorus: i. 9. 15].

That Perseus' attack is mother-murder as well is evident from the close association between Perseus and Orestes. Aeschylus, for example, when the chorus is galvanizing Orestes to slay his mother, has them exhort him to "hold in thy breast such heart as Perseus had" [*The Choephori* 831]; and Neumann points out the essential identity of the Erinyes' pursuit of Orestes and the Gorgons' pursuit of Perseus: "like [Orestes], Perseus becomes a hero because he has killed the Terrible Mother" [1954, p. 215; cf. also Harrison, 1957, 223–36].

Presumably mother-murder myths which culminate in some sort of stabbing reflect a higher proportion of incestuous desire to terrified rage than does a "castration" myth like that of Perseus, in which the hero is far more concerned with destroying sexuality than with gratifying it.[14] But the castration theme must have some additional meaning for the myth since it is repeated in the stealing of the eye and the tooth from the Graeae. We recall that Kenneth Elton's adult seducer was a "powerful" woman often observed chopping wood, and can hypothesize that the castration symbol is a talionic revenge (cf. the eye and tooth of the Graeae) upon a mother who is viewed as "castrating." More enlightening is an incident in the well-known tale from the Grimms' collection, "The Seven Ravens." A girl, seeking to disenchant her older brothers, who are imprisoned in a glass mountain, is given a bone by the Morning Star to use as a key. She loses it, and is only able to effect the rescue by cutting off her own little finger. A group of my students, attempting to analyze this myth in conjunction with two similar ones ("The Twelve Brothers," "The Six Swans"), noted the pregnancy symbolism of the glass mountain and puzzled over what they saw as a "double castration" (losing the key and cutting off the finger). They finally concluded that the initial loss was an expression of penis envy (which is usually marked in girls with older brothers), and that the second expressed the idea that only by relinquishing the wish for a penis was it possible

---

[14] Ovid's atypical rendering of the Callisto myth, for example, captures the core emotional dynamic of the Perseus myth but does not contain the castration aspect. Zeus seduces the nymph Callisto, who subsequently gives birth to Arcas. In revenge, Hera turns her into a bear. When Arcas is grown he unknowingly encounters his mother in the forest:

> He stepped back from the staring eyes that held him,
> Eyes that seemed fixed to pierce his gaze forever,
> And with that look a wordless fear possessed him.
> He poised a deadly spear aimed at her heart . . .
>   [*Metamorphoses* ii. 490ff. Gregory trans.]

Here the mother's sexuality is represented by her animal form (which is, after all, a consequence of it). The same preoccupation with looking, with immobility, with terror at the sight of the mother is portrayed, but the apparent resolution of mother-murder is forestalled by Zeus in deus ex machina fashion.

to enter the state of motherhood. While there is more to the incident than this, I would subscribe to their interpretation, and suggest that the castration in the Perseus legend may have a similar aim: to divest the mother of those male-envying and male-hating attributes which corrode the mother-son relationship.

Now it is possible to see all of this as directed toward some sort of "healthy" outcome. The mother is unsexed so that other objects can be sexualized, and she is rendered benign in her attitude toward males so that the son can be benign in his approach to females. The hostile side of the ambivalence has been expressed so that positive sexual feelings are now freed. This is the view taken by Neumann, who sums it up by saying, "Perseus must kill the Terrible Mother before he can win Andromeda" [1955, p. 38; 1954, pp. 216ff.]. He interprets the winged horse as the freeing of the hero's libido from the Great Mother, as well as its "spiritualization." He speaks of "soaring creative forces," and argues that the slaying of the Medusa represents making the unconscious conscious [1954, pp. 218–19].

I cannot suppress a certain skepticism about this viewpoint, although as a general model of hero myths it has much to recommend it. In the first place, Perseus' act of "raising the image to consciousness" is rather too half-hearted to serve as a prototype of truth-seeking confrontation. Consciousness would be represented by looking *directly* at the object; and I am struck by the fact that it is precisely this contentment with mirror images which limits the utility of Jungian theories. The myth is never allowed to be reduced to its dynamic components and their sources in objective reality. Any influence by real family or personal experiences, or real social structures, must be denied, so that the myth can preserve some of its mysterious quality—never tied to reality, only to other segments of the mythological realm itself. The "archetype" is the Athene's shield of Jungian analysis, preventing the analyst from being overwhelmed by the concrete and immediate significance of the symbols with which he plays so bravely in a looking-glass land detached from the crudities of everyday life.

Second, Perseus seems to me a poor example of heroic health or creativity. Neumann is of course talking primarily about the raw symbolism of the myth, rather than the subtleties of character development added by poets; but these later imaginings were inspired by something in the myth, after all, and if Pegasus is a symbol of creativity, as Neumann argues, one wonders why none of it rubs off on Perseus. He is in fact a singularly unattractive hero, lacking the intense humanness of a Gilgamesh, the suffering of an Oedipus or a Heracles, the cleverness and loneliness of an Odysseus or a Prometheus, the urbanity of a Theseus. He has no special virtues or capabilities save the ability to do as he is told and to utilize in an obvious way the implements he is given. He is a phallic nine-year-old's hero par excellence and his conquest of Medusa which, if it is nothing else, is a mythical representation of clitoridectomy [cf. Chapter I, footnote 29], expresses masculine sexual timidity in its most brutal and repellent form.

But the most serious question to be raised about Neumann's view concerns the degree to which the maternal conflict is actually resolved. If Perseus really overcomes his maternal conflict, why cannot he permit his real mother to marry? The logical resolution for this part of the tale would be for Danaë and Dictys, the two fugitives, to marry when Dictys is made king—was Dictys not, after all, her rescuer and protector? For so natural an outcome to be avoided, and for Perseus to drag his mother with him back to Argos, argues strongly against an anagogic interpretation. It requires considerable neurotic conservatism to maintain the Perseus myth's ultimate warp.

Furthermore, Andromeda is hardly lacking in maternal attributes, leading one to wonder if she is not really just a mother who has been "castrated"—purified of her punitive and sexually demanding characteristics. For Andromeda must be "castrated" also, in the sense of being permanently separated from the she-monster which threatens to turn her lovely nakedness into a fearsome menace. More important, however, is the fact that Perseus must compete with the same kind of avuncular rival for Andromeda as he does for his mother.

Indeed, if there is one unwavering consistency in the Perseus myth it is the oedipal quality of its relationships. Leaving Perseus himself aside, we note that Danaë is said, in one version, to have copulated with her father's twin, Proetus, and in all versions Acrisius has her imprisoned in his house to keep her from other men. This pattern is replicated on Seriphus, where Polydectes similarly imprisons her and tries to keep her for himself, and where she similarly has an ambiguous relationship with the king's brother (Dictys) who, like Proetus, is dispossessed. And are we to say that Andromeda represents a new departure, when we find her betrothed to her father's brother? And is this a very different kind of father who, like Acrisius, sacrifices his daughter for his own welfare, while at the same time placing an almost insuperable barrier between her and any possible suitor? Far from detaching his libido from the mother, Perseus appears to have married her, almost as surely as did Oedipus upon slaying *his* monster. We may find some corroboration of this statement in the name "Andromeda" itself, which is most reasonably translated as "ruler of men," and which contains within itself an echo of Medusa. That he kills both men (Acrisius, Polydectes) who stand in the nearest relation to fatherhood to him also attests to the oedipal character of the tale.

We should not leave the Perseus myth without observing the usual salient role played by narcissistic attitudes. The sea-serpent is sent as a consequence of Cassiopeia's vanity, and

Perseus' confrontation with the Medusa results from his *hubris* in boasting to Polydectes of his valor.[15]

Bellerophon

This is the most appropriate place to discuss the closely related myth of Bellerophon, who is connected with Perseus not only as a monster-slayer and the rider of Pegasus, and by his association with Proetus, but also through several dynamic parallels.

The origins of Bellerophon are rather misty. He starts, in a sense, with his name, which he acquired by killing the equally vague Bellerus, a tyrant of Corinth. To be purified of this murder, or of the accidental killing of his brother, variously named, he came to Proetus at Tiryns. There Anteia (or Stheneboea), Proetus' wife, fell in love with him, and when he rejected her advances played out the usual Potiphar's-wife sequence. Proetus, unable to kill a suppliant, sent Bellerophon to Anteia's father, Iobates, with a sealed death warrant, but since Iobates did not open it until he had shared food with Bellerophon for nine days, he also was forced to use indirect means.[16] He first sent Bellerophon to kill the Chimera, a

[15] The plethora of serpents in the story by now requires no comment, but a word or two may be added regarding the shower of gold. This incident is usually associated with folk beliefs and tales about impregnation by the sun's rays, and I would concur with this interpretation. Kerényi points out [1960, p. 129] that Athene was born in a similar shower [Pindar: *Olympian Odes* vii. 34], which helps account for her involvement in the tale. I might add, however, that a urethral definition of impregnation is quite in keeping with the infantile sexual level of the myth as a whole [cf. Jones, 1959, pp. 303ff. and *passim* for an integration of these views]. We are familiar, from clinical literature, with the conjunction of enuresis, exhibitionism, maternal seductiveness, and the inability to tolerate the accumulation of sexual tension [cf. e.g., Menninger, 1941].

[16] The tradition "which forbade those who had eaten together to kill each other," noted by Frazer in his notes on Apollodorus [Vol. I, p. 151], may be an extension of the idea of "milk" siblings—unrelated children suckled by the same woman [cf. Patai, 1959, p. 196].

three-headed, fire-breathing, serpent-tailed she-monster, believing he would be killed in the act. On the advice of a seer, Bellerophon sought the aid of Athene to tame Pegasus, and the goddess gave him a golden bridle with which to do so. Riding the winged horse, Bellerophon slew the Chimera, some say by thrusting a lump of lead between her jaws with his spear so that her fiery breath melted it and broiled her own innards. On similar orders from Iobates, Bellerophon defeated armies of Solymi and Amazons, and finally slew a group of palace guards sent by Iobates to ambush him on his return. He was only routed when a group of Xanthian women raised their skirts and exposed their genitals to him. But Iobates now relented and gave Bellerophon his daughter and made him his heir. Bellerophon then flew to Tiryns, enticed Anteia to ride with him and threw her into the sea. His final exploit was to attempt to fly to Olympus and join the gods, for which presumption he was thrown by Pegasus down to earth, and passed the rest of his life miserable and hated by the gods, wandering alone and "avoiding the paths of men" [Apollodorus: ii. 3. 1–2; Homer: *Iliad* vi. 155–203; Pindar: *Olympian Odes* xiii. 63–90 and *Isthmian Odes* vii. 44; Hesiod: *Theogony* 319ff.; Graves, 1955, I, p. 253; Kerényi, 1959, p. 83; Plutarch: "Bravery of Women" 248].

The cause of Bellerophon's initial difficulties is, once again, a seductive woman. Like the Biblical Joseph, he appears quite willing to forego this oedipal prize for the sake of establishing a positive dependent relationship with a paternal figure. But note how different are the outcomes. Joseph plays the sycophant, gains and retains the Pharaoh's favor and lives to lord it over all his enemies as virtual prime minister of the world. Bellerophon slays monsters and defeats armies, but when he tries to approach the "father" (Zeus) he is punished for his *hubris* (surely no greater than Joseph's dreams exhibit) and dies alone and neglected. This reveals the difference between a patriarchal woman-derogating culture in which the father actually plays a strong and salient role in the family, and one in which he is more detached. Paternal authority is never far from Joseph—despite the machinations of women and siblings he can always count upon it and knows how to appeal to it. Bellerophon, on the other hand, struggles alone, largely against feminine opponents (Anteia, the Chimera, the Amazons, the Xanthian women), with a father figure (Iobates) who misunderstands and tries to destroy him. He does not know how to placate or please the father, and in seeking him is rejected by him. In other words, the maternal threat in the Biblical family was cushioned by the provision of a strong male role model,[17] while in Greece it was not, producing a more brittle, phallic, and narcissistic male, longing for a father but unable to tolerate one.

The Potiphar's-wife theme appears no less than five times in Greek mythology, usually with tragic results [Apollodorus: ii. 3. 1, iii. 13. 3 and *Epitome* iii. 24; Hyginus: *Astronomica* ii. 20; Euripides: *Hippolytus*].[18] Two of these tales (Astydamia and Peleus, Demodoke and Phrixus) have several elements in common with the Bellerophon myth, and may have a common base, but the others (Phaedra and Hippolytus, Phylonome and Tenes) are rather distinct. The male is always the innocent victim of these seduction efforts, although "paternal" wrath is usually aroused, and often (as in Kenneth Elton's case) utterly blameless females (typically sister-figures) suffer as much as or more than the hero.

[17] A cushion which was in part retained by the Jews through centuries of wandering and persecution, although the lack of relation of the male role to the practical issues of everyday life often made it a rather thin one [cf. Zborowski and Herzog, 1962, 131–41, 331]. The combination of emigration and assimilation often eliminated this cushion, producing a rich mythology of seductive, possessive, castrating, and generally overwhelming mothers, and some fantasies and life-styles similar to those I have been discussing.

[18] The frequency is not surprising, for the theme captures the combination of maternal seductiveness and maternal vindictiveness, and the attempt to weaken the father-son relationship. A sixth example [Apollodorus: iii. 15. 3] contains two of these three elements.

The emotional consequences are narcissism and misogyny. Bellerophon striving for Olympus on Pegasus represents the boy "puffed up" with phallic pride, only to be cast down by parental scorn. Like Perseus, he depends upon the anti-maternal Athene to achieve his victories, and like Perseus, he fears to look upon the maternal genitalia. His conquest of the she-monster, however, is considerably more spectacular, and this is perhaps why the myth of Bellerophon ends unhappily. Bellerophon is both more overtly phallic and more overtly sexual than Perseus. The incident with the molten lead expresses this: the fire of the maternal monster's passion is consuming, like that of Grendel's mother or Althaea; but in Bellerophon's flight and spear-thrust one is to understand that the sexual advance is returned in kind, and the Chimera's fire is finally extinguished. Bellerophon's conquest is thus a true oedipal rape, although one based upon infantile sexual theories. Where Perseus cautiously and surreptitiously unsexes the mother, Bellerophon reciprocates her rapacity, and must therefore be deflated later on.[19] Like Peleus, he masters the threatening female, but only to be ultimately cast away and neglected. In Greek fantasy, only Zeus could be allowed such a victory.

[19] Bunker interprets his revenge on Anteia (riding with her and hurling her down) as incestuous intercourse [1944, pp. 203-4].

CHAPTER XII

The Multiple Defenses
of Heracles

For not even the mighty Herakles escaped death,
albeit most dear to Kronian Zeus the King, but
Fate overcame him and Hera's cruel wrath.
[Homer: *Iliad* xviii. 115. Lang, Leaf,
and Meyers trans.]

Will there ever be words for the vicissitudes
of the milk and the suffering of the mouth?
[Rosen, 1953, vi]

THE GLORY OF HERA" was chosen as the title of this book because it translates the name "Heracles," and hence captures the bitter irony of the Greek mother-son relationship, inasmuch as Hera was also the hero's chief persecutor. Nilsson, while accepting the derivation as incontrovertible, argues that the name is of no importance and antedates the myth itself:

> Because Hera plays such a prominent part in his myth, Heracles has often been thought to be a descriptive name; but if we consider the matter closely, it will be found to be a forced and improbable explanation that Heracles should have been called "The Fame of Hera" or "The Man who became famous because of Hera," while this goddess dealt the severest

337

blows to him and imposed pain, grief, and labor upon him [Nilsson, 1932, pp. 191–92].

Yet we now recognize that such vicarious narcissistic strivings are in no way incompatible with a persecutory attitude, and in the Greek mother-son relationship were almost inseparable from it.[1]

The choice of title was also based on the centrality of Heracles to my interpretation. Not only does he have attached to him a larger body of myth than any other figure in Greek mythology, but these myths include virtually all of the themes discussed in previous chapters. While other gods and heroes display a variety of responses, more or less peculiar to each, with only partial overlap and duplication, Heracles exemplifies every mode of response to maternal threat. Like Zeus, he is a sexual athlete, and fears not to copulate with the serpent. Like Apollo, he affects a masculine antisepsis against matriarchy, femininity, and chthonic forces everywhere. Like

[1] It is plausible to suggest that Heracles was originally the adolescent consort of Hera the mother-goddess, as Tammuz was to Ishtar, Adonis to Astarte, Attis to Cybele [cf. Guthrie, 1955, p. 66n.; Harrison, 1962, p. 491]. This alone would explain the ambivalence, which is undisguised in the latter myths. The male consort in these cases acts as a kind of intermediary between man and deity, just as Christ and Mary do in Christianity. Thus Heracles was both man and god, and could be used as a charm against chthonic forces [Guthrie, 1955, p. 240]. Similarly, in Malekula, a boar is sacrificed to a devouring female deity as a surrogate for a dead man, who thereby purchases his passage to the land of the dead, intact. The boar is seen as given to man by the goddess' consort, Taghar, "*both in defence against, and also in honour of, Le-hev-hev,*" the goddess [Levy, pp. 154–62. Italics mine]. This statement would serve equally well to describe Heracles' labors.

In general it seems unwise to use accident as an explanatory principle. It may be true that the Heracles legend, as Nilsson suggests [1932, p. 192], attached itself early to some individual who just happened to be named Heracles, or that the name was once as common as Jack or Hans or other names typical in folklore. But the Heracles legend is an amalgamation of many such, which means that this one name stuck while the others dropped out; and this survival must also be explained. In modern times, for example, Heraclean heroes in Greek folktales *are* called Jack [Lawson, 1964, p. 281]. Survival is never automatic.

Orestes, he attacks the mother directly—the very breast that suckled him. Like Hephaestus, he emasculates himself and plays the servant and buffoon. Like Dionysus, he identifies with the mother and becomes feminine. Like Perseus, he "castrates" the mother. But more specifically than these others, Heracles represents a kind of compulsive assertion of strength, or, to put it the other way around, a vigorous denial of weakness in the face of maternal hostility. Even today he symbolizes exaggerated masculine differentiation, with emphasis on secondary rather than primary sex characteristics: muscularity rather than virility per se [cf. Harnik, 1924]. As such, he is difficult for an urban people to take altogether seriously—a difficulty we share with the Athenians of the classical period. In a way this is unfortunate, since the Heracles that emerges from the total agglomeration of Greek myth is a far more complex and interesting figure than someone like Achilles, who is merely a wellborn gorilla.[2] While Heracles is often boorish and a being of gross appetites and homicidal passions—perhaps because of his Bearson origins, as Carpenter suggests [Carpenter, 1958, pp. 191–92], he is also portrayed as a culture hero: ridding the world of monsters and lawless creatures, ending human sacrifice, and performing useful engineering feats [cf. Graves, 1955, II, pp. 123–24, 133, 135, 137, 144, 167, 176]. Vestiges of a primitive dactylic nature, even somewhat trickster-like (as in the tale of the Cercopes, where he becomes "Blackbottom"), combined with his treatment (in Attic drama) as a kind of good-natured oaf, lend him humorous qualities [cf. Kerényi, 1956, pp. 176, 186,

---

[2] I do not wish to slander gorillas, who are actually rather mild-mannered beasts. I use the term in its colloquial sense of "thug" or "goon." It is perhaps unfair to single out Achilles, however, since most of the Greek heroes in the *Iliad* operate with the values and assumptions of a delinquent gang—a similarity nicely captured by Sol Yurick in *The Warriors* [1965]. Achilles' necrophiliac passion for Penthesilia [Apollodorus: *Epitome* v.1] is the functional equivalent of a gang-bang.

189; Kerényi, 1959, pp. 126, 194–95; Euripides: *Alcestis*
747ff.; Aristophanes: *The Birds* 1575ff. and *The Frogs*
103ff.]. But it has been said that his most distinctive quality
is his role as the conqueror of death [Fontenrose, 1959,
pp. 110, 113–14, 323ff., 358; Kerényi, 1959, pp. 132–82].
The consistent, overt, manifest theme in the Heraclean tales,
however, is his laboring and his suffering. It is this which
makes him human and meaningful.

Like Dionysus, Heracles is attacked in the womb, as an infant, and as a grown man, with Hera once again the persecutor. The attack which destroys him, however, comes after
all of these, in his gruesome death on Mount Oeta. Even his
labors are an expression of maternal malevolence, as well as
many of the supplementary difficulties which he must endure
in carrying them out.

Hera's enmity toward Heracles is supposed initially to have
been aroused by Zeus's affair with Alcmene. This is an ab-
surdly weak reason, since Zeus's infidelities were legion, while
no one suffered Hera's wrath so persistently as Heracles. But
we are not to expect too much reason and coherence from such
a mélange of unrelated and contradictory traditions. What
we do know is that the relation between Hera and Heracles is an intense one, and by no means always negative. That
we are left with the contradictions, largely unrationalized,
suggests that such ambivalence did not seem altogether
strange to the Greeks—that it tapped something meaningful
in their experience.

The skeleton of the story is as follows: When Zeus boasted
that a son of his would be born that very day and would rule
the land, Hera made him swear an oath to this effect. She
then hurried to Argos and delivered, prematurely, a grandson
of Perseus (and thus a descendant of Zeus), Eurystheus, while
at the same time delaying Heracles' birth [Homer: *Iliad* xix.
95ff.]. This "attack in the womb," while less devastating than
that perpetrated on Dionysus, determined the entire course of

Heracles' future, since he was forced to serve Eurystheus, a weak and cowardly man, for most of his adult life.

Heracles was born with a twin, Iphicles, the son of Alcmene's husband, Amphitryon, whom Zeus had impersonated in fathering Heracles. One night when the twins were less than a year old, Hera sent two serpents to destroy the hero, but Heracles awoke and strangled them [Pindar: *Nemean Odes* i. 38ff.; Diodorus Siculus: iv. 10; Apollodorus: ii. 4. 8].

Upon reaching manhood—after some military victories, marriage to his first wife (Megara) and the fathering of several offspring—Hera drove Heracles mad, so that he murdered all his children and two sons of Iphicles. In some versions he also slew Megara [Apollodorus: ii. 4. 12; Euripides: *Heracles* 922ff.]. When he recovered from his madness, the oracle at Delphi instructed him to serve Eurystheus for twelve years and perform whatever labors were set for him. No sooner were these accomplished, however, than Heracles committed another murder, to expiate which he was sold into slavery to Queen Omphale. While serving in this capacity he achieved several more heroic exploits, and followed up his slavery with a military expedition to Troy, the killing of a sea-monster, further battles, and a new marriage—one which was to bring his death.

Seeing such a life story today, divested of its supernatural elements, one would undoubtedly comment on the repetitive self-destructive behavior, the lack of impulse control, and so on. It is in fact very reminiscent, in style if not in content, of the case history of a talented delinquent. The father (Zeus) is somewhat in the background, important primarily as procreator and doing very little to "protect" the son against the pathogenic demands of the mother (Hera). The son is impulsive and depends heavily on peer relationships for support (Iolaus, Hylas, Telamon). He is restless and mobile, but his independence is spurious since he is almost always in some sort of servitude. Like so many criminals, he completes a long term of thraldom only to forfeit his new freedom at the first opportunity. And, of course, like all other Greek heroes, he is utterly dependent upon feminine aid, usually in the form of the ubiquitous and ever-helpful Athene. Thus in the *Iliad* the goddess rails against Zeus for not appreciating "all those many times I rescued his own son, Herakles, when the tasks of Eurystheus were too much for his strength. And time and again he would cry out aloud to the heavens, and Zeus would send me down in speed from the sky to help him" [Homer: *Iliad* viii. 362–65. Lattimore trans.]. Yet this, too, is only a part of the picture, for when he is *not* crying for help he appears, and seems to feel, invincible.

The contradictions in Heracles begin with his ambivalent relationship with Hera. Of this, two separate questions may be asked. We may inquire how the contradictory aspects of the relationship came to exist in the first place, and we may ask why they were retained in the surviving myths. To the first question Kerényi suggests the reasonable answer that part of the Heracles legend derives from a myth in which Heracles is simply a divine servant of the mother-goddess [Kerényi, 1959, pp. 126ff.; cf. also Fontenrose, 1959, p. 322]. Heracles is, as Fontenrose points out [*Ibid.*, pp. 321–23] a composite figure, and his story, "a peg on which a great number of related, unrelated, and contradictory myths have been hung" [Graves, 1955, II, p. 88]. Anomalies in the legend can be "explained" by tracing the dissonant parts to their varied origins, as was done even in ancient times [*Ibid.*].

But to explain the origin of a contradiction is not to explain its survival. Why were these myth-components hung on such incongruent "pegs"? Why were not the contradictions purified out, as in Biblical stories, or at least better rationalized? When one finds an inconsistency in a myth one must be prepared either to argue that nothing in a myth ever gets lost or changed (a patent absurdity), or to assume that its survival is in some way motivated. Furthermore, it is here, more than anywhere else, that socio-psychological interpretations are likely to carry most weight, since some emotional pressure is necessary to counteract the desire for congruence.[3] In the case of Heracles, I would argue that the positive and negative versions of the Hera-Heracles relationship were retained together because it made sense to the Greeks for a maternal figure to use a male both as an extension of herself and as an object of persecution.

But how much material that defines a positive relationship or one of identification do we really have? There is, as already noted, Heracles' name, and the fact that Hera's temple at Paestum was decorated with his exploits [Kerényi, 1959, p. 131]. There is the story that Heracles built a shrine to Hera at Sparta and sacrificed to her, allegedly because she had not thwarted him in his campaign against the sons of Hippocoön [Pausanias: iii. 19. 9]—a weak explanation, since there were a number of other exploits in which Hera did not oppose him. There are also two episodes in which Heracles defended Hera against attack: once against the giant Porphyrion, who attempted to rape her during the Giants' revolt [Apollodorus: i. 6. 1–2]; and once against a group of Sileni with similar intentions, as portrayed in vase paintings and on the temple at Paestum [Kerényi, 1960, p. 159 and Plate VIa; Kerényi, 1959, pp. 197–98].

Some of the "positive" themes are rationalized by the story that Hera and Heracles were reconciled on Olympus following the hero's apotheosis [Apollodorus: ii. 7. 7]. Some such device was necessary to account for Heracles' marriage to

---

[3] By "congruence" I do not refer to rules of logic, but simply to the need to give a myth some sort of internal coherence. All myths tolerate more coexistence of opposites than Western rationalism is comfortable with, but there is a tendency for this increasingly to assume a form which the listener feels "hangs together" in some way. Trickster is now the sharper, now the patsy, now male, now female, now creative, now destructive; but he is a recognizable unity, one which we would feel had been violated if, for example, too much impulse control were suddenly attributed to him.

Hebe, the daughter of Zeus and Hera. Given Heracles' Christlike suffering and persecution, it became increasingly important to imagine a joyous resurrection, and the peaceful heavenly marriage with the innocuous Hebe was a seldom-omitted feature of the Heracles legend [Homer: *Odyssey* xi. 602ff.; Hesiod: *Theogony* 950ff.; Pindar: *Isthmian Odes* iv. 59 and *Nemean Odes* i. 69 and x. 17; Euripides: *Heracleidae* 915ff.]. Since Hera was a marriage-goddess, her role in this event was crucial; and since Hebe "walketh for ever in Olympus beside her mother" [Pindar: *Nemean Odes* x. 18], it was necessary that he and his stepmother be defined as at peace with one another, to convince us that Heracles' sufferings were really over.[4] One might wonder who Heracles was really marrying here, and Kerényi argues explicitly that Hebe was simply another aspect of Hera [1960, p. 98; 1959, p. 204].

Some versions of the tale go further, saying that Hera performed an adoption ceremony, taking the hero beneath her skirts, feigning labor, bringing him out again, and suckling him [Kerényi, 1959, p. 204; Diodorus Siculus: iv. 39].

Others place the suckling of Heracles earlier. There is an old tradition that Hera was tricked into nursing the infant hero, thus becoming his foster mother as well as his stepmother and mother-in-law.[5] There are two versions of the involuntary suckling. In one, Heracles was smuggled to Olympus and put to the breast while Hera was asleep. In the other, Alcmene, fearing Hera's jealousy, had exposed the child on what is now called "The Plain of Heracles." Athene took the Queen of the Gods for a supposedly aimless stroll where they would

[4] This repressed insight, that the sufferings of Heracles were really endless (because a part of his character), reveals itself in the notion that despite his blissful sporting on Olympus he also had a shade in the underworld who strode about fiercely, as in life, frightening the other spirits [Homer: *Odyssey* xi. 602ff.].

[5] Graves argues that Alcmene is in fact merely a title of Hera's, an idea suggested by the worship of the former at Thebes [Graves, 1955, II, pp. 88, 209, 211].

encounter the infant, and persuaded Hera to suckle him. In both versions, Heracles sucked so hard that Hera threw him off in agony, causing a spurt of milk to fly either from Hera's breast or the greedy Heracles' mouth, creating the Milky Way. The milk, in any case, made Heracles immortal, so that while it was Hera who destroyed the hero, it was also Hera who saved him from death [Diodorus Siculus: iv. 9; Pausanias: ix. 25. 2; Hyginus: *Astronomica* ii. 43].

This story does more than affirm the mother-son relationship of Hera and Heracles. It also provides a missing psychological link with the major events in Heracles' later career, which form a meaningful symbolic pattern when this piece is added. This is not to say that the suckling story was old, or one of the original components of the Heracles myth. One suspects, in fact, that it was added rather late. What I am suggesting is that as initially unrelated myth fragments began to agglutinate in terms of prevailing cultural preoccupations, a gap was formed which had to be filled.

The incident itself suggests a hostile, depriving mother and a deprived, devouring child. Its significance is perhaps most simply illustrated by a modern parallel, drawn from the same case history I discussed at the end of Chapter X. It will be recalled that the child, Eric, met, at birth, "a mother who had no wish to meet him," and who had experienced pregnancy as a humiliating defeat. After he was born, these feelings introduced an element of deprivation into the mother-child relationship: "When she felt him at the breast, the fantasies of being sucked dry and emptied out by him were uppermost; she experienced feeding as a fight for survival and her flow of milk remained inadequate" [Hellman, 1960, p. 371]. Hera's milk is not inadequate, simply withdrawn, but the parallel of the "fight for survival" seems appropriate to their relationship.

Yet this in itself does not take us very far. Hera is not so much a depriving mother as a malevolent, persecuting one.

She resembles the "schizophrenogenic" mother, who gives love but with conditions attached which are destructive to the child's personality. In the fantasies of psychotic patients this appears symbolically as "poisoned milk" or the "poisoned breast." The conditions may be demands that reality be misperceived, that contradictory instructions be followed, that the child be sick, bad, or unhappy, that the child not exist as an entity independent of the mother but be an extension of her, and so on [Bateson, *et al.*, 1956; Lidz, *et al.*, 1966; Limentani, 1956; Searles, 1961; Wynne, *et al.*, 1958].

The baldest statement of the matter comes from John Rosen, who remarks that "psychotics live immediately under the shadow of the breast" [1953, p. 8]. Only "oral" questions —that is, those of obtaining uncontaminated nurturance from the mothering one—have any meaning to them. At the root of the schizophrenic psychosis is the feeling of being poisoned by a Perverse Mother who is unable to love and empathize with her child [*Ibid.*, pp. 99ff.].

We know that some time after the suckling incident, Hera sent two serpents to devour Heracles. I have argued that serpents always represent some aspect of the oral-narcissistic conflict, and malevolent serpents are usually defined as poisonous. We have also seen that this conflict is aroused in the mother by the boundary violations of pregnancy and childbirth, and again by the incessant demands of the hungry infant who feeds on her body. Thus the serpent in the "Eros and Psyche" story preferred women close to delivery, as Leto was when Hera sent Python to kill her. Apollo had to slay this serpent, just as Heracles slew his—that is, they had to overcome the malevolent terror which they aroused in the mother. At the same time, the hunger of the abandoned Heracles confirms the maternal fear: suckling in this case *is* a fight for survival.

I have often noted that the oral-narcissistic dilemma is a reciprocal one. Mother and child threaten the integrity of each other's boundaries, since they now wish to be one (as they once were) and now wish to be separate. Clytemnestra and Orestes both saw each other as serpents, and this is duplicated with Hera and Heracles. Hera is a serpent by virtue of the frequency with which she inflicts them upon him, Heracles by virtue of injuring the breast, just as did the serpent-Orestes in Clytemnestra's dream [Aeschylus: *The Choephori* 530–33].[6]

One further connection between deprivation, poison, and the serpent symbol is revealed by cross-cultural literature on weaning practices. Unlike our own society, in which weaning is typically early and attended with few concomitant changes, weaning in many primitive societies involves a total transformation of the child's world, from a warm, loving, and protective one to a rejecting and indifferent one. Since weaning, which is likely to occur somewhere in the third year, is usually instigated by the advent of a new pregnancy, it is often accompanied by a sharp (sometimes total) diminution in physical affection and warmth—not only by the mother, but sometimes by the entire community. The child loses not merely the physical breast but also the "symbolic breast" of general maternal nurturance. He often ceases to sleep with the mother at this point, is no longer the center of attention, is ignored by everyone when he cries, and may be required to assume onerous responsibilities. This has a profound effect on

[6] One can of course find other indices. Heracles kills his enemies with the venom of a serpent, fathers a serpent on the princess Pyrene [Fontenrose, 1959, pp. 48–49], and wears on his shield "heads of snakes unspeakably frightful" which "used to frighten the tribes of men on earth whosoever made war against the son of Zeus; for they would clash their teeth when Amphitryon's son was fighting" [Hesiod: *The Shield of Heracles* 161ff.], not to mention the Gorgons [*Ibid.*, 230ff.]. But, as I noted in the previous chapter, such representations were common on shields: Menelaus also had one [Graves, 1955, II, p. 211]. Furthermore, all heroes became serpents upon death, as Jane Harrison observes [1957, pp. 133, 325ff.], and had a chthonic nature due to their close association with ancestor worship [*Ibid.*, pp. 232ff., 325ff.]. Finally, "the dragon-slayer is of the dragon's seed" [Harrison, 1962, p. 435], or becomes identified with it through conquest, just as Perseus carries the Gorgon head, or Heracles wears the lion skin, or Apollo speaks through a Pythoness.

the child—so much so that the last child to be born often has a personality markedly different (happier, "healthier") from the others (this perhaps accounts for the near-universality of folktales in which the youngest of a group of siblings is the only one to be successful). Ethnographers remark upon the dramatic changes in children who have just been weaned in such societies—from being happy, good-natured, confident, and affectionate they become sullen, whining, touchy, suspicious, and apathetic. Illness and death are frequent after weaning [Whiting, 1963, pp. 146–51, 473–80, 646–51, 827–33; Stephens, 1963, pp. 362–65].[7]

Weaning is obviously not a trivial deprivation in such societies, and is often achieved with some difficulty. Complete separation from the mother is sometimes necessary, but the most frequent coercive device is to place some substance on the breasts which is or is said to be unpleasant or poisonous, such as red pepper, ginger, sour juices, dirt, manure of various kinds, or bitter herbs. Sometimes the breast is made frightening by coloring it, covering it with black paper or human hair, pretending it is injured, bleeding, and so on. The child may also be threatened with bogies who will eat him, cut out his tongue or heart, and so on [Whiting, 1963, pp. 149, 321, 474–75, 648, 829–30; Mead, 1953, p. 189]. Particularly interesting, however, is the following account of the Kwoma:

> They tell the child that huge, snakelike monsters which cause storms dwell in the swamp, and that it is dangerous to go near their dwelling places. This danger is brought within the sphere of experience of the child when his mother tells him that a *marsalai* occupies her breast and vivifies the story by putting a leech on it [Whiting, 1941, p. 35. Quoted by Stephens, 1963, p. 379].

[7] The susceptibility of the newly weaned to infection may in some areas be due to the fact that it will never again have so adequate a diet. Yet the same tendency toward illness and death is also found in orphanages with the most nutritious of diets and impeccably antiseptic conditions, when affectionate mothering and social stimulation are lacking [cf. Spitz, 1964].

Thus, when deprivation is necessary, the *threat* of poisoning or of boundary-dissolution is invoked.

A comparable monster was the Hydra, a snaky, venomous, multiheaded being which "Hera nourished, being angry beyond measure with the mighty Heracles" [Hesiod: *Theogony* 313–15]. It, too, dwelt in a swamp, at Lerna, the entrance to the underworld.[8] Heracles killed it with much difficulty and used its gall as poison to tip his arrows. This poison was so venomous and unbearably painful that when Heracles accidentally wounded Cheiron, who was immortal, Cheiron forfeited his immortality to escape the agony [Apollodorus: ii. 5. 4].

Since Hera reared the Hydra specifically in anger against Heracles (and since its venom ultimately killed him), one might accept this as a sufficient indication of a "poisoned milk" theme. But there is another incident which solidifies the connection. It is said that Heracles, during the battle for Pylus (in which the gods participated), wounded Hera in the right breast with a three-barbed arrow, causing her unassuageable pain [Homer: *Iliad* v. 392–94]. Nothing is said of Hydra venom, nor are the wounds of the other gods hit by Heracles' arrows similarly described, nor is there any other mention of Hera's injury. What the passage suggests, however, is that Hera suffered the same affliction as did Cheiron. Kerényi even translates the pain as "incurable" [1959, p. 165]. We thus find a poisoned breast after all, albeit retroactively; and a hero who is nourished by it becomes psychotic, and dies of it. The Greek mother's ambivalence is thus nicely realized in the suckling episode. Hera's hostility toward Zeus, displaced onto Heracles, destroys him, while her need to make

[8] As noted earlier, the serpent, since it represents boundary ambiguity, will tend to appear wherever nature suggests birth, death, or boundary ambiguity itself: oceans, lakes, swamps, caves, tombs. The Lernean swamp was a natural location, since it contained springs, pools that were considered bottomless, and was the road to Tartarus.

him a husband-substitute and a narcissistic self-extension, makes him ambitious, glorious, and immortal. Small wonder that there was such confusion over Heracles' post mortem fate—that he had to be split in two. The shade in Tartarus is the Heracles destroyed by the poison, while the Olympian Heracles is the part made immortal by the divine milk.

The Heraclean suckling story may profitably be compared with that of the infant Krishna:

> A certain goblin named Putana came in the shape of a beautiful woman, but with poison in her breasts. She entered the house of Yasoda, the foster mother of the child, and made herself very friendly, presently taking the baby in her lap to give it suck. But Krishna drew so hard that he sucked away her life, and she fell dead, reassuming her huge and hideous form [Campbell, 1956, p. 327].

All of the elements I have struggled so laboriously to connect are tightly fused in this tale, which undoubtedly bears a genealogical relationship to the story of Heracles' suckling. But the Queen of the Gods cannot be portrayed as a demon with poison in her breasts, however malevolent her attitude. Thus the poison is detached—temporally by having the venom enter the breast only later, and spatially by using venomous emissaries, such as the pair of serpents and the Hydra. Further masking appears in the idea that the suckling was involuntary on the part of the goddess. Hera cannot be a two-dimensional representation of the Bad Mother; she is the Greek mother *in toto*, and must be supplied with motives for her malevolence.

One interesting facet of the Hindu myth is its articulation of the relation between sheer deprivation and contaminated love. Krishna is not destroyed by the poison; indeed, in the "fight for survival" he is victorious. What this seems to say is that if there is enough love, it does not matter whether it is "poisoned" or not, the ego can somehow muddle through.[9] Krishna takes *all* the milk, and survives. He is even strong enough to subsequently redeem the demon [*Ibid.*], as if to show that the mother-child relationship can display a benign as well as a pathological spiral. Heracles fares less well with his abrupt "weaning," but Hera survives, redeemed or not.

We still have not considered the curious specification that Hera was wounded in the *right* breast, a detail which is perhaps trivial, save that questions of left and right appear elsewhere in the Heraclean myths. Right and left are assigned relative values throughout the Western world: right is good or primary, left is evil or secondary. Since Heracles had a twin, Iphicles, who was in every way a lesser figure, the specification is perhaps a way of identifying the right breast more particularly as that which pertained to the hero. We may also recall that the Amazons were alleged to cut off the right breast to facilitate drawing the bow and shooting the javelin [Diodorus Siculus: ii. 45 and iii. 53; Apollodorus: ii. 5. 9]. Indeed, almost the only time Hera intervened in person in the affairs of Heracles was when she disguised herself as an Amazon to stir up these warriors against him [Apollodorus: ii. 5. 9]. The main point here, however, is the not surprising association between a woman being masculine and warlike and lacking nurturance (the name "Amazon" means "without breasts").

These associations become more meaningful when we examine the events surrounding Heracles' marriage with Deianeira, the wife who was to kill him. Kerényi points out that Deianeira's name itself implies "a virgin hostile to men, not merely warlike," and that one might have predicted that she

---

9 The same notion is found in the remark Euripides puts in the mouth of Theseus, that love is proof against magical pollution [*Heracles* 1234], whether the line be interpreted as referring to Heracles and Theseus or, as Lawson argues, to Heracles and his children [1964, pp. 470–71].

would be a dangerous wife [Kerényi, 1959, pp. 114, 198].
She was a very masculine bride, who drove a chariot and was
a huntress and warrior [Apollodorus: i. 8. 1]. Fontenrose
compares her with Atalanta, and observes that she helped
Heracles fight the Dryopes [1959, p. 354]. Such a masculine
helpmate might seem desirable to a Greek, inasmuch as she did
not have maternal qualities—another Electra or Athene. Yet
masculine women are a mixed picture in Greek mythology;
for every Athene there is an Artemis, and Atalanta was, after
all, the indirect cause of the destruction of Meleager and her
many suitors. As in the case of the parallel cousin in the Arab
tales, the defense does not succeed, and although the masculine woman initially seems more satisfactory, the underlying
anxiety usually breaks through. Orestes' mad scene with
Electra (see Chapter V) illustrates this process. The male
not only wishes to avoid the Bad Mother—he also wishes to
find a Good (nurturant) Mother, and when the warlike maiden
fails to satisfy this need he finds himself wishing for what he
fears the most.

Heracles might have been warned by Deianeira's familial
background. Her father was the mother-mad Dionysus and
her mother the filicidal Althaea [Apollodorus: i. 8. 1]. Worst
of all, it was the ghost of Deianeira's brother Meleager who
had persuaded Heracles to make the match, when Heracles
went to the underworld to bring up the hound Cerberus
[Bacchylides: xxxiii. 56ff. and 165–75]. Thus not only was
the match made in Hell [Apollodorus: ii. 7. 5 note 2] but the
woman given was the duplicate of she who was the undoing
of the giver.[10] When Heracles rescued Deianeira from Achelous and Nessus (as he had rescued Hera from Porphyrion

[10] But the mismatched and unhappily married are always the most ardent
matchmakers.

Meleager, like many a man, fell in love with the double of his sister. Like
Deianeira, Atalanta was masculine, was attacked by Centaurs, was the prize
in a lethal competition of suitors, and caused her lover's death [Kerényi,
1959, 117ff.].

and the Sileni) he was rescuing his own Delilah [Fontenrose, 1959, pp. 354–55].

But it was a characteristically Greek Delilah—devoid of soft seductive wiles which would have frightened away the prey before it was trapped. More man than woman, Deianeira is in everything but birth an Amazon. Indeed, Heracles actually killed an Amazon named Deianeira during his Ninth Labor, when he fought the warrior women for Hippolyte's girdle [Diodorus Siculus: iv. 16]. According to Sophocles, Deianeira even committed suicide like a man, with a sword instead of a rope [*The Trachiniae* 929].

A maternally persecuted man might well find comfort in such a warrior-maiden. But what of the maternally *deprived* man? It is noteworthy that Heracles is said by some to have preceded his marriage by obtaining the cornucopia from Achelous. This river-god was a suitor for Deianeira, so fearful in appearance that she later used him to justify her overpowering fear of marriage [Sophocles: *The Trachiniae* 6ff.]. When Heracles threw the bull-headed god he turned into a serpent, which the hero proceeded to strangle, whereupon Achelous turned into a huge bull. Heracles wrestled the bull to the earth and tore off the right horn [Ovid: *Metamorphoses* ix. 1–88].

There is some confusion about whether this horn itself became the horn of plenty, or whether Achelous got his own back by giving Heracles the true cornucopia of his sister Amaltheia [Ovid: *loc. cit.*; Apollodorus: ii. 7. 5]. Heracles, in any case, won the inexhaustible receptacle along with his bride, and is often portrayed carrying it instead of his club [Kerényi, 1959, p. 199].

This horn is at once phallic and breast-like, representing both inexhaustible potency and oral plenty. There is nothing extraordinary about this—when the preoccupations are oral the two are not distinguished. Playing a male sexual role becomes a question of having enough, rather than seeking pleasure; while a woman's sexuality is experienced as vampiresque, and intercourse as feeding or giving [cf. Rosberg and Karon, 1958]. Nor is it only schizophrenics who operate on such assumptions. The belief that it takes forty drops of blood to make one drop of semen is widespread in the East, and Weakland [1956] has shown how absorbed the Chinese have long been with this question. According to Weakland, the female Yin essence is viewed as inexhaustible, while the male Yang essence must be carefully hoarded. Restraining ejaculation returns the semen to the brain, while loss of semen can be only partially restored by proper eating [1956, pp. 240–41]. A good woman is nurturant, mild, and sexually undemanding, and the sex handbooks suggest that the penis movement in intercourse "should resemble that of an infant nibbling its mother's breast" [pp. 242–43]. It is believed that through practice the forces of the woman can be sucked in through the urethra, but a woman who can prevent this can live without food [pp. 243–44; cf. also Heyer, 1953, pp. 221–34]. Wolfenstein relates this attitude to prolonged feelings of connection with the mother's body, stimulated by the practice of pre-chewing the infant's food, and by the mother's rather active participation in the child's excretory activities. If a parent becomes extremely ill a child may try to revive him or her with a soup in which the child has cooked a piece of his own flesh [Wolfenstein, 1963b, pp. 363–67].

We are not disappointed in our expectation that the Greeks must have shared some of these notions, an expectation which is reinforced by their homosexuality and preference for unripe women. Women were indeed expected to be sexually moderate [Ehrenberg, 1951, p. 194], and a declaration of passion was likely to produce instant flight [Plutarch: "Dialogue on Love" 753b]. Aristotle devotes considerable thought to the matter and argues that semen is a "secretion of useful nutriment." Thus "the exhaustion consequent on the loss of even a very little of the semen is conspicuous because the body is deprived of the ultimate gain drawn from the nutriment" and "in most men and as a general rule the result of inter-course is exhaustion and weakness" [Aristotle: "On the Generation of Animals" i. 18]. A similar view can be found in Plato [*Laws* viii. 841], and a pale reflection of it in sixteenth-century England [Stone, 1964, p. 174].

That the cornucopia is phallic is suggested by its association with a phallic animal and phallic deities such as Hermes, Pan, and Dionysus [Fontenrose, 1959, pp. 350ff.]. Furthermore, when Heracles tore off the horn, the drops of blood shed by Achelous became the Sirens, just as the blood from the castration of Uranus produced the Erinyes [Kerényi, 1960, p. 56]. But here the phallus means fertility—the horn is, after all, filled with inexhaustible food and drink. It is the inexhaustibility which is important, whether one thinks in terms of food or of semen. Heracles must securely establish his potency before mating with so warlike a woman, and remove any feelings of deprivation or insecurity before taking so unnurturant a wife. The seized right horn of Achelous nullifies both the withdrawn and poisoned right breast of Hera and the absent right breast of the Amazon wife. Since his maternal experiences make the Greek male feel rejected, deflated, and deprived, he must be continually replenished.

The connection with Amaltheia supports this interpretation. Another version of the Milky Way's origin is that it was created when Rhea suddenly weaned Zeus [Graves, 1955, II, p. 94]. Following this deprivation the King of the Gods was nursed by this same Amaltheia, either on her milk or from her horns, one of which yielded ambrosia, the other nectar [Hyginus: *Astronomica* ii. 13; Apollodorus: ii. 7. 5 note 4]. She also bears traces of the Terrible Mother, so Gorgonesque that Zeus used her hide as an aegis to frighten the Titans [Fontenrose, 1959, pp. 353–54].

The cornucopia represents only the symbolic solution to the Greek dilemma. The interpersonal solution is equally characteristic: Heracles avoids his wife as much as possible, just as he did his earlier one, spending all his time in battles and casual sexual encounters [Sophocles: *The Trachiniae* 28–48 and 459–60]. His death, furthermore, shows a similar consistency in its symbolic and interpersonal "causes." Let us consider the symbolic aspect first.

A few years after his marriage to Deianeira, Heracles killed a kinsman of his father-in-law and exiled himself to Trachis. While en route the couple had to cross the river Evenus, and the Centaur Nessus offered to ferry Deianeira across. Heracles agreed, but Nessus attempted to violate Deianeira and Heracles killed him with an arrow. As he was dying, Nessus told Deianeira that if she would mix the blood from his wound with the semen he had spilled on the ground it would be an infallible love charm which would work on Heracles if his affections should ever wander [Apollodorus: ii. 7. 6; Sophocles: *The Trachiniae* 555–81; Diodorus Siculus: iv. 36].

Some years later, Deianeira had occasion to use the charm, for Heracles, having sacked Oechalia and killed its king, Eurytus, took the princess, Iole, captive. Iole had attracted him even before his marriage to Deianeira, and he had won her in an archery contest from her father and brothers. They refused to give her up, however, on the grounds that he was a known madman and would kill any children she bore. Heracles submitted to the verdict, but later killed one of the brothers—the one most sympathetic to his cause—in a fit of rage (it was this murder for which his slavery to Omphale was penance). Now he took his full revenge, killing the remaining brothers along with the father. Sending his captive home to Deianeira with a herald, he also requested that his wife send him some fine clothing with which to perform sacrifices. Deianeira, upon apprehending what Iole's true role in the household was to be, smeared the tunic with the Centaur's charm. No sooner had the heat from the sacrificial flames reached the tunic than the Hydra's venom from the

Centaur's wound began to consume his flesh [cf. Sophocles: *The Trachiniae* 770–71].

> Then as he tried to strip the shirt away,
> His flesh came with it. Horror to his sight,
> It seared his bones and clung or stripped them bare;
> Like white-hot rods thrust into icy water,
> His blood steamed with the heat of Hydra's venom,
> Its flames burned inward to his vital parts,
> And darkened sweat poured from the restless furnace
> That covered lungs and belly, even the marrow
> Of bones turned into steaming, brackish water;
> And all his limbs turned black with hidden fires.
>
> [Ovid: *Metamorphoses* ix. 166ff.
> Gregory trans.]

On learning of her mistake, Deianeira fell on her sword. Heracles demanded of their son, Hyllus, that he immolate his father on a pyre atop Mount Oeta, and marry Iole. The immortal part of Heracles then ascended to Olympus [Apollodorus: ii. 6. 1–2 and ii. 7. 7; Sophocles: *The Trachiniae* 749–1256; Diodorus Siculus: iv. 38].

Heracles is slain by his own Hydra-envenomed arrow—that is, by the Centaur's lust, his own lust, Deianeira's jealousy, Hera's jealousy, Hera's poisoned breast. At the symbolic level all of these refer to the oral-narcissistic conflict. That he was killed by his own arrow and his sexual desire are two ways of saying the same thing. For sexual love kindles oral conflicts and hence is felt by the oral personality as dangerous—as threatening to psychological boundaries: "If I love, if I desire, if I 'cleave to another,' will I still be intact, or will I devour and be devoured by my hunger and that of the other?" Penis and vagina are both feared because both appear to violate the boundaries of the object [cf. Ehrenzweig, 1949, pp. 117–18]. Thus a dormant oral-narcissistic conflict may be inflamed by sexuality, just as the fire activated the Hydra's venom. Without such a flame, detached, narcissistic, and bellicose individuals like Heracles and Deianeira could stave off the conflict. This is another reason the serpent is such a superb symbol for the oral-narcissistic syndrome: it is cold-blooded, and remains sluggish in the absence of heat, like the Hydra's venom.

Heracles' own needs and maternal malevolence thus destroyed him. Deianeira in this respect simply duplicates Hera, with Iole in the role of Alcmene. In vain does Heracles attempt to placate the mother's hatred (for how can a displaced hatred be appeased?):

> Perhaps the savage wife of Jove is sleepy,
> Has strained her mind inventing labours for me,
> Which even now I'm willing to attempt . . .
> [Ovid: *Metamorphoses* ix. 198–99.
> Gregory trans.]

Only by the father can the son be saved, and this is the symbolic solution in Heracles' apotheosis:

> All that his mother gave him burned away.
> Only the image of his father's likeness
> Rose from the ashes of the funeral pyre;
> Then as a snake sloughs off his elder skin
> And glories in new dress with glittering scales
> So Hercules stepped free of mortal being,
> And took on greater stature with his honours,
> And with an air of gravity and power
> Grew tall, magnificent as any god.
> [*Ibid.*, 264–70]

Rebirth is so often symbolized by the serpent because rebirth "solves" the oral-narcissistic conflict. In this fantasy the two sides of the ambivalence are expressed through temporal alternation: the individual dissolves into another, but is reconstituted, usually with improvements. In Heracles' case the dissolution is selective: part of the self is relinquished to the devouring mother; the rest, purified by being freed from the mother's hold, grows stronger than before. It is, in effect, the same fantasy that we found at the root of many circumcision rites, wherein the organ "sloughs off" its "feminine" component (the foreskin), which is given to the mother to devour, leaving the penis more purely "masculine," appropriate for the assumption of an adult male role in the society. Presumably the apotheosis myth originally defined a pubertal circumcision rite.

But in the Heracles myth the narcissism which, according to Harnik [1924], males usually center in the phallus, has been transferred to the body as a whole. This is often associated with the fantasy of being someone else's phallus—the well-performing and admired ego-extension of another person, usually the mother. Heracles' name expresses this. Yet in order to perform well as a male it is necessary to have male models, and the individual who sees himself as a maternal extension must occasionally transfer that parasitism to an object who will bolster up his sense of masculinity. Heracles gets this "refueling" from Zeus, but in the world of reality the role may be played by any available male figure. A patient of Katan was incapable of performing competently in the intellectual sphere unless in close contact with an interested teacher, who would "give him a pep talk, which the patient called and experienced as 'being pumped up.' Then he felt 'erected' and capable for a very short while . . ." [Katan, 1960, pp. 210–11].

Let us now examine the story of Heracles' death from a simple interpersonal viewpoint, as an incident originating in the relationship between two individuals—for which purpose we may turn to Sophocles' drama, *The Women of Trachis*. As the play opens, Deianeira is recounting her unhappy life, beginning with her dread of marriage ("greater than any maiden in Aetolia") which was aroused by her suitor Achelous—so unprepossessing that she continually prayed for death. Even Heracles has brought her nothing but worry, and now that his labors are over his whereabouts is uncertain. She also makes the characteristic complaint that her husband is never at home, scarcely even knows his children: "like a farmer working an outlying field, who sees it only when he sows and when he reaps" [*The Trachiniae*, 33–35. Jameson trans.].

Into this scene of feminine deprivation and neglect the absent Heracles sends his new concubine. Deianeira is intensely sympathetic to the captive girl until she learns her true position in the household, and even then her rather mild resentment is directed entirely at Heracles. The murder of Heracles, furthermore, is made virtually unconscious. While it is clear to everyone else that this is the last straw for Deianeira and that she is destroying her husband in a fit of jealous rage [cf. Bacchylides: xv. 30ff.], she herself becomes aware of it only afterward. In part, this is a powerful dramatic device, but it also reveals the Greek horror of mariticide, upon which I commented in the chapter on Orestes. Medea can premeditate the murder of her children and Jason's new bride and father-in-law, but the deliberate murder of a husband is impossible for a sympathetic character, no matter how great the provocation. Although Heracles is portrayed as a brutal and insensitive lout, and although Deianeira's suffering and misery receive constant and effective stress, her act must nonetheless be defined as unwitting (however much this strains our credulity). Her son, furthermore, although aware of her plight, and scarcely acquainted with his father, automatically sides with Heracles and condemns her unequivocally [Sophocles: *The Trachiniae* 734ff.]. While idealization of the "absent father" may play a part in this, it strikes one as a little overdrawn, and perhaps reflects Sophocles' moralizing horror at such uxorial rebellion.

The effect of this is to give the drama a strangely modern ring. The self-pitying, self-justifying, pseudo-reasonable, well-intentioned malevolence of Deianeira's speech to the chorus, announcing her intention to use the Centaur's charm, requires only a Southern or a Yiddish accent to be fully contemporary. It is beautifully set up by the preceding lines of the chorus, which describe Deianeira waiting piteously for the outcome of the battle between the two suitors and then being parted from her mother "like a calf that is lost" [*Ibid.*, 526–30]. This serves to remind the audience that marriage was a trauma for the Greek bride, regardless of the nature of the husband. It is picked up again in the speech itself [*Ibid.*, 555ff.] when she tells of obtaining the charm from Nessus when "still only a child."

She begins her speech by saying that she is talking with them (the chorus) secretly to tell them "what these hands have devised" and to gain their sympathy for her suffering [*Ibid.*, 531–35]. She observes that Iole has come not as a maiden but as a mistress of the household, and that this is intolerable.

> So now the two of us lie under the one sheet waiting for his embrace. This is the gift my brave and faithful Heracles sends home to his dear wife to compensate for his long absence! And yet, when he is sick as he so often is with this same sickness, I am incapable of anger. But to live in the same house with her, to share the same marriage, that is something else. What woman could stand that?
>
> [*Ibid.*, 539–46. Jameson trans.]

She goes on to point out her competitive disadvantage with a younger woman, but then argues that no sensible woman should give way to rage, and finally reveals her solution. She protests, "may deeds of wicked daring be ever far from my thoughts, and from my knowledge," and asks the women if they think she is acting rashly. (These remarks are the first indication that she has some dim awareness of what she is doing.) Her women respond in the fashion of advisory committees everywhere, supporting her plan cautiously and remarking rather fatuously that one cannot judge a plan's wisdom except by carrying it out [*Ibid.*, 547–93].

But Deianeira soon encounters evidence of her true intentions that cannot be ignored. The ball of wool used to smear Heracles' tunic—cast aside into the sunlight—she now finds disintegrated into dust, and from the earth beneath it clots of bubbling foam. Suddenly she realizes the true purpose of Nessus' charm. The audience, of course, is surprised at her surprise. Could she really have deceived herself into imagining that " 'blood clotted in my wounds, wherever it is black with the bile of the Hydra, the monstrous serpent of Lerna, in which he dipped his arrows' " [*Ibid.*, 572–75] could be a love charm? Why did she think the Centaur laid so much stress on taking blood that was full of the Hydra's poison? And what did she imagine to be the purpose of the Centaur's instruction to keep the charm away from heat, an instruction she repeats so carefully to the hapless herald Lichas [*Ibid.*, 604–9]? Like official killers today, she takes refuge in the exactitude with which she has followed orders [*Ibid.*, 684ff.], but awareness of her guilt becomes increasingly difficult to repress:

> From what possible motive, in return for what,
> could the dying beast have shown me kindness,
>   when he
> was dying because of me?
>
> [*Ibid.*, 707–9]

It is indeed strange that this thought has never before occurred to her, and that she has heretofore ignored the fact that whatever the poison touches it kills [*Ibid.*, 713ff.]. When Hyllus accuses her and describes Heracles' death she kills herself without a word, accepting the guilt and fulfilling her son's parting curse [*Ibid.*, 734–820 and 899ff.].[11]

At the interpersonal level, then, one finds the usual strains

---

[11] It may be objected that in a "shame culture" such as this it is the deed and not the intent which is important, hence the suicide would, in any case, be automatic. Deianeira's responses prior to the suicide, however, show elements of true guilt.

in the Greek marital relationship: the husband's neglect, the wife's jealousy, the lack of communication, the pervasive sex antagonism. Deianeira's fear and hatred of men is matched by Heracles' feelings about women, for although he collects a number of them, he lives with none voluntarily, and destroys those he does not give away. As he dies his major concern is that he has not died a manly death—that he has been destroyed by a woman and has become a woman in his weakness. His language recalls Agamemnon's death, and he makes the same complaint about it:

> . . . the false-faced daughter of Oeneus has fastened
> upon my shoulders, a woven, encircling net
> of the Furies, by which I am utterly destroyed.
> It clings to my sides, it has eaten away
> my inmost flesh; it lives with me and empties
>   the channels
> of my lungs, and already it has drunk up
> my fresh blood. . . .
>
> > [*Ibid.*, 1050–1056]

No warrior, beast, or monster has ever slain him—only:

> A woman, a female, in no way like a man,
> she alone without even a sword has brought me down.
>
> > [*Ibid.*, 1062–1063]

He is mortified to be "moaning and weeping like a girl," and boasts that never before has he behaved like this, despite all his hardships. But: "Now in my misery I am discovered a woman" [*Ibid.*, 1071–1075].

Narcissism and sex antagonism receive their strongest statement in the fantastic passage where Heracles asks Hyllus to bring his mother to him:

> . . . that I may know clearly whether it pains you more to
> see *my* body mutilated or *hers* when it is justly tortured.
>
> > [*Ibid.*, 1066–1069]

In few cultures could a man dying in agony, even on stage, absorb himself in such petty invidiousness.[12]

Madness and Murder

Let me now backtrack a little, and consider some other examples of maternal malevolence in the Heracles myths. The most prominent of these, in the hero's adult life, is his attack of madness—like Dionysus', a result of Hera's enmity.

Of Heracles' marriage to Megara one is told very little. She was the daughter of Creon, King of Thebes, and was given to Heracles as a reward for his defeat of the Minyans [Apollodorus: ii. 4. 11]. Her name, like Deianeira's, tells us something, for it refers to those chasms in the earth into which swine were thrown during the Thesmophoria ritual and recovered when their flesh had rotted, to be used in fertility magic. These clefts were said to be inhabited by snakes and were associated with death, ghosts, and the underworld [Harrison, 1957, pp. 38, 122–23]. Thus it is a chthonic name, suffused with the mysteries of the womb. Megara is an aspect of the Earth-Mother—a duplicate of Hera.

Madness is sent to Heracles in serpentine form, and hence repeats the earlier attack in the cradle:

> O gorgon of Night, O hiss
> of a hundred snakes! O madness,
> whose look makes stones of men!
> [Euripides: *Heracles* 882–84.
> Arrowsmith trans.]

Indeed, madness was always associated with snakes in the ancient world, perhaps because it involved boundary-confusion, but also because this was the way maternal hatred was traditionally symbolized, and madness was sensed as a mater-

---

[12] Similar outbursts occur in Euripides' *Heracles* [1241ff. and 1306ff.] when the hero recovers from his disastrous madness and discovers that he has slaughtered his family.

nally induced disease. We find Ovid describing Tisiphone, one of the Erinyes, in similar fashion when she arrives to wreak Hera's vengeance on Athamas and Ino:

> Vipers were darting bracelets round her arms,
> And as she shook her head the waking serpents
> Fell to shoulder, breast, spit blood and vomit,
> And forked their hissing tongues. Then from her head
> She plucked two snakes and aimed them with true art
> At man and wife. The gliding creatures crawled
> Over the breasts of both, kissing their lips,
> Pouring black serpent's breath into their lungs;
> Nor was their flesh seared, but their minds were pierced.
>
>   [Ovid: *Metamorphoses* iv. 491–99.
>   Gregory trans.]

The effect of this attack on Athamas matches Heracles' in that he murders his own eldest son, Learchus, while Ino boils the infant Melicertes in a cauldron [Apollodorus: iii. 4. 3].[13] Heracles' psychotic episode is of more heroic proportions, in keeping with his stature and appetites: he kills his three sons, and Megara, and attempts the life of his earthly father, Amphitryon [Euripides: *Heracles* 922ff.]; or eight sons alone [Pindar: *Isthmian Odes* iv. 62–64]; or an unspecified number of children and an attempt on his nephew, Iolaus [Diodorus Siculus: iv. 11]; or all his own children and two of Iphicles' [Apollodorus: ii. 4. 12].

I have already discussed in detail the reasons why Heracles' sons should be the central victims of the tragedy (see Chapter VIII): the husband in a patriarchal society is attacked through his children, his immortality. This is made quite explicit by Euripides, when he has Iris instruct Madness to:

> . . . drive him, goad him, shake out the sails of death
> and speed his passage over Acheron,

---

[13] While there are various motives offered for Hera's persecution of Athamas [Apollodorus: iii. 4. 3; Ovid: *Metamorphoses* iv. 464ff.], all share the elements of narcissistic injury and jealousy.

Where he must take his crown of lovely sons.
Let him learn what Hera's anger is . . .
                    [Euripides: *Heracles* 836–40.
                                    Arrowsmith trans.]

The children, like Heracles himself, are slain by the poison of
the Hydra in Euripides' version [*Heracles* 1188–1190]. Narcissistic injuries to Hera, aggravated by Heracles' achievements
[Apollodorus: ii. 4. 11–12], are matched by Heracles' own
humiliations. The rationalizing Diodorus even makes these
humiliations the source of his madness, Hera's visitation being
only a precipitating factor [Diodorus Siculus: iv. 11].

The theme of paternal inadequacy is also present in Euripides' drama. The earthly father, Amphitryon, is weak and
helpless, relying on Heracles for his own protection; while
Zeus, the powerful divine father, is conspicuous in his absence
throughout. Indeed, Heracles himself is an absent father, and
the tragedy opens with Megara describing to Amphitryon her
difficulty in answering her children's constant queries about
their father's whereabouts [Euripides: *Heracles* 71ff.].
Threatened with death by the usurper Lycus while Heracles
is in Tartarus seeking Cerberus, Amphitryon is verbose but ineffectual, even in debate [cf. *Ibid.*, 188ff.]. Megara is a more
vigorous figure, and tries to bolster the courage of her father-
in-law, who is able only to berate Zeus for not standing by
them [*Ibid.*, 275ff. and 339ff.]. When Heracles arrives and
asks his father about the general distress, Megara quickly
interrupts and maintains control over the conversation [*Ibid.*,
533ff.].

Here we have the fundamental structural flaw in the Greek
family: the father is effective only outside the home. Within
the family circle the thin patriarchal veneer tends to collapse,
and the child does not experience paternal adequacy where it
is needed. Indeed, Heracles is soon struck by the same insight,
protesting that all of his glorious deeds are pointless if he is in-

capable of fulfilling the most elementary male role—protecting his wife and children [*Ibid.*, 574–81].

Heracles does kill the tyrant, however, and Hera, feeling he is too puffed up with success, sends his affliction. Euripides has the hero try to kill Amphitryon as well as Megara and the children, but at this point he is put out of action by Athene, who as usual supports traditional patriarchal values. When Heracles awakes from his attack Amphitryon is again terrified and indecisive, but eventually communicates to his son the true state of affairs. Theseus (whom Heracles had rescued from the underworld) now appears, and Heracles hides his head under his robes in shame. The two heroes then have a long philosophical discussion and Theseus takes Heracles off to Athens, the rescued becoming the rescuer [*Ibid.*, 734ff. 821ff. 1001ff. 1068ff. and 1159ff.].

The oedipal ambivalence we saw in the Perseus myth is thus repeated here. The need for paternal protection against an overwhelming mother is great, but involvement with the latter is too strong for a competitor to be tolerated. Heracles' attempt to kill Amphitryon is not a trivial by-product of his madness, for he later compares himself with Ixion, the upstart mortal befriended by Zeus, who attempted to seduce Hera herself [*Ibid.*, 1297–1298; Pindar: *Pythian Odes* ii. 40ff.]. Yet anger at paternal neglect is a constant theme in the drama.[14] Amphitryon complains: "O Zeus, do you see these deeds Hera has done?" [Euripides: *Heracles* 1127], while Heracles bitterly rejects the world on the grounds that Hera rules it; accusing Zeus of having procreated him merely as a butt for Hera's hatred, and disowning him as a father [*Ibid.*, 1253, 1263–1265].

[14] The theme of aggressive insistence on paternal assistance also appears during Heracles' labors. He shoots an arrow at Helius, whose rays are too hot, and is rewarded with a goblet with which he later crosses the ocean; and to find the garden of the Hesperides he seizes the sea-god Nereus, clinging fast to him despite many transformations, until he reveals its location [Apollodorus: ii. 5. 10 and ii. 5. 11].

Let the noble wife of Zeus begin the dance,
pounding with her feet Olympus' gleaming floors!
For she accomplished what her heart desired,
and hurled the greatest man of Hellas down
in utter ruin.

[Ibid., 1303–1308]

He is affectionate toward the hapless Amphitryon, however, who even at the end is fretting over his own immortality *[Ibid.,* 1408ff. and 1419]. The nearest to a real paternal protector is Theseus, and as he leaves Heracles describes himself as: ". . . towed in Theseus' wake like some little boat . . ." *[Ibid.,* 1424], a phrase he uses earlier about his own children as they follow him into his house *[Ibid.,* 631ff.].

Madness is also invoked by some authors to justify Heracles' murder of Iphitus [cf. Apollodorus: ii. 6. 2], but in fact the Heraclean myths are full of acts of violence and brutality. While these tales may merely reflect the barbarous state of society during the millennium preceding the classical age, their retention in more or less undiluted form argues a psychological congruence with the other facets of the hero's legend.

These acts of violence begin with the killing of Linus, who struck Heracles while teaching him to play the lyre [Apollodorus, ii. 4. 9; Diodorus Siculus: iii. 67]. Also provoked, but equally extreme, was Heracles' handling of the Minyan heralds, whose ears, noses, and hands he cut off and hung with ropes about their necks in lieu of the tribute usually paid them by the Thebans [Apollodorus: ii. 4. 11; Diodorus Siculus: iv. 10]. The murder of Iphitus, however, was entirely unprovoked. In search of his father's stolen mares, Iphitus came to Heracles (who had obtained them, through one means or another) and was received as a guest by the hero, who hurled him from a tower to his death [Homer: *Odyssey* xxi. 13ff.; Apollodorus: ii. 6. 2; Diodorus Siculus: iv. 31]. Heracles also treacherously ambushed and killed the Molionides, valiant twins whom he had been unable to best in battle [Apollodorus:

ii. 7. 2; Pindar: *Olympian Odes* x. 26ff.]; petulantly killed Eunomus, a kinsman of Oeneus, for spilling water on him [Diodorus Siculus: iv. 36; Apollodorus: ii. 7. 6]; and crushed the skull of the herald Lichas for his innocent part in bringing Deianeira's poisoned tunic [Sophocles: *The Trachiniae* 772–82; Apollodorus: ii. 7. 7; Diodorus Siculus: iv. 38]. These incidents do much to preserve Heracles' rude pre-civilized character. His poor impulse control and brute rages still had resonance for the Greeks even at the height of their cultural flowering, for they never lost their quarrelsomeness and sensitivity to insult. Thus Lysias, in one of his many assault cases, remarks on the wisdom of Solon in not making injuries resulting from street fights grounds for banishment, since otherwise Athens would have been depopulated [Lysias: "Against Simon" 42].

Responses to the Maternal Threat

While Heracles' crude hypermasculinity is perhaps unique to him, his other modes of reaction are, as I observed at the opening of the chapter, similar to those of other mythical figures.

Like Zeus, Heracles copulates with the serpent. For it is told that when Heracles was driving the cattle of Geryon back to Mycenae he rested in Scythia, unharnessing the mares from his chariot. When he awoke, they were gone, and in searching for them he found in a cave a viper-maiden, a woman above her loins, a snake below. She told him she had his mares and would return them if he would lie with her. To this Heracles agreed, and fathered three children on her, one of them Scythes, the eponymous hero of the Scythians [Herodotus: iv. 8–10; cf. Fontenrose, 1959, pp. 97–98]. In another version it is Zeus who lies with the serpent-woman [Diodorus Siculus: ii. 43]. Graves points out that this tale is a variant of the "Laidley Worm" ballad, in which the monster turns into a beautiful woman when kissed [Graves, 1955, ii,

p. 144; cf. also "Prince Lindworm," Henderson and Oakes, 1963, pp. 167ff.]. The psychological message of the myth, like that of Zeus and Rhea (see Chapter III), is that the malevolent mother may be rendered benign by gratifying her libidinal needs. Such a resolution being beyond the capacity of a child, he who achieves it must be cast as a sexual prodigy—a Zeus or a Heracles.

Heracles' claim to this distinction is based upon his encounter with the daughters of Thespius. The latter, wishing to have grandchildren by the hero (who was still a boy), sent all of his daughters in to sleep with his guest, one by one. All conceived sons, save one, who resisted Heracles' advances and became his priestess [Diodorus Siculus: iv. 29; Apollodorus: ii. 4. 10 and ii. 7. 8; Pausanias: ix. 27. 5–7].

What is interesting about this story is that it is the precise complement of the myth of the Danaids. Danaus had reluctantly agreed to wed his fifty daughters to the sons of his brother Aegyptus, but gave each of the maidens a dagger to slay her bridegroom. All did, save the eldest, Hypermnestra, who spared her husband Lynceus because he had not deflowered her [Pindar: *Nemean Odes* x. 6; Apollodorus: ii. 1. 5]. Both myths reflect the "taboo of virginity" of which Freud speaks [1918b, 217–35]. The horror of mariticide is also expressed in the punishment accorded the Danaids in the Kingdom of Hades [Ovid: *Metamorphoses* iv. 462–63]. Heracles essentially undoes their crime, as well as compensating for the defeat of the sons of Aegyptus by the hand of a woman. The hero successfully braves the ire of the deflowered virgin, as he braved the sexuality of the serpent-mother. But just as a fragment of love filtered through Greek sex antagonism in the myth of the Danaids, so a fragment of sex antagonism mars the hero's sexual feat (which is, of course, itself based on sex-antagonistic assumptions).

Heracles resembles Orestes in his murderous attacks on women: his wounding of Hera, his murder (in Euripides' version) of Megara, and his apparently unprovoked slaying of Hippolyte and other Amazons [Apollodorus: ii. 5. 9; Diodorus Siculus: iv. 16]. But these incidents are merely episodes in an extensive anti-feminine career, one which in this regard most closely resembles Apollonian myth. Plutarch even tells us of a shrine of "Heracles the Woman-Hater" in Phocis [Plutarch: "The Oracles at Delphi" 20], an aspect of the hero which is also revealed in his refusal to participate in the Argonauts' revelry with the Lemnian women, and his insistence on ending this idyll and sailing away [Apollonius Rhodius: i. 852ff.].

Like Apollo, Heracles is anti-chthonic and a serpent-slayer. Indeed, the latter attribute is so central that "Ophioctonus," or serpent-killing, is one of his titles [Graves, 1955, II, p. 206]. In addition to the serpents which attack him in his cradle he kills the Hydra, the sea-serpent of Troy, the hundred-headed serpent Ladon which guards the apples of the Hesperides, and the dragon of the river Sangarios; he also defeats Achelous in his serpent form [Apollodorus: ii. 5. 2; ii. 5. 9 and ii. 5. 11; Fontenrose, 1959, p. 109]. Even when not specifically combating serpents he is fighting their brood, since most of the monsters which figure in the Heraclean myths are introduced to us as offspring of those ancestral serpent-monsters, Typhon and Echidna. The Nemean Lion, the Hydra, the eagle which attacked Prometheus' liver, the hound Cerberus, Ladon, and Geryon's two-headed dog Orthrus are all children of Typhon and Echidna. All save Cerberus were slain by Heracles, along with the triple-bodied Geryon, Echidna's brother [Hesiod: *Theogony* 287–332; Apollodorus: ii. 5. 1 and ii. 5. 10–11; Apollonius Rhodius: iv. 1396; Euripides: *Heracles* 355–424; Sophocles: *The Trachiniae* 1092ff.]. The lion and the Hydra were reared by Hera, however [Hesiod: *Theogony* 313ff. and 326ff.], supporting Fontenrose's statement that "we see Hera inciting dragons and demons against Heracles just as she did against Apollo" [1959, p. 357].

The viper-maiden who seduced Heracles and became the

mother of Scythes was also called an "echidna" [Herodotus: iv. 8], although it is not known whether the name preceded the term or vice versa. Echidna, also, was a beautiful maiden above and a serpent below—"great and awful, with speckled skin, eating raw flesh beneath the secret parts of the holy earth" [Hesiod: *Theogony* 298–300]. Echidna epitomizes the Greek view of the malevolent and devouring yet seductive mother, and her progeny are comparably ravenous and serpentine. In some cases their orality is expressed through the traditional device of multiple heads [Hydra, Cerberus, Ladon, Orthrus], but often it is more explicit. The eagle devotes himself entirely to pecking at Prometheus' liver, while the hound of Hades swallows those who try to escape the underworld [Apollodorus: ii. 5. 12; Hesiod: *Theogony* 770–73]. When Heracles captured Cerberus he was bitten by its serpent-tail [Apollodorus: ii. 5. 12]. The venomous Hydra was assisted by a giant crab which, as the Hydra immobilized Heracles by wrapping itself around his ankles, bit the hero on the foot [Apollodorus: ii. 5. 2]. The Nemean Lion bit off one of Heracles' fingers, according to one version, before he was able to strangle it [Graves, 1955, II, pp. 104, 106–7]. This provides a curious parallel to the Orestes myth, since the lion episode immediately follows Heracles' attack of madness in all but the Euripidean version. For Orestes is said to have bitten off a finger to placate the Erinyes when they drove him mad following his murder of Clytemnestra [Pausanias: viii. 34. 1–3]. One might expect the Angry Ones to demand a more extensive sacrifice; and a similar view of the Nemean Lion (as agent of Hera, after all) seems to have appealed to vase painters, who most often show Heracles holding the lion in a stranglehold with the animal baring his teeth in close proximity to the hero's genitals. The association between jealousy and castration is hardly remote: the ancients believed that an herb called the Nymphaean heracleon, named after a nymph who was deserted by Heracles and died of jealousy, would make a man impotent [Graves, 1955, II, p. 155; cf. also Lawson, 1964, pp. 18–21].

Heracles most resembles Apollo in his peculiarly ambivalent relationship to earth. His enemies are almost entirely chthonic, and the story of his apotheosis stresses his being burned on a mountaintop, instead of receiving the usual hero's fate of burial, transformation into a serpent, and libations poured on the ground. Yet, as Graves points out: "canals, tunnels, or natural underground conduits were often described as the work of Heracles" [1955, II, p. 124]. He is also a drainer of swamps and a creator of them—a dam-builder [Pausanias: ix. 38. 6–8 and viii. 14. 1–3; Apollodorus: ii. 5. 5; Diodorus Siculus: iv. 18, 22, and 35]. He is said both to have widened and to have narrowed the Straits of Gibraltar, to let in the ocean or to keep out sea-serpents [*Ibid.*, iv. 18]. As Fontenrose points out, this contradiction simply expresses the fact that the conquest of Chaos brings about control over natural forces, either for repressive or utilitarian purposes [1959, pp. 343–44].

In general, however, Heracles is least secure and effective in the context of soft or moist earth. His archenemy Eurystheus, on the other hand, is quite the opposite, hiding himself in what can only be interpreted as a tomb-jar—half-buried in the earth—whenever Heracles appears following the successful completion of one of his labors [Apollodorus: ii. 5. 1; Fontenrose, 1959, p. 357; Harrison, 1957, pp. 36ff.].

An example of Heracles' insecurity in the bosom of the earth is an incident in his encounter with the Ligurians—a story told by Aeschylus in his lost tragedy, *Prometheus Unbound*, and quoted by later authors. Heracles, out of arrows, knelt on the ground looking for stones to hurl at the attacking Ligurian forces, but the earth was soft and he could find none. Miserable and wounded, he would have been overwhelmed had not Zeus taken pity on him and sent down a shower of stones with which he drove the Ligurians off [Aeschylus: Fragment 112; Frazer's note to Apollodorus: ii. 5. 10]. A similar bewilderment occurred in both of the labors associated with swamps. He was almost overcome by the Hydra in the Lernean marsh, and was forced to call for help from his nephew Iolaus. The latter brought fire to cauterize the Hydra's severed necks and prevent them from sprouting new heads [Apollodorus: ii. 5. 2]. In the Stymphalian marsh Heracles again was baffled, this time by his inability to drive off the Stymphalian birds with arrows. This time Athene came to his aid with a pair of brass castanets, which frightened them away [Apollodorus: ii. 5. 6; Apollonius Rhodius: ii. 1052; Pausanias: viii. 22. 3–9]. In his battle with the Centaurs, their mother, Nephele ("cloud"), the misty duplicate of Hera,[15] sent a heavy rain which made the ground slippery underfoot; the mud created little difficulty for the four-legged Centaurs but much for Heracles [Diodorus Siculus: iv. 12]. Earth also undermines our hero in the story of Antaeus, the headhunting giant with whom Heracles wrestled in Libya. Whenever Heracles threw him down he rose up stronger than ever—some said because Gaea was his mother and revived him. Heracles finally lifted him off the ground entirely and bear-hugged him to death [Apollodorus: ii. 5. 11]. A somewhat similar story is told of Heracles' struggle with Alcyoneus during the Giants' revolt [Apollodorus: i. 6. 1].

Antaeus is the "opposite" of Heracles, in that he draws strength from that which weakens the hero.[16] Antaeus looks

***

[15] Nephele was created by Zeus to fool the ungrateful Ixion, who attempted to seduce Hera when Zeus invited him to dine. Zeus formed a cloud into the likeness of Hera, and Ixion failed to notice the deception. Zeus punished Ixion by binding him to a fiery wheel which rolled endlessly through the sky; but from his union with Nephele came the monster Centaurus, the progenitor of the Centaurs, several of whom Heracles slew, but one of whom slew Heracles [Pindar: *Pythian Odes* ii. 21–49].

[16] A contrast is also drawn between their modes of preparing for combat. Heracles rubs himself with oil, in the Olympic mode, while Antaeus covers himself with sand to increase his contact with Earth [Lucan: iv. 612–53]. The first facilitates separateness, the second contact. In Ovid's account of Heracles' battle with Achelous both fighters are first covered with sand

to the Earth-Mother for help, Heracles to the Sky-Father. We saw how the myth of Apollo stresses the danger of *mana* draining away into the earth. Heracles suffers from a similar vulnerability: soft earth weakens him, and he requires celestial aid to preserve his powers, which are similarly based on the illusion of narcissistic independence from the mother. One is reminded of Kenneth Elton's association between his childhood seduction and sinking into quicksand.

The Heraclean myths also include the self-abasing strategy discussed in connection with Hephaestus. This is inferred, not from his appearance as a buffoon in Attic drama, but from his role as a servant of the gods and a slave to women. He consistently performs "dirty work" for others, killing pests, cleaning the Augeian stables, herding cattle, reaping grain, and so on. Indeed, his entire life is one of suffering, servitude, and degradation, relieved only by his achievements and final apotheosis. From the slave of the cowardly Eurystheus he becomes the slave of Omphale, and is constantly being cheated of his wages (e.g., by Eurystheus, Augeias, Eurytus, and Laomedon).

Like Hephaestus, furthermore, Heracles both attacks and defends Hera. Kerényi, in fact, derives Heracles' more general role of rescuer of women from his archaic servant character [Kerényi, 1959, pp. 197–98]. Many other parallels can also be drawn, although it is a somewhat sterile exercise to do so: his engineering feats, his leg wound [Pausanias: iii. 19. 7 and viii. 53. 9], his rejection and exposure at birth, and so on. Aside from Heracles' servant role, however, the only really im-

---

[*Metamorphoses* ix. 35–36]. One is reminded of the modern ritual of baseball batters, who rub their hands with dirt before gripping the bat. Like so much contemporary magic, this practice is rationalized, being alleged to provide a more satisfactory degree of friction. This is as easy to disprove as it is to test, but there is no doubt that it "feels" better and more under control, probably because the batter's awareness of his own anxiety (sweating palms) is reduced. Modern athletes are thus not above seeking an assist from Mother Earth, albeit unconsciously.

portant parallel with Hephaestus is his habit of sharing his women with other men—usually sons or son-like figures, as if to emphasize that it is oedipal competitiveness that is being denied. After slaying his children, for example, he gave Megara to his favorite nephew and charioteer Iolaus [Apollodorus: ii. 6. 1; Diodorus Siculus: iv. 31]—the same Iolaus that he had murderously attacked (in this version) during his madness [Diodorus Siculus: iv. 11]. Oedipus killed his father and took his mother to wife; Heracles killed his sons and gave his wife to a son-surrogate. The homosexual character of this reversal is revealed by the fact that immediately following this bestowal he sought a new bride (Iole) with the same name as his nephew [Apollodorus: ii. 6. 1; Diodorus Siculus: iv. 31; Fontenrose, 1959, p. 109].

But Iole in turn is bestowed upon Heracles' son Hyllus, much to the latter's consternation. Heracles' last instructions to his son are, in fact, that Hyllus "become" Oedipus—killing his own father by lighting the pyre, and marrying his step-mother—his father's beloved new bride [Sophocles: *The Trachiniae* 1193–1251]. Hyllus, too, affects a sharply "un-oedipal" character, taking Heracles' side against Deianeira and professing hatred for Iole; but he gives in after forcing his father to command him and make it a pious act [*Ibid.*, 1245–1251]. Sophocles seems to suggest a "return of the repressed," however, in his description of Hyllus mourning for his dead mother:[17]

---

[17] Another son of Heracles, Telephus, also participates in an oedipal incident. Heracles had violated Auge, the virgin-priestess of Athene (another parallel with Hephaestus), and she was punished (in the usual double-standard fashion) by being sold into slavery, narrowly escaping death. Telephus, having been exposed on a hillside, was suckled by a doe and upon reaching manhood won his mother as a reward for martial valor. Auge took a sword into the bedchamber, resolved to slay her bridegroom, but the gods sent a serpent between them and before Telephus could repay her intent, their identities were made known [Diodorus Siculus: iv. 33; Apollodorus: ii. 7. 4 and iii. 9. 1; Pausanias: viii. 4. 9 and viii. 47. 4; Hyginus: *Fabulae* 100]. Thus once again a heterosexual encounter was blocked by a serpent.

. . . he threw himself
upon her lips and there, pressing his side to hers,
he lay and groaned over and over that he
had struck her thoughtlessly with a cruel
accusation . . .

[*Ibid.*, 937–40. Jameson trans.]

Finally, I will mention here Heracles' gift to Telamon of Hesione, whom he had won at such great cost, killing a dragon and fighting a war [Sophocles: *Ajax* 1299–1303; Apollodorus: ii. 5. 9 and ii. 6. 4; Diodorus Siculus: iv. 32 and iv. 42]. Telamon was a helper, like Iolaus, and had also been threatened with death by Heracles, in this case out of jealousy because Telamon had been the first to breach the walls of Troy [Apollodorus: ii. 6. 4].

Thus, while Heracles may compare himself to Ixion, he seems compulsively to deny any such oedipal presumptuousness. Yet elements of the underlying rivalrous and murderous feelings continue to creep back in, as if to remind us of that against which all this negation is directed.

Heracles also displays the Dionysian response of identification with the aggressor. This is expressed not only by his name, and by the fact that he achieves many of his victories clad in the Nemean Lion's skin, and with arrows tipped with Hydra venom; but also by the fact that, driven mad, he kills his children, just as Hera tried to kill him in his cradle [cf. Euripides: *Heracles* 839–40].[18] His experiences with Hera are indeed strikingly similar to those of Dionysus, as already noted. But of more immediate relevance is his homosexuality. For this most virile and compulsively masculine of all heroes was also famous as a transvestite and pederast—Licht claims fourteen boy-loves for him, and he was even said by one third-century poet to be the lover of Eurystheus [Licht, 1963, pp. 10, 464].

[18] This is also Jung's interpretation of the incident [1957, p. 539].

*"Et Héraclès ne se contentait pas des femmes . . . il aima
son jeune neveu et compagnon Iolaos, et c'est pourquoi, à
Thèbes, érastes et éromènes échangeaient serments et gages de
foi sur le tombeau d'Iolaos. Il aima aussi 'le gracieux Hylas,
l'enfant aux belles boucles' "* [Flacelière, 1960, p. 52; cf. also
p. 80; Theocritus: *Idylls* xiii]. It was, in fact, for love of Hylas that Heracles abandoned the expedition of the Argonauts,
a sharp contrast to his impatience when his comrades were
dallying with the Lemnian women. Hylas was carried off in
Mysia by water-nymphs and Heracles went to search for
him. He threatened to lay waste the land unless the Mysians
continued to search after he himself had given up and re-
sumed his labors. He even took several young men with him as
hostages, who eventually founded Trachis. The Mysians continued to cry "Hylas" vainly and perpetually, until the act
became proverbial [Apollonius Rhodius: i. 1207ff.; Apollodorus: i. 9. 19; Aeschylus: *The Persians* 1054; Aristophanes:
Plutus 1127]. This may be the origin of the French *"hélas"*
and the English "alas," although they are usually derived in a
more complicated fashion.

There are two transvestite episodes in Heraclean myth: the
first takes place on the Island of Cos. Having sacked Troy,
Heracles set sail for home, but Hera lulled Zeus to sleep and
raised a storm which drove the hero off course. Landing on
Cos, he was attacked, wounded, and almost killed. Some say
he was rescued by Zeus, who chained Hera up with anvils
tied to her feet in revenge [Homer: *Iliad* xv. 18–30; Apollodorus: i. 3. 5 and ii. 7. 1]. Others say that he escaped by hiding in a Thracian woman's house, in whose clothes he dressed
himself and fled. Later, victorious, he married Chalciope in the
same garb, thus inaugurating an old Coan custom [Plutarch:
"The Greek Questions" 58]. This story is reminiscent of
Dionysus hiding from Hera by dressing as a girl, and the elements of maternal persecution, paternal rescue, and marital
hatred are also familiar.

The second episode occurs in conjunction with Heracles' term as Omphale's thrall. "Omphale" is a chthonic name, the feminine form of *omphalos*, or navel. Claims to be the Earth's navel were supported in places like Delphi by breast-shaped stone *omphaloi*, indistinguishable in form and meaning from tomb-mounds [Harrison, 1957, pp. 61–62; Fontenrose, 1959, p. 109]. It is in fact as a sojourn in the land of death that Fontenrose interprets Heracles' period of servitude. He suggests that Omphale is the Lydian Echidna, and points out her sinister character as a homicidal seductress in one version [Fontenrose, 1959, pp. 108–10].

But whatever menacing overtones may or may not be present, there is general agreement that Heracles was Omphale's slave and lover, and there are many stories concerning the effeminacy to which the hero was reduced during this bondage. Later authors describe, and painters show, how the couple exchanged clothes—Omphale donning the lion pelt, Heracles her golden gown, slippers, and jewelry [Plutarch: "Whether an Old Man Should Engage in Public Affairs" 785E]. There are various elaborations on this theme, such as Heracles being forced to spin or carry Omphale's parasol, and a mistaken sexual approach by Pan, but these are decidedly of later origin [Ovid: *Heroides* ix. 55–118 and *Fasti* ii. 305–58]. Both of Heracles' transvestite episodes can probably be traced to confused descriptions of wedding customs, and the story of the hero's slavery may well describe a period of expiation as a temple-slave, as Graves suggests [1955, II, p. 167]. But the retention and elaboration of the story expresses Greek concern with the emasculating impact of dominant and passionate females—Graves points out that the navel was regarded in classical times as the seat of feminine desire [*Ibid.*].

The male child impotent in the face of adult female passion recalls Perseus, and here, too, one finds several resemblances. According to Pindar [*Isthmian Odes* vii. 5–6], Heracles also was conceived in a golden rain, and we are told that he also confronted the Gorgon Medusa, drawing his sword against her shade in the land of Hades [Apollodorus: ii. 5. 12]. But it is as the slayer of the female dragon, the "castrator" of the mother who separates her from her sexuality, that Heracles truly adopts Perseus' characteristic response and posture. This occurs in two of his monster-slaying exploits. The first is the slaying of the Hydra, which recalls the Medusa battle not only because the hero requires help, is threatened with immobility, and uses the same weapon—a sickle—to perform the deed [Kerényi, 1959, p. 144]; but also because he makes the monster's power his own: the head for Perseus, the venom for Heracles. By "castrating" the mother, in other words, the hero gains potency; destroying her sexuality engenders his own.

The Hydra also resembles the Gorgon through its innumerable serpent heads—a hundred, according to Euripides [*Heracles* 1190]—connoting maternal hunger and maternal entanglement. Its location in a swamp is analogous to Medusa's residence in a sea cave, and recalls Kenneth Elton's dreams of being trapped in sea-grass, quicksand, and pubic hair.

The second exploit, the rescue of Hesione, is an almost exact duplicate of Perseus' rescue of Andromeda: the god's wrath, the sea-serpent, the king's daughter chained to a rock and exposed to the monster in an effort to placate the god, the hero's timely rescue of the maiden, and even the king's subsequent attempt to renege on the agreement [Apollodorus: ii. 5. 9].

An even closer link is provided by a vase painting, reproduced by Kerényi [1959, Plate 31], which shows the hero grasping the monster's tongue and preparing to cut it off with his sickle-shaped sword. In another variant, Heracles leaped into the dragon's mouth and spent three days in its belly, finally hacking his way out, but re-emerging without any hair on his head [Frazer's note to Apollodorus: ii. 5. 9, Kerényi, 1959, p. 161]. Fontenrose interprets this loss as one of potency, comparing it to Samson's downfall and Zeus' loss of his sinews to Typhon; but he also views the sojourn in the monster's belly as a descent into the land of death [Fontenrose, 1959, p. 348].[19] From this perspective, the hairlessness might suggest rebirth, but one could also fuse these viewpoints by interpreting the episode as derived from circumcision ritual. The complementary version, in which Heracles cuts out the monster's tongue, would represent the female counterpart of circumcision, clitoridectomy—performed in cultures in which males feel too great a danger from feminine passion.

Sibling Rivalry

Since sibling rivalry plays such an overpowering role in most mythologies, and certainly in those geographically and culturally most closely related to Greece, it is surprising to realize how muted it is in the richest mythology of all. For the most part sibling rivalry in Greek myth provides a kind of historical background to the central events, but does not arise in the major myths themselves. The heroes are usually only-children, or, if they have siblings, are united in amity with them. Sibling rivalry among the gods is even more insignificant.

The reasons for this are difficult to ascertain. We know that the patriarchies of the Biblical and Moslem cultures intensified sibling rivalry, and one might wonder whether the difference is related to the emergence of democratic institutions. Conflicts in Greek myth seem to cross generation and sex lines, as we have seen, and oedipal aspirations are subordinated to sibling unity. The most reasonable explanation for this is that mythology gradually incorporated the Greeks' antidote to their pathogenic family pattern—the homosexual male brotherhood discussed in Chapter I. Father-son and

[19] Mopsus also loses his hair when he is fatally bitten by one of the Libyan serpents spawned by the Medusa's blood [Apollonius Rhodius: iv. 1513–1536].

brother-brother rivalry, necessarily violent in the old dynastic tales (witness Atreus and Thyestes, Oedipus and his sons), often tended to be muted somewhat or submerged in cross-sex conflicts. Thus Jason-Medea supplants Jason-Pelias in interest; Agamemnon-Clytemnestra supplants Agamemnon-Aegisthus; Creon-Antigone supplants Eteocles-Polyneices, and so on.

In any case, the story of Heracles and his twin illustrates the process of censorship quite strikingly. What is remarkable about Iphicles is that nothing whatever is known about him, save that he married a daughter of Creon when Heracles did, had Iolaus by a previous marriage, lost some children through Heracles' madness, and died in the battle against the Lacedaemonians [Apollodorus: ii. 4. 11–12 and ii. 7.3]. That he should be overshadowed by Heracles is not surprising, but this degree of vagueness seems rather suspicious. Heracles had many helpers, particularly Iphicles' son Iolaus. Why did not Iphicles himself appear more prominently in this role? There seems to be no reason why such a theme should be suppressed unless the relationship were originally rivalrous.

There is, in fact, one very early suggestion that the relation between the twins was not altogether harmonious. In the *Shield of Heracles* the two brothers are described most invidiously, and it is said of Iphicles that "from him Zeus took away sense, so that he left his home and his parents and went to do honour to the wicked Eurystheus—unhappy man! Deeply indeed did he grieve afterwards in bearing the burden of his own mad folly; but that cannot be taken back" [Hesiod: *Shield of Heracles* 48–56 and 87–92]. There is no material which would illuminate this cryptic comment, but it suggests that Iphicles was at one time and in some way the enemy of Heracles.[20]

Twins in Greek myth are usually amicable, but such is not the case in many other mythologies. Questions of precedence are particularly likely to arise in cultures with primogeniture.

---

[20] He was probably a hero in his own right at one time, since his name implies strength.

The book of *Genesis* is almost totally devoted to this problem, with several generations of rival brothers, the younger often gaining the elder's rights: Jacob over Esau, Ephraim over Manasseh, Joseph over his elder brothers. Jacob and Esau were twins who fought in the womb [*Genesis* 25:22–23], and concerning Zerah and Perez, there was considerable ambiguity about who was really the eldest: "And when she was in labor, one put out a hand; and the midwife took and bound on his hand a scarlet thread, saying, 'This came out first.' But as he drew back his hand, behold, his brother came out . . ." [*Ibid.*, 38:28–29].

Interestingly enough, this issue is never raised with Heracles and Iphicles. But it *is* raised between Heracles and Eurystheus. There is a struggle to see who will be born first, and who will thereby obtain the right to rule. The father is deceived into cheating his favorite, just as Isaac was deceived into cheating Esau. Heracles, like Esau, is a hunter, while Jacob, like Eurystheus, is "a quiet man, dwelling in tents" [*Ibid.*, 25:27]. To impersonate Esau, who is hairy, Jacob wears the skins of animals, just as Heracles wore a lion's skin [*Ibid.*, 27:11–16]. Both Heracles and Esau are rejected by the mother and lead a life of suffering: "By your sword you shall live, and you shall serve your brother; but when you break loose you shall break his yoke from your neck" [*Ibid.*, 25:28, 27:40]. The Heracles myth is thus a version of the vicissitudes of Esau, ignored in the Biblical tale.

From this it is clear that Iphicles and Eurystheus were originally the same. Their near-simultaneous birth, their common descent from Perseus, and the fight over birthright make it clear that Heracles and Eurystheus are the functional twins (no attention is given to Iphicles' claims, for example). Hesiod's story of Iphicles going to serve Eurystheus is a residue of their original identity.[21] Heracles is the deprived abandoned twin who leads a life of suffering. Eurystheus-

---

[21] Fontenrose also regards Iphicles as "the forerunner of Eurystheus as Herakles' rival" [1959, p. 403], although he does not give his reasons.

Iphicles is the favored twin from the brother's viewpoint: weak, cowardly, protected, hiding behind the mother's skirts (i.e., in the earth). Only after Heracles' death is vengeance achieved: Hyllus cuts off Eurystheus' head and Alcmene gouges out its eyes, a punishment which suggests the nature of the crime [Apollodorus: ii. 8. 1].

Sibling rivalry becomes, from this perspective, a rather essential feature of the Heraclean myths, albeit a disguised one. It also illuminates a number of peculiarities and regularities in the legend as a whole.

The most notable of these is the murder of Iphitus. Even granting the importance of the rules of hospitality, Iphitus' friendliness, and Heracles' treachery, it seems odd that of all Heracles' provoked and unprovoked murders this one should be singled out as requiring expiation. It is also the only one, aside from his murder of his children and other kin, that evoked the excuse of madness from mythographers [cf. Apollodorus: ii. 6. 2]. One cannot help wondering if behind this incident lies a story of sibling murder. The name itself is a variant of Iphicles, as Fontenrose points out [1959, p. 403], and Eurystheus had a brother named Iphitus, as well as a son Iphimedon [Diodorus Siculus: iv. 48; Apollodorus: ii. 8. 1].

The story of Iphitus takes place after Heracles has given Megara to Iolaus and gone to win Iole. Both Iole and Iphitus were children of Eurytus, who had promised his daughter to whoever could defeat his sons and himself in archery. When Heracles had done so, Eurytus reneged, and he and his sons threw Heracles out of the house. Only Iphitus supported the hero's cause. Later, Iphitus came to Tiryns in search of some stolen mares and Heracles invited him to be his guest. There is disagreement among mythographers as to whether (a) Heracles in fact had the mares and (b) if so, whether he had stolen them from Eurytus. In any case, taking Iphitus up to a tall tower, Heracles hurled him to his death [Apollodorus: ii. 6. 1-2; Diodorus Siculus: iv. 31; Sophocles: *The Trachiniae* 260ff.; Homer: *Odyssey* xxi. 28ff.].

It is the meaninglessness of this crime which undoubtedly led to ideas of Heracles' madness or uncontrollable rage over false accusations. The fact that Iphitus had supported Heracles gave the mythographers some trouble in explaining Heracles' crime, just as its expiation had caused difficulty. But the problems of motivation and heinousness both disappear if one assumes the crime disguises the murder of a sibling. Iphitus' friendly espousal of Heracles' cause, the contest itself, the question of injustice, the theft, the punishment—all these are issues of sibling love and sibling hatred. Heracles' rage is a jealous rage, just as was Daedalus' when he hurled his nephew and pupil Talos from the Acropolis [Apollodorus: iii. 15. 8].

While this conclusion may seem arbitrary, it gains strength when we see how often the theme is repeated. For there is always one son of each of his enemies who supports him: Nestor when he tries to get Neleus to purify him of the murder of Iphitus, Priam when Laomedon cheats him of his reward for killing the sea-serpent, Phyleus when Augeias refuses to pay him for cleaning out his stables. In all of these cases, Heracles eventually kills the father and all the other sons, while his supporter inherits the kingdom [Diodorus Siculus: iv. 31; iv. 32 and iv. 33; Apollodorus: ii. 5. 5; ii. 6. 4; ii. 7. 2; ii. 7. 3 and ii. 7. 7]. Thus while each enemy cheats, tricks, and deprives him, a small piece of the enemy loves and supports him. Iphicles also has a son who assists Heracles: Iolaus, his inseparable companion and charioteer.

But if his enemies are not without friendship, so Heracles is not without enmity toward his friends. He tries to kill Iolaus when he goes mad, and starts to kill Telamon when the latter succeeds in breaching the walls of Troy before the hero can do so. It is only by abandoning the enterprise and pretending to build an altar to Heracles that Telamon averts death at the hands of his jealous companion [Apollodorus: ii. 6. 4].

Heracles is in general a dangerous friend—Cheiron and Pholus owe their deaths to him [Apollodorus: ii. 5. 4]—and an

even worse master, for he kills Lichas, Eunomus, and Cya-
thus, and indirectly causes the deaths of others. While he is
attached to youthful companions such as Iolaus and Hylas,
and attracts youthful support from enemies, he is also a jealous
filicide. The attraction to youth is not only a homosexual
response, but also one expressing an intolerance of competition, of equality. And even this defense periodically breaks
down, revealing the oedipal and sibling rivalry beneath. One
of the complexities inherent in fantasy products is that the
strains they reflect are mutually reinforcing (the more of one
the more of all the others) while the defenses against them
tend to be competitive (one strain overt, others denied or
counteracted in some way). It is this dialectic that generates
much of the richness of a concrete fantasy.

The Evolution of Heracles

The problem of dating myth fragments is almost insuperable,
and demands a depth of knowledge and scholarship well beyond the bounds of this work. Yet it would help to know
which aspects of the Heraclean myth are most likely to have
been earlier and which later, since the later ones should most
clearly reveal the attempt to mold earlier ideas to fit the
psychological realities of the pre-classical and classical periods.

If we restrict ourselves to those historical inferences which
seem most cautious, the development of Heracles does show
some increase in preoccupation with the ambivalent mother-
son relationship. Although much of the myth is already present in Homer, the Deianeira story is missing, as well as
Heracles' death and apotheosis [Nilsson, 1932, pp. 199, 205].
Nilsson suggests that Hera's enmity is a late feature, the
original problem being a simple conflict between a sovereign
(Eurystheus) and a vassal (Heracles), similar to that between
Agamemnon and Achilles [*Ibid.*, pp. 209–11]. Yet it is difficult to make much of this, since Hera's enmity is well-
developed in Homer. Nilsson also sees Heracles' madness as a

late attempt to rationalize his brutality [*Ibid.*, p. 202], although again, the idea seems to have been present at least in the post-Homeric epics [Proclus: *Chrestomathy* i].

One can perhaps best summarize the myth's evolution by saying that Heracles changes (although not altogether) from a bumptious, impulsive, gross, immoderate, and quarrelsome hero, appropriate to a coarse and uncivilized era, to a hag-ridden sufferer—persecuted, unstable, and self-defeating. Narcissism and sex antagonism are present throughout, but are increasingly elaborated; while other themes, such as sibling rivalry, tend to diminish in importance or are suppressed.

One curious feature of the myth is the fact that only Heracles, among Greek heroes, becomes a god. This is in keeping with his character change from a trickster or Stupid Hans to a Promethean and Christlike figure, suffering and sacrificing himself in order to confer boons upon mankind. Yet crossing the great dividing line is not only an unheard of form of social mobility [cf. Finley, 1959], but also a kind of oedipal presumption; for the prototype of all social mobility is the passage from the low, sexless status of the child to the high, fully sexual status of the adult; and dramatic social mobility always has oedipal overtones, both in myth and in everyday life. This is why Heracles must so often renounce his women in favor of son-figures and become a slave for others: the oedipal challenge must be denied. Heracles is Bellerophon inverted—instead of presuming to Olympus and being punished, he is punished and then taken to Olympus.

There is still another reason why such a blasphemous duality was permitted to endure. Heracles, more than any other figure, was a symbol of Greece itself. His progress from Gargantuan bully to suffering culture-hero, and from hero to deity, reflects the development of Greek civilization out of Dorian vulgarity [cf. Arrowsmith, 1959, p. 273]. He symbolizes, without achieving, the instinctual renunciations that are involved in the development of urban life and mastery over nature—in the transition from a "shame culture" to a "guilt culture" [cf. Dodds, 1957, pp. 28–50]. This is perhaps why his apotheosis is associated with so little sense of rejoicing, and his suffering so little regarded as a means to an end:[22] it is never in the least clear, as Freud pointed out [1930, pp. 87, 143], that the achievement is worth all the trouble.

In any case, Heracles presents us with a curious contradiction. On the one hand he is all impulse, with his gross appetites and lack of restraint or foresight. On the other, he is a man engaged in chronic labor, with no release from suffering, no real love or enjoyment of life—a kind of unwitting adherent of the Protestant Ethic. The qualifying adjective, of course, invalidates this anachronistic categorization, but Heracles is perhaps as close to such a position as ancient mythology could get. Heracles is a civilizing force, but not civilized. He is proto-urban but not urban, chronically industrious without the capacity for sustained effort and self-denial. His is the blind and uncontrolled narcissistic ambition out of which the capacity for civilization may accidentally arise. From his blocked pleasure derives the energy for cultural achievements.

Yet he is, as noted, *proto*-urban, the force but not the product. He is like the crude lower-class racketeer who achieves economic success but not social respectability, and is rejected by his children for the very origins from which his success has insulated them. So Heracles was in part rejected in favor of the rather pale but more cultured figure of Theseus, to whom we now turn.

Theseus

The attempt to make out of Theseus a local Athenian hero who would supplant Heracles in the imagination of men was

---

[22] Such thinking would presuppose the existence of the very guilt culture whose advent is symbolized. The development of internalized restraints, of long-range foresight, of the ability almost permanently to postpone gratification, lies at the very end of this process.

never altogether successful. If Heracles was too vulgar and old-fashioned for cultured Athenians he nonetheless signified "hero" to them in a way that Theseus never could. Theseus' very civility deprived him of emotional interest, so that in the dramas he is seldom more than a background figure—a kind of idealized ruler who defends the weak and counsels the strong.

Nilsson points out [1932, pp. 163–64] that in the archaic period Heracles is still the dominant figure in Greek art, with Theseus gradually gaining ground until, by the fifth century, he has become a founder of the Athenian state and of democratic institutions. Arguing from the evidence of vase paintings and political annexations, Nilsson maintains that most of the Thesean myths—those which imitate Heracles and those which support local political claims—cannot be older than the earlier historical period, although others, such as the various abductions and the Cretan myth, are of Mycenean origin [*Ibid.*, pp. 165–80].

In any case, the Theseus who comes down to us seems to be primarily a negative idealization of Heracles. Most of the latter's coarse and impulse-ridden attributes are stripped away, with only his courage and civilizing proclivities retained (thus Theseus rids the Isthmus of monsters and brigands and unifies Attica). As a result, Theseus never appears in comedy [Ehrenberg, 1951, p. 264]. Euripides adds a noble spirit, generosity, kindness, and rationality, so that the total picture is a pleasing though somewhat colorless one. Theseus can never quite escape the deliberateness of his manufacture; the older myths about him have lost the kind of rich symbolic detail that adheres to the Perseus legend, while the newer ones are too self-conscious and purposive to evoke the interpersonal elaboration found in the later Heraclean myths.

Theseus, then, is a kind of pastel Heracles, and with all of his artificiality one should expect to find comparable themes in his myths. Yet, considering his exemplary character (aside

from his inveterate proclivity for rape), one might also antici-
pate some element in his history which would mitigate the
usual maternal menace in some way. Both predictions are confirmed in the late myth of Theseus' arrival in Athens—his encounter with his father, Aegeus, and his stepmother, Medea.

Theseus, like most Greek heroes, was for all practical purposes fatherless. Like Heracles, he had a mortal and an immortal sire, his mother having copulated in the same night
with Aegeus, King of Athens, and Poseidon. He was reared
in a mother-child household and upon reaching manhood
acquired, through a trial of strength, the sword and sandals
Aegeus had left for him, with which he proceeded to Athens.
On his way he cleared the Isthmus of various ogres and arrived after many adventures in his father's city. Medea, who
had sought shelter with Aegeus after her rupture with Jason
and had ultimately married her benefactor, now saw her position threatened by the newcomer, and persuaded Aegeus of
Theseus' wicked intentions. The hero was received with a
cup of poison, and would have perished had not Aegeus
recognized his sword and dashed the cup from his hands.
Medea was banished and Theseus received as Aegeus' son and
heir [Apollodorus: iii. 15. 7; iii. 16. 1–2 and *Epitome:* i. 1–6;
Bacchylides: xvii. 16–30; Callimachus *Hecale* fragment 66;
Plutarch: *Theseus* 3–12; Lycophron: *Alexandra* 494–95 and
1322–1323].

What is familiar in this story is the absent father, the uncertain paternity, the mother-child household, and the maternal threat, appropriately displaced onto a stepmother. What
is unique is that Theseus actually finds and keeps a mortal
father for himself, one who accepts him, adopts him, who
reigns, and whom he can succeed as king. Unlike the shadowy
mortal and immortal fathers of other heroes, Aegeus actually
protects Theseus—even tries to overprotect him [Kerényi,
1959, p. 225]. The salience of a paternal figure in the Theseus
myth is in keeping with the relative scarcity of serpentine

monsters and other representations of maternal malevolence. Zeus, for all his power, is unable to protect Heracles from Hera, while Aegeus not only saves Theseus from Medea but banishes the latter in his favor.

The preoccupation with paternity is also exhibited in Bacchylides' narrative of the encounter between Theseus and Minos in Crete. When Minos made advances toward one of the Athenian maidens Theseus reproached him, whereupon the Cretan overlord sneered at Theseus' claim of being a son of Poseidon. Minos prayed for a sign from his own father, Zeus, and received it in the form of a flash of lightning. He then threw a golden ring in the ocean and demanded that Theseus prove his origins by recovering it. Theseus dove into the sea, was carried by dolphins to the palace of the king of the sea and was given not only the ring but a golden crown by Amphitrite [Bacchylides: xvi; Pausanias: i. 17. 3]. Thus both of his fathers support and sustain him, which is congruent with the fact that most of the women in Theseus' life are relatively benign. It is Ariadne who enables him to kill the Minotaur and escape from the Labyrinth, giving him, like Amphitrite, a sign.

This is not to say that fear of the mature female is altogether absent from the Theseus cycle. Theseus' venture through the Labyrinth and the killing of the Minotaur can be construed as a reversal of the birth journey—the hero returning to the woman, encountering a phallic paternal object therein, and destroying it. This seems to be the same symbolic process that one finds in the Perseus story: the male child separates the mother from her sexuality, her need for adult genital satisfaction. But in this case the hero's motivation seems more classically oedipal, since it is more explicitly the father against whom this effort is directed. In the Perseus myth the child wishes to eliminate a force with which he is unable to cope—to create a mother who is *only* a mother. The father is not recognized as that factor which will fulfill this desire to the degree that it is realistically attainable. In the Minotaur myth the father is associated with the secrets of women, and his secondary importance in the eyes of the small child is apparent in the fact that he, too, is contained within the recesses of the all-encompassing mother.

The first real symptom of gynephobia is, however, Theseus' abandonment of his helper and bride, Ariadne, on the Island of Naxos. The Homeric version of this tale has Ariadne slain by Artemis at the request of Dionysus [Homer: *Odyssey* xi. 321–25], but later versions show Theseus intentionally or accidentally deserting the princess [Theocritus: *Idylls* ii. 45; Plutarch: *Theseus* 20]. This alteration reflects the emergence of classical modes of masculine defense against the fear of women. Theseus must flee Ariadne because she is tainted with maternal attributes: she knows the secret of the Labyrinth. Furthermore, her feeling for Theseus is so intense that she is willing to betray her father and sacrifice the life of her brother (the Minotaur); such depth of feminine passion had little appeal for the Greek male. Jason deserts Medea who makes a similar sacrifice, Minos himself kills Scylla for her love-inspired parricide, and Amphitryon similarly rewards Comaetho [Kerényi, 1959, p. 230; Apollodorus: i. 9. 24; i. 9. 28; ii. 4. 7 and iii. 15. 8].

Theseus also has a preference for youthful and boyish women. We are told that, with the help of his bosom companion, Peirithous, he abducted Helen when she was only twelve years old—an appealing age for Athenian males as well as for Nabokovian heroes [Apollodorus: *Epitome* i. 23; Plutarch: *Theseus* 31]. While it might be argued that this assignment of extreme youth to Helen is merely an attempt to reconcile conflicting chronologies, one must then explain why with all the striking anachronisms in Greek myth such precision was required in this single instance. The youth of Helen is in fact the focal point of an otherwise rather meaningless episode, and is stressed by almost all sources. Whatever its origin, its retention must be credited in part to Greek sexual preoccupations.

Theseus also had an Amazon bride, Antiope, whom he eventually killed when she jealously threatened to disrupt his wedding to Phaedra [Apollodorus: *Epitome* i. 17]. She is also said to have fought at his side when he repelled the Amazonian invasion of Attica [Plutarch: *Theseus* 27].[23]

Athenian sex antagonism necessitated the assignment to Theseus of the victory over the Amazons, whatever other factors, including history, may have contributed to it.[24] This victory seems to have been regarded with even more reverence than Theseus' alleged democratic innovations and the unification of Attica [Kerényi, 1959, pp. 240–42; Thucydides: ii. 15ff.; Lysias: "Funeral Oration," 4–6; Pausanias: i. 3. 3; Plutarch: *Theseus* 24–27]. That Athens' rise should be tied to a victory over women seems quite in keeping with the misogyny of Athenian thought.

The danger of mature feminine passion is also portrayed in the story of Theseus' wife Phaedra and her stepson Hippolytus, the son of Antiope. This is the familiar Potiphar's-wife theme—the lustful mother figure posed against the innocent son, whom she falsely accuses of her own seduction attempt. There are, however, three unusual features about it. The first is the extreme emphasis placed on Hippolytus' asceticism and hatred of women [Apollodorus: *Epitome* i. 18; Euripides: *Hippolytus* 1off.]. The second is the fact that it is not a hero

---

[23] Theseus' own masculinity is called into question in one tale. When he first arrived in Athens, dressed in a long tunic and with his hair plaited, some workmen asked him why a young maiden was allowed to walk about unescorted. Theseus tossed some oxen into the air by way of reply [Pausanias: i. 19. 1–2].

[24] There is a little too much ethnographic and circumstantial detail about the Amazons and the Amazon war to dismiss the entire episode as pure myth [cf. Lysias: "Funeral Oration," 4–6; Xenophon: *Anabasis* iv. 4, 16–17; cf. also Briffault, 1959, p. 100]. Yet it seems likely that the Victory Over The Women, so conspicuous in Athenian lore, primarily describes an event in the emotional life of each male child.

but a hero's son who is the central character in the tale—the same tendency to invert the oedipal drama that we found in Heraclean myth. The third is the savage punishment inflicted on the son by his father, Theseus, and his grandfather, Poseidon [Apollodorus: *Epitome* i. 19; Euripides: *Hippolytus* 1199ff.]. Of all the Potiphar's-wife heroes, Hippolytus is the only one to be killed.

This severe paternal retribution is symptomatic of the stronger father element in the myths of Theseus. Oedipal rivalry is commensurately more direct than in the myths of Perseus and Heracles.

One example of this is the mad expedition of Theseus and Peirithous to the underworld to steal Persephone from their divine uncle, Hades. Peirithous here serves as a handy object of displacement, with most of the responsibility for this act of *hubris* being laid at his door. Yet it is Theseus who is the famous abductor of women, and as Kerényi points out [1959, p. 238], the adventure is really a duplicate of the Ariadne myth, the Labyrinth also representing the land of the dead. Ariadne, furthermore, was also the bride of a chthonic god (Dionysus).

Hades pretended to welcome the heroes, but bade them sit on the throne of forgetfulness, to which their flesh grew fast while coils of serpents held them. In some versions this was the end of both heroes; in others, Theseus was saved by Heracles; in still others, both Theseus and Peirithous were rescued [Diodorus Siculus: iv. 26 and iv. 63; Apollodorus: ii. 5. 12 and *Epitome* i. 24; Euripides: *Heracles* 619]. In any case, nothing is heard of Theseus after this incident—except his death on Scyros.

In this limited sense, then, Theseus falls victim to the serpent as a consequence of his oedipal pretentions. Immobilized, entangled, boundaries dissolved (growing into the stone), he experiences those same perils which threaten other heroes.

The other version of Theseus' death also has oedipal overtones, for Theseus dies the same death as his father. On his return from Crete Theseus forgot to hoist the white sail which was to signal his safe return, and Aegeus, seeing the boat approaching with a black sail, assumed he was dead and threw himself to his death, either off the Acropolis or into the sea [Apollodorus: *Epitome* i. 10–11; Pausanias: i. 22. 5; Plutarch: *Theseus* 22]. Thus Theseus became king by killing his father through an act of omission, and it is therefore quite fitting that he himself should die by being hurled from a high rock into the sea by King Lycomedes of Scyros [Plutarch: *Theseus* 35; Pausanias: I. 17. 6; Lycophron: *Alexandra* 1323–1325; Apollodorus: *Epitome* i. 24].

But how is one to interpret all of this falling?[25] We find it again in the story of Theseus' struggle with the brigand Sciron, who used to force travelers on the Isthmus to wash his feet, whereupon he would kick them into the sea to be eaten by a huge turtle. But Theseus seized the tyrant by the feet and hurled him over the cliff, serving him as he had served others [Apollodorus: *Epitome* i. 2–3; Pausanias: i. 44. 8]. A vase painting, however, shows Theseus riding on the back of the turtle; so in some early version he must actually have been hurled down like the other travelers and been *rescued* by the turtle [cf. Kerényi, 1959, p. 221 and Plate 49]. Sciron stands to Theseus in the relation of master to servant, and the servant revolts—just as the son causes the father to be hurled down and takes his place.

It is pride and presumption that precede a fall—the fall itself being caused here by masculine jealousy. Daedalus hurls down Talos, Heracles Iphitus. Icarus and Bellerophon are similarly punished for their *hubris*. Theseus, who is hurled down after his bold oedipal insult to Hades, bears many resemblances to Bellerophon: like him he defeats the Amazons, and after an impudent adventure, which ends disastrously, is neglected and dies obscurely.

One can best understand the importance of this theme of

[25] The story of Icarus' presumption and his fall into the sea also occurs in the context of the Theseus myth [Apollodorus: *Epitome* i. 12–13].

height and falling by considering a study by Erikson of the play configurations of pre-adolescent children [Erikson, 1963]. Erikson found that in this age group only boys build towers, and that the concern with height is intimately connected with that of "downfall"—ruins, collapse, madness, suicide, and so on. He concludes that *"the variable high-low* is a *masculine variable,"* and relates it to doubts about masculinity [*op. cit.,* p. 334]. It is at this age that boys in our culture show most similarity to the Greeks in their boastfulness, their narcissism, their misogyny, their fear of involvement, their homosexuality, their athleticism, their quarrelsomeness, their dreams of glory. It is an age when separation from the mother is being won and identification with the father is strong, yet it is also an age in which the preoccupation with masculine potency is great, and the desire to surpass the father equally compelling. All of these motives seem to be fused in the myths of the fall. Bellerophon and Icarus fly too high, Talos surpasses his uncle Daedalus in skill and has an incestuous relationship with his mother. Theseus also shows this ambivalent pattern of needing the paternal model and protector but being unable to resist trying to surpass it.

Part Three

QUANTIFICATIONS, GENERALIZATIONS, AND IMPLICATIONS

CHAPTER XIII

Familial Emphases in Greek Myth: A Statistical Analysis

IN THE PRECEDING CHAPTERS I have conducted my investigation with a fine humanistic freedom—dwelling upon those examples which illustrate the argument most convincingly, and making generous use of symbolic substitutions. But such a procedure can be misleading, just as long descriptions of gales and hurricanes can distort an estimate of annual rainfall.

In this chapter I shall attempt to test one of the central generalizations I have made about the Greek family system: that its principal strains were in the cross-sex parent-child dyads, as both cause and consequence of the sex antagonism prevailing in the culture as a whole. I shall conduct three tests of this hypothesis, making as few assumptions as possible and using indicators which allow the smallest leeway for interpretive intervention. Even if the hypothesis is confirmed, I cannot, of course, assume the generalization to have been demonstrated, since the tests are of necessity inferential. But some such statistical analysis seems necessary to lend a fiber of credibility to an otherwise highly "artistic" interpretive fabric.

The three tests I have chosen by no means exhaust the possibilities. They were merely those that immediately occurred to me as expressing most directly and simply the processes I have been discussing on a more "clinical" level. They concern, respectively, the distribution of physical injury or homicide among parent-child dyads, the distribution of psychotogenesis among god-mortal dyads, and the distribution of interaction and affect among parent-child dyads in Greek tragedy.

Aggression

The first test is the simplest and makes the fewest assumptions. It states that if the cross-sex dyads involve the most strain they should display the most aggression. "Aggression" is defined operationally in the most stringent manner possible, excluding "psychological" aggression entirely. "Parent-child" means just that—no surrogates or step-parents are included. These limitations remove almost all ambiguity from the tabulation process and make the test a highly rigorous one.

The "sample" for this test was Apollodorus, including the *Epitome*. Three kinds of aggression were tabulated: successful homicide, assault producing permanent injury (there was no other kind), and unsuccessful homicide. No attempt was made to decipher motivation or intent: accidental killing, mistaken identity, sacrifice to the gods, and deliberate murder were all treated in the same manner. "Unsuccessful homicide" was used when the homicide failed through the escape of the victim, rescue by a third party, or whatever. It similarly ignores intent or purpose. Successful and unsuccessful homicide both include placing the victim in a situation in which death would normally occur, such as exposing an infant or instructing a third party to carry out the murder. The instructions must be explicit, however: if a king sends his daughter to another king with a written note to kill her, the father is scored as the agent; but if a stepmother accuses her stepson of rape and his father kills him, the father is again scored as the agent, since, although the stepmother may have known that the killing would result, she did not explicitly instruct the father to do it. These precautions also serve to counteract any bias in favor of the hypothesis.

When this technique is used, 47 instances of aggression in parent-child dyads result. Table 1 shows the distribution of these examples--the complete list appears in Appendix I.[1]

Since we expect males to engage in physical aggression more than females we should not be surprised to see that the father-son dyad involves the largest number of cases, the mother-daughter dyad the smallest number. Indeed, the single mother-daughter case comes about by omission—Apollodorus not specifying the sex of the children devoured by the Argive women (in all other such cases they are male). This sexual differentiation is illustrated by the fact that the predominance of the father-son dyad in Table 1 is dependent upon five cases in which the aggression was directly instigated by a female: what the woman is not expected to do herself she must provoke the male to do.[2]

[1] There were five questionable cases. One was the sons of the Amazons, who are not explicitly said to have been exposed, although this is obvious from the statement that only the girls were reared. The second was Antiope, who fled her father when he "threatened" her. This was assumed to be an attempt at homicide but might be considered purely verbal. The third was Hippolytus, whose father's prayer to Poseidon was treated as an "instruction." The fourth was Tantalus' slaughter of Pelops, which Apollodorus never specifically mentions, although he comments on Pelops' reconstitution. The fifth was Hippodamia, the nature of whose instruction to Myrtilus was ambiguous. Since the most dubious cases (second, fourth, and fifth) fall on both sides of the hypothesis, and since there is no pattern of inclusion or exclusion which would alter the statistical significance of the results, I decided to include them all.

There is also some ambiguity about whether Cronus' devouring of his children and Tantalus' destruction of Pelops should be coded as "successful" or "unsuccessful." The assumption made here was that Cronus' children were never actually destroyed but that Pelops was. This is certainly debatable, but a change would not significantly alter the results in either case.

[2] There is no comparable tendency to instigate cross-sex aggression. Electra is not presented by Apollodorus as the instigator of Orestes (an omission balanced by the fact that Apollodorus has Laius rather than Jocasta expose Oedipus). Both sexes are equally prone to be the indirect

TABLE I

Distribution of Aggression in Parent-Child Dyads

Dyad	Success-ful Homi-cide	Unsuc-cessful Homi-cide	Assault Producing Permanent Injury	Total	Total for Dyad
Father-Son	6	4	3	13	
Son-Father	4	0	1	5	18
Mother-Son	7	3	0	10	
Son-Mother	2	0	0	2	12
Father-Daughter	1	10	0	11	
Daughter-Father	5	0	0	5	16
Mother-Daughter	1	0	0	1	
Daughter-Mother	0	0	0	0	1
Total	26	17	4	47	47

There are a number of interesting trends in Table 1. Notice, for example, that all four of the assaults with mutilation occur in the father-son dyad—quite in accord with traditional psychoanalytic ideas (they include a castration, a crippling, and two blindings, even without any assistance from Oedipus and Laius). More interesting is the fact that while males and females are equally likely to commit successful homicides, males are overwhelmingly more likely to be the victims ($X^2 = 11.12, p < .001$).

The ratio of successful to unsuccessful homicides also shows interesting patterns. Note that while the parents are on the whole slightly more often unsuccessful than successful, the

cause of aggression: through oracles, by being fought over, or by inducing madness; but only females directly instigate in the manner described. Males have a monopoly on accidental killings: there are three cases in which sons kill fathers through nonrecognition. This of course has no bearing on the test being made here, but it is interesting as an expression of Greek resistance to recognizing father-son hostility and rivalry.

children never fail ($p = .003$, exact test). It is the fathers rather than the mothers who are responsible for these failures ($X^2 = 3.05, p < .10$) and they fail more often with daughters than with sons ($X^2 = 4.03, p < .05$). But, as we have seen, mothers do not share this cross-sex carelessness, nor do the daughters reciprocate the paternal pattern. Note also that the total of attempted and consummated father-daughter homicides exceeds all of the other categories, so that no affectionate impulse is in question. A unique peculiarity of these father-daughter attempts, however, is that they are so often thwarted.

My primary question, however, is still unanswered. Are cross-sex aggressions more common than same-sex aggressions? We can see from Table 1 that they are, and this is made somewhat clearer in Table 2 (since the direction of difference was predicted, a one-tailed test is used). Competition between family members of the same sex—a cornerstone of orthodox psychoanalytic thinking—is completely overwhelmed in Greek culture by antagonism between the sexes.

TABLE 2

Aggression in Cross-Sex and Same-Sex Dyads*

	Victim		
Agent	Male	Female	Total
Male	18	13	31
Female	15	1	16
Total	33	14	47

* Tendency for aggression to cross sex lines significant at .01 level, using Fisher's exact test, one-tailed.

Madness

In Chapter 1 I suggested that psychosis tended to be inflicted along cross-sex lines in Greek myth, and this will now be tested more systematically. For madness in Greek mythology does not occur spontaneously, but is always visited upon a mortal by a god or goddess. As in the case of physical aggression, then, we have an agent and a victim for each instance of madness. But here, unfortunately, I will have to make an additional assumption, since there are no cases in which biological parents and children inflict madness on one another.[3] I will assume that the god-mortal relation "inherits" the characteristics of the parent-child relation and can be interpreted in the same manner. I will predict that madness is visited significantly more often upon persons of the sex opposite to the divine agent.

The problem of sampling is also more difficult here. Apollodorus records only fourteen cases, which probably, nonetheless, surpasses other ancient sources. Among modern compendia Graves probably has the largest collection (nineteen), but some of these involve considerable poetic license. I finally decided to combine these two "samples," which have an overlap of eleven cases.[4] All of Apollodorus' cases were used, whether or not included in Graves, and his attributions were used in case of conflict. Of eight cases in Graves which are not found in Apollodorus, all those were retained for which ancient sources could be found.

Like all such procedures, this is somewhat arbitrary, excluding some cases which are, and including some which are not, unequivocally old and Greek. But it is desirable to limit in some way the exercise of too much (potentially biased) discretion in choosing cases. Limiting the sample to Graves and Apollodorus eliminates several cases which would favor the hypothesis, mostly involving Dionysus and various groups of

[3] Except indirectly, as in the two cases in which a mother's Erinyes drive the son mad.

[4] Since the idea for this analysis came from reading Graves, the first test was performed on his data. The results confirmed the hypothesis somewhat more resoundingly than does the test in Table 3, but further investigation led to doubts about the validity of some of Graves' attributions, and suggested the advisability of a more stringent test. The small number of cases in the Apollodorus sample, however, makes it difficult to achieve statistical significance even with a favorable distribution.

women (Carya's sisters, the women of Attica). The restriction on Graves eliminates three cases: the sons of Halia, Pentheus, and the Argive women. Pentheus' "madness" is Graves' own invention, serving the same purpose as Murray's hypnotism theory, and there is only the slightest justification for treating the daughters of Proetus and the Argive women as separate incidents.

One final problem concerns two cases in which alternative agents were suggested. While Apollodorus cites Dionysus as the source of Lycurgus' madness, Graves claims Rhea. As far as I can tell, however, Graves' choice is gratuitous, and was therefore ignored. The second case is more difficult, since there are two genuine traditions—both mentioned by Apollodorus—regarding the daughters of Proetus: one, that Dionysus drove them mad; the other, that Hera did. Here Dionysus was again chosen, on the grounds not only that his is the more accepted tradition, but also that if Hera were chosen one would have to reinstate the separate story of Dionysus and the Argive women—since the larger group is far more clearly tied to Dionysus. Diodorus even attaches the latter incident to Anaxagoras rather than Proetus [Diodorus Siculus: iv. 68; cf. also Pausanias: ii. 18. 4]. The two attributions thus cancel out each other.

Where several persons are driven mad together, they are treated as one case, with the single exception of Athamas and Ino, who are of different sexes and behave somewhat differently. A complete list of the cases is shown in Appendix II.

Table 3 shows the results of the analysis. The hypothesis is confirmed at the .05 level, using a one-tailed version of Fisher's exact test. As in Table 2, females attack males more often than the reverse. Here, however, females tend *in general* to be the aggressors, while in Table 2 males predominate as agents. In *both* tables, however, males tend to be victims more than twice as often as females.

TABLE 3

Madness in Cross-Sex and Same-Sex Dyads*

| | Victim | | |
Agent	Male	Female	Total
Male	2	4	6
Female	11	2	13
Total	13	6	19

* Tendency for madness to be inflicted on a cross-sex basis significant at .05 level, using Fisher's exact test, one-tailed.

Dyadic Emphasis in Tragedy

My third test concerns the emphasis on various parent-child dyads in Greek tragedy. It makes the assumption that drama concerns itself with issues and relationships which are problematic and conflict-laden, and which generate ambivalent responses. One would therefore expect to find that cross-sex parent-child dyads are treated more often, more thoroughly, and with more emotionality, than same-sex parent-child dyads. As in the first test, only actual parent-child cases are used— no surrogates, step-parents, or in-laws. The only exception is the case where a god is alleged to be the child's father: here the child's sociological (and mortal) father is used. There are only two such cases—Xuthus-Ion and Amphitryon-Heracles— both of which work against the hypothesis since both are father-son dyads involving some ambivalence and are treated at some length.

There are two additional factors working against the hypothesis. Greek society was a masculine society and a sex-segregated society, and insofar as drama reproduced everyday conditions, one might expect more interactions to occur between same-sex individuals, and particularly between males. Socially, in other words, the father-son relationship was the most conspicuous one for the Athenians, and this might offset to some extent the factor with which I am concerned here.

The procedure was as follows: from the thirty-three extant plays of the three great dramatists, sixty-five parent-child dyads were extracted. Only persons actually appearing on stage were used, whether speaking or mute. In most of the dramas the children are individuated in some way, but in some half-dozen cases the children are not designated by name but appear as a group, and in these instances I treated the group as a single case (e.g., the daughters of Danaus, the sons of Heracles, Polymestor, and Medea). Both parent and child had to appear on stage, however, to be included.

I also coded the number of lines actually directed by each member of the dyad to the other, using three categories: no interaction, one to twenty-five lines, and over twenty-five lines. Mourning over a corpse was included if the words were clearly directed toward the deceased, and if the latter was a living character at some time during the play.

I also made an attempt to code the intensity of positive and negative affect expressed by the members of the dyad toward each other. This was based not only on direct interaction but also on behavior occurring offstage and attitudes expressed to third parties. A score of "1" was assigned if the feeling was neutral or absent or unexpressed or unknown. A positive score of "2" was given to moderate expressions of affection, and a negative score of "2" to moderate expressions of anger and resentment. Scores of "3" were used for intense expressions of love and nurturance on the one hand, and violent, murderous hatred on the other. Two conventions were also adopted: affection expressed to a corpse was always rated 2, no matter how intense, on the assumption that (a) there is a formal element of exaggeration in mourning, and (b) loss accentuates positive feelings; killing was always rated 3, whether done in sorrow, in madness, or in anger.

These codes are the most subjective measure used in this chapter and should be viewed with a certain amount of skepticism. It would be difficult to obtain full agreement between any two individuals even with so simple a set of categories, given the multiplicity of interpretations of the emotional significance of any given Greek drama. I feel little confidence that my own ratings would be precisely the same were I to do them again after a year or so. At the same time, it seemed important to make some distinction between an intense dyadic relationship, such as that between Medea and her sons, and a relatively bland one, such as that between Aethra and Theseus. In any case, all of the ratings made for the dramas are presented in Appendix III, and the reader is invited to try his own hand at it.

Two final variables were included as a kind of afterthought: the age and mortality of the "child" in the dyad.[5] I had predicted that cross-sex dyads would more often involve young children and/or children who died—both conditions being presumed to reflect a greater insecurity, anxiety, and sense of inadequacy on the part of the offspring in the dyadic relationship.

The results of these tabulations are shown in Table 4. All variables show the same trend, with the mother-son dyad being highest on each, the mother-daughter dyad lowest. The father-son dyad is second, however, and all of the differences are much reduced for the dyads involving the largest amount of interaction. While on every variable the cross-sex dyads score a higher total than the same-sex dyads, none of the differences are statistically significant.

The strongest effect in Table 4 is obviously the difference between sons and daughters, the latter being clearly of less importance. Parent-son dyads are more common, treated at greater length, and involve more emotion than parent-daughter dyads (perhaps because the playwrights were male). Sons are more often small children, and die with much greater frequency. It is only within the context of this gross difference that the weaker tendency toward cross-sex emphasis might be

[5] More than two-thirds of the "children" in the sample are full-grown.

TABLE 4

Parent-Child Dyads in Greek Drama

Dyad	Cases	*Amount of Interaction**				*Total Af-fect***	*Ambiva-lence****	*Child Not Full-Grown*	*Child Dies*
		Parent		*Child*					
		1+	25+	1+	25+				
Mother-Son	23	19	8	12	7	148	7	7	9
Father-Son	17	15	7	10	7	106	6	6	8
Father-Daughter	14	9	6	7	6	81	3	3	2
Mother-Daughter	11	8	4	6	5	63	1	2	2

* Number of lines addressed to other member of dyad.

** Obtained by adding together positive and negative affect from both parent and child.

*** Number of cases in which parent or child expresses both positive and negative affect (score of "2" or "3" on each) toward other member of dyad.

said to occur: mother-son being higher than father-son, father-daughter higher than mother-daughter.

Thus, while Table 4 certainly does not contradict the hypothesis, it provides little support. It seems likely that the masculine orientation of the culture plays an important part in diluting this effect, if indeed it exists. The more satisfactory results from the first two tests, however, provide a certain amount of cartilage for my interpretations,[6] and encourage me to ask to what extent these interpretations can be generalized beyond the specific context of classical Greece.

[6] I am speaking here to the social scientist, for I am well aware that to most humanists this chapter will seem not only unnecessary but offensive, with its statistical intrusions, its callous dissection of organic wholes, and its operational definitions which stubbornly ignore context. The social scientist will perhaps object for precisely opposite reasons.

CHAPTER XIV

A Cross-Cultural Analysis of Maternal Ambivalence and Narcissism[1]

W F. HAVE REPEATEDLY OBSERVED that the phenomena under consideration here are by no means limited to the culture of classical Greece. One may now ask, how general are they? More precisely, do these processes that I have claimed to be dynamically related in Greek culture appear similarly linked in other societies? Do sex antagonism, maternal ambivalence, gynephobia, and masculine narcissism generally occur together?

Even a casual perusal of the sociological and anthropological literature suggests that some of the relationships for which I have argued have wide applicability. Komarovsky, for example, shows that in the American working class sex segregation is far more marked than in the middle class, and that the marital bond is a relatively weak and distant one. In many cases the "overlapping of interests is so narrow . . . that neither partner can serve as a satisfactory audience for the other" [Komarovsky, 1964, pp. 149ff.; cf. also Bott, 1957; Young and Willmott, 1964]. This is associated with a strong mother-daughter bond, weak ties between child and father,

[1] An earlier version of this chapter appeared in the *Merrill-Palmer Quarterly* [Slater and Slater, 1965].

and an ambivalent mother-son relationship—one in which the son is sometimes made a substitute for an inadequate husband [Komarovsky, 1964, pp. 208ff., 243ff., 260ff.]. On the whole, however, the mother-son bond does not seem to be so intense (in either respect) as in Greece.

Bayley and Schaefer, on the other hand, see a general tendency, at least in American society, toward greater tension in the mother-son than in the mother-daughter relationship:

"Several studies indicate that mothers express greater warmth toward girl babies, but permit more aggression in boys. As for specific techniques of training, boys usually get more physical punishment and girls are more often controlled by the giving or withholding of approval or love . . . mothers feel more assured with their daughters and freer to control them" [Bayley and Schaefer, 1960, p. 61].

This suggests that there is more anxiety in the mother-son relationship, as well as less warmth. The mother feels "freer" to control the daughter because she is unconflicted in her attitude toward her. She may in many cases permit aggression in the boy because she wishes him to express her own frustrated needs for achievement. But resentment is exhibited in her preference for "fear-oriented" socialization techniques.

The authors also report that for children from birth to three years old: "such sex differences as there are point toward a slightly more autonomous, cooperative, equalitarian treatment of daughters and more irritable, punitive, ignoring treatment of sons. Such differences would be in the same direction as reported in other studies" [Bayley and Schaefer, 1960, p. 70].[2]

The anthropological literature is rich in examples of so-

[2] For children between the ages of nine to fourteen these sex differences tend to reverse themselves [*Ibid.*, p. 74]. This may be due to the fact that the boys are reaching the age where they can more successfully serve to satisfy vicariously the unfulfilled ambitions of the mother, while the girls are entering a period in which they can compete with the mother in the only area in which women in our society are generally expected to achieve, i.e., sexual popularity.

cieties with at least some pieces of the Greek constellation. I observed earlier, for example, that Trobriand women practiced pubic depilation, while the males evinced some fear of feminine sexual rapacity and carried Medusa-like shields into war (See Chapters I and XI). They are also extremely vain, ambitious, easily offended, and jealous of any undue prominence on the part of a peer [Malinowski, 1959, pp. 29, 91, 95]. There is great fear of flying witches and a belief in female secret societies from which men are excluded and which "subject men to degradations and mutilations"; but despite "considerable tension between the sexes," there is far more freedom and sexual comfort than seems to have existed in Greek society [Kardiner, 1939, p. 98; Malinowski, 1929, pp. 273–79].

The Marquesans believe in female ogres (*vehini-hai*) who, like Lamia, steal and devour small children (although in reality it was enemy warriors who at times captured and sacrificed a child). Males are touchy, terrified of ridicule, and invidious. There is a strongly oral definition of sexuality, a fear of the intensity of feminine sexual hunger, and a magical temptation to matricide [Kardiner, 1939, pp. 165–66, 175–79, 189–93, 226–27]. Yet the Marquesans are a polyandrous society in which women have considerable power.

These examples show the difficulty one encounters in attempting to extract a generalized hypothesis from the analysis of a single case. Every society is both unique and complex —how does one know which items are significant and which extraneous to a given constellation? Does one say it exists when two elements are present, or three, or four? Or should one insist, like Lévi-Strauss and others [1963, pp. 8–14], that all must coexist? The simplest answer is that this is a poor way to proceed; we must disregard the totality I have portrayed and try instead to extract the most important variables for which I have posited some sort of causal interrelationship, and test this relationship across a number of societies.

We will never find another Athens, after all, but any two societies will share *some* common elements.

An even more serious problem is the achievement of an appropriate level of abstraction. Concrete phenomena have many determinants, only some of which will be relevant to the variables under study, and social-psychological pressures may produce a variety of mutually substitutable forms. Phenomena such as depilation or mythical female ogres are far too specific to be used in themselves, although they might conceivably serve, among many others, as indicators of some more general tendency.

Stephens' study of menstrual taboos exemplifies this problem. One might take his finding of a positive correlation between the prolonged postpartum sex taboo (which he quite reasonably views as a likely cause and indicator of maternal seductiveness) and the severity of menstrual taboos (a plausible index of male fear of women) as corroborating an implicit hypothesis in my present analysis [Stephens, 1962, pp. 3–5, 79–99]. I might also note with satisfaction Benedict's contrast between the modest, cooperative, pacific Zuni, who have very mild menstrual taboos, and the egregiously narcissistic Kwakiutl, whose entire lives are devoted to "megalomanic" self-glorification, invidious economic display, and the humiliation of rivals, and for whom "menstrual blood was polluting to a degree hardly excelled in the world." According to Benedict, the Kwakiutl "recognized only one gamut of emotion, that which swings between victory and shame," and death frequently resulted from the latter [Benedict, 1953, pp. 110ff., 167, 173–86, 198–204].[3] Yet as nearly as one can tell, the Greeks themselves had neither a prolonged postpartum sex

[3] Kwakiutl narcissism is perhaps more reminiscent of the fifth-century Athenian variety than that of any other contemporary primitive society. One is not surprised, therefore, to find that the serpent is pervasive in Kwakiutl mythology, nor that it is associated with antagonism between the sexes, with bisexuality, and with devouring [Locher, 1932, pp. 6ff., 27–34, 83].

taboo nor elaborate menstrual taboos.[4] Any such concrete indicator is thus bound to miss some important cases.

As I shift then to a cross-cultural approach, I must alter my emphasis, and try to find the most general terms for my interpretive scheme. Mead, for example, in discussing variation across seven societies with which she has personal familiarity, makes general statements which can be applied to my analysis with little qualification:

> . . . [in] those societies which have emphasized suckling . . . there is the greatest symbolic preoccupation with the differentials between men and women, the greatest envy, overcompensation, ritual mimicry of the opposite sex, and so on. . . . When in addition male separateness from women has been developed into a strong institution, with a men's house and male initiation ceremonies, then the whole system becomes an endlessly reinforcing one, in which each generation of little boys grows up among women, identified with women, envying women, and then, to assert their endangered certainty of their manhood, isolate themselves from women. Their sons again grow up similarly focussed on women, similarly in need of overcompensatory ceremonial to rescue themselves" [Mead, 1955, pp. 73-74].

What is implicit here is the notion that societies vary between two poles, one of which accents the mother-child relationship, the other the marital bond. Each produces its own pattern of self-maintaining circularity, although there are numerous idiosyncratic variations on each, as well as many compromise patterns, and others that perhaps escape the polarity altogether through some ingenious mechanism.

[4] Unless one takes as a menstrual taboo Hesiod's admonition not to bathe in water a woman has used [*Works and Days* 753-55]. Briffault maintains that primitive Greece had severe menstrual taboos, some of which were retained during the classical period [Briffault, 1959, p. 241]. But even if one does not treat Hesiod's dictum as a menstrual taboo, it obviously expresses the same kind of concern.

In this volume I have been describing a pattern of the mother-child type. Sex segregation and antagonism are of primary importance in differentiating the two poles, since they weaken the marital bond and redirect the mother's libidinal interest onto her children; and I have stressed the threefold interrelationship of sex antagonism, maternal ambivalence, and male narcissism.

Beatrice Whiting discusses some aspects of this constellation in a recent paper on violence. She notes that several studies of lower-class culture have commented upon the prevalence of the female-based household conjoined with an "almost obsessive lower class concern with 'masculinity.' " She then calls attention to a cross-cultural study of the correlates of crime [Bacon, Child, and Barry, 1963], in which personal crime was found to be correlated with variables reflecting barriers to a boy's identification with his father, such as polygynous mother-child households and mother-child sleeping arrangements. She argues that this compulsive male "reaction formation" will occur only in societies in which males are viewed as more powerful and prestigious than women in the adult world. Analyzing six societies studied with an integrated ethnographic strategy [B. Whiting, 1963], she points out that two of them (Gusii and Rajputs) show a much higher incidence of assault and homicide than the other four. They also have a pattern of severe sex segregation: men and women neither eat nor sleep nor work nor play together, in sharp contrast to the other four societies. The father, furthermore, plays almost no part in infant care. Both societies are patrilocal, however, and women must behave in a deferent manner toward males.[5] As Whiting points out, the early female identi-

[5] Whiting makes the interesting statement, regarding the lack of confidence felt by women isolated from their own family (wives were sometimes taken from distant villages or enemy clans), that "it may well be that a woman's behavior to her children alters when her husband is present" [B. Whiting, 1965, p. 136]. She does not elaborate this point, so central to my argument.

THE GLORY OF HERA

fication creates a difficulty for the boy only if the society makes sharp role distinctions between males and females and only if men are viewed as more important and powerful—both of which conditions obtain among the Rajputs and Gusii but not among the other four. Whiting concludes, as I have, by emphasizing the "never-ending circle. The separation of the sexes leads to a conflict of identity in the boy children, to unconscious fear of being feminine, which leads to 'protest masculinity,' exaggeration of the difference between men and women, antagonism against and fear of women, male solidarity, and hence to isolation of women and very young children" [B. Whiting, 1965, pp. 124–37].

Whiting's chain omits one link upon which I have placed great stress—maternal ambivalence—and her concept of "protest masculinity," while it broadly overlaps my description of Greek narcissism, is not quite identical with it. At this stage of our knowledge, however, it is inappropriate to attempt too detailed a specification of terms, since the indices available to represent them are, in any case, imprecise enough to stand for any of several closely related formulations. This is a mistake often made in the behavioral sciences, one of whose conventions is to insist upon great precision at every point except the operational definition of the variables—very much as if we were to try to launch one of our intricate rockets with incantations. It has become customary for us to allow each other to wear these blinders—measurement problems are inordinately difficult in the social sciences, and this courtesy allows us both to feel like scientists and to produce. Ultimately, however, this etiquette creates both anarchy and a false sense of progress, and it might be more useful in the long run to admit that looseness anywhere is looseness everywhere—to allow at the start for a whole constellation of possible interpretations. It is at present unclear to me whether Whiting's cycle is meaningfully different from the one I have proposed; let alone trying to decide which explains the data most satisfactorily. I emphasize maternal ambivalence and the term "narcissism" here only to provide continuity with what has gone before, but with full awareness that considerable refinement of these hypotheses is both possible and necessary.

The two central hypotheses are as follows:

(a) In societies with a structural pattern that tends to weaken the marital bond, ambivalent maternal involvement with sons will be high.

(b) Such ambivalent involvement will tend to generate a modal male personality of a "narcissistic" type (which will in turn favor structural patterns tending to weaken the marital bond).[6]

Method

There are a number of common structural patterns which can be regarded as weakening the marital bond, such as segregation of the sexes in daily activities, or institutionalized sex antagonism of various kinds. There is a considerable literature, for example, on what Stephens [1962, pp. 2ff.] has called "diluted marriage variables." These include long (one year or more) postpartum sex taboos and prolonged (one year or more) exclusive mother-son sleeping arrangements [Whiting, Kluckhohn, and Anthony, 1958]; amount of polygyny [Murdock, 1962; Whiting, 1964]; mother-child households; and similar institutions—all of them reflecting the relative degree of physical or emotional distance between mother and father as compared with that between mother and child. While all of these variables are intercorrelated [Stephens, 1962; Whiting, 1964], the postpartum sex taboo, because of the unequivocal sexual barrier it places between husband and wife, is closest to a structural analogue of the Greek family syndrome

[6] Perhaps it has not been made sufficiently explicit that there are two bases for this narcissistic pattern. The first is the instability of the self-concept resulting from the mother's ambivalent responses. The second is the boundary anxiety induced by the mother's involvement.

and hence was expected to show the strongest relationship with "narcissism." On the other hand, it seems to provide no parallel for the resentment toward males which I posited for the Greek mother. This might be more adequately reflected in the institution of polygyny, which implicitly assigns (although uncorrelated with other indices of) a slightly inferior status to women and entails some sexual deprivation of some wives by the husband [Stephens, 1962, pp. 6–7]. I am not daunted by the fact that classical Greece constitutes a negative case for both of the structural patterns I chose as synthetics for it, but it might be noted that one could regard both these institutions as productive, not of ambivalence, but merely of maternal seduction. This is in fact the view taken by Stephens [*Ibid.*, 39ff.]. In order to choose between these two interpretations we will require additional information about maternal behavior.

My data for both measures come primarily from Whiting [1964, pp. 528–33] and secondarily from Stephens [1962, p. 245]. A "long" postpartum sex taboo is eleven months or more; a "short" one is less. Polygyny is "high" if more than 30 per cent of the wives are thus married; "medium" if more than 5 per cent of the wives are polygynously married; and "low or absent" otherwise. (The two polyandrous societies in the sample were excluded from this computation.) Where Whiting's codings were ambiguous or his categories did not match mine, Stephens' ratings were used to "break the tie." Thus, Whiting treats as "low" anything under 15 per cent, while I wished to include in my lowest category only those societies in which polygyny could be viewed as essentially nonexistent. Hence, whenever Whiting scored a society as "low" and Stephens rated it as "absent," I placed it in my lowest category.

My major problem was to find some way of assessing the degree of male "narcissism" in a culture. On the basis of traits emphasized in the study of Greece, we concentrated our attention on three broad characteristics: self-display, sensitivity, and ambition. We then drew up a list of about twenty-five indicators which might conceivably be discussed by ethnographers with enough regularity, detail, and specificity to be coded. After testing, redefining, combining, and subdividing these variables in a pilot study, we found seven which were both usable and bore a strong manifest relation to my original conceptualization.

The abandoned indicators were dropped for a variety of reasons. Some, such as "ambitiousness" or "pursuit of rank," were difficult to code because they depended upon a quantitative assessment by the ethnographer in the context of some specific behavioral example, and tended to be noncomparable from one ethnography to another. Others were noted too infrequently. Thus, we originally tried to code all kinds of exhibitionistic display—oratory, drama, athletic contests, and so forth—but these are seldom discussed in detail. Furthermore, they take so many alternative forms (exhibitionistic display may be buried away in some religious ritual, for example) that it would be difficult to put together an exhaustive combined index. One cannot solve the problem in this way, since the fact that an ethnographer fails to mention a trait can rarely be assumed to indicate its absence. Display in ornamentation and clothing was dropped because they are relatively invariant, being always present to some extent and with differences in degree too complex and subtle to assess. In short, some variables were simply too vague and diffuse to measure, others too minute and specific to receive consistent attention by ethnographers. Although the seven scales that survived the pretest manage, as a group, to convey quite satisfactorily what I intend by the term "narcissism" in the present context, they owe their existence as much to ethnographic habits as anything else.

The seven scales, briefly defined, are listed below. A complete description of the coding instructions is presented in Appendix IV. Scales two, four, and six are rated only for presence or absence, the others are on a three-point scale.[7] As I have attempted to show, they are for the most part highly relevant to aspects of ancient Greek life, both Homeric and classical.

(1) *Sensitivity to Insult:* scored high when public humiliation or interpersonal insults often lead to suicide, homicide, or other disastrous consequences; or ethnographer specifically describes tribal members as easily offended. We were at first somewhat surprised that this relatively intangible variable should prove so easy to code, but it is, of course, a matter of great personal importance to an ethnographer. One hardly needs to call attention to the prominence of this trait for ancient Greece—its mythology, literature, and history are filled with examples. Indeed, it is still a pronounced Greek characteristic: a common Greek phrase is "you molested my *philotimo*" (roughly equivalent to "honor," and closely related to the concept of *machismo* in Latin countries); "doubting one's *philotimo* is deeply resented and can easily lead to violence" [Pollis, 1965, p. 35; cf. Gouldner, 1965, pp. 98ff.].

(2) *Invidious Display of Wealth:* scored high when displayed wealth and invidious liberality are prominent features of the society and important sources of prestige. Huizinga points out the wide distribution of "competitions of unbridled liberality," and observes that the essential feature of the potlatch (which is its most extreme expression) is winning —that wealth and power are subordinated, even sacrificed, to pure glory, to a moment of richly savored superiority in

[7] These codes have been modified slightly since this study was carried out (scale two is now a three-point scale, for example), and additional societies have been rated. Ultimately each society will be independently coded by three raters, as part of another study, and this may produce minor alterations in these results.

which one's rival is humiliated [1955, pp. 59ff.].[8] While the Greeks may never have approached the Kwakiutl or the Tlingit in this respect, it was certainly an important feature of Greek culture at all periods. "One measure of a man's true worth was how much he could give away in treasure. Heroes boasted of the gifts they had received and of those they had given as signs of their prowess. That is why gift-objects had genealogies" [Finley, 1959, pp. 129–30]. And Gouldner refers to the "almost potlatch type of honorific public expenditure" which drove wealthy Athenians of the classical period to the verge of bankruptcy [Gouldner, 1965, p. 67].

(3) *Pursuit of Military Glory:* scored high when death is sought in battle as a source of glory, or is preferred to defeat, or when military virtues (valor, recklessness) or trophies are particularly emphasized in the society. Thus what this scale seeks to tap is the warrior ethos, and it is hence much more characteristic of the Homeric than of the classical period, and of Sparta than of Athens. Finley points out that from the point of view of the battle as a whole, the Homeric habit of pausing to strip a slain opponent's armor was "almost treasonable"; but "it is a mistake . . . to see the battle as the goal, for victory without honor was unacceptable," and trophies provided the evidence for such honor [1959, pp. 126–28]. The Spartan tendency to prefer death to defeat, while by no means reliable, was at least demonstrable.

(4) *Bellicosity:* scored high when the society is viewed by the ethnographer or its neighbors as a chronic aggressor, or when its adult males spend most of their time warring or raiding. This scale is obviously closely related to the former, but refers to the frequency of war rather than the style in

[8] Huizinga makes the astute observation that the potlatch spirit is universal to boyhood [1955, p. 60], but of course the same could be said of most of these variables. Delinquent gangs, men in warrior societies, and militarists in all societies, merely remain fixated in what is for the average middle-class American male a rather tiresome pre-pubertal interlude.

which it is pursued. The Homeric Greeks could be so classified, and Athens was viewed in this manner by its neighbors during the latter half of the fifth century. Furthermore, as Gouldner points out, war and piracy were relatively constant during the classical period: "peace is viewed as a time between wars rather than war being viewed as a disruption of peace" [1965, p. 144].

(5) *Bloodthirstiness:* scored high when the society engages habitually in the prolonged torture of prisoners. This scale was not initially conceived as an attribute of narcissism, although it fits some conceptualizations [cf. Stuart, 1955, pp. 118–22]. It emerged as an entity from the last and most viable of several trial combinations of war-related variables, and was retained out of an independent interest in the correlates of cruelty. It later proved to correlate with the other six measures, however, and was hence included in the present study. The Greeks would not receive a high rating on this measure despite sporadic episodes of torture in their mythology and history, and despite the fact that slaves were habitually tortured for pragmatic reasons. But although pragmatism may have had the major voice in such matters, there is no doubt that the Greeks had a strong streak of cruelty. Finley points out that Homer and his audience "lingered lovingly over every act of slaughter" [1959, p. 127], and this is even more true of Sophocles and Euripides. Greek mythology in general has an unusual amount of bodily mutilation.

(6) *Institutionalized Boasting:* scored high when boasting is habitual and accepted behavior, or institutionalized in ceremonial forms. Usually, as Huizinga points out, this pattern tends to become agonistic, assuming the shape of the scoffing match—"a collision of offended honours" [1955, p. 65]—and scorning others is also included in this scale. It hardly needs to be pointed out that the Greeks, from Achilles to Alcibiades, were notorious braggarts.

(7) *Exhibitionistic Dancing:* scored high when dancers are

differentiated and individual skill is recognized and rewarded in competitive terms. Of the more benign, bodily forms of narcissistic striving this was the only one which proved to be measurable. Although it is incorrect to say, as Licht does, that *all* ancient Greek dancing was exhibitionistic, the theatrical, spectator form was certainly highly developed in ancient times [Licht, 1963, pp. 161–66].

Ninety societies, representing fifty-five of Murdock's sixty culture areas [Murdock, 1957, 1962], were coded on these seven scales.[9] Reliability was tested in two ways. First, a preliminary check on a subsample of thirty societies was carried out using Swanson's technique [Swanson, 1960] of having a second rater (the author in this case) code the excerpted material used as the basis for the first rater's codings. This is less satisfactory here than in the case of Swanson's material; the narcissism ratings involved more global qualitative judgments, and hence depended more on context. Frequently, for example, it was necessary to weigh opposing indications, which only a more extended familiarity with the culture would permit. Since the second coder did not know from which culture the excerpts were taken, and thus had access only to the most immediate cues, this was often difficult to do. In any case, agreement was satisfactory, averaging about 76 per cent perfect accord and less than 2.5 per cent opposite ratings. Only one scale (Exhibitionistic Dancing) fell markedly below the average for complete agreement (63.3 per cent), while all but one of the completely discordant ratings fell on "Invidious Display of Wealth," which would undoubtedly be improved by adding to it an intermediate category. Inspection of the disagreements suggested that the aforementioned absence of context accounted for the overwhelming majority, and the original codings were hence retained.

Subsequently, a subsample of thirty-six societies was re-

---

[9] All of the ratings were done by Dori A. Slater.

coded independently from scratch by a second rater.[10] Agreement here averaged 64 per cent perfect accord, 5 per cent opposite ratings. Once again the latter occurred almost entirely on two-point scales, and would probably be eliminated by converting to a three-point scale.[11]

When the first seventy-one societies had been coded, the seven scales were dichotomized (in such a way as to maximize the equality of the distributions) and intercorrelated by means of *phi* coefficients.[12] The resulting matrix was factor analyzed, using Thurstone's complete centroid method [Thurstone, 1947]. Two measurable factors were extracted and left unrotated. The first was a general factor which accounted for 31 per cent of the total variance, the second a bipolar factor accounting for 12 per cent. The first factor can be measured by adding all seven scales together, which produced estimated loadings of .90 on Factor I and .00 on Factor II, using Thomson's pooling square technique [1949]. The second factor can be similarly measured by adding together scales three, four, and five, and subtracting the remainder. This yields estimated loadings of .76 on Factor II and .11 on Factor I. The second factor, which seems to discriminate between war-related narcissism and forms involving competition within the society under peaceful conditions, is not fully understood, and will not be dealt with here.

Factor I scores, which were treated as a composite index of narcissism[13] for the society, were computed for all ninety

[10] There was no overlap with the first subsample. This sample was coded by Elizabeth Lozoff.

[11] Conversion of scale two is in process, and thus far fully confirms this prediction.

[12] This analysis was a by-product of the ratings having been included in a preliminary computer run for Textor's *Cross-Cultural Summary* [1967].

[13] This is thus a slightly different measure than the composite narcissism index which will appear in Textor's study. It might be objected that scales three and four contain a built-in tendency toward "dilution" of the marital

cultures, and then correlated with the "diluted marriage" variables. The number of cases varies from table to table, however, according to the availability of data for these variables.

Of the tests which follow, Tables 5–8 and 13–14 correlate narcissism with variables reflecting the intensity of marital intimacy. Maternal ambivalence is merely an inferred intervening variable. Tables 9–11 and 15 attempt to relate narcissism more directly to aspects of maternal ambivalence. The remaining tests also concern maternal ambivalence but are, again, more indirect.

Results

The relationship between the narcissism score and the duration of the postpartum sex taboo is shown in Table 5. It is in the expected direction and significant at the .01 level.

TABLE 5

Relationship Between Narcissism and Postpartum Sex Taboo

		Narcissism		
		High	Medium	Low
PPST	Long	15	12	6
	Short	8	9	23

$X^2 = 11.96, p < .01$

Table 6 shows the relationship between the narcissism score and polygyny. This association is transparently weaker than the preceding, and only reached the .10 level of confidence.

---

bond, since warring and raiding often (though by no means necessarily) involve prolonged separation of husband and wife. These two scales do *not*, however, correlate more highly with the "diluted marriage" variables than do the four non-military scales. Factor II, moreover, shows no correlation with any of the diluted marriage variables.

TABLE 6

Relationship Between Narcissism and Polygyny

	Narcissism		
	High	Medium	Low
High Polygyny	12	9	9
Medium Polygyny	10	12	7
Polygyny low or absent	5	5	14

$X^2 = 7.87, p < .10$

Since the two "independent" variables are far from perfectly correlated, it might be worthwhile to examine their combined relationship to narcissism. One might assume, for example, that a structural pattern which linked a sexual deprivation for the wife with a built-in transfer of the libidinal interest of the husband to an alternate sexual object would intensify her ambivalent involvement with her son in a way that would surpass the impact of either of these two variables taken separately. The combined relationship is shown in Table 7.

TABLE 7

Relationship of Narcissism to Polygyny and Postpartum Sex Taboo Combined

	Narcissism		
	High	Medium	Low
High or Medium Polygyny, Long PPST	13	10	4
Mixed cases*	6	9	14
Polygyny low or absent, Short PPST	1	2	10

$X^2 = 16.91, p < .01$

* High or medium polygyny with short PPST, and low or absent polygyny with long PPST.

Table 7 does show a tightening of the relationship, reducing the number of clear negative cases to five.

One further finding should be reported here, for although it was not predicted beforehand, the variable is of the same order as the postpartum sex taboo. This variable is the length of exclusive mother-son sleeping arrangements [Whiting, Kluckhohn, and Anthony, 1958]. Like the postpartum sex taboo it would seem to have a primarily seductive impact on the child.

Table 8 indicates that this relationship also is a strong one.[14]

TABLE 8

Relationship of Narcissism to Length of Exclusive Mother-Son Sleeping Arrangements

Exclusive mother-son sleeping arrangements	Narcissism High	Medium	Low
Long (> 1 year)	8	7	2
Short (< 1 year)	5	3	10

$x^2 = 7.56, p < .05$

We are still faced with the problem, however, of eliminating a number of possible alternative interpretations of these findings —particularly the possibility that it is not maternal ambivalence but seductiveness alone that is associated with narcissism. To support the hypotheses with which we began, we need corroborating answers to two questions:

(1) What evidence is there of a negative or conflictful aspect to the mother-son relationship?

(2) What evidence is there that the mother is alternately inflating and deflating the ego of the male child?

To answer these questions I shall draw upon material provided by Textor's *Cross-Cultural Summary* [1967]. From this point on, therefore, my findings are of the post hoc variety, although they follow logically from my interpretations of the Greek family system.

Let us first take up the question of ambivalence. Is there

[14] The incidence of mother-child households—a less direct measure—is also related to narcissism in the expected direction, but the relationship is not significant.

anything which would contradict the notion that male narcissism is a direct outgrowth of pure maternal libidinal attachment to the son?

One clear test suggests itself. Stephens [1962, pp. 11–12] found that "societies 'high' on all three diluted marriage variables—frequency of polygyny, frequency of mother-child households, and duration of the postpartum sex taboo—tend strongly to be 'high' on 'initial indulgence of dependency.'" My analysis of the Greek family, however, would predict that *despite* the positive relationship between diluted marriage and indulgence of dependency, and between the former and narcissism, narcissism should be *negatively* related to any form of nurturance on the part of the mother. In other words, while diluted marriage may in general produce such indulgence, only when it is combined with hostility (as expressed in the tendency to frustrate and deprive the child) will it generate a narcissistic personality.

Table 9 shows the results of a test of this hypothesis, and provides modest support for it. Despite the positive relationship each holds with diluted marriage, they are negatively related to one another.[15]

TABLE 9

Relationship of Narcissism to Initial Indulgence of Dependency

Initial Indulgence of Dependency	Narcissism High	Medium	Low
Low	6	7	3
High	5	4	11

$X^2 = 5.00, p < .10$

This point may be generalized by referring to Table 10, in

[15] This relationship remains when we restrict the sample to those societies with ratings on all three variables. The correlation between "narcissism" and "initial indulgence of dependency," with "diluted marriage" (polygyny and the postpartum sex taboo) held constant, is —.37.

which the narcissism index is correlated with Bacon, Barry, and Child's rating of "overall indulgence in infancy," which is in turn a summary of seven variables reflecting nurturance, protection, and need-satisfaction on the part of the mother toward the infant child [Bacon, Barry, and Child, 1952; Barry, Bacon, and Child, 1957]. The correlation is again negative, and this time clearly significant.

TABLE 10

Relationship Between Narcissism
and Overall Indulgence in Infancy

Indulgence	High	Narcissism Medium	Low
High (12–14)	1	6	11
Low (2–11)	15	9	11

$\chi^2 = 8.41, p < .02$

The gross relationship shown in Table 10, however, masks an apparent selectivity in the nonindulgence of mothers in narcissistic societies. Table 11 shows the relationship of narcissism to the initial satisfaction of five types of needs, using the ratings of Whiting and Child [1953]. Note that although on four of the measures (as well as the combined rating) the non-narcissistic cultures are higher, the relationship is reversed for aggression (although the difference fails to reach significance), with the narcissistic societies showing the higher score. Apparently, mothers in such societies do not frustrate all needs, but may act in such a way as to channel libidinal energy into aggressive activities. This is of course speculative, and the problem should be examined more fully. Stuart [1955, pp. 34–41, 89ff.], for example, places great emphasis on the transformation of love-hunger into aggression in narcissistic pathology, and argues that narcissism springs largely from a deprivation of early pleasurable sensation. Without challenging this interpretation, it would be useful to examine the extent to which this transformation is facilitated by the socialization process itself. The only other kind of "indulgence" which appears to be higher in the narcissistic cultures is also one which would directly reinforce a narcissistic adjustment—I refer to the later age at which modesty training is initiated. While the numbers are too small to permit any confidence in the relationship, I include it for what it is worth.[16]

TABLE II

Relationship Between Narcissism and Need-Satisfaction in Infancy

		Narcissism			
		High	Medium	Low	P
Oral satisfaction	High (14–18)	7	9	13	
	Low (6–13)	7	7	2	.10
Anal satisfaction	High (12–16)	5	9	9	
	Low (3–11)	5	4	4	NS
Sexual satisfaction	High (12–20)	6	10	9	
	Low (6–11)	7	6	5	NS
Dependence satisfaction	High (15–18)	5	6	12	
	Low (9–14)	7	10	3	.05
Aggression satisfaction	High (12–17)	7	9	4	
	Low (5–11)	6	7	11	.20
Overall satisfaction	High (13–17)	6	6	9	
	Low (10–12)	4	7	4	NS
Modesty training initiated	After age 6	2	2	2	
	Before age 6	0	4	4	NS

One further group of data may add contextual detail and

[16] It may well be that it is also the lack of concern with modesty in the more narcissistic cultures which dilutes the trend with regard to sexual and anal indulgence. As in many other instances, some of the component narcissism scales do correlate significantly (and negatively) with the sexual-satisfaction potential. Space does not permit consideration of these more specific relationships.

understanding to this negative side of the mother-son relationship in narcissistic societies. In my analyses of Greece and medieval Islam I observed the importance of progeny to the narcissistic male, and his consequent vulnerability to attacks on his sons. While I have no way of capturing this constellation with these data, I can at least determine whether the concern with progeny is particularly marked.

Textor's *Summary* includes two sets of variables relevant to such concern. The first is from Ayres' study of pregnancy taboos [1954], the second from Ford's study of reproduction [1945]. From the former, I examined the relationship of narcissism to (a) the strength of the desire for children, and (b) the presence of practices to protect the neonate from harmful influences. From the latter, I examined its relation to attitudes toward twins. All three were in the expected direction, as Table 12 indicates, although only one achieved significance.[17]

TABLE 12

Relationship Between Narcissism and Concern with Progeny

| | Narcissism | | | |
	High	Medium	Low	P
Children strongly desired	8	2	4	
Children not strongly desired	4	8	6	.10
Practices to protect neonate present	5	6	3	
Practices to protect neonate absent	7	2	8	NS
Twins welcome	5	2	0	
Twins unwelcome, killed	1	6	4	.02

17 Although the numbers are so small that explanation of minor variations is perhaps futile, the poorer showing of the second variable in Table 12 may reflect the general lack of nurturance in narcissistic societies. The attitude toward twins in primitive societies is sharply bimodal, as Frazer points out in his notes on Apollodorus [Vol. II, pp. 376–83]. While occasionally viewed as having fertilizing virtue, "far more usually the birth of twins is viewed with horror and dismay as a portent which must be expiated by the death of the twins and sometimes by that of the mother also."

These findings suggest that in narcissistic societies conditions exist which would favor the employment of the Greek scapegoating mechanism, and we have seen evidence that mothers in such societies do in fact treat their children more harshly. But this provides little basis for assuming real hostile intent. We do not even know that feminine hostility toward males exists in these societies. Polygyny generally bespeaks a certain social distance between the sexes, but polygyny correlates only weakly with narcissism. It would be helpful to have some more direct indication that tension between the sexes exists in narcissistic cultures.

Such evidence is available in the form of two sets of unpublished ratings by Whiting and his associates [1962 and 1963]. The first deals with the frequency with which husband and wife normally eat together in the culture—a traditional index of solidarity the world over. The second concerns the incidence and frequency of wife-beating. Both of these correlate with narcissism as one would expect, the first negatively, the second positively. The results are given in Tables 13 and 14.[18]

TABLE 13

Relationship Between Narcissism and Husband-Wife Eating Arrangements

| | Narcissism | | |
Husband and Wife Eat Together	High	Medium	Low
Usually or always (3–4)	6	10	12
Sometimes (2)	2	7	2
Rarely or never (0–1)	10	3	5

$X^2 = 10.69, p < .05$

Let us now turn to the second of the two questions mentioned earlier in this chapter, regarding the availability of evi-

---

[18] I am in the process of developing new scales of sex segregation: in work, in recreation, and among children.

TABLE 14

Relationship Between Narcissism and Frequency of Wife-Beating

	Narcissism		
Frequency of Wife-Beating	*High*	*Medium*	*Low*
Frequent (4–5)	6	7	3
Occasional (2–3)	4	7	7
Rare or absent (0–1)	0	0	6

$X^2 = 12.4, p < .02$

dence that mothers in narcissistic societies may alternately inflate and deflate the self-concepts of their male children. For answers to this question I turn once again to the ratings of Bacon, Barry, and Child—this time to their treatment of what they call "substitute behavior," i.e., behavior which replaces childhood dependency. This includes, specifically, the inculcation in children of nurturance, responsibility, self-reliance, achievement, and obedience. Looking first for signs of attempts to build up the male child, one would naturally be most interested in the achievement ratings. Happily, these ratings were made separately for boys and girls, and include five separate variables: (1) positive pressure toward achievement; (2) anxiety over failure to achieve (generated by severity and frequency of punishment for such failure); (3) anxiety over achievement (generated by negative consequences of successful achievement); (4) conflict over achievement (generated by the relative equality of forces rewarding and punishing achievement); and (5) frequency of achievement behavior.

It would seem at first glance as if this set of variables would answer both parts of our question at once: that we would predict all of the variables to correlate positively with narcissism, as a clear reflection of maternal ambivalence and inconsistency in the mother's vicarious ambitions for her male child to be a "big man." Unfortunately, however, the Bacon, Barry, and Child ratings of anxiety over achievement focus on negative pressures from contemporaries, rather than on ambivalent responses from the mother. We are thus primarily interested in the achievement ratings as evidencing attempts to "build up" the male child in narcissistic cultures.

Table 15 provides strong corroboration for the hypothesis. But we are still left in something of a quandary with regard to maternal tendencies toward deflating or belittling sons in narcissistic societies. Assuredly they build them up, but what evidence is there that they also tear them down?

TABLE 15

Relationship Between Narcissism and Achievement Variables

Achievement Variables	Narcissism			P
	High	Medium	Low	
Positive pressure toward achievement				
High (12–15)	11	5	5	
Low (3–11)	3	8	15	.01
Anxiety over nonachievement				
High (10–13)	10	3	3	
Low (2–9)	4	10	16	.01
Anxiety over achievement				
High (6–11)	11	6	8	
Low (3–5)	3	7	9	.15
Conflict over achievement				
High (6–11)	7	6	6	
Low (2–5)	7	7	11	NS
Frequency of achievement behavior				
High (11–14)	12	5	6	
Low (3–10)	2	10	12	.01

This is unquestionably the weakest link in the entire series. I cannot derive any comfort from the slight positive relationship between narcissism and anxiety over performance, because we know that this is largely a function of peer-responses and intrinsic sacrifices associated with achievement. The best we can do is to assume that the general harshness of maternal behavior in narcissistic societies might include this kind of belittling, until some more conclusive evidence can be found for or against this notion.

One final relationship might be noted briefly, since it bears so directly on my theory. I suggested that as a consequence of the intense and ambivalent relationship with the mother, males in narcissistic societies would show a generalized fear of women, and would, like their counterparts in classical Greece, marry late. This proves to be the case, as Table 16 indicates. The data are once again drawn from Textor's *Summary*, ultimately, in this case, from Harley's cross-cultural study of adolescent peer groups [1963].

TABLE 16

Relationship Between Narcissism and Age of Males at Marriage

Age of Males at Marriage	High	Narcissism Medium	Low
Over twenty	9	3	2
Under twenty	7	9	10

$x^2 = 5.39, p < .10$

Discussion

Up to this point we have been working within the rather confining structure of a complex individual constellation: trying to find, in a series of cross-cultural relationships, analogues of a specific cultural pattern. Actually, we have done rather well with it, suggesting perhaps that part of the fascination with Greek fantasy life which still obtains today is due to some kind of modality which this pattern epitomizes. Yet the pattern itself is idiosyncratic, and there is no reason to expect all aspects of it to appear together when it arises in a new setting. By "connecting the dots" of a series of not quite perfectly relevant correlations we have been able to reproduce a crude outline of the theory of the self-perpetuating cycle of maternal ambivalence, male narcissism, and "diluted marriage." But not all of the relationships were equally strong, and not all of my operational definitions were equally convincing. And even of the strongest, we must ask: In how many other ways could these be interpreted?

On the basis of the stronger relationships found, the following statements seem reasonable:

(1) There is a positive correlation between male narcissism and a distant or dissentient marital relationship.

(2) There is a negative correlation between male narcissism and nurturant indulgence or gratification of infants.

(3) There is a positive correlation between maternal sexual deprivation and male narcissism.

(4) There is a positive correlation between male narcissism and close physical mother-son contact during such deprivation.

(5) There is a positive correlation between male narcissism on the one hand, and pressure for the child to achieve, anxiety over failure to achieve, and frequency of achievement behavior, on the other.

One might attempt to account for all these relationships in terms of one of the "only-just" theories popular in sociology and psychology. One could say that males of the sort I have described would be unlikely to form close or intimate relationships with their wives, might be more likely to beat them, and would be particularly pleased at having more than one. One could also say that such men would want to pressure their sons to achieve (although one would think they might also shun such competition), and could perhaps find some way to get their wives to do the same. One could even say that the lack of indulgence of infants is "only" a reflection of male narcissism, somehow transplanted to women. One could say, in other words, that these findings are "just" consequences of a set of personality characteristics caused by something else. It would be a little difficult, however, to see how male narcissism would "cause" a postpartum sex taboo or prolonged mother-child sleeping arrangements—in fact, one would anticipate some resistance to such institutions on the part of narcissistic males who had no particular sexual anxieties. But perhaps these phenomena could be explained away in terms of some other set of considerations, so that one would not "need" to employ a psychodynamic theory of any sort.

It is difficult to see any advantage in this exercise-in-closing-one-eye, aside from furthering sociological imperialism. A theory which explains how x influences a, b, and c would seem manifestly inferior to one which explains how x influences a, b, c, d, and e, and also how these in turn influence x. Since I have no vested interest in denying the body, it is toward the latter type of theory that I will strive.

In doing so, there is no reason to exclude the notion that male narcissism has an impact on the marital relationship. On the contrary, this is a crucial factor in maintaining the cycle. I would also suggest that the self-aggrandizing characteristics of males in the narcissistic societies make it impossible for them to provide the kind of support for their wives that many feel is a pre-condition of a nurturant attitude on the part of the latter toward their children [cf., e.g., Caplan, 1955, pp. 63–64].[19] Finally, if the narcissism includes negative or fearful attitudes toward women, it would explain the tolerance of males for their own deprivation and exclusion in the postpartum setting.

The effect of male narcissism on child-rearing characteris-

[19] This factor might be diluted in cultures where the wife is strongly supported by feminine members of an extended family group of some kind (a situation notably lacking in classical Greece), although my data suggest that the marital bond may be crucial in this regard, even where it is otherwise unimportant. This can easily be determined empirically.

tics must perforce be indirect, since it is maternal rather than paternal behavior which is involved in the overwhelming majority of cases, particularly, of course, in the narcissistic societies. What my findings suggest is that the mother's relationship to the child is, in some way or other, influenced by her own marital relationship.

My original theory about the nature of this process was perhaps too detailed, and some of this detail receives only mild and inferential support from the data. While it seems likely that a constellation such as I have described is not altogether uncommon in narcissistic societies, a modification of this picture, emphasizing the more powerful relationships, would give it greater generality. The notion of the mother treating the male child as a husband-substitute, and alternately seducing and castrating, inflating and deflating his self-concept is perhaps made eminently plausible by these data; but all we can say with any certainty is that in narcissistic societies the mother is rather depriving and non-nurturant toward her son, that she makes heavy and apparently successful demands for achievement-behavior on his part, and that she sleeps with him a long time under conditions of sexual deprivation. We may then hypothesize of the mother that:

(a) Being deprived leads to depriving behavior.

(b) Being deprived leads to demanding behavior.

(c) These responses are directed toward the male child.[20]

While it strains credulity to ignore the likelihood of maternal seductiveness under these circumstances, this formulation does not require those who shun psychoanalytic interpretations to break their pledge.

The third link in my circular chain is the creation of a narcissistic personality by these maternal responses. Nurturant indulgence is denied the little boy, and achievement-behavior is demanded. These are the pre-conditions for narcissism as

[20] It would be interesting to investigate the manner in which girls are raised in narcissistic societies.

outlined by Stuart [1955], particularly in view of the fact
that the components of the Bacon, Barry, and Child scale are
of a highly physical nature: display of affection, protection
against environmental discomforts, degree, immediacy, and
consistency of satisfaction of basic needs ("hunger, thirst,
etc."), constancy of presence of the nurturing agent, and absence of pain from the nurturing agent.

"Pleasure . . . becomes a key-word. But its existence, far
from indicating a state of narcissism, is precisely the condition
which will prevent such a state from later arising to any detri-
mental extent. And pleasure, at this time, and for this purpose,
is to be understood in the quite primary sense of comfortable
physical sensation. . . ." [Stuart, 1955, p. 34].

Deprived of such pleasure, the child, like the mother, seeks
compensation through self-aggrandizement—renouncing love
for admiration—and in this he is encouraged by the achievement pressure placed upon him, and presumably by the
myriad narcissistic role models he finds around him. He becomes vain, hypersensitive, invidious, ambitious, aggressive,
cruel, boastful, and exhibitionistic. As a consequence of these
traits he is a poor husband and father, and the cycle is repeated
until some outside force impinges upon it:

> My love is as a fever, longing still
> For that which longer nurseth the disease;
> Feeding on that which doth preserve the ill,
> The uncertain sickly appetite to please.
> [Shakespeare, *Sonnet 147*]

CHAPTER XV

Cultural Pathology and Cultural Development

What kind of town is this
What sort of streets are these
Who invented this
who profits by it. . . .

[Weiss, *Marat/Sade*, Act II]

What land is this? what race of men? Who is it
I see here tortured in this rocky bondage?
What is the sin he's paying for? Oh tell me
to what part of the world my wanderings have brought me.
[Aeschylus: *Prometheus Bound* 561–64. Grene trans.]

I HAVE TRIED in the preceding chapters to sketch a circular family pattern common to many societies—one which was in part present in Homeric times but seemed to intensify during the Athenian civilization, and was reflected in Greek mythology and elaborated by Greek tragedians. In the last chapter some effort was made to test the generality of these observations, and to take cognizance of the fact that the various components of the pattern are not tied to one another with bonds of homogeneous inevitability. In this final chapter I would like briefly to consider some of the implications of these explorations.

My first task is to resist the temptation to attribute to maternal ambivalence and narcissism the unique cultural explosion that caused Athens to become a generic term for conspicuously civilized communities.[1] For can we not argue that it was the narcissistic striving generated by maternal ambivalence that drove the Athenians to their fifth- and fourth-century heights? Thus far I have concentrated heavily on the pathological consequences of maternal ambivalence, but could it not also have had more benign consequences? Heracles, while tormented and destructive, also "civilized the world" and rid it of its pests—"spurred by Hera's goads" [Euripides: *Heracles* 20–21]. Was he not "the Man who became famous because of Hera" [Nilsson, 1932, p. 191]? Did we not find, in the preceding chapter, a correlation between narcissism and the tendency to demand and obtain achievement responses from the male child?

There is, indeed, a considerable amount of support for such a view. Alexander argues that socially mobile sons of immigrant families derive their "inordinate ambition," their "insincerity . . . unfairness in competition, disloyalty" and "ruthless" careerism [cf. ancient characterizations of Athenian politicians] from a family pattern in which the son "usurps the father's place in the mother's affection as well as in economic importance" [Alexander, 1952, pp. 197–99].[2] Gouldner argues specifically that "the 'glory that was Greece' was, in some important measure, born of this violent competitive-

1 Many fine explanatory vehicles have been driven into the ground in this fashion by otherwise clearheaded thinkers. The universally relevant concept is the philosophers' stone of intellectual life. Even Havelock, in his brilliant analysis of the impact of literacy on Greek culture, cannot resist imputing Greek intelligence to the survival of oral techniques, despite the existence of comparable conditions elsewhere without comparable results [Havelock, 1963, pp. 126–27]. Insofar as Greek culture is not unique, it can be explained by many different factors; but insofar as it is unique, it cannot be accounted for by any testable hypothesis, since it cannot be repeated.

2 Alexander's explanation of the interpersonal and intrapsychic dynamics, however, is rather different from mine.

ness," and ties Greek rationalism, Greek energy, and the Greek ability to break with tradition to aspects of the contest system [1965, pp. 13, 44–45, 59, 70–71]. He also observes its negative consequences, however, remarking that "of all the Greek talents, by far their greatest is mutual destruction" [*Ibid.*, p. 60].

The strongest evidence for assigning to narcissistic attitudes a civilizing function comes from McClelland's study of achievement motivation and cultural development. McClelland attributes rapid economic growth to social factors which increase the need for achievement. The family is once again an intervening variable: "all our evidence suggests that external events affect motivational levels primarily as they affect the family . . ." [McClelland, 1961, p. 387].[3] The need for achievement, as McClelland defines it, overlaps considerably with narcissism as I have defined it: there is the same need for self-aggrandizement, the same inflated self-concept, the same invidiousness and competitiveness; and while militarism must be subordinated to economic pursuits in McClelland's scheme, the latter tend to be defined in militaristic terms [*Ibid.*, pp. 40, 97, 114, 222–24, 230, 290]. Yet there are important differences as well, and while the problem is too complex to discuss fully here, it seems fair to say that the differences center on the ability to control impulses, delay gratification, orient oneself to long-range goals, and so on—an ability which is an essential part of achievement behavior but which is irrelevant to narcissism as I have defined it.

---

[3] McClelland goes on to specify "the values and childrearing practices of the parents," but one need not follow him into this error. Students of socialization suffer from an occupational infirmity—a rather poignant eighteenth-century faith in the power of conscious values and deliberate parental techniques to influence personality formation. While these various kinds of good intentions no doubt play some role, they are only a fragment of the total family interaction. It is a little like trying to understand the locomotion of birds by analyzing their feet—one can find a few correlations, but it hardly seems strategic.

McClelland makes a good case for the role of achievement needs in the rise and decline of Greek civilization [*Ibid.*, pp. 108–29], but obviously we cannot do the same for narcissism. While there may have been a decline during the Hellenistic and Roman Ages in the kinds of behavior and attitude which we call narcissism, these are certainly quite conspicuous in modern Greece and show no signs of contributing anything to a cultural revival. Furthermore, the cross-cultural study yielded a number of highly "narcissistic" societies, and although some may exhibit a certain luster in a nonliterate sample it is clear that the most profound narcissism is no guarantor of a cultural explosion. At times narcissistic tendencies actively interfere with cultural development: note the frequency with which important innovations are rejected because they violate "machismo" norms.

Perhaps the best tentative hypothesis is that "narcissism" in a society is a contributory but not a sufficient condition for cultural development. Like a new weapon, it can facilitate growth or disrupt the society altogether. The more intense it is the more it may stimulate individuals to perform unusual feats, which may be creative, or destructive, or simply futile. What seems most closely related to Greek narcissism is not the rise of Athens but its instability—the rapidity of its rise and fall. There are many societies with nothing whatever to show for centuries of braggadocio, and that the Greeks did leave us something is surely due to other factors which, for a brief instant in time, captured and channeled their narcissistic strivings.

This point might be made clearer by an example on the individual level. Social scientists have long recognized that in disadvantaged groups the most talented individuals are often the most troublesome. Life for the ambitious slum child is the most difficult of all, since his aspirations usually outstrip both his limited opportunities and the impulse control necessary to exploit these opportunities. This breeds a cycle of increasingly

violent and foolhardy strategies, followed by increasingly cata-
strophic failures; although he may be a leader as long as those
around him can see no real solution to their life's problems. He
may, in other words, be a rebel martyr, although he will
rarely possess the control to be a successful revolutionary.
Hence the latter are usually middle-class renegades.

On this crude analogy we could say that many societies foster individuals with grandiose aspirations, and that perhaps a
great society must have a similar tendency. But it must have a
good deal else as well. The Greek achievement involved a relatively brief period of time in which Greek narcissism was
infused with something that transformed its empty vain-
gloriousness into a palpable moment of real glory, only to be
lost again.

Many writers, both ancient and modern, have attributed the
Athenian triumph to some aspect of its democratic institutions. McClelland sees democracy itself as a product of an increase in the need for achievement—the desire to substitute
achieved for ascribed status [*Ibid.*, p. 124]. This again is an
extremely complex question which lies outside the scope of
this book and I would like merely to make a brief comment
about what might be the relationship of narcissism to democratic institutions.

In general, the narcissistic pattern described operationally in
Chapter XIV seems to be more strongly associated with authoritarianism than with democracy. Indeed, Pollis argues
that it is Greek *philotimo* which makes democratic govern-
ment impossible in modern Greece [Pollis, 1965, pp. 36ff.].[4]

[4] Pollis' gloomy prognosis has since been supported by events, although
one cannot help wondering what might have happened if American aid had
not continually reinforced authoritarian elements in the society. That the
United States which, whatever its shortcomings, maintains a democratic
ethos on the largest scale ever known, should pursue a foreign policy that
supports Fascist elements wherever in the world it is possible to do so,
reflects the familiar fact that international relations are everywhere conducted on *philotimo* assumptions.

In a narcissistic society authoritarianism often seems the only alternative to an anarchy of individualism—an explanation perhaps of the fact that academic institutions are the most undemocratic in our society.

Authoritarian societies frequently consist of a narcissistically oriented warrior class and a relatively non-narcissistic peasantry. Classical Greece is in this respect an anomaly. At some point the narcissistic attitudes of the aristocracy seem to have been diffused throughout the free urban population, so that the bulk of the society, not merely the privileged elite, became addicted to narcissistic self-aggrandizement. This perhaps helped to energize the populace, but it also multiplied the problems of social integration and solidarity.

There is a rough analogical similarity between this diffusion of narcissistic assumptions and Weber's description of the diffusion of asceticism—previously monopolized by monastic specialists—among those engaged in worldly activities [Weber, 1930, p. 121]. Both, of course, are merely special cases of the familiar "inchworm" pattern of cultural development: an individual (or a small group of individuals) is placed in a protected, favored, or withdrawn position in the society and develops new attitudes or skills, which, in the second phase of the process, are diffused into the society at large. The process may also take place between groups—that is, a society may perform this function for the species as a whole. This is the meaning of the common idea that evolution is best served by the existence of many, small, isolated groups living fairly close together; this provides an opportunity to evolve independent solutions to environmental problems. Indeed, the specialization-generalization peristalsis is found at every biological level.

In any case, it is futile to speculate here how the Greeks managed to combine their shame-culture narcissism with democratic institutions, even for so brief a time, or why this diffusion occurred when it did, or precisely what combination of ingredients brought about the Athenian ascendancy. This is a task best left to historians, who have been struggling with it for centuries and will continue to do so for centuries more.[5] Whether or not sex antagonism, maternal ambivalence, and narcissism made any positive contribution to the Greek triumph, they most assuredly made a negative one, and it would be more profitable to pursue this issue, which has some significance for our own era.

Sex segregation, carried to as great an extreme as was true of fifth-century Athens, is an expensive social pattern. It interferes with many natural rhythms and responses and is enormously inconvenient in daily life.[6] It tends to breed fear and mistrust between the sexes, which leads to the subordination and derogation of one or the other. As Margaret Mead observes: "to the extent that either sex is disadvantaged, the whole culture is poorer, and the sex that, superficially, inherits the earth, inherits only a very partial legacy" [Mead, 1955, pp. 272–73].

But Mead goes much further than this, suggesting that the price may be civilization itself: "It may even be that one of the explanations which lie behind the decline of great periods of civilized activity, when philosophies fail, arts decline, and religions lose their vigour, may be found to be a too rigid

---

[5] McClelland's theory [1961, pp. 127–28], that the achievement needs which produced a new wealthy class were vitiated by the use of slaves to rear children, is ingenious as well as plausible, since it posits a self-extinguishing process (always a useful tool in analyzing social change).

There has also been a recent flurry of renewed interest in the more general problem of the conditions which bring about sudden cultural flowering. This is usually put in terms of economic development, with a none-too-casual glance at contemporary Asia and Africa; but for an interesting sociological approach to the more subtle issue of artistic achievement, see Kavolis [1964, 1965, and 1966].

[6] This is true of all avoidance patterns, but particularly when they involve the separation of two people who would under other circumstances be closely bound by their mutually intimate relationship with a third.

adherence to the insights and gifts of one sex." This rigidity, she argues, creates a split between the narrow sex-linked definition of one's creative life and one's personal existence. "The deeper the commitment to a creative activity becomes . . . the more the participating individuals will seek wholeness in it" [*Ibid.*, p. 280]. It may be, as I have argued elsewhere [Slater, 1963], that some artificial barriers between the sexes are necessary to maintain the intactness of large social systems—redirecting libidinal involvement from dyadic to multiple channels. But at some point, the costs in individual misery—in the hatred, destructiveness, and scarcity mentality which such emotional deprivation produces—begin to outweigh the advantages; and the solidarity-building mechanism becomes a source of disruption and dissolution.

This same double-edged quality appears in McClelland's discussion of the relationship of family patterns to the need for achievement. He observes, on the one hand, that children from mother-child households have a low need for achievement and tend toward "homosexuality, poorly developed superegos . . . and high frequency of personal crimes." Yet on the other hand, he presents evidence showing that boys with "more powerful fathers" show a low need for achievement, and suggests that conditions which reduce paternal presence in the family—such as war and seafaring—tend to increase achievement motivation [McClelland, 1961, pp. 330, 352, 374, 404–6]. How can this contradiction be resolved? How is it that intensification of the mother-son bond can produce with equal facility schizophrenia, homosexuality, unscrupulousness, and high achievement motivation?

The basis of the multiple effects of maternal overinvolvement is clear from my own analysis, and McClelland provides an explanation for the choice of outcome. Intensification of the mother-son bond seems consistently to generate a narcissistic personality structure, of which all four outcomes are variant forms. Two things seem to affect the outcome: the role of the father and the behavior of the mother. It seems to be important to achievement motivation that the father not be dominant or authoritarian. The mothers of high achievers, however, *are* dominant. They tend to push their sons earlier toward independence and self-reliance, although permissive in other respects. Their own achievement needs tend to be of an intermediate intensity, reflecting the finding that too much achievement pressure can have as negative results as too little. The mothers of achievers also express more warmth, especially as a reward for the son's achievement [*Ibid.*, pp. 342, 346, 348–49, 351–53].

The maternal involvement and dominance, the secondary role of the father, the combination of warmth with an attempt to accelerate the son's ability to play an adult male role—all of these are found in the family pattern so laboriously elaborated in this volume. But, although it is difficult to make fine distinctions with concepts and measures as crude and imprecise as those available to us, there do seem to be some modifying factors present in the case of McClelland's high achievers. The mothers of high achievers do not appear to be infantilizing or deflating or rejecting, nor do they seem to require some denial of reality or maintenance of pseudo-relationships. They are stable, supportive, consistent, "strict and severe in training practices, controlled and moderate in warmth and affection," with a well-defined value system, and the sons usually have available to them alternative male models who are important to them [*Ibid.*, pp. 330–31, 404–6].

These findings help resolve the puzzling contradiction between these facts: that high achievers so often come from mother-child households, and that children from such households tend so often to be impulsive, unstable, conscienceless, and, particularly, unable to delay gratification [cf. Mischel, 1958]. The mothers of the high achievers seem more controlled, less likely to vent their ambivalent feelings directly onto the child. The "buffer" between mother and son, which the father usually provides, is in this case provided by the mother herself, sometimes aided by the presence of an important male relative. Hence the son feels less danger of being overwhelmed or invaded by her involvement with him, is able to internalize her controls or those of the male relative, and has an opportunity to organize his own narcissistic strivings around relatively long-range goals.

This still leaves many unanswered questions. The not-too-little-not-too-much kind of explanation is a bit unconvincing, and it is disconcerting that the mothers of high achievers are first said to be more affectionate and then portrayed as rather controlled in this regard. Some of the answers will be obtained by asking more refined questions, based upon subtler concepts, and by using more precise measures ("warmth" and "dominance" are rather inclusive notions, after all). But I strongly suspect that some of the confusion arises from viewing as opposite traits that are really very closely allied. Just as the patriarchal father is closer to the absent father than to the dedifferentiated monogamous couple, so the high achiever is probably closer to the homosexual, the schizophrenic, and the unscrupulous psychopath than to the average man of good heart and good conscience. His goals may appear more orderly and respectable and long-range, but underneath all this is the same oedipal yearning, the same self-aggrandizement, the same inability to become deeply and lastingly involved with others. Our society puts a premium on high achievers, while it winks at the swindler and regards the schizoid and the homosexual as a menace. Other societies reverse these priorities for reasons just as compelling.

The relevance of this point becomes clearer when one considers American middle-class family patterns. Sex segregation is not highly developed in this group, and the sexual division of labor is theoretically slight, with males playing an active and affectionate role in the child-rearing process. These practices should form a strong barrier against the kinds of pathology I have been discussing in this volume.

Unfortunately, however, the picture is somewhat more complicated. Despite male involvement in the family, reality factors often keep the father out of the picture somewhat. Typically, he works away from home, and if he lives in a new suburb of the age-graded type, the son grows up in as female-dominated an environment as a harem child, or, as that of a boy in some primitive tribe, too young to live in the men's house. Sex segregation may thus exist, even though it is neither valued nor a recreational pattern.

Most important of all is a set of factors highly conducive to maternal ambivalence, although in a form unique to our era, and with consequences which can therefore not be predicted. In our society equality of the sexes is a value to which lip service is constantly paid and which is implemented even where it is not really endorsed. The result is equality in education through the college years, increasing numbers of women in the work force, except in the professions, and equalitarian family norms. But there is a serious reservation in this trend: the proportion of educated middle-class women entering the academic, medical, and legal professions has actually declined in the past few decades. The educated female is thus underemployed; her knowledge, intelligence, and sophistication underutilized. Along with this frustration goes a new emphasis and a redirection of energies: the middle-class female in modern America is expected to make a full-time activity out of a task—child rearing—which, throughout the history of mankind, has had to be worked into the interstices of a busy life. Whatever her talents, then, she tends to be hired as a kind of maternal Pygmalion—a molder of live persons. This is a task for which she may or may not be suited, but into which some frustration and resentment must inevitably creep, since she is unable, in such a setting, to realize her talents and is barred from the kinds of stimulation which her husband obtains through his work.[7] As in the case of the Greeks, the male child is the logical vehicle for these frustrated aspirations, as well as the logical scapegoat for her resentment of the masculine monopoly in the major professions. The results of this pattern seem to be worked out primarily in the arena of education—the middle-class mother exhibiting a bizarre and fanatical obsession with the child's educational environment and achievements, the child often responding to this with an increasing awareness that he is merely an extension of the mother; and ultimately abandoning the enterprise, temporarily or permanently. When this occurs in college it is popularly labeled an "identity crisis," but it often means nothing more than an attempt to answer the question, "am I in college for me or for my mother?"

There are many differences between the American middle-class male, with his elaborate controls, and the impulsive fifth-century Greek. Yet the most important differences are only quantitative—the qualitative differences are merely stylistic. Buried beneath every Western man is a Greek—Western man is nothing but Alcibiades with a bad conscience, disguised as a plumber.

Modern society is a mechanism which more effectively harnesses the kind of energy that narcissism makes available. The addition of a more elaborate control system—that is, the invention of chronic guilt—was successful in separating narcissistic striving from the impulsive, heroic, quixotic, self-

---

[7] The mass media are filled with joking references to the multiple roles and skills which a "mere housewife" performs ("nursemaid, mechanic, chauffeur, teacher," and so forth), as a way of denying the emotional and intellectual poverty of the role. The condescension implied in this device is barely disguised; to say that a housewife must be a Jack-of-all-trades is a sop to her desire to be a master of one. She is thus placed in a position like that of the unemployed Negro, who is alleged to be happy-go-lucky, with music in his soul. Indeed, detergent and floor wax are to the American female what watermelon is to the American Negro. Yet, despite the fact that no minority group has ever been portrayed as unflatteringly as is the American female in television commercials, this insult has gone unprotested.

defeating gestures one usually associates with it. But there is no *motivational* difference between an Achilles and a Carnegie, an Agamemnon and a Lyndon Johnson, an Alcibiades and a Ford, an Alexander and a Getty, an Ajax and a Morgan. The need to surpass others, to aggrandize oneself, to prove one's worth and manhood are just the same. The only difference is that the Greeks usually threw away their successes through some ill-considered act, while Americans usually do not.

Ah, but this difference, one might object, is profound. This willingness to sacrifice everything, these intense emotions, these dramatic gestures—this is what makes the Greeks heroic, romantic, fascinating. Their absence is what makes Americans pedestrian and dull.

I suspect that we are dull because we are here, and they are fascinating only because they are not. If their skeletons are fleshed out with our fantasies, is it we or they who are fascinating? But my main objection to this argument is its assumption that there is nothing romantic or quixotic in spending one's life in the unflagging pursuit of power, wealth, and fame. To be pedestrian is to be practical, sensible, realistic. What could be more romantic and fantastic than to amass great wealth and wear old clothes? What more quixotic than to acquire the means of obtaining pleasure and never use them? What more self-defeating than to sacrifice one's entire life in the service of an oedipal fantasy? At short range it is difficult to see such heroics as anything other than sheer stupidity or perversion, but time and distance lend power to the domain of infantile fantasy, until ultimately we are all in its grip. We do not have the opportunity to look at Achilles or Alexander from the viewpoint of the common soldier, as Shakespeare looked at Henry V ("Ay, he said so, to make us fight cheerfully, but when our throats are cut, he may be ransom'd and we ne'er the wiser"), or as "Old Blood and Guts" General Patton's soldiers looked at him ("his guts and our blood").

What I am saying is that the change from classical to modern, from "shame-culture" to "guilt-culture," from Pagan to Christian, or however one wishes to characterize the differences between Greek and modern industrial society, is not, as far as basic motivational structure goes, a change from x to y, but a change from x to $x + y$. We tend, when looking at a culture pattern built around a flamboyant style of male narcissism, to say, "this is something that pertains to a shame culture, as opposed to the guilt culture we 'enjoy.' These are qualitatively different—in fact opposite—patterns." I am arguing here that the one springs directly from the other—that the motivational basis of our own society is simply an advanced stage of the same disease that dominated Greek life. We seem less narcissistic than the Greeks for the same reason that a prospective paretic looks less syphilitic than someone who has recently acquired the disease. Modern narcissism is a spirochete that has produced a facsimile of cure by abandoning its most visible manifestations, burrowing beneath the surface, diffusing itself, and establishing an elaborate dominion over the host organism. Narcissistic motivation is no less pervasive now than in ancient Greece—only its forms have changed, being farther and farther removed from the simplest bodily expressions.

This raises a number of questions:

(1) How can we best conceptualize the difference between the ancient and modern form?

(2) What caused the change?

(3) Since the family systems of classical Greece and modern America differ markedly, is it not necessary to sharpen or qualify this theory of the familial origins of narcissism?

(4) If modern society is also narcissistically based, what are the implications for the future of our civilization?

These are broad questions—questions which take me far beyond the scope of this volume—and I cannot examine them with the care and in the detail typical of the previous chapters. I can only hypothesize and speculate in a rough way—my conclusion must be left as a beginning. Still, one cannot avoid drawing implications—Western civilization needs all the help it can get—and I myself would be less than honest were I to pretend a disinterest in these questions, or to forego, in the service of a specious elegance, any discussion of the future paths this study has suggested to me.

Earlier in this chapter I commented on the fact that maternal dominance in the home seems to generate, with equal facility, homosexuality, schizophrenia, and achievement drive. I also made some effort to discover factors that might differentiate among these varied outcomes, while at the same time recognizing that the desire to do so may be nothing more than the venerable human effort to devise classification systems that will put "good" things and "bad" things in different categories. Perhaps the issue demands a more serious look.

What binds together homosexuality, schizophrenia, and the need for achievement is a deep concern and doubt about the integrity and value—not in moral terms but in something closer to a monetary sense—of the self. We call this concern, together with the various devices developed to obviate it, narcissism. I have attempted to show that its roots lie in an overloaded mother-child relationship that prevents the development of clear but flexible and permeable boundaries. We need, now, to identify the dimension that distinguishes between ancient and modern forms of this disease.

One can quite easily arrange the various manifestations of narcissism along a continuum which expresses the degree to which the narcissistic behavior is detached from immediate bodily gratification.[8] The most simple, primitive, and socially

---

[8] Those readers familiar with my paper "On Social Regression" [1963] may have experienced some confusion over a shift in my usage of the term "narcissism." At that time I used the term to refer to the negative end of a dimension (libidinal diffusion) which combined gratification delay and multiple cathexes, whereas here it has been used as if it were either independent of, or positively related to, gratification delay. I have found it more profitable to conceive of gratification delay and multiple cathexes as or-

benign type of self-preoccupation, for example, is body adornment: clothing, cosmetic alteration, and so on. Here, the covert goal of all narcissistic manifestations—to make oneself lovable, to obtain nurturance, caresses, and physical gratification without endangering the separateness and integrity of the organism—is rather easily discerned and more or less immediate. One tries to enhance one's attractiveness while at the same time donning a kind of bodily armor, making oneself more desirable and less available.

As we move farther along the continuum—farther from the body and toward a longer delay in the (imagined) gratification cycle—we find the type of narcissism I have been discussing throughout the bulk of this volume, most specifically in Chapter XIV.[9] The goal is the same but the procedure more

---

thogonal dimensions and apply the term "libidinal diffusion" only to the latter. Thus if one imagines a two-dimensional plot with libidinal diffusion as East and gratification delay as North, narcissism in the earlier sense would appear as Southwest and narcissism as used here (and as Grace Stuart conceives it) as Northwest. This is not surprising: I have found, in factor analytic work, that all long-used, richly connotative terms are conceptually bloated, spreading their corpulent posteriors over 90°, and sometimes even 135°, of a two-dimensional plot, and giving rise to endless controversies between social scientists who attempt to give them narrower meanings of one kind or another. There is really no point in such an effort, since their richness is what gives such concepts value and makes them difficult to relinquish. Terms like narcissism, identification, oedipus complex, bureaucracy, gemeinschaft, authoritarian, romanticism, and primitive are useless as dimensional concepts but are highly evocative. A huge orange dome in a playing field would not be very helpful as a goal-line marker, but it would at least tell us where the game was being played. In a subsequent work I will attempt, nevertheless, to abandon the term "narcissism" and work only with its dimensional components.

9 This requires some qualification. Exhibitionistic dancing is close to body adornment, while boasting also involves a somewhat shorter gratification cycle. Some aspects of the military glory syndrome, on the other hand, are much farther along the continuum than the group as a whole. The narcissism variables were defined before this dimension was conceptualized, and the codes for a given scale may involve a considerable range of points along it.

detached, symbolic, roundabout. The individual enhances his attractiveness by displaying his possessions and trophies, or his courage and skill, and once again, that which makes him desirable also makes him less accessible, less vulnerable. But here he must make more sacrifices and postpone gratification longer. He also takes more risks, for the higher the building, the more likely it is to fall. Just as a euphemism eventually absorbs the obscene connotation it is intended to forestall, so narcissistic defenses become increasingly self-defeating as they increasingly remove themselves from their motivational source.

But in this type of narcissism the self-aggrandizement is still short-run. The warrior suffers and sacrifices, but he can win (or lose) his glory in a single battle. Even in the economic area, where greater postponement is necessary, the feast is given when it can be, the wealth exhibited and expended. As we move further along the continuum we find more modern phenomena appearing: gratification postponed for years, or even a whole lifetime. Wealth is amassed but never spent, and power accumulated but used only to gain more power.

Finally, at the upper extreme of this continuum we find the most pathological and bizarre of all forms of narcissism, in which the focus becomes other-worldly, and the gratification delay therefore permanent. Self-denial becomes the end rather than the means: the body is abandoned altogether, and the goal is simply to aggrandize the psychological self—to increase the sexual desirability of the spirit while at the same time making it inaccessible to any human overture. The ascetic nun rejects all human caresses, and makes herself worthy to be a bride of Christ. The pilgrim brutally abandons his earthly family to aggrandize his immortal soul (to use extreme examples).

We may conceptualize the change from ancient to modern narcissism, then, as one involving greater detachment from the body—a more elaborate circuitry of displacement and delay between the behavior and its ultimate and original goal.

Any age, of course, will contain individuals who fall at every point along the continuum. Greece had its saints and martyrs, its misers and power-hoarders, and modern industrial society has its fops and dandies, its daredevils and big-time spenders. In fact, a whole generation of social commentators have been deploring (or applauding) what they see as a movement away from the Calvinistic extreme of the continuum back to a point nearer the Greek position. But it is still too early to tell whether this phenomenon really betokens a curative trend or if, as Martha Wolfenstein suggests [1963a], it is merely a more insidious form of the disease. (I shall return to this question a little later.) In any case, it seems fair to say that despite these variations, Greek narcissism was more impulsive and less detached from bodily pleasure than the modern form.

This brings us to the second question, concerning the causes of the change. Since this issue is the subject of work currently in progress, I would like now merely to advance two hypotheses. The first is that the detachment of narcissistic concerns from the body and the increase in gratification delay is part of a generalized increase in libidinal repressiveness which has characterized Western civilization since its inception, and which is, indeed, an attribute of all civilizations in comparison with nonliterate societies taken as a whole. The second is that such repressiveness has tended to prevail in human society as a result of natural selection—the more repressive societies supplanting the less repressive through their greater aggressiveness.

By libidinal repressiveness I refer to any social interference with any kind of bodily gratification: restrictions on times, places, and partners for sexual activities; touching taboos; restrictions on eating, sleeping, excretion, and so on. Some of these restrictions, such as the incest taboo, are virtually universal, while others, such as the rule that sexual intercourse be confined to the marital relationship, are relatively uncommon. The variety of restrictions is so great, however, that it is difficult to evaluate the overall difference between one society and another. Furthermore, it will be objected that many nonliterate societies are highly Puritanical. All the evidence that has ever been brought to bear on this question, however, argues very strongly for the hypothesis [cf. Slater, 1965]. While an increase in sexual repressiveness is clearly not a sufficient condition for the achievement of a higher level of cultural development, a good case can be made that—up to this point in cultural history at least—it is a necessary one.

Historians writing about the movements and conflicts of nations often talk about one people being more "energetic" or "virile" than another, as a way of evading serious causal questions. While it is not good form to respond literally to polite conventions, it might repay us to ask just what is meant by saying that one man is more "energetic" than another. Obviously it does not mean that he *has* more energy, or cultural evolution could be entirely predicted by diet. It means that he *expends* more energy—that he utilizes more of what he has.

Cottrell [1955, p. 4ff.] points out that virtually all known societies exert more energy than is required to subsist and procreate, but that many have not exploited the external energy sources at hand. He also points out the relative uselessness of energy that is only intermittently available. If one were a demiurge, then, seeking the cultural development of a people, one would seek some way to increase the output of human energy (necessary to exploit other forms) and to make it chronic rather than intermittent. This is essentially a motivational problem.

Biological drives, in their pure form, do not lend themselves to chronic energy production, since they are too easily and fully extinguished. If I were a demiurge interested in tapping human energy more fully, I would be discontented with this source, which is excessively spasmodic. After eating, drinking, or copulating, my primeval man becomes inert and quiescent. I need clearly to find *some way of motivating him so that he will never be satisfied, never stop expending energy, which can then be tapped for social purposes.* Were I such a demiurge I would try to block these bodily sources of gratification and shift his attention to others. I would first make some spontaneous desires taboo, or I might find some way to attach them to substitute objects, which would be less satisfying—or, better yet, to attach them to symbolic objects, which provide no bodily gratification whatever. If I could get him to associate sexual gratification with buying an automobile or smoking a cigarette or waxing a floor, for example, my problem would be entirely solved. Another device would be to shift his attention from activities in which self-gratification simultaneously gratifies others to activities in which self-gratification simultaneously deprives others (i.e., from sexuality to the pursuit of fame or power. A particularly effective mechanism would be to combine a taboo with some means of increasing the desire to violate it: an example would be any of those societies, mentioned in Chapter XIV, which tended to force libido away from the husband-wife relationship and onto the parent-child relationship in the face of the incest taboo.

Looking about the world today such a demiurge would be pleased at the success of his efforts, but at the same time he might be so dismayed at the destructiveness that seemed to accompany his success as to immolate himself in shame.[10]

To translate this image into more mundane terms: I am suggesting that restrictions on libidinal gratification—arising from any variety of more or less accidental sources [cf. Whiting, 1964]—tended to be rewarded in intersocietal competition by increasing the energy output, the restlessness, of those restricted. I am assuming here the psychoanalytic concept of instinctual plasticity—that blocked drives push toward the nearest available substitute: the more elaborate forms I have mentioned follow automatically from this assumption.

[10] This is the only contribution that will be made here to God-Is-Dead theology.

Let us now turn to my third question: How must we modify my theory of the familial antecedents of narcissism to absorb the sharp differences between ancient Greek and modern American family patterns? I have discussed the differences between "ancient" and "modern" narcissism and their family correlates, but I have also stressed their similarity. What similarities are there in the family patterns? For example: narcissism has been linked to cultural patterns which intensify the mother-son relationship at the expense of the husband-wife relationship. Yet surely the reverse is true of American society, which probably places more emotional burdens on the husband-wife relationship than any culture in the history of the world. The mobility and transience of American life have forced American couples to seek from each other the gratification of needs which, in more stable societies, are satisfied severally by kinship and neighborhood.

Why, then, has our society also produced the most voluminous literature on pathological mother-son relationships of any society since ancient Greece? It appears that the either-or model of family emphasis, while useful in comparing societies of a more or less comparable degree of cultural complexity, is not adequate to the present task. It seems more likely that the factors leading to an emotional overload in the marital relationship might similarly affect *all* nuclear family relationships. Probably at no time in history have children been so exclusively dependent upon their parents (as opposed to other adults in the community), for the satisfaction of emotional needs.

Furthermore, America is a future-oriented society, and although social mobility may be far less than most Americans imagine, it is a powerful force in the minds of parents and children. By and large, children in most European societies do not expect to outstrip their parents, while American children do. Even more important, *parents* expect to be surpassed by their children—in income, education, sophistication, and material comfort.

Since husband and wife are so exclusively dependent on each other they cannot help but be disappointed in some degree. In most societies spouses are expected to be minimally compatible and to procreate, but ask little of each other beyond this. There are many emotional buffers between husband and wife, and between parent and child. In American society these buffers are weakened by the absence of lifelong stable communities. Unlike the Greek mother the American mother more often has a marital relationship which is satisfying. But when it fails her, as it often must, she is similarly isolated from enduring alternatives.

What is more important is that both family systems tend to produce male children who are highly oedipal. The systems are alike in depriving women of contact with and participation in the total culture, and in creating a domestic pattern peculiarly confining and unfulfilling. They thus encourage a vicarious involvement of the mother in the life of the son. Both systems, furthermore, place an emotional overload on the mother-son relationship: the Greek system by forcing the mother to put the son in the father's place, the American by making child rearing a full-time occupation and removing the child in its earliest years from other socializing agents.

But what does it mean to be "highly oedipal"? Essentially, it means to be oriented toward an unattainable goal, to be trapped in fantasy, alienated from experience. It means to be competitive, dissatisfied, grandiose. There are, of course, social advantages to this: much of what we most value in both cultures has come from "dreaming great dreams"—from trying to force reality into fantasy molds, from pursuing the nonexistent. Cultures which are extremely low in this quality always seem a little earthbound, a little unimaginative and literal-minded.

This brings us to the final question: What are the implications of a narcissistic orientation for modern society? I argued at the beginning of this chapter that Greek narcissism could not have been the crucial factor in producing Greek civiliza-tion—although it may have provided some of the raw material —but that it certainly was heavily responsible for its demise. I have since suggested that maternal overinvestment in the mother-son relationship, a resulting commitment to oedipal fantasies, and a narcissistic orientation to the world, all tend to produce societies which historians would call "energetic"—restless, fitful, and competitive—and that under optimal condi-tions this output of energy can lead to what are usually felt to be positive cultural achievements, even if in the majority of cases it leads only to some extremely unpleasant dead ends. Clearly, there are so many question marks about the relation-ship between narcissism—in any of its forms—and cultural evo-lution, that it would be premature to pass judgment on its cur-rent social value.

Since I nonetheless feel impelled to do so, I will make the question a hypothetical one—a kind of game. Let us ask it in this way: If it were demonstrated that both ancient Greek and modern American civilizations could not have come into being without the prior emergence of a narcissistic motivational structure, has it been worth it?

To this question I would reluctantly answer "no." A few great works of art, a large body of knowledge, and a great deal of machinery, seem inadequate compensation for the chronic suffering and joylessness narcissism engenders. If it would take twice as long to produce half as much culture, a five per cent reduction in the human commitment to narcis-sism would seem well worth the price.

One obvious reason is that it would reduce the danger of nuclear war. Since war invariably costs more than whatever material advantages it might bring, it represents an almost pure expression of narcissistic motivation. Even Americans are slowly coming to recognize the high cost of national vanity.[11]

But even if war were not in question, the cost of narcissism in daily unhappiness seems too great. Because it is subordinated to fantasy, life is not savored, and the joys of the many are sacrificed to the achievements of the few. What narcissism makes possible is the emergence of a small number of notable individuals—"great men"—most of whom are vicious and destructive and are admired because they succeeded heroically in making an impact on the world, rather than by having improved the lot of mankind. And the price of enabling these few to embody the narcissistic fantasies of the many is that the bulk of mankind is left disappointed, frustrated, and miserable because they operate, with fewer advantages, on the same premises.

It may be objected that although the great political and military figures of history left the world no better than they found it, the same cannot be said for artists, scientists, inventors. (Here the relationship with narcissism is far less clear, but I shall stay with my assumption.) Yet great artistic or literary achievements are important to us precisely because we are narcissistically oriented and shackled to fantasy. They are a substitute for living, and having deprived ourselves of life we shrink from the thought of also losing what we have put in its place. For art exists, emotionally, to supply what a narcissistic orientation takes away—it provides seasoning for the

[11] A therapist once remarked of one of his patients that he was "so narcissistic he gives away the game for the rest of us"; and American Vietnam policy seems to have played a similar role. As this goes to press, the State Department and the North Vietnamese have been unable to agree upon a site for peace talks. The spectacle of two grown individuals in such a dilemma would reduce us to helpless laughter, but we have long condoned an infantilism in international relations which would be shocking in the business community. I have often amused myself by re-translating diplomatic pronouncements into the language of warring slum gangs, for although the phraseology differs, the psychology is identical.

air-pudding of fantasy with which we feed ourselves.[12] Without it we would experience our starvation, but were we fed,
we would not need it. By "fed" I mean, if it were possible for
people to live in the present, experiencing their world as it is.

Perhaps less needs to be said about science and technology,
since disillusion with "progress" has become relatively widespread. Yet, quite recently [1968], David Sarnoff, of the
Radio Corporation of America, delivered an encomium on the
subject, quite in the nineteenth-century manner, arguing that
before the year 2000, all mankind could be raised to "much
higher levels of prosperity, health, and education." He argued
that malnutrition and starvation could be banished and allow
a large increase in the world's population; that atomic energy
could provide abundant power; that the ocean could be
tapped for minerals and chemicals; that electronic organs
could replace real ones; that new drugs could be developed;
that communication media could become global; and knowledge centralized. He did not say why we should be pleased
at the thought of living in one big city, of the demise of other
species, of the development of new ways to poison ourselves

[12] Much of what is newest in all forms of artistic expression today seems
to recognize this fact, and push against it, making the creative act more
important than the product, and saying that every man is an artist. What it
may express, however, is a change from a condition in which some live and
some imitate living, to one in which *all* imitate living. The mass diffusion of
a principle is usually mistaken by humanists (who tend toward a seesaw
model of history) as a reaction against that principle, since its form is altered
in the process of diffusion. A good example of this is the diffusion of Puritan
attitudes toward erotic expression—a trend usually regarded as the "liberal-
ization of sexual norms." Yet the sexualization of soap, the growth of touching taboos, and the linking of sexual expression to sexual ideology do far
more to inhibit erotic gratification than simple, straightforward (and generally violated) prohibitions.

I would not deny that art—the (narcissistic) impulse to adorn—would
add a certain intensity and savor to life in any society, and might be missed
in a hypothetical society devoid of narcissism; I am stating the case in
extreme terms to make the issues clear. But it should perhaps be emphasized
that I am advocating a reduction in, not the elimination of, narcissistic
motivation.

and others, of becoming ersatz organisms, of becoming inundated in our junk, of the homogenizing of mankind, of the possibility for unheard-of concentrations of power in a few hands, and so on. There is no word about the enjoyment of living in all this. "Prosperity, health, and education" are to be increased, for mankind is viewed here as a machine or a domesticated animal—ways are being found to improve his level of functioning, both through better resources and improved motivation. The vision of human life is that of a modern poultry farm in which the animals are raised more or less like plants. But since no one is to eat these fat and healthy and well-educated humans, one wonders what it is all for. The answer is: it is a measurable achievement. And in a narcissistic society, achievement is the end, not the means. An increase in dollars earned, in man-hours endured inside a school, in years lived (however tediously) can be assigned to someone's record, and he can be rewarded and praised, regardless of how much the (unmeasurable) misery of mankind has been raised.

Whether one subscribes to General Sarnoff's view or my own, the question I have posed here: Is our culture worth what its narcissism has cost us? is the central one of our era. More traditional questions, such as whether Capitalism is superior to Communism, or whether God exists, are becoming dwarfed. Capitalism and Communism are no longer relevant categories, for in every major country in the world the young are fighting with the old, demanding that the old justify their leadership in some way. Although obscured by local differences, the fundamental split between generations is increasingly one between the old who embrace the narcissistic pattern, yearning for mastery, lost in competitive dreams of glory, seeking libidinal expression in vicarious violence, and the young who are trying to escape the pattern, who are yearning for a world of cooperation and brotherhood, of simple sensual pleasure and experiential immediacy. The conflict is confused, inchoate, the arguments inappropriate, inconsistent, the coalitions shifting and uncertain, as is always the case in periods of major potential change. But for perhaps the first time in Western history, the major premises of our civilization are being widely questioned. The slogan, "Make Love Not War," is the most radical rejection of Western culture ever made, for it challenges a priority system which has existed ever since the classical age—a priority system so strong that it was able to absorb Christianity and completely invert its initial thrust. This system places competition before co-operation, mastery before pleasure, conceptualization before sensation.

We have been admiring the products of this system for twenty-three hundred years, in a variety of manifestations. The oldest one seems always to charm us the most, perhaps because it was its first flowering. Were destruction to threaten what remains of Greek culture I would sacrifice much to save what I could, as I would—although far more selectively—of my own. Yet, were I to find that some part of this depended upon the preservation, intact, of Western narcissism I would, not without tears, let it disappear. Greek narcissism, with all its drama and poignancy, was a disease. Through various metamorphoses it has survived the decay of several civilizations, always transmitting itself to a new bearer and burrowing into its favorite spot, close to the heart of Western culture. It is still fascinating and seductive, but it is still a disease, one in which we luxuriate at considerable peril and with great discomfort.

> For I have sworn thee fair, and thought thee bright,
> Who art as black as hell, as dark as night.

APPENDIXES

Appendix I   Aggression in Parent-Child Dyads in Apollodorus

Agent	Victim	Dyad Type*	Aggression Type**	Reference
Cronus	Uranus	SF	API	i. 1. 4
Cronus	Hestia, Demeter, Hera	FD	UH	i. 1. 5
Cronus	Pluto, Poseidon	FS	UH	i. 1. 5
Zeus	Hephaestus	FS	API	i. 3. 5
Oeneus	Toxeus	FS	SH	i. 8. 1
Althaea	Meleager	MS	SH	i. 8. 3
Hipponous	Periboa	FD	UH	i. 8. 4
Athamas	Phrixus	FS	UH	i. 9. 1
Tyro	Pelias, Neleus	MS	UH	i. 9. 8
Lemnian women	Their fathers	DF	SH	i. 9. 17
Pelias' daughters	Pelias	DF	SH	i. 9. 27
Medea	Sons	MS	SH	i. 9. 28
Acrisius	Danaë	FD	UH	ii. 4. 1
Cepheus	Andromeda	FD	UH	ii. 4. 3
Comaetho	Pterelaus	DF	SH	ii. 4. 7
Heracles	Sons	FS	SH	ii. 4. 12
Amazons	Sons	MS	SH	ii. 5. 9
Laomedon	Hesione	FD	UH	ii. 5. 9
Agelaus, Eurypylus, Callias	Temenus	SF	SH	ii. 8. 5
Althaemenes	Catreus	SF	SH	iii. 2. 2
Athamas	Learchus	FS	SH	i. 9. 2; iii. 4. 3
Ino	Melicertes	MS	SH	iii. 4. 3
Lycurgus	Dryas	FS	SH	iii. 5. 1

Agave	Pentheus	MS	SH	iii. 5. 2
Argive women	Sons	MS	SH	iii. 5. 2
Argive women	Daughters	MD	SH	iii. 5. 2
Nycteus	Antiope	FD	UH	iii. 5. 5
Antiope	Zethus, Amphion	MS	UH	iii. 5. 5
Laius	Oedipus	FS	UH	iii. 5. 7
Oedipus	Laius	SF	SH	iii. 5. 7
Alcmaeon	Eriphyle	SM	SH	iii. 7. 5
Aleus	Auge	FD	UH	iii. 9. 1
Iasus	Atalanta	FD	UH	iii. 9. 2
Priam	P:ris	FS	UH	iii. 12. 5
Amyntor	Phoenix	FS	API	iii. 13. 8
Thias	Smyrna	FD	UH	iii. 14. 4
Procne	Itys	MS	SH	iii. 14. 8
Phineus	Plexippus, Pandion	FS	API	i. 9. 21; iii. 15. 3
Chione	Eumolpus	MS	UH	iii. 15. 4
Erechtheus	Daughter	FD	SH	iii. 15. 4
Scylla	Nisus	DF	SH	iii. 15. 8
Theseus	Hippolytus	FS	SH	Epitome i. 19
Tantalus	Pelops	FS	SH	Epitome ii. 3
Hippodamia	Oenomaus	DF	SH	Epitome ii. 6–7
Agamemnon	Iphigenia	FD	UH	Epitome iii. 22
Orestes	Clytemnestra	SM	SH	Epitome vi. 25
Telegonus	Odysseus	SF	SH	Epitome vii. 36

* F = father, M = mother, S = son, D = daughter; the first letter refers to the agent, the second to the victim.

** SH = successful homicide, UH = unsuccessful homicide, API = assault with permanent injury.

Appendix II Greek Madness

Agent	Victim	Principal Source	Graves Reference
Athene	Herse, Aglauros	Apollodorus: iii. 14. 6	Vol. II, p. 322
Athene	Ajax	Apollodorus: *Epitome* v. 6	Vol. II, p. 27
Artemis	Broteas	Apollodorus: *Epitome* ii. 2	Vol. II, p. 77
Artemis	Alopecus, Astrabacus	Pausanias: iii. 16. 9	
Artemis	Teuthras	Plutarch: *Of the Names of Rivers and Mountains,* 21	Vol. II, pp. 188–89
Erinyes	Alcmaeon	Apollodorus: iii. 7. 5	Vol. II, p. 22
Erinyes	Orestes	Apollodorus: *Epitome* vi. 25	Vol. II, p. 67
Rhea	Demophon	Apollodorus: *Epitome* vi. 16–17	Vol. II, p. 349
Mother of the Gods	Sagaris	Plutarch: *Of the Names of Rivers and Mountains,* 12	
Hera	Heracles	Apollodorus: ii. 4. 12	Vol. II, p. 164
Hera	Athamas	Apollodorus: i. 9. 2; ii. 4. 3	Vol. II, p. 100
Hera	Ino	Apollodorus: ii. 4. 3	Vol. I, p. 104
Hera	Dionysus	Apollodorus: iii. 5. 1	Vol. I, p. 104
Dionysus*	Lycurgus	Apollodorus: iii. 5. 1	Vol. I, p. 104
Dionysus	Agave	Apollodorus: iii. 5. 2	Vol. I, p. 105
Dionysus	Tyrrhenian Pirates		
Dionysus	Antiope	Pausanias: ix. 17. 6	Vol. I, p. 257
Dionysus	Minyas' Daughters	Plutarch: *The Greek Questions* 38	Vol. I, p. 105
Dionysus**	Proetus' Daughters (and Argive women)	Apollodorus: i. 9. 12; ii. 2. 2; iii. 5. 2	Vol. I, pp. 234–35

* Rhea in Graves
** Or Hera (for Proetus' daughters alone)

Appendix III Family Dyads in Greek Drama

Drama	Dyad	Amount of* Interaction		Affect**				Child*** Not Full-Grown	Child**** Dies
		Parent	Child	Parent Pos.	Parent Neg.	Child Pos.	Child Neg.		
AESCHYLUS									
The Suppliants Maidens	Danaus-Daughters	2	2	2	1	2	1	A	L
Prometheus	Oceanos-Daughters	0	0	1	1	1	1	A	L
The Persians	Darius-Xerxes	0	0	1	1	1	1	A	L
The Persians	Atossa-Xerxes	0	0	2	1	1	1	A	L
The Choephori	Clytemnestra-Orestes	2	2	1	3	1	3	A	L
The Choephori	Clytemnestra-Electra	0	0	1	1	1	3	A	L
The Eumenides	Clytemnestra-Orestes	0	0	1	3	1	2	A	L
SOPHOCLES									
Ajax	Ajax-Eurysaces	1	0	2	1	1	1	C	L
Ajax	Tecmessa-Eurysaces	1	0	2	1	1	1	C	L
Oedipus Tyrannus	Jocasta-Oedipus	2	2	2	1	2	1	A	L
Oedipus Tyrannus	Jocasta-Daughters	0	0	1	1	1	1	C	L
Oedipus Tyrannus	Oedipus-Daughters	1	0	3	1	2	1	C	L
Oedipus at Colonus	Oedipus-Antigone	2	2	3	1	3	1	A	L
Oedipus at Colonus	Oedipus-Ismene	2	2	2	1	2	1	A	L
Oedipus at Colonus	Oedipus-Polyneices	2	2	1	3	1	1	A	L
Antigone	Creon-Haemon	2	2	2	2	2	3	A	D
Antigone	Eurydice-Haemon	0	0	2	1	1	1	A	D
The Trachiniae	Heracles-Hyllus	2	2	1	1	2	3	A	L
The Trachiniae	Deianeira-Hyllus	2	2	1	1	2	3	A	L
Electra	Clytemnestra-Orestes	1	0	1	2	3	3	A	L
Electra	Clytemnestra-Electra	2	2	1	2	3	3	A	L
Electra	Clytemnestra-Chrysothemis	0	0	1	1	1	2	A	L

[continued on 472]

| | | Amount of* Interaction | | Affect** Parent | | Child | | Child*** Not Full- | Child**** |
Drama	Dyad	Parent	Child	Pos.	Neg.	Pos.	Neg.	Grown	Dies
EURIPIDES									
Alcestis	Admetus-Eumelus	1	1	1	1	1	1	C	L
Alcestis	Alcestis-Eumelus	1	1	1	1	2	1	C	L
Alcestis	Alcestis-Daughter	1	0	2	1	1	1	C	L
Alcestis	Admetus-Daughter	0	0	1	1	1	1	C	L
Alcestis	Pheres-Admetus	2	2	1	3	1	3	A	L
Medea	Jason-Sons	1	0	2	1	1	1	C	D
Medea	Medea-Sons	2	0	3	3	1	1	C	D
Hippolytus	Theseus-Hippolytus	2	2	2	3	2	1	A	D
Heracles	Amphitryon-Heracles	2	2	3	1	3	3	A	L
Heracles	Heracles-Sons	1	0	2	3	2	1	C	D
Heracles	Megara-Sons	1	0	2	1	1	1	C	D
Hecuba	Hecuba-Polydorus	1	1	2	1	2	1	A	D
Hecuba	Hecuba-Polyxena	2	2	3	1	3	1	A	D
Hecuba	Polymestor-Sons	1	0	1	1	1	1	C	D
Andromache	Menelaus-Hermione	0	0	1	1	1	1	A	L
Andromache	Andromache-Molossus	1	1	3	3	3	1	C	L
Trojan Women	Hecuba-Cassandra	1	2	1	1	1	3	A	L
Trojan Women	Andromache-Astyanax	1	0	2	1	1	1	C	D
Ion	Creusa-Ion	2	2	3	3	3	3	A	L
Ion	Xuthus-Ion	2	2	3	1	2	2	A	L
Rhesus	Terpsichore-Rhesus	2	0	2	1	1	1	A	D
Suppliants	Aethra-Theseus	2	2	1	1	1	1	A	L
Suppliants	Iphis-Evadne	1	1	2	1	2	1	A	D
Orestes	Menelaus-Hermione	0	0	1	1	1	1	A	L
Orestes	Helen-Hermione	1	0	1	1	1	1	A	L
Orestes	Tyndareus-Helen	0	0	1	2	1	1	A	L
Iphigenia in Aulis	Agamemnon-Iphigenia	2	2	3	3	3	1	A	D
Iphigenia in Aulis	Clytemnestra-Iphigenia	2	2	3	1	2	1	A	D

472

Play	Relationship	Lines*	Positive**	Negative	Lines*	Positive**	Negative	Age***	Fate****
Iphigenia in Aulis	Clytemnestra-Orestes	1	0	2	1	1	1	C	L
Iphigenia in Aulis	Agamemnon-Orestes	0	0	1	1	1	1	C	L
Electra	Clytemnestra-Orestes	1	0	1	2	2	3	A	L
Electra	Clytemnestra-Electra	2	2	2	1	2	3	A	L
Phoenissae	Jocasta-Oedipus	0	1	1	1	2	1		
Phoenissae	Jocasta-Antigone	1	1	1	1	2	1	A	L
Phoenissae	Oedipus-Antigone	2	2	2	1	3	2	A	L
Phoenissae	Oedipus-Polyneices	1	1	2	1	2	1	A	D
Phoenissae	Oedipus-Eteocles	1	0	1	1	1	2	A	D
Phoenissae	Jocasta-Eteocles	2	2	2	1	2	2	A	D
Phoenissae	Jocasta-Polyneices	2	2	3	1	2	1	A	D
Phoenissae	Creon-Menoecus	1	1	1	1	1	1	A	D
Phoenissae	Teiresias-Daughter	1	0	1	1	1	2	C	L
The Bacchae	Agave-Pentheus	1	1	2	3	1	2	A	D
The Bacchae	Cadmus-Agave	2	2	1	1	2	2	A	L

* 2 = more than 25 lines directed to other person
1 = one to 25 lines directed to other person
0 = no interaction with other person

** For positive affect:
1 = neutral,1 polite, expedient, or no data
2 = moderate warmth, affection expressed (includes mourning)
3 = intense love, affection, nurturance

For negative affect:
1 = neutral or no data
2 = moderate anger, resentment expressed
3 = violent, murderous rage or hatred expressed (includes killing, regardless of affect)

*** A = full-grown, marriageable age
C = infant or young child

**** L = child lives throughout play
D = child dies during or at conclusion of play

1 "Neutral" here means with regard to the love-hate dimension. Other affects, such as anxiety, despair, and so forth, may have been expressed.

Appendix IV   Narcissism Codes

General Instructions

(1) Proceed culture-by-culture, making all ratings for a given culture before moving to the next. The most efficient order for acquiring information on the basis of the Human Relations Area File (HRAF) system is as follows: *Always* check categories 181 and 183 first, then 152, 156, and 157, which are relevant to several of the codes and often provide cues for where to look further. Then look under categories listed under specific ratings. Begin with N–9, then N–6 and N–11, leaving N–1A to the last.

(2) This system, while most efficient, necessitates guarding very carefully against halo effect. Every rating made should be based upon a specific criterion in the coding instructions, in conjunction with a specific statement or passage in the ethnography. Each passage used in making the rating should be copied from the ethnography and recorded.

(3) When no material can be found on which to base a rating, the coder should record "O."

(4) When information can be found which supports making ratings at both extremes of a variable, "X" should be recorded (unless the conflict can be resolved: see below).

(5) If the conflict exists between specific practices and an evaluative comment by the ethnographer, the former should be given greater weight unless it is an isolated instance. One should be particularly cautious about a common practice of ethnographers: arguing that a given item of behavior does not reflect the attitude that it seems to reflect. Words are imprecise, and the ethnographer who claims that some bit of behavior is "not based on pride," for example, may merely be concerned with differentiating the behavior from a similar pattern in another culture—i.e., making a much finer distinction than we are concerned with here. On the other hand, when not concerned with drawing such distinctions, ethnographers may use "narcissistic" language very broadly, and this should be examined very closely. It may be said, for example, that some individual "committed suicide out of shame" in response to some economic failure, when despair at being unable to achieve some personal goal or meet familial obligations is at issue. Narcissistic motives are always present in suicide, and any failure will be accompanied by an emotion which could be called "shame." We wish to distinguish here between the man who commits suicide because his business has gone bankrupt and the one who commits sui-

cide because he dropped the pop fly which let in the winning run in the decisive World Series game. Both failures may be viewed as irremediable, although neither in fact is, but the latter is more likely to be defined purely as something which cannot be "lived down."

In general, one should never use key words such as "pride," "shame," "respect," "ambition," and so forth, as evidence in themselves, although they may point the way to evidence which *can* be used.

(6) If conflict arises through the existence of subgroups in the culture, the following rules should apply:

(a) Occasionally an ethnographer will make passing references to a neighboring culture, or to the larger and perhaps urbanized society in which the more primitive group is embedded. The coder should make certain that his ratings are *not* based on this material, which is not kept separate in the HRAF.

(b) The most general rule to be applied with regard to divisions *within* the culture is that the ratings should be made on whatever group of adult males is given most attention by the ethnographer generally, or is equated by him with the culture as a whole.

(c) Special occupational categories, such as chiefs, shamans, and so forth, or any numerically small subgroup, should never be made the basis of any ratings.

(d) When a society is divided into nobles and commoners, the former group being of considerable size, every effort should be made to establish what is common to both. If irreconcilable differences nevertheless exist, and rule (b) above cannot be applied, an intermediate code category should be chosen wherever possible. Otherwise, code "X."

(7) In coding all of the variables below, one should take care to avoid making a positive rating on the basis of idiosyncratic behavior. Most of the reactions involved in these variables are universal in some degree, and therefore will be found in some individuals everywhere.

(8) In the specific instructions listed below, only those HRAF category numbers are listed which have not already been checked. That is, the numbers listed under N–1A do *not* include 181, 183, and so forth, or relevant numbers which have already been checked in looking up N–9, and so forth.

Variable N–9: Sensivity to Narcissistic Wounds HRAF Categories 626, 578, 762, 576

CODE 3 (HIGH) IF:

(1) Public humiliation *frequently* leads to suicide or some other violent response. Or,

(2) Interpersonal insults, slights, snubs frequently lead to suicide, homicide, vendetta, permanent estrangement, or demand for heavy remuneration (because of narcissistic wounds, not because of malediction, and so forth). Or,

(3) Ethnographer explicitly says they are acutely sensitive to narcissistic wounds, easily take offense, and so forth, (*not* if merely "easily hurt"—there must be some indication that pride is wounded, or vanity, *not* merely that they feel rejected, unloved, or deprived). Or,

(4) Abnormally elaborate etiquette precautions designed to avoid giving offense are present (not limited to specific groups or relationships).

CODE 1 (LOW) IF NONE OF THE ABOVE ARE PRESENT AND:

(1) Ridicule and shame are specifically excluded as important public sanctions. Or,

(2) Incidents are specifically mentioned (as typical) by ethnographer, in which insults, scorn, and so forth, are received without marked reaction. Offenses can be erased with small gifts, and so forth. Or,

(3) Ethnographer specifically describes them as phlegmatic, serene, easygoing, not easily offended, quick to forgive slights, and so forth.

CODE 2 (MODERATE) IF NONE OF THE ABOVE ARE PRESENT BUT:

(1) Ridicule and shame are nevertheless important public sanctions. Or,

(2) Insults, slights, snubs, and so forth, are explicitly mentioned as giving rise to sulking, tears, or anger of brief duration. Or,

(3) There is mention of mild etiquette precautions for face-saving. Or,

(4) Ridicule may yield suicide *attempts*, but actual suicide is rare, Or,

(5) Ethnographer characterizes culture as "shame culture."

Variable N–6A: Invidiousness
HRAF Categories 554, 556, 431

CODE 2 (PRESENT):

(1) When ethnographer states explicitly that one of the central values attached to wealth in the society is its use in display, or if he refers to the importance of "conspicuous consumption," or if he states that ambition, social mobility, and competitiveness are focused upon the ability to display wealth or the symbols of wealth. Or,

(2) When prestige, rank, and power in the society are dependent

upon displayed wealth, or displayed wealth is said to be a major goal in the society. Or,

(3) When gift-giving and hospitality in the society are essentially invidious (e.g., the potlatch). That is, liberality is not conceived as an obligation or a kindness but as an act of self-aggrandizement and ostentation.

(Displayed wealth includes subsistence goods, currency, luxuries, servants or retainers, or anything which symbolizes the ability of the individual to command wealth.)

CODE 1 (ABSENT) WHEN NONE OF THE ABOVE ARE CONSPICUOUS AND:

(1) Ethnographer states that gradations of wealth are unimportant, static, or minimized by those who possess it. Or,

(2) Wealthy persons have no prestige in the society or are regarded as immoral. Or,

(3) There is a norm that surplus wealth must be shared, and that the accumulation of wealth confers prestige upon the group rather than the individual. Or,

(4) The value of wealth is seen as residing altogether in the security it provides, or the power to procure goods and services. Or,

(5) Ethnographer says that ostentatious approach to wealth is frowned upon or looked down upon. Or,

(6) Gift-giving is closely regulated on the basis of reciprocity and obligation.

Note: Since invidiousness is virtually universal, one should be cautious about making a positive rating on the basis of scanty support.

Variable N–11A: Pursuit of Military Glory
HRAF Categories 721, 703, 701

CODE 3 (HIGH):

(1) When ethnographer says that members of the tribe seek death in battle, or regard it as preferable to defeat and behave accordingly, or see it as the principal road to earthly or other-wordly glory. Or,

(2) When war is said to be considered by the tribe as glorious, the primary source of status and prestige, or to be waged principally for the purpose of obtaining rank, honor, or fame. Or,

(3) When military virtues, such as valor, recklessness, fighting skill, and so forth, are said to be the most important ones in the society.

(4) When military trophies are said to be the principal source of rank or prestige in the society.

CODE I (LOW) WHEN NONE OF THE ABOVE ARE PRESENT AND:
(1) Ethnographer says military virtues are not valued. Or,
(2) Some indication is given that saving one's own life in battle is considered normal and appropriate behavior. Or,
(3) War is regarded as abhorrent.

CODE 2 (MODERATE) WHEN NONE OF THE ABOVE ARE PRESENT BUT:
(1) *Defensive* virtues are said to be valued—military resistance, endurance, fortitude, and so forth. Or,
(2) Values other than military ones predominate, though the latter are important.
(3) Contests of bravery, skill, or endurance (e.g., ability to withstand pain) are an important feature of masculine relationships.
(4) Raids, and so forth, are frequent, but conducted primarily for economic reasons.

Note: These values must apply to the present, not to the past. That is, they must currently exist as attitudes, even though actual warfare has disappeared from tribal life. ("Present" refers to the time of the ethnographer's report.)

Variable N–11B: Collective Pugnacity HRAF Category 628

CODE 2 (HIGH):
(1) When ethnographer explicitly describes the tribe as currently belligerent or warlike. Or,
(2) When the majority of adult males are said to spend most of their daily life engaged in or preparing for war, raids, or homicidal vendettas.
(3) When ethnographer says the tribe is feared by surrounding tribes as an aggressor.

CODE I (LOW) WHEN NONE OF THE ABOVE ARE PRESENT AND:
(1) War is said to be defined as waged primarily in revenge, or defensively, in response to the presence of warlike neighbors. Or,
(2) When tribe is described as peaceful, meek, friendly, nonaggressive, and so forth. Or,
(3) War, raids, vendettas, and so forth, are said to be absent.

Note: References to a distant warlike past are *not* sufficient. The behavior must have existed within the memory of some person living at the time of the ethnographer's report.

Variable N–11C: Bloodthirstiness
HRAF Category 727

CODE 3 (HIGH):

(1) When members of the tribe habitually take prisoners in warfare or raids for the explicit purpose of torturing them. Or,

(2) When prolonged or elaborate torture of captives is mentioned as a common phenomenon. Or,

(3) When prisoners are regularly sacrificed under conditions that approximate torture (slow, painful death, dismemberment while still alive, eaten alive, and so forth). Or,

(4) When particularly large numbers of prisoners are slaughtered in ways that produce a rapid but especially painful or terrifying death.

CODE 2 (MEDIUM) WHEN NONE OF THE ABOVE ARE PRESENT BUT:

(1) Warriors are said never to take prisoners in battles or raids but have a policy of killing all of their enemies on the spot. Or,

(2) Headhunting or scalp-collecting is said to be practiced on a wide scale, and provides a major source of prestige and status. Or,

(3) Killing is a prerequisite of manhood.

CODE 1 (LOW) WHEN NONE OF THE ABOVE ARE PRESENT AND:

(1) The tribe is described as peaceful, gentle, kindly, and so forth. Or,

(2) Prisoners are taken and kept as slaves, or otherwise incorporated into the society. Or,

(3) There is no consistent policy regarding prisoners. Or,

(4) Prisoners are not taken but battles or raids are typically concluded before everyone is killed, i.e., when some objective is obtained, or when ritual expression of defeat is rendered by the enemy. Or,

(5) Wars and raiding are rare.

Note: References to a distant bloodthirsty past are *not* sufficient. The behavior must have existed within the memory of some person living at the time of the ethnographer's report.

Variable N–1A: Boasting and Scorning
HRAF Categories 521, 555

CODE 2 (PRESENT):

(1) When ethnographer refers to the tribe as generally boastful. Or,

(2) When ethnographer says boasting is typical at certain times (feasts, bragging after battles, crowing over achievements, and so forth), or describes instances in which this is general and accepted behavior. Or,

(3) When ethnographer describes, as typical, instances of boasting-by-contrast, i.e., the speaker scorns, taunts, or ridicules others for not possessing attributes, achievements, or goods which the speaker possesses.

CODE 1 (ABSENT) WHEN NONE OF THE ABOVE ARE PRESENT AND:

(1) When ethnographer refers to the tribe as modest, unassuming, humble, and so forth. Or,

(2) When ethnographer explicitly says they do not boast over triumphs, achievements, and so forth, or describes incidents, *in detail*, of triumph, achievement, and so forth, following which the speaker speaks modestly, and so forth. Or,

(3) When ethnographer says boasting or scorning is negatively sanctioned.

Variable N–1B: Exhibitionistic Dancing
HRAF Category 535

CODE 3 (HIGH):

(1) When ethnographer reports that most dancing is performed individually, with an audience present. Or,

(2) When there is strong emphasis on being a good performer, with prestige or material rewards going to the best individual dancer. Or,

(3) When there is considerable competitiveness with regard to costume among dancers.

CODE 1 (LOW):

(1) When dancing is primarily social—men and women dancing together, with no attention paid to individual skill. Or,

(2) When dancing is primarily ritual and ceremonial, with no audience, and most members participating. Or,

(3) When emphasis is placed primarily on ritual exactitude rather than skill.

CODE 2 (MEDIUM):

(1) When social-ceremonial and exhibitionistic elements seem to be about equal.

BIBLIOGRAPHY

Abraham, Karl. "The Experiencing of Sexual Traumas as a Form of Sexual Activity" (1907), in *Selected Papers of Karl Abraham*. New York: Basic Books, 1957, 47–63.

―――. "Dreams and Myths" (1909), in *Clinical Papers and Essays on Psychoanalysis*. New York: Basic Books, 1955, 151–209.

―――. "A Complicated Ceremonial Found in Neurotic Women" (1912), in *Selected Papers*, 157–63.

―――. "Mental After-Effects Produced in a Nine-year-old Child by the Observation of Sexual Intercourse Between Its Parents" (1913a), in *Selected Papers*, 164–68.

―――. "Restrictions and Transformations of Scoptophilia in Psychoneurotics: with Remarks on Analogous Phenomena in Folk-Psychology" (1913b), in *Selected Papers*, 169–234.

―――. "Manifestations of the Female Castration Complex" (1920), in *Selected Papers*, 338–69.

―――. "The Spider as a Dream Symbol" (1922), in *Selected Papers*, 326–32.

―――. "Two Contributions to the Study of Symbols" (1923), in *Clinical Papers*, 81–85.

Aeschylus. Translated by Herbert Weir Smyth. (Loeb Library.) 2 vols. Cambridge: Harvard University Press, 1952.

―――. *Agamemnon*.

―――. *The Choephori*.

―――. *The Eumenides*.

―――. *The Persians*.

―――. *The Suppliant Maidens*.

Alexander, Franz. *Our Age of Unreason*. rev. ed. Philadelphia: Lippincott, 1952.

Anthony, E. J. "A Study of 'Screen Sensations,'" *Psychoanalytic Study of the Child*, XVI. New York: International Universities Press, 1961, 211–41.

Apollodorus of Athens. *The Library*. Translated by Sir James

George Frazer. (Loeb Library.) 2 vols. Cambridge: Harvard University Press, 1921.

Apollonius of Rhodes. *The Voyage of Argo*. Translated by E. V. Rieu. Baltimore: Penguin, 1959.

Apuleius. *The Golden Ass*. Translated by Robert Graves. New York: Pocket Books, 1951.

Archilochus of Paros. In *Greek Lyrics*. Edited and translated by Richmond Alexander Lattimore. 2nd. ed. Chicago: University of Chicago Press, 1961, 1–6.

Ariès, Philippe. *Centuries of Childhood*. New York: Knopf, 1962.

Aristophanes. Translated by Benjamin Bickley Rogers. (Loeb Library.) 3 vols. Cambridge: Harvard University Press, 1950.

———. *The Birds*.

———. *Ecclesiazusae*.

———. *The Frogs*.

———. *Lysistrata*.

———. *Plutus*.

———. *Thesmophoriazusae*.

Aristotle. "Ethica Nicomachea," in *The Basic Works of Aristotle*. Edited by Richard McKeon and translated by W. D. Ross. New York: Random House, 1941.

———. "On the Generation of Animals," in *Basic Works*. 665–80.

Arrowsmith, William. "Introduction to *The Bacchae*," in *The Complete Greek Tragedies*. IV. Edited by David Grene and Richmond Alexander Lattimore. Chicago: University of Chicago Press, 1960, 530–41.

———. "Introduction to *Heracles*," in *The Complete Greek Tragedies*, III. 266–81.

Aymar, Brandt (ed.) *Treasury of Snake Lore*. New York: Greenberg, 1956.

Ayres, Barbara C. "A Cross-cultural Study of Factors Relating to Pregnancy Taboos." Unpublished Ph.D. dissertation, Radcliffe College, 1954.

Bacchylides. In *Lyra Graeca*, III. Translated by J. M. Edmonds, rev. ed. (Loeb Library.) Cambridge: Harvard University Press, 1952.

———. "Paean on Peace," in *Greek Literature in Translation*.

Edited by G. Howe *et al.* and translated by John Addington Symonds. rev. ed. New York: Harper, 1948, 179.

Bach, George R. "Father-Fantasies and Father-Typing in Father-separated Children," *Child Development*, XVII (1946), 63–80.

Bacon, Margaret K., *et al.* Unpublished ratings of socialization practices. Department of Psychology, Yale University, 1952.

————. "A Cross-cultural Study of Correlates of Crime," *Journal of Abnormal and Social Psychology*, LXVI (1963), 291–300.

Barry, H. A. III, *et al.* "A Cross-cultural Survey of Some Sex Differences in Socialization," *Journal of Abnormal and Social Psychology*, LV (1957), 327–32.

Baruch, Dorothy. *One Little Boy*. New York: Julian Press, 1952.

Barzini, Luigi. *The Italians*. New York: Bantam, 1967.

Bateson, Gregory, *et al.* "Toward a Theory of Schizophrenia," *Behavioral Science*, I (1956), 251–64.

Baudelaire, Charles. *Flowers of Evil*. Translated by George Dillon and Edna St. Vincent Millay. New York: Harper. 1936.

Baum, L. Frank. *The Magic of Oz*. Chicago: Reilly and Lee, 1919.

Bayley, Nancy, and Schaefer, E. S. "Relationships Between Socio-economic Variables and the Behavior of Mothers Toward Young Children," *Journal of Genetic Psychology*, XCVI (1960), 61–77.

Beauvoir, Simone de. *Le Deuxième Sexe*. Paris: Gallimard, 1949.

Benedict, Ruth. *Patterns of Culture*. New York: Mentor Books, 1953.

Bettelheim, Bruno. *Symbolic Wounds*. London: Thames and Hudson, 1955.

————. *Truants from Life*. Glencoe, Ill.: Free Press, 1955.

Bettelheim, Bruno, and Sylvester, Emmy. "Parental Occupations and Children's Symptoms," in *A Modern Introduction to the Family*. Edited by N. W. Bell and E. F. Vogel. Glencoe, Ill.: Free Press, 1960, 499–509.

Bible. Revised Standard Edition. New York: Thomas Nelson and Sons, 1953.

Bibring, Grete L., *et al.* "A Study of the Psychological Processes in Pregnancy and of the Earliest Mother-Child Relationship,"

Psychoanalytic Study of the Child, XVI. New York: International Universities Press, 1961, 9–72.

Bieber, Irving. "Clinical Aspects of Male Homosexuality," in *Sexual Inversion*. Edited by J. Marmor. New York: Basic Books, 1965, 248–67.

Bird, Brian. "A Study of the Bisexual Meaning of the Foreskin," *Journal of the American Psychoanalytic Association*, VI (1958), 287–304.

Blake, William. "The Mental Traveller," in *Selected Poems*. Edited by Ruthven Todd. New York: Dell, 1960.

Blood, Robert O. "The Husband-Wife Relationship," in *The Employed Mother in America*. Edited by F. I. Nye and Lois W. Hoffman. Chicago: Rand, McNally, 1963, 282–305.

Blümner, H. *The Home Life of the Ancient Greeks*. Translated by Alice Zimmern. New York: Funk and Wagnalls, n.d.

Boccaccio, Giovanni. *The Decameron*. Bibliophilist Society, n.d.

The Book of the Thousand Nights and a Night. Translated by Richard F. Burton. London: Burton Club, 1885.

Bott, Elizabeth. *Family and Social Network*. London: Tavistock, 1957.

Bowlby, John. "Grief and Mourning in Infancy and Early Childhood," *Psychoanalytic Study of the Child*, XV. New York: International Universities Press, 1960, 9–52.

Briffault, Robert. *The Mothers*. abr. ed. New York: Macmillan, 1931.

———. *The Mothers*. Abridged by G. R. Taylor. Macmillan, 1959.

Brody, Sylvia. *Patterns of Mothering*. New York: International Universities Press, 1956.

Budge, E. W. *Literature of the Egyptians*. New York: Dutton, 1914.

Bunker, H. A. "Mother-Murder in Myth and Legend," *Psychoanalytic Quarterly*, XIII (1944), 198–207.

Burton, R. V., and Whiting, J. W. M. "The Absent Father and Cross-Sex Identity," *Merrill-Palmer Quarterly*, VII (1961), 85–95.

Callimachus, in *Callimachus and Lycophron, Aratus*. Translated by A. W. Mair and G. R. Mair. (Loeb Library.) New York: Putnam, 1921.

Campbell, J. F., and Henderson, G. (trans.) *The Celtic Dragon Myth*. Edinburgh: John Grant, 1911.

Campbell, Joseph. *The Hero with a Thousand Faces*. New York: Meridian Books, 1956.

———. *The Masks of God*. New York: Viking, 1959.

Caplan, Gerald. *Mental Health Aspects of Social Work in Public Health*. Berkeley: University of California, School of Social Welfare, 1955.

Carpenter, Rhys. *Folk Tale, Fiction, and Saga in the Homeric Epics*. Berkeley: University of California Press, 1958.

Clark, L. P. "Unconscious Motives Underlying the Personalities of Great Statesmen and Their Relation to Epoch-making Events; III. The Narcism of Alexander the Great," *Psychoanalytic Review*, X (1923), 56–69.

Clift, Charmian. *Mermaid Singing*. New York: Bobbs-Merrill, 1956.

Collingwood, S. D. *The Life and Letters of Lewis Carroll*. New York: Century, 1899.

Cottrell, F. *Energy and Society*. New York: McGraw-Hill, 1955.

Daly, C. D. "The Psycho-Biological Origins of Circumcision," *International Journal of Psychoanalysis*, XXXI (1950), 217–36.

Dante, Alighieri. *The Divine Comedy*. Translated by L. G. White. New York: Pantheon, 1948.

Devereux, George. "The Psychology of Feminine Genital Bleeding. An Analysis of Mohave Indian Puberty and Menstrual Rites," *International Journal of Psychoanalysis*, XXXI (1950), 237–57.

———. "Why Oedipus Killed Laius," *International Journal of Psychoanalysis*, XXXIV (1953), 132–41.

Diodorus of Sicily. Translated by C. H. Oldfather. (Loeb Library.) 12 vols. Cambridge: Harvard University Press, 1953.

Dodgson, Charles Lutwidge. *Alice's Adventures in Wonderland* by Lewis Carroll [pseud.] New York: Random House, 1946.

———. *The Annotated Alice*. Edited by Martin Gardner. New York: Potter, 1960.

————. *The Diaries of Lewis Carroll.* Edited and supplemented by Roger Lancelyn Green. 2 vols. London: Cassell, 1953.

Dodds, E. R. *Euripides' Bacchae.* 2nd ed. London: Oxford Press, 1960.

————. *The Greeks and the Irrational.* Boston: Beacon Press, 1957.

Dooley, Lucile. "The Genesis of Psychological Sex Differences," *Psychiatry*, I (1938), 181–95.

Dundas, Sir Charles. "History of Kitui," *Journal of the Royal Anthropological Institute*, XLIII (1913), 480–549.

Ehrenberg, Victor. *The People of Aristophanes.* Oxford: Basil Blackwell, 1951.

Ehrenzweig, Anton. "The Origin of the Scientific and Heroic Urge (the Guilt of Prometheus)," *International Journal of Psychoanalysis*, XXX (1949), 108–23.

Ekstein, R., *et al.* "Countertransference in the Residential Treatment of Children," *Psychoanalytic Study of the Child*, XIV. New York: International Universities Press, 1959, 186–218.

Elwin, Verrier. *The Baiga.* London: John Murray, 1939.

Empedocles of Acragas. *Fragments.* Translated by W. E. Leonard. Chicago: Open Court Publishing Co., 1908.

Engle, Bernice S. "Lemnos, Island of Women," *Psychoanalytic Review*, XXXII (1945), 353–58.

Erikson, E. H. "Sex Differences in the Play Configurations of American Pre-Adolescents," in *Childhood in Contemporary Cultures.* Edited by Margaret Mead and Martha Wolfenstein. Chicago: University of Chicago Press, 1963, 324–41.

Euripides. Translated by Arthur S. Way. (Loeb Library.) 4 vols. Cambridge: Harvard University Press, 1919, 1925, 1947.

————. *Alcestis.*

————. *The Bacchæ.*

————. *The Cyclops.*

————. *Electra.*

————. *Hecuba.*

————. *Heracleidae.*

————. *Heracles.*

————. *Hippolytus.*

————. *Ion.*

————. *Iphigeneia in Aulis.*

————. *Iphigeneia in Tauris.*

————. *Medea.*

————. *Orestes.*

————. *Phoenissae.*

————. *Suppliants.*

Feldman, Thalia. "Gorgo and the Origins of Fear," *Arion*, IV (1965), 484–94.

Ferenczi, Sándor. "Symbolism" (1912), in *Selected Papers, I.* New York: Basic Books, 1950, 253–81.

————. "The Symbolism of the Bridge" (1921), in *Selected Papers, II.* New York: Basic Books, 1952, 352–56.

————. "On the Symbolism of the Head of Medusa" (1923), in *Selected Papers, II*, 360.

————. *Thalassa: A Theory of Genitality*, New York: Psychoanalytic Quarterly, 1938.

————. "On Epileptic Fits" (1939), in *Selected Papers, III.* New York: Basic Books, 1955, 197–204.

Finley, M. I. Review of "Enter Plato," *New York Review of Books*, VII (August 18, 1966), 27–29.

————. *The World of Odysseus.* New York: Meridian, 1959.

Flacelière, Robert. *L'Amour en Grèce.* Paris: Hachette, 1960.

Flugel, J. C. "Polyphallic Symbolism and the Castration Complex," *International Journal of Psychoanalysis*, V (1924), 155–96.

Fontenrose, Joseph. *Python: a Study of Delphic Myth and Its Origins.* Berkeley: University of California Press, 1959.

Ford, C. S. "A Comparative Study of Human Reproduction," *Yale University Publications in Anthropology*, No. 32 (1945).

Fortune, R. F. "The Symbolism of the Serpent," *International Journal of Psychoanalysis*, VII (1926), 237–43.

Frazer, Sir James George. *Adonis, Attis, Osiris.* London: Macmillan, 1906.

————. *The New Golden Bough.* Edited by T. H. Gaster. New York: Criterion Books, 1959.

Frenkel-Brunswik, Else. "Differential Patterns of Social Outlook and Personality in Family and Children," in *Childhood in Contemporary Cultures.* Edited by Margaret Mead and Martha

Wolfenstein. Chicago: University of Chicago Press, 1963, 369–402.

Freud, Sigmund. *The Interpretation of Dreams* (1900). New York: Basic Books, 1955.

————. *Totem and Taboo* (1913). New York: Norton, 1962.

————. "On Narcissism: an Introduction" (1914), in *Collected Papers, IV*. London: Hogarth, 1953, 30–59.

————. "One of the Difficulties of Psychoanalysis" (1917), in *Collected Papers*, IV, 347–56.

————. "From the History of an Infantile Neurosis" (1918), in *Collected Papers*, III, London: Hogarth, 1956, 473–605.

————. "The Taboo of Virginity" (1918), in *Collected Papers*, IV. 217–35.

————. "The 'Uncanny'" (1919), in *Collected Papers*, IV, 368–407.

————. *A General Introduction to Psychoanalysis* (1920). Garden City, N.Y.: Garden City Books, 1952.

————. "Medusa's Head" (1922), in *Collected Papers*, V. London: Hogarth, 1953, 105–106.

————. *Civilization and Its Discontents* (1930). London: Hogarth, 1953.

————. "Female Sexuality" (1931a), in *Collected Papers*, V, 252–72.

————. "Libidinal Types" (1931b), in *Collected Papers*, V, 247–51.

————. *New Introductory Lectures on Psycho-analysis*. London: Hogarth, 1933.

Friedl, Ernestine. *Vasilika, A Village in Modern Greece*. New York: Holt, 1964.

Friedman, J., and Gassel, Sylvia. "Orestes," *Psychoanalytic Quarterly*, XX (1951), 423–33.

Fromm, Erich. *Escape from Freedom*. New York: Rinehart, 1941.

————. *The Forgotten Language*. New York: Grove Press, 1951.

Fustel de Coulanges, Numa D. *The Ancient City*. Garden City, N.Y.: Doubleday, 1956.

Galt, W. E. "The Male-Female Dichotomy in Human Behavior," *Psychiatry*, VI (1943), 1–14.

Gomme, Arnold W. *Essays on Greek History and Literature.* Oxford: Basil Blackwell, 1937.

Gouldner, A. W. *Enter Plato.* New York: Basic Books, 1965.

Graves, Robert. *The Greek Myths.* 2 vols. Baltimore: Penguin, 1955.

Green, A. "The Middle Class Male Child and Neurosis," *American Sociological Review,* XI (1946), 31–41.

Greenberger, Ellen Silver. "Fantasies of Women Confronting Death: A Study of Critically Ill Patients." Unpublished Ph.D. dissertation, Harvard University, 1961.

Grene, David, and Lattimore, Richmond (eds.) *Aeschylus* in *The Complete Greek Tragedies.* Chicago: University of Chicago Press, 1959.

———. *Euripides* in *The Complete Greek Tragedies.*

———. *Sophocles* in *The Complete Greek Tragedies.*

Grote, George. *Mythology of the Greeks.* New York: William L. Allison Co., n.d.

Gundlach, R. H., and Riess, B. F. "Self and Sexual Identity in Men and Women in Relationship to Homosexuality," in *Development and Evolution of Behavior.* Edited by L. Aronson and J. Rosenblatt. New York: Freeman, 1966.

Guntrip, H. "A Study of Fairbairn's Theory of Schizoid Reactions," *British Journal of Medical Psychology,* XXV (1952), 86ff.

Guthrie, W. K. C. *The Greeks and Their Gods.* Boston: Beacon Press, 1955.

Hall, E. T. *The Hidden Dimension.* Garden City, N. Y.: Doubleday, 1966.

Harley, J. K. "Adolescent Youths in Peer Groups: A Cross-cultural Study." Ph.D. dissertation, Harvard Graduate School of Education, 1963.

Harnik, J. "Narcissism in Men and Women," *International Journal of Psychoanalysis,* V (1924), 66–83.

Harrison, Jane Ellen. *Mythology.* New York: Harcourt Brace, 1963.

———. *Primitive Athens as Described by Thucydides.* Cambridge: Harvard University Press, 1906.

————. *Prolegomena to the Study of Greek Religion.* New York: Meridian Books, 1957.

————. *Themis.* Cleveland: Meridian Books, 1962.

Havelock, Eric A. *Preface to Plato.* Cambridge: Harvard University Press, 1963.

Hawthorne, Nathaniel. *Short Stories.* Edited by Newton Arvin. New York: Knopf, 1961.

Hebb, D. O. *The Organization of Behavior.* New York: Wiley, 1949.

Heer, D. M. "Dominance and the Working Wife," in *The Employed Mother in America.* Edited by F. I. Nye and Lois W. Hoffman. Chicago: Rand, McNally, 1963, 251–62.

Hellman, Ilse. "Simultaneous Analysis of Mother and Child," in *Psychoanalytic Study of the Child,* XV (1960), 359–77.

Henderson, J. L., and Oakes, Maud V. *The Wisdom of the Serpent.* New York: Braziller, 1963.

Henry, G. W. *Sex Variants.* New York: Hoeber, 1948.

Herodotus. *The Histories.* Translated by Aubrey de Sélincourt. Baltimore: Penguin, 1954.

Hesiod. In *Hesiod, The Homeric Hymns and Homerica.* Translated by H. G. Evelyn-White. (Loeb Library.) Cambridge: Harvard University Press, 1959.

Heyer, Virginia. "Relationships Between Men and Women in Chinese Stories," in *The Study of Culture at a Distance.* Edited by Margaret Mead and Rhoda Métraux. Chicago: University of Chicago Press, 1953, 221–34.

Hoffman, Lois W. "The Father's Role in the Family and the Child's Peer-Group Adjustment," *Merrill-Palmer Quarterly,* VII (1961), 97–105.

————. "Parental Power Relations and the Division of Household Tasks," in *The Employed Mother In America.* Edited by F. I. Nye and Lois W. Hoffman. Chicago: Rand, McNally, 1963, 215–30.

Homer. *The Iliad.* Translated by Andrew Lang, *et al.* New York: Modern Library, 1950.

————. *The Iliad.* Translated by Richmond Lattimore. Chicago: University of Chicago Press, 1951.

————. *The Odyssey*. Translated by S. H. Butcher and Andrew Lang. New York: Modern Library, n.d.

————. *The Odyssey*. Translated by Robert Fitzgerald. Garden City, N.Y.: Doubleday, 1961.

Homeric Hymns. In *Hesiod, The Homeric Hymns and Homerica*. Translated by H. G. Evelyn-White. (Loeb Library.) Cambridge: Harvard University Press, 1959.

Horney, Karen. "The Dread of Woman," *International Journal of Psychoanalysis*, XIII (1932), 348–60.

————. "On the Genesis of the Castration Complex in Women," *International Journal of Psychoanalysis*, V (1924), 50–65.

Howey, M. O. "The Serpent as a Phallic Emblem," in *Treasury of Snake Lore*. Edited by Brandt Aymar. New York: Greenberg, 1956, 42–49.

Huizinga, Johan. *Homo Ludens*. Boston: Beacon Press, 1955.

Hyginus. *Astronomica*. Edited by E. Chatelain and P. Legendre. Paris: Libraire Honoré Champion, 1909.

————. *Fabulae*. Edited by H. J. Rose. Leyden: Sythoff, 1933.

Jacobson, E. "The 'Exceptions': An Elaboration of Freud's Character Study," *The Psychoanalytic Study of the Child*, XIV. New York: International Universities Press, 1959, 135–54.

James, Henry. *The Turn of the Screw*. New York: Modern Library, 1930.

Jones, Ernest. *On the Nightmare*. New York: Grove Press, 1959.

Jung, Carl G. *Psychology of the Unconscious*. New York: Dodd, Mead, 1957.

Kafka, Franz. "The Burrow," in *Selected Short Stories of Franz Kafka*. Translated by Willa and Edmund Muir. New York: Modern Library, 1952, 256–304.

————. "The Green Dragon," in *Parables and Paradoxes*. New York: Schocken, 1961, 150–51.

————. "Josephine the Singer, or the Mouse Folk," in *The Penal Colony, Stories and Short Pieces*. New York: Schocken, 1961, 256–277.

Kardiner, Abram. *The Individual and His Society*. New York: Columbia University Press, 1939.

Karpman, Benjamin. *Case Studies in the Psychopathology of Crime*, II. Washington: Medical Science Press, 1944.

――――. *The Sexual Offender and His Offenses*. New York: Julian Press, 1954.

Katan, Anny. "Distortions of the Phallic Phase," *Psychoanalytic Study of the Child*, XV. New York: International Universities Press, 1960, 208–14.

Kavolis, V. "Economic Correlates of Artistic Creativity," *American Journal of Sociology*, LXX (1964), 332–41.

――――. "Political Dynamics and Artistic Creativity," *Sociology and Social Research*, XLIX (1965), 412–24.

――――. "Community Dynamics and Artistic Creativity," *American Sociological Review*, XXXI (1966), 208–17.

Keiser, S. "Body Ego During Orgasm," *Psychoanalytic Quarterly*, XXI (1952), 153–66.

Kerényi, Károly. *The Gods of the Greeks*. Translated by N. Cameron. New York: Grove Press, 1960.

――――. *The Heroes of the Greeks*. Translated by H. J. Rose. New York: Grove Press, 1959.

――――. "The Trickster in Relation to Greek Mythology," in Paul Radin, *The Trickster*. New York: Philosophical Library, 1956, 173–91.

Kisker, G. W. "A Study of Mental Disorder in Ancient Greek Culture," *Psychiatry*, IV (1941), 535–45.

Kitto, H. D. F. *The Greeks*. Baltimore: Penguin, 1960.

Klein, Melanie. *Our Adult World*. New York: Basic Books, 1963.

Kluckhohn, Clyde. "Recurrent Themes in Myths and Mythmaking," *Daedalus* (Spring, 1959), 268–79.

Knight, R. P. "A Discourse on the Worship of Priapus" (1786), in *Sexual Symbolism*. New York: Julian, 1957.

Komarovsky, Mirra. *Blue-Collar Marriage*. New York: Random House, 1964.

Kopit, A. L. *Oh Dad, Poor Dad, Mamma's Hung You in the Closet and I'm Feelin' So Sad*. New York: Hill and Wang, 1960.

Lampl-de Groot, Jeanne. "On Defense and Development: Normal and Pathological," *Psychoanalytic Study of the Child*, XII. New York: International Universities Press, 1957, 114–26.

Lancaster, Evelyn. *The Final Face of Eve*. New York: McGraw-Hill, 1958.

Larousse Encyclopedia of Mythology. New York: Prometheus Press, 1959.

Lawson, John C. *Modern Greek Folklore and Ancient Greek Religion.* New Hyde Park, N.Y.: University Books, 1964.

Leach, Edmund R. "Lévi-Strauss in the Garden of Eden," in *Reader in Comparative Religion.* Edited by W. A. Lessa and E. Z. Vogt. 2nd ed. New York: Harper & Row, 1965, 574–81.

Leach, E. R. "A Trobriand Medusa," *Man,* LIV (1954), 103–05.

Lennon, Florence B. *Victoria Through the Looking-Glass.* New York: Simon and Schuster, 1945.

Lévi-Strauss, Claude. "The Structural Study of Myth," in *Reader in Comparative Religion.* Edited by W. A. Lessa and E. Z. Vogt. 2nd ed. New York: Harper & Row, 1965, 562–74.

———. *Totemism.* Translated by Rodney Needham. Boston: Beacon Press: 1963.

Levy, Gertrude R. *The Gate of Horn.* New York: Book Collectors Society, n.d.

Licht, Hans. *Sexual Life in Ancient Greece.* New York: Barnes and Noble, 1963.

Lidz, Theodore, *et al. Schizophrenia and the Family.* New York: International Universities Press, 1966.

Limentani, D. "Symbiotic Identification in Schizophrenia," *Psychiatry,* XIX (1956), 231–36.

Linton, Ralph. *The Tree of Culture.* New York: Knopf, 1959.

Locher, G. W. *The Serpent in Kwakiutl Religion.* Leyden: E. J. Brill, 1932.

Lucan. *The Civil War.* Translated by J. D. Duff. (Loeb Library.) Cambridge: Harvard University Press, 1951.

Lycophron. In *Callimachus and Lycophron, Aratus.* Translated by A. W. Mair and G. R. Mair. (Loeb Library.) New York: Putnam, 1921.

Lysias. Translated by W. R. M. Lamb. (Loeb Library.) Cambridge: Harvard University Press, 1957.

Mace, David R., and Vera. *The Soviet Family.* Garden City, N.Y.: Doubleday, 1964.

Malinowski, Bronislaw. "Baloma: The Spirits of the Dead in the Trobriand Islands," in *Magic, Science, and Religion and Other Essays.* Garden City, N.Y.: Doubleday, 1948, 149–274.

————. *Crime and Custom in Savage Society*. Paterson, N.J.: Littlefield, Adams, 1959.

————. *The Sexual Life of Savages*. New York: Harcourt, Brace, 1929.

Mauss, Marcel, and Hubert, Henri. "On Magic and the Unknown." Translated by J. R. Pitts. In *Theories of Society*, II. Edited by Talcott Parsons, *et al.* New York: Free Press, 1961, 1088–91.

McClelland, D. C. *The Achieving Society*. Princeton, N.J.: Van Nostrand, 1961.

McLuhan, H. Marshall. *The Mechanical Bride*. Boston: Beacon Press, 1967.

Mead, Margaret. *Growing up in New Guinea*. New York: Mentor, 1953.

————. *Male and Female*. New York: Mentor, 1955.

Mellaart, J. "Deities and Shrines of Neolithic Anatolia," *Archeology*, XVI (1963), 29–38.

Menninger, Karl A. "Factors in Urination and Genito-Urinary Afflictions," *Psychoanalytic Review*, XXVIII (1941), 117–29.

Mills, T. M. "Authority and Group Emotion," in *Interpersonal Dynamics*. Edited by Warren G. Bennis *et al.* Homewood, Ill.: Dorsey, 1964, 94–108.

Milton, John. "Paradise Lost," in *The Poetical Works*. New York: Crowell, 1892.

Mischel, W. "Preference for Delayed Reinforcement: An Experimental Study of a Cultural Observation," *Journal of Abnormal and Social Psychology*, LVI (1958), 57–61.

Murdock, G. P. "Ethnographic Atlas," *Ethnology*, I (1962), Nos. 1–4.

————. "World Ethnographic Sample," *American Anthropology*. LIX (1957), 664–87.

Murray, Gilbert. *Five Stages of Greek Religion*. Garden City, N.Y.: Doubleday, n.d.

Nemecek, Otto. *Virginity: Pre-Nuptial Rites and Rituals*. New York: Philosophical Library, 1958.

Neubauer, P. B. "The One-Parent Child and His Oedipal Development," *The Psychoanalytic Study of the Child*, XV. New York: International Universities Press, 1960, 286–309.

Neumann, Erich. *The Great Mother.* Translated by Ralph Manheim. (Bollingen Series, XLVII.) New York: Pantheon Books, 1955.
———. *The Origins and History of Consciousness.* New York: Pantheon Books, 1954.
Nilsson, Martin Persson. *The Dionysiac Mysteries of the Hellenistic and Roman Age.* Lund, Sweden: Svenska Institute i Athen, 1957.
———. *Greek Folk Religion.* New York: Harper, 1961.
———. *A History of Greek Religion.* 2nd ed. Oxford: Clarendon Press, 1949.
———. *Minoan-Mycenean Religion.* London: Oxford University Press, 1927.
———. *The Mycenaean Origin of Greek Mythology.* Berkeley: University of California Press, 1932.
Nonnos, Panopolitanus. *Dionysiaca.* Translated by W. H. D. Rouse. (Loeb Library.) 3 vols. Cambridge: Harvard University Press, 1940.
Nunberg, Herman. "Circumcision and Problems of Bisexuality," *International Journal of Psychoanalysis,* XXVIII (1947), 145–79.
Oates, W. J., and O'Neill, Eugene, Jr. (eds.) *The Complete Greek Drama.* 2 vols. New York: Random House, 1938.
Ovesey, Lionel. "Pseudohomosexuality and Homosexuality in Men: Psychodynamics as a Guide to Treatment," in *Sexual Inversion.* Edited by Judd Marmor. New York: Basic Books, 1965, 211–33.
Ovid. *Fasti.* Translated by Sir James George Frazer. (Loeb Library.) Cambridge: Harvard University Press, 1951.
———. *Heroides and Amores.* Translated by Grant Showerman. (Loeb Library.) Cambridge: Harvard University Press, 1947.
———. *The Metamorphoses.* Translated by Horace Gregory. New York: Mentor, 1960.
———. *Metamorphoses.* Translated by Frank Justus Miller. (Loeb Library.) 2 vols. Cambridge: Harvard University Press, 1946.
Patai, Raphael. *Sex and Family in the Bible and the Middle East.* Garden City, N.Y.: Doubleday, 1959.

Pausanias. *Description of Greece*. Translated by W. H. S. Jones. (Loeb Library.) 5 vols. Cambridge: Harvard University Press, 1954-55.

Peller, Lili. "Daydreams and Children's Favorite Books," in *Psychoanalytic Study of the Child*, XIV. New York: International Universities Press, 1959, 414-33.

Pindar. *Odes*. Translated by Sir John Sandys. (Loeb Library.) Cambridge: Harvard University Press, 1957.

Plato (?). *Alcibiades I and II*, in *The Dialogues of Plato*, II. Translated by Benjamin Jowett. 2 vols. New York: Random House, 1937, 733-72 and 793-806.

———. *Charmides*, in *The Dialogues*, I, 3-27.

———. *Crito*, in *The Dialogues*, I, 427-38.

———. *Laws*, in *The Dialogues*, II, 407-703.

———. *Phaedo*, in *The Dialogues*, I, 441-501.

———. *Phaedrus*, in *The Dialogues*, I, 233-82.

———. *Republic*, in *The Dialogues*, I, 591-879.

———. *Symposium*, in *The Dialogues*, I, 301-45.

Plutarch. "Bravery of Women," in *Moralia*, III. Translated by Frank Cole Babbitt. (Loeb Library.) 15 vols. Cambridge: Harvard University Press, 1949, 474-581.

———. "Dialogue on Love," in *Moralia*, IX, 306-441.

———. "The E at Delphi," in *Moralia*, V, 198-253.

———. The Greek Questions," in *Moralia*, IV, 176-251.

———. "Isis and Osiris," in *Moralia*, V, 6-191.

———. *Lives of the Noble Grecians and Romans*. Translated by John Dryden and revised by Arthur Hugh Clough. New York: Modern Library, 1932.

———. *Lives*. Translated by B. Perrin. (Loeb Library.) 11 vols. Cambridge: Harvard University Press, 1914.

———. "The Obsolescence of Oracles," in *Moralia*, V, 350-501.

———. "Of the Names of Rivers and Mountains, and of Such Things as Are to Be Found Therein," in *Miscellanies and Essays*. Edited by W. W. Goodwin. Boston: Little, Brown, 1889, 477-509.

———. "The Oracles at Delphi," in *Moralia*, V, 258-345.

———. "Whether an Old Man Should Engage in Public Affairs," in *Moralia*, X, 76-155.

Pollis, A. "Political Implications of the Modern Greek Concept of Self," *British Journal of Sociology*, XVI (1965), 29–47.

Pritchard, James Bennett. *Ancient Near Eastern Texts Relating to the Old Testament.* 2nd ed. enl. Princeton, N.J.: Princeton University Press, 1958.

Proclus, Diadochus. *Chrestomathy,* in *Hesiod, The Homeric Hymns and Homerica.* Translated by H. G. Evelyn-White. (Loeb Library.) Cambridge: Harvard University Press, 1959, 488–95.

Radin, Paul. *The Trickster.* New York: Philosophical Library, 1956.

Rank, Otto. *The Myth of the Birth of the Hero.* New York: Brunner, 1952.

Ransom, J. C. "First Travels of Max," in *Modern American Poetry.* Edited by Louis Untermeyer. New York: Harcourt, Brace, 1950, 431–32.

Reich, Annie. "Pathologic Forms of Self-Esteem Regulation," *Psychoanalytic Study of the Child*, XV. New York: International Universities Press, 1960, 215–32.

Riviere, Joan. "On the Genesis of Psychical Conflict in Earliest Infancy," in *Developments in Psychoanalysis.* Edited by Melanie Klein *et al.* London: Hogarth, 1952, 37–66.

Rodrigué, E. "The Analysis of a 3-year-old Mute Schizophrenic," in *New Directions in Psychoanalysis.* Edited by Melanie Klein *et al.* New York: Basic Books, 1957, 140–79.

Róheim, Géza. "Totemism and the Fight with the Dragon," *International Journal of Psychoanalysis*, V (1924), 407–408.

Rolker, A. W. "The Story of the Snake," in *Treasury of Snake Lore.* Edited by Brandt Aymar. New York: Greenberg, 1956, 274–83.

Root, N. N. "A Neurosis in Adolescence," *Psychoanalytic Study of the Child*, XII. New York: International Universities Press, 1957, 320–34.

Rosberg, J., and Karon, Bertram P. "The Oedipus Complex in a Case of Deteriorated Schizophrenia," *Journal of Abnormal and Social Psychology*, LVII (1958), 221–25.

Rose, H. J. *A Handbook of Greek Mythology.* New York: Dutton, 1959.

————. *Primitive Culture in Greece*. London: Methuen, 1925.

Rosen, J. N. *Direct Analysis*. New York: Grune and Stratton, 1953.

Rostand, Jean. *Bestiaire d'Amour*. London: Routledge and Kegan Paul, 1961.

Russell, Bertrand. *A History of Western Philosophy*. New York: Simon and Schuster, 1945.

Sachs, Hanns. "The Delay of the Machine Age," *Psychoanalytic Quarterly*, II (1933), 404–24.

Sanders, I. T. *Rainbow in the Rock*. Cambridge: Harvard University Press, 1962.

Sarnoff, D. "Science and Technology Eliminating the World's Poverty, Disease, Ignorance." *Barbados Advocate*, February 4, 1968.

Schaffner, B. (ed.) *Fourth Conference on Group Processes* (1957). New York: Macy Foundation, 1959.

Scott, J. P. *Animal Behavior*. Chicago: University of Chicago Press, 1958.

Searles, H. F. "The Evolution of the Mother Transference in Psychotherapy with the Schizophrenic Patient," in *Psychotherapy of the Psychoses*. Edited by Arthur Burton. New York: Basic Books, 1961, 256–84.

Semonides of Amorgos, in *Greek Lyrics*. Translated by Richmond Lattimore. 2nd ed. Chicago: University of Chicago Press, 1961.

Shakespeare, William. *Antony and Cleopatra*.

————. *King Henry V*.

————. *Sonnets*.

Simmel, Georg. *The Sociology of Georg Simmel*. Edited and translated by Kurt H. Wolff. Glencoe, Ill.: The Free Press, 1950.

Slater, P. E. "Cultural Attitudes Toward the Aged," *Geriatrics*, XVIII (1963), 296–314.

————. "Culture, Narcissism, and Sexuality." Unpublished manuscript, Brandeis University, 1965.

————. "Displacement in Groups," in *The Planning of Change*. Edited by W. G. Bennis *et al*. New York: Holt, 1961, 725–36.

————. "On Social Regression," *American Sociological Review*, XXVIII (1963), 339–64.

————. "The Social Bases of Personality," in *Sociology: an Introduction*. Edited by N. J. Smelser. New York: Wiley, 1967, 545–600.

Slater, P. E., and Bennis, W. G. "Democracy Is Inevitable," *Harvard Business Review*, XLII (1964), 51–59.

Slater, P. E., and Slater, Dori A. "Maternal Ambivalence and Narcissism: a Cross-Cultural Study," *Merrill-Palmer Quarterly*, XI (1965), 241–59.

Smith, Lillian. *Killers of the Dream*. Garden City, N.Y.: Doubleday, 1961.

Smith, W. Robertson. *The Religion of the Semites*. New York: Meridian, 1957.

Sophocles. Translated by F. Storr. (Loeb Library.) Cambridge: Harvard University Press, 1951.

————. *Ajax.*

————. *Electra.*

————. *Oedipus Tyrannus.*

————. *The Trachiniae.*

Spiegel, L. A. "The Self, the Sense of Self, and Perception," in *Psychoanalytic Study of the Child*, XIV. New York: International Universities Press, 1959, 81–109.

Spitz, R. A. "Hospitalism," in *The Family: Its Structure and Function*. Edited by Rose L. Coser. New York: St. Martin's, 1964, 399–425.

Stein, Leopold. *Loathsome Women*. New York: McGraw-Hill, 1959.

Stephens, W. N. *The Family in Cross-Cultural Perspective*. New York: Holt, 1963.

————. *The Oedipus Complex*. New York: Free Press, 1962.

Stewart, Harold. "Jocasta's Crimes," *International Journal of Psychoanalysis*, XLII (1961), 424–30.

Stone, L. "Marriage Among the English Nobility," in *The Family: Its Structure and Function*. Edited by Rose L. Coser. New York: St. Martin's, 1964, 153–83.

Strato. "Musa Puerilis," in *The Greek Anthology*. Translated by

W. R. Paton. (Loeb Library.) Vol. V. Cambridge: Harvard University Press, 1948, 280–413.

Stuart, Grace. *Narcissus*. New York: Macmillan, 1955.

Swanson, G. E. *The Birth of the Gods*. Ann Arbor: University of Michigan Press, 1960.

Taylor, G. R. "Historical and Mythological Aspects of Homosexuality," in *Sexual Inversion*. Edited by Judd Marmor. New York: Basic Books, 1965, 140–64.

Textor, Robert B. *A Cross-Cultural Summary*. New Haven: Human Relations Area Files Press, 1967.

Theocritus. In *The Greek Bucolic Poets*. Translated by J. M. Edmonds. (Loeb Library.) Cambridge: Harvard University Press, 1950.

Thigpen, C. H., and Cleckley, H. M. *The Three Faces of Eve*. New York: McGraw-Hill, 1957.

Thompson, Clara. "Some Effects of the Derogatory Attitude Towards Female Sexuality," *Psychiatry*, XIII (1950), 349–54.

Thomson, Sir Godfrey Hilton. *Aeschylus and Athens*. London: Lawrence and Wishart, 1950.

Thomson, G. *The Factorial Analysis of Human Ability*. London: Houghton Mifflin, 1949.

Thucydides. *The Complete Writings: The Peloponnesian Wars*. Edited by J. H. Finley, Jr. New York: Modern Library, 1951.

Vogel, E. F. and Bell, N. W. "The Emotionally Disturbed Child as the Family Scapegoat," in *A Modern Introduction to the Family*. Glencoe, Ill.: The Free Press, 1960, 382–97.

Wahl, C. W. "The Psychodynamics of Consummated Maternal Incest," in *Patterns of Incest*. Edited by R. E. L. Masters. New York: Julian, 1963, 179–89.

Walter, E. V. "Theories of Terrorism and the Classical Tradition." Paper delivered at the meetings of the American Political Science Association, New York City, 1966.

Warner, W. L. *The Living and the Dead*. New Haven: Yale University Press, 1959.

Watt, I. "The New Woman: Samuel Richardson's *Pamela*," in *The Family: Its Structure and Function*. Edited by Rose L. Coser. New York: St. Martin's, 1964, 267–89.

Weakland, J. H. "Orality in Chinese Conceptions of Male Genital Sexuality," *Psychiatry*, XIX (1956), 237–48.

Weber, Max. *The Protestant Ethic and the Spirit of Capitalism.* Translated by Talcott Parsons. New York: Scribner, 1930.

Webster's New International Dictionary of the English Language, 2nd ed. Springfield, Mass.: G. and C. Merriam Co., 1947.

Weigert-Vowmkel, E. "The Cult and Mythology of the Magna Mater from the Standpoint of Psychoanalysis," *Psychiatry*, I (1938), 347–78.

Weiss, Paul. *The Persecution and Assassination of Jean-Paul Marat as Performed by the Inmates of the Asylum of Charenton under the Direction of the Marquis de Sade.* Translated by G. Skelton and A. Mitchell. New York: Pocket Books, 1966.

Whiting, Beatrice, (ed.) *Six Cultures: Studies of Child Rearing.* New York: Wiley and Sons, 1963.

———. "Sex Identity Conflict and Physical Violence: A Comparative Study," *American Anthropologist*, LXVII (December, 1965 supp.), 123–40.

Whiting, J. W. M. *Becoming a Kwoma.* New Haven: Yale University Press, 1941.

———. Unpublished ratings of wife-beating practices. Harvard University, 1962.

———. Unpublished ratings of eating arrangements. Harvard University, 1963.

———. "Socialization Process and Personality," in *Psychological Anthropology*. Edited by F. L. K. Hsu. Homewood, Ill.: Dorsey, 1961, 355–80.

———. "Effects of Climate on Certain Cultural Practices," in *Explorations in Cultural Anthropology*. Edited by W. H. Goodenough. New York: McGraw-Hill, 1964, 511–44.

Whiting, J. W. M., and Child, I. L. *Child Training and Personality*. New Haven: Yale University Press, 1953.

Whiting, J. W. M., *et al.* "The Function of Male Initiation Ceremonies at Puberty," in *Readings in Social Psychology*. Edited by E. E. Maccoby *et al.* New York: Holt, 1958, 359–70.

Wolfenstein, Martha. "Fun Morality: An Analysis of Recent

American Child-Training Literature," in *Childhood in Contemporary Cultures*. Edited by Margaret Mead and Martha Wolfenstein. Chicago: University of Chicago Press, 1963, 168–78.

————. "Some Variants in Moral Training of Children," in *Childhood in Contemporary Cultures*. Edited by Margaret Mead and Martha Wolfenstein. Chicago: University of Chicago Press, 1963, 349–68.

Wright, T. "The Worship of the Generative Powers" (1866), in *Sexual Symbolism*. New York: Julian Press, 1957.

Wynne, L. C., *et al.* "Pseudo-Mutuality in the Family Relations of Schizophrenics," *Psychiatry*, XXI (1958), 204–20.

Xenophon. *Anabasis*. Translated by C. L. Brownson, in *Xenophon*. (Loeb Library.) Cambridge: Harvard University Press, 1947.

————. *The Persian Expedition*. Translated by Rex Warner. Baltimore: Penguin, 1949.

————. *Memorabilia and Oeconomicus*. Translated by E. C. Marchant. (Loeb Library.) Cambridge: Harvard University Press, 1953.

————. *Symposium*. Translated by O. H. Dodd, in *Xenophon*. (Loeb Library.) Cambridge: Harvard University Press, 1947.

Yates, Sybille L. "An Investigation of the Psychological Factors in Virginity and Ritual Defloration," *International Journal of Psychoanalysis*, XI (1930), 167–84.

Young, Michael, and Willmott, Peter. *Family and Kinship in East London*. Baltimore: Pelican, 1964.

Yurick, S. *The Warriors*. New York: Holt, 1965.

Zborowski, Mark, and Herzog, Elizabeth. *Life Is with People*. New York: Schocken, 1962.

Zilboorg, Gregory. "Masculine and Feminine," *Psychiatry*, VII (1944), 257–96.

INDEX